LEMON-AID PERSONAL COMPUTERS

BUYING, SELLING, AND UPGRADING YOUR PC

JIM SANDERSON

Stoddart

Published in 1998 by Stoddart Publishing Co. Limited
34 Lesmill Road, Toronto, Ontario M3B 2T6
Toll-free tel. for Ontario and Quebec 1-800-387-0141
Toll-free tel. for all other provinces and territories 1-800-287-0172
Fax (416) 445-5967
Email Customer.Service@ccmailgw.genpub.com

02 01 00 99 98 1 2 3 4 5

Canadian Cataloguing in Publication Data

Sanderson, Jim 1953–
Lemon-aid personal computers: buying, selling, and upgrading your PC

ISBN 0-7737-5953-0

1. Microcomputers – Purchasing. 2. Selling – Computers.
3. Microcomputers – Upgrading I. Title.

QA76.5.S255 1998 004.16'029'7 C97-932565-X

Cover design: Bill Douglas @ The Bang
Text design & page composition: Tannice Goddard

Printed and bound in Canada

CONTENTS

FOREWORD

Twenty-six years ago, when I wrote the first Lemon-Aid car guide, personal computers were still a decade away from becoming available to North American consumers. Little could anyone then have foreseen the tremendous growth that would occur in the PC marketplace in the '80s and '90s. With that growth has developed a need for a reliable, trustworthy consumer's guide to personal computers – a need that Jim Sanderson's book is here to fill. I wish *Lemon-Aid Personal Computers* had been around when I bought my first computer ten years ago; I would have saved a bundle.

Jim takes the mystery out of buying, selling, and upgrading personal computers without using the "techno-babble" found in most computer guides. He is an expert in the real world sense, having owned and managed his own computer store and acted as a consultant and teacher. This guide follows the Lemon-Aid tradition of giving readers a hard-hitting, unbiased analysis of what's good and what's not good in the PC marketplace. If you've got a beef with your computer hardware or software, there's even a sample complaint letter you can copy and send off to get a refund.

All in all, this book is a delight to read. I only regret that it wasn't around a decade ago.

Phil Edmonston
Author, Lemon-Aid auto guides

Preface

The *Lemon-Aid Personal Computers* buyer's guide is designed to help you buy, sell, or upgrade your computer by offering useful, up-to-date information about what to look for, how much to pay, how much to charge, and what to avoid. The book is divided into sections on everything from the task of assessing your computer needs, to problems to watch for when dealing with warranties and repairs, to the specifications and prices of major lines of Canadian personal computers, monitors, and printers available in 1998. We'll look at specific steps in the evaluation and successful purchase of a PC, and consider what to do with the one you may already own.

In Chapter 1 we start with the rise of the personal computer, the evolution of the marketplace, different classes of manufacturers, and what constitutes a "balanced" system. In Chapter 2 we help you decide what you need by asking five key questions about the kind of computer *you* want to buy, not what someone else says you need. In Chapter 3 we explain the main technical terms you'll encounter when shopping, and the relative importance of essential components such as motherboards, hard drives, compact disc (CD-ROM) drives, digital video (DVD) drives, and different kinds of computer memory. In Chapter 4 we look at some of the tricky problems you can encounter when choosing and buying software: different applications, the physical forms in which they're available, and the temptations and pitfalls of pirated programs. In Chapter 5 we look at common home and small-business scenarios, at why some people use their computers productively and others don't, and at the hardware and software needed to perform such tasks as wordprocessing, faxing, setting up a home office, and accessing the Internet.

After examining your needs, we turn in Chapters 6 and 7 to the problem of finding good new and used computer equipment: how to approach wholesalers, dealers, the private market, leasing companies, mass marketers, and corporations that are upgrading. We look at how to advertise your intentions when buying privately, and how to use the Internet to advantage when gathering product information. We consider how to judge a system's performance and determine whether it's worthwhile paying for a third-party evaluation. And if a system checks out, we even describe how to negotiate the best price for it and bring it home. Chapter 8 is what Lemon-Aid guides are all about: what to do in case of trouble. What if the PC you just bought doesn't work properly? What if it was misrepresented or contains inferior parts? What if your vendor disappears before his warranty does? We look at options available from manufacturers, alternative resellers and service providers, and even a worst-case scenario in small claims court.

And after all that, what about your old computer? Perhaps you're thinking of keeping it. Chapters 9 and 10 help with the pros and cons of upgrading versus selling: different types of upgrades, how they improve a computer's performance, how they don't, and whether they're worth it. If you find yourself thrown onto the seller's side of the market, you'll also want to know how to prepare your PC for sale, research a competitive price for it, demonstrate it, and sell it for maximum value. In Chapters 11 and 12 we look at service and warranty issues and even hazard some predictions about the computer marketplace of the future. Finally, in the product-review section of the guide, we consider a broad range of Canadian desktop computers, printers, and monitors: their specifications, list prices, street prices, and other characteristics. So don't forget to make a note of our email address and website (PClemonaid.com) and send us your comments and questions. We look forward to your feedback for future editions of *Lemon-Aid Personal Computers*.

As you might imagine, this guide is the result of the combined efforts of many people. Special thanks are due to Paul Roberts and Larry Hoffman for assisting with the project at the concept stage. The product review section would not have been possible without the efforts of Lawrence Wade, Chris Bernard, and especially Steve Halinda and his colleagues at the Canada Computer Paper Test Labs, all of whom helped me understand the rapidly changing PC marketplace in Canada. Thanks also to David Hong, Frankie Chan, and Neal Primeau for their input to the technical sections in the book, as well as Myles Whyte, whose own books *How to Buy a Computer* and *How to Avoid Buying a Computer* are excellent sources of information on the high-tech marketplace; still, it is important to note that any errors or omissions in this book are my own responsibility. Appreciation is due to Bruce Westwood, and to the team at Stoddart Publishing, including Kevin Linder, Marnie Kramarich, Sue Sumeraj, and Lloyd Davis for their most patient editing, and to Nelson Doucet, without whose support the project would still be a few sheets of paper resting peacefully in the idea bin. I must also acknowledge the contributions of my family, including my father and brother, who are also my colleagues at work, and my wife and boys, who have had to spend a lot more time without me in the last two years than any of us liked. Each has helped with this book in his or her own special way. Finally, this preface would certainly not be complete without mention of Phil Edmonston, who wrote the first Lemon-Aid guide twenty-six years ago. Honest and accurate information has made his books invaluable to car buyers throughout the years and I can only hope this first volume in the *Personal Computer* series continues the tradition.

PART I

PC LEMON-AID

1

An Introduction to the PC Marketplace

THE SUCCESS OF THE MICROCHIP

There is no doubt how important computer technology has become to all of us in the '90s. From our traffic lights and telephones to our automobiles and ovens, every day it seems that more and more of our actions are being affected by electronics. Computers have become essential to a degree that continues to surprise most of us, and is even starting to frighten a few. Today's descendants of the Altair, Apple, and other prototypes of the '70s have begun to rival the telephone and television as instruments of business and communication. What is it about microcomputers that has made them so successful, so essential? Perhaps it's the same set of qualities that make them so exasperating. They are logical to a fault. When they're working properly they can be counted on to do exactly what they are programmed to do, whether we like it or not. They can mimic with startling accuracy almost every form of audiovisual communication. They are even beginning to approximate such uniquely human activities as the creation of works of art.

The more we work with PCs, it seems, the more we need to remind ourselves that they are merely inanimate collections of switches (memory and motherboard), guided by precise instructions (software), displayed on a treated screen (monitor), and controlled by an input device such as a keyboard, microphone, or mouse. These basic elements have together given rise to an identity which sometimes leads us to expect more from computers than we should. Every technical support person has a favourite list of humorous, silly, even downright frightening stories about the strange and wonderful ways these methodical little monsters are creeping into our lives.

Of course, while PCs have continued to evolve, questions surrounding the successful purchase of one today are much the same as when the first products appeared some twenty years ago. Just what is it that makes one computer a better buy than another?

A GOOD COMPUTER SHOULD . . .

A good computer should contain quality parts of recent specifications at a competitive price. Its processor type and speed, memory, hard drive storage, motherboard, video card, multimedia components, and other significant characteristics should be in line with those of its true competitors in the marketplace. Its subsystems should be balanced so that no one of them is over- or under-powered in comparison to the others.

A good computer should work properly when you get it. All of its hardware should fit together correctly and be optimized for performance with the included software. It should work perfectly with all other software and hardware with which it is claimed to be compatible.

A good computer should be easy to upgrade and repair. It should be reasonably compatible with "aftermarket" (i.e., after the original purchase) RAM (random-access memory), video cards, and hard drives used in other systems in its class so it can be improved or fixed without expensive proprietary parts.

A good computer should come with proper, clearly written documentation. It should be accompanied by either separate manuals or one complete book or compact disc describing its main characteristics: motherboard, RAM, video subsystem, hard drive, case, power supply, bundled software, and other components.

A good computer should come with a good warranty, which should protect it for an absolute minimum of one year, but preferably two or three, and cover all parts and labour. The warranty should be transferable from user to user and be at least national, and preferably international, in scope. The warranty terms should be clearly stated: when it does and does not apply; what the owner has to do in case of failure; who to call; and where to go. Warranty claims should be easy to make. If there is a hotline, it should be accessible without too long a wait. Both manufacturer and vendor should be available for after-sale support as well as upgrades and repairs.

A good computer should last. It should run for at least ten years or until it can't be upgraded anymore and becomes too underpowered to use.

But how well do the people manufacturing computers understand these requirements? Probably pretty well, perhaps better than the folks running the car business, to which the microcomputer business is sometimes compared. PC assembly comes from different roots – the academic, aerospace, and defence communities, aided by a significant amount of garage-workbench tinkering. It is also inextricably married to the unique and confusing business of software development. All of these factors have given computer manufacturing a character unlike any other: dynamic, fast-changing, at the edge of innovation.

THE EVOLUTION OF THE PC MARKETPLACE

Once upon a time, all computers were large, cumbersome, and expensive. Then, around 1980, Apple's, and IBM's, first personal computers appeared. Revolutionary, groundbreaking, they burst upon the office equipment world with all the excitement and promise of a brand-new industry. Processing at a screaming 4.77 MHz (megahertz, or million cycles per second), with 256K (kilobytes, or thousand bytes) of RAM and two 360K floppy drives, IBM's machines were introduced to the North American public at street prices of up to $5,000. The company's marketing plan included new retail stores complete with chrome, glass, and slick displays of their latest products.

Of course, it wasn't long before microcomputers of increased power were issued by IBM's competitors, especially Compaq, and so it was that the character of the PC market was established: innovation, mass production, and emulation. Successive generations of computers appeared in following years, based on new generations of Intel and Motorola processors including the 8088, 80286, 80386, 80486, Intel Pentium, Pentium MMX, and Pentium II processors.

Alongside each successful breakthrough product inevitably appeared copycats, or "clones," a term borrowed from the science of microbiology, meaning "to reconstruct or duplicate something from a single part of its original form." The result was that all of a sudden, a group of items which had already earned a reputation for being unfamiliar and complex got even more complicated to buy. Because shoppers didn't really have a handle on high-tech products, one of the most daunting tasks confronting a salesperson back then was convincing his customers that they actually needed a computer in the first place. How many times did couples stand in showrooms and have the old conversation about the relative merits of writing recipes in a book versus storing them on the PC they were thinking of buying for the kitchen? Wasn't there something else this expensive new gadget could do to make life easier, like maybe connect them to a bulletin board with one of those old acoustic couplers (a forerunner of today's modems) blasting data back and forth at a whopping transmission speed of 300 baud?

It was interesting to hear shoppers viewing this new group of products in terms of other items with which they were more familiar. I was reminded of the European explorers of old who, when first exposed to new animals in Africa, painted them as amalgamations of beasts they already knew: the hippopotamus drawn as a pig with a horselike head, or the giraffe with a doleful face like a dog. Even today, shoppers find it hard to get a handle on the PC marketplace. One example of this is the mistaken assumption that a new and improved "lineup" will be issued each year at the same time, as happens with automobiles. Unfortunately, developments in microelectronics are relentless and erratic, which is one of the main reasons why the PC market is so hard to evaluate on any given day. Is there a "good" or "bad" time to buy a computer? Not that I know of. There have been good and bad times in the past, to be sure, but these were identifiable only to the lucky few with the ability to see into the future. There are, however, effective ways to seek the best buy among the products currently available.

THE STEPS IN A SUCCESSFUL PC PURCHASE

Microcomputers are difficult items to shop for, new or used. They are costly: a recent survey identified the home computer as one of the most expensive household items the average North American family will buy in 1998, ranking only behind the automobile. They are complicated: even a superficial approach to the average purchase involves decisions on several items – things like a system's processor, its RAM, hard drive, monitor, operating system, software, and printer. And because a PC purchase is a technical endeavour, intelligent discussion about it with a salesperson usually involves terms and concepts which most shoppers would rather avoid having to learn. Characteristics and dollar values of things like VRAM (video random-access memory), DRAM (dynamic random-access memory), external cache memory, and monitor refresh rates are usually viewed with weariness by customers who also have to factor in price distinctions between competing brands. Most of the significant manufacturers have addressed this by offering packaged, or "bundled," products – complete systems including hardware and software, all ready to take home, unpack, and put to work. This has been a major development in the new-computer market of the '90s.

What are the key steps to ensure a successful microcomputer purchase? We'll be looking at the nuts and bolts of the purchase process in detail in Chapters 6 and 7, but by way of introduction, here are the main points to keep in mind:

1. Do some soul-searching. *Before* you start shopping, ask yourself, or your advisor, why you want the computer, and what tasks you want it to perform.
2. Assess your budget. If you have only a limited amount of money to spend – and who doesn't? – determine just how much. PCs are available in a wide variety of shapes, sizes, stripes, colours, and of course, prices. Without at least a ballpark figure in mind, the process becomes much more difficult.
3. Think about software. Buying a PC is a bit like getting a VCR: if you take the thing home and play a bunch of bad movies on it, the whole experience is pretty terrible. So give some thought to the programs you want to run. In most cases, they will help you determine the computer you need.
4. Survey the product market. No matter how daunting the task may seem, spend at least a little time and effort acquainting yourself with what's out there *today.* You lay yourself open to all kinds of difficulties by hurrying into the first "great" deal you come across.
5. Seek a balanced system. In descending order of importance, look for the following: the fastest processor you can afford, the biggest and best monitor, the most RAM, the biggest hard drive, the fastest modem, and the best multimedia components (compact disc or digital video disc and sound card).
6. Survey possible suppliers. Once you have an idea of the equipment that will suit your needs, shop around! It's a free country, isn't it? A good method is to request written quotes (via fax if possible; prices change quickly) from at least three likely vendors. And be sure you get prices on everything you need.
7. Survey your chosen supplier. Once you've found a vendor you like who offers the equipment you want at a good price, ask a few pointed questions. Find out what type(s) of payment he or she accepts, how long it will take to get possession of the goods, and what after-sale support and warranty are offered.

8. Finally, how does that song go? Don't worry, be happy. If you're concerned that whatever you buy is going to be hideously, horribly obsolete in about six months, you're absolutely right. We're all on the same train, and there's nothing anyone can do about it. So forget about it. Worrying about obsolescence when buying a personal computer is fruitless, so do your best to purchase good equipment at a good price from a vendor you like, and then take your new system home and enjoy it.

Of course, not everyone is going to have the time and energy to execute all of these steps when purchasing a PC. Life is hectic, and we all have limited resources to devote to an exercise like this. But try to consider as many of the above guidelines as you can; they'll increase your chances of ending up with a PC you like – and can afford.

GENERIC AND BRAND-NAME PCs

When considering either the new or the used computer marketplace, it's important to know the difference between generic, or "clone," systems, and brand-name, or "original manufacturer," ones. As broad terms which refer to loosely defined groups of products, these labels are somewhat arbitrary. Nevertheless, they are useful to help provide direction through a very diverse market.

Brand-name computers can be classed as those produced in quantity, usually by large companies that assemble their products under some conditions of quality control. These are systems which are normally manufactured from standardized components and come with specific documentation, proper packaging, and support from the manufacturer as well as the vendor. PCs of this type tend to be more expensive, and in many cases are more proprietary, which is to say they contain components designed for them alone. This last characteristic has implications when a dealer or individual attempts to repair or upgrade them later. Proprietary components, while sometimes better built and tested in the first place, are often more expensive than generic parts.

Of course, there are different kinds of brand-name computers. Big companies such as IBM, Compaq, and AST produce wide ranges of PCs. When trying to make some sense out of this often confusing field, it's useful to subdivide brand-name computers into two further groups: home products and office-grade systems. The difference between these is largely, though not completely, one of configuration and marketing. Home systems such as Compaq's Presario series and IBM's Aptivas are complete PCs which are usually sold with a monitor from the same manufacturer, a large and varied complement of software on several compact discs, a modem, speakers, a sound card, and a microphone – a fully loaded purchase.

Perhaps having taken note of Apple's success, IBM helped pioneer the concept of home, or "integrated," systems back around 1988 with its attractive little Personal System 2. An all-in-one design, this computer was constructed so that its twelve-inch VGA monitor was built right onto a small base which contained the other main components: motherboard, hard and floppy drives, and modem. It came complete with Microsoft Works software and a very responsive IBM mouse. Not long after the appearance of this product, all sorts of other manufacturers started getting into the act. Even typewriter builder Smith Corona had a fling with the computer business about this time, turning out a conventionally designed SCM PC (actually manufactured by the ACER computer corporation) marketed in North America with Smith Corona's own wordprocessing software as well as Microsoft Works and some other extras. Unfortunately, this product was not quite successful enough to save SCM from the difficult financial times it would experience a few years later.

Today, the home market has become filled with entries from most major computer corporations. In the background, however, remain "office," or industrial, lines from manufacturers like IBM and Compaq, two companies that remain pre-eminent in this field. These customizable systems are aimed at large- and medium-sized businesses with networking and other, more specialized applications in mind where higher-quality components and manufacturer support are an absolute must. Originally, computers like these inherited a share of the academic and defence mainframe markets, and were promoted in much the same way, to companies through computer consultants and professionals. Over time, however, the pre-eminence of these kinds of brand-name PCs has been eroded by the generic market. But with home computer packages filled with goodies, the large manufacturers can be more competitive. Alliances with software companies have enabled them to offer heaps of product at a price most generic manufacturers simply can't match.

In the established lines of industrial desktop computers such as the Compaq Deskpro series, the AST Bravos, and the IBM 700 series, users are presented with a heaping measure of quality and support. Unfortunately, in most cases, they are also presented with a price which is difficult for families and small businesses to justify when no extra products are involved. As a result, industrial lines are losing ground to generic systems in some business and networking applications where they once were king. One way that some manufacturers are seeking to bridge this gap is to offer custom-designed systems and sell them direct, in a sales and marketing plan borrowed from smaller, local assemblers. This can be an attractive alternative if you are looking for the safety offered by a large manufacturer and the ability to have a system built to specification. Prices will still be higher than the cheapest locally assembled product you can find, but then again, the cheapest PC is not always the best buy, especially if it's a "no-name." Notable corporations in the attractive custom-assembly market are Dell and, more recently, NEC.

Clone or generic computers, on the other hand, are a different group of products than their better tested, better documented, and more slickly marketed brand-name counterparts. Nevertheless, they can perform as well – sometimes even better, depending on certain factors.

In almost every city around the world, there are now computer-savvy entrepreneurs who purchase parts locally or directly from the world computer centres of California, Hong Kong, Malaysia, Singapore, Taiwan, and China. They are able to assemble remarkably fast and inexpensive PCs out of compatible components that happen to fit together. It still never fails to amaze me how much power is available for so little money in the generic, or "locally assembled," computer market. Of course, with all that firepower for the dollar, and common parts that are so easily changed or upgraded, there's a pretty strong case to be made for purchasing one of these kinds of no-name systems, isn't there? Well, sort of. The key to comparing generic computers to their better known brand-name counterparts is to remember that, as in most choices in life, each option poses advantages and disadvantages. It's wise to weigh these carefully and fairly before deciding on one or the other.

If you absolutely must have maximum processing power for the lowest price, and are an experienced enough computer shopper to talk to your vendor about different kinds of components and their properties, then you should probably look at a locally assembled system. But don't neglect to take at least some care to purchase it from a reliable source. As I have often advised shoppers seeking generic PCs, there is nothing wrong with looking for a good deal, but in this part of the market it's usually a mistake to buy the cheapest system you can find. To do this is to throw the quality part of the equation out the window, and this is perilous when there is no reliable manufacturer to fall back on for support. So the assembler figures pretty heavily in this picture. Is he honest? Does he know what he's doing when he screws all those hotshot components together? Will he actually take responsibility for them if they don't work?

If you are seeking a brand-name system in which all of the parts in a model in one store are guaranteed to be exactly the same as those in the same model in another store, it really doesn't matter from whom you make the purchase. In this case, by all means, shop until you drop and pry the best price out of every vendor in town. After all, you're dealing with a known quantity. But when addressing the clone market, when you and your assembler will probably discuss a set of ten or fifteen specifications, and you'll probably not know as much as he does about any of them, it's a good idea to resist the temptation to select the cheapest quote in the pile. Much safer is to go with a medium-priced assembler who scores highly on support points as well. How can you rate prospective suppliers? Ask some questions:

- What is the reputation of the store or assembly company?
- How long has it been in business?
- Does it use components from recognized manufacturers?
- What are its warranty claims, and does it live up to them?
- Finally, how do you like the sales associate or proprietor? Do you and he or she communicate effectively and in a friendly, straightforward manner?

Buying a computer is different from purchasing almost any other household or small-business object. As soon as you get it home, set up, and running, one of the first things you're going to want to do is call the store and talk to the people who sold it to you, if only just to hear a reassuring voice. If you can make a reasonable deal with a friendly, reputable vendor, then he or she won't mind hearing from you afterward to help you with problems. To forget this benefit or trade it away in favour of a few dollars at the head of the purchase is fine if you are buying a refrigerator or other "plug-and-play" appliance. It is, however, an invitation to disaster when buying a generic PC which has been assembled by a small company.

PACKAGED COMPUTER SYSTEMS

What if you are a novice user who needs a complete package and would like to be able to rely on the extra support and pre-tested components that come with a brand-name system such as an IBM Aptiva, Compaq Presario, or AST Advantage? Then by all means go for this kind of deal, and be secure in the knowledge that you have not only your dealer to call but someone behind the help desk at the support centre as well, even if it does take an hour or two to get through on the phone. In brand-name systems like these, the industry standard is to offer pre-tested and factory-installed (or at least factory–set up for you to install easily) software, standardized components, better documentation, stronger packaging, and – I offer this observation cautiously – lower rates of failure.

Of course, these advantages usually result in a higher price, but not always. A successful choice in any marketplace depends on the ability to make accurate comparisons. The real advantage of generic or locally assembled systems, next to price, is their flexibility: you can specify exactly what you want, and even more important, exactly what you don't! With many of the brand-name packages, on the other hand, you may find yourself purchasing software and other features that you don't really want. You are buying a configuration that marketing experts at the manufacturer think will appeal to the maximum number of people and yield the greatest profit.

In some situations these extras are not only unwanted but actually detrimental. Consider, for example, the case of Frank, a graphic designer who is very experienced with a specific program, Corel Draw, and is looking for a system on which to work in his home office. He plans to use his PC with a colour scanner to capture, store, and retouch pictures, drawings, and photographs. Probably his best option is to invest in the most powerful and specific hardware he can afford, and purchase only the software he needs to get his job done. That way, if his requirements later expand, he will stand the best chance of being high enough on the hardware ladder to run other, newer programs. In this case a brand-name package complete with all sorts of neat little software features like smart wake-up and voice recognition are really a waste, and they will detract from the value of the hardware Frank can afford.

On the other hand, consider the case of Betty, an executive who wants to do some spreadsheets, wordprocessing, and presentation programming at home but who also has a husband and two children who want to use their new computer for the Internet and games. In her case a home package complete with software is probably a good route to take.

We tried an interesting experiment at Dominion Business Machines recently, faithfully price-comparing one of our own, locally assembled

Pentium 233 MHz systems that contained all of the features in a well-known brand-name package. The result was surprising. By the time we had accounted for the complement of software (about ten CDs), the systems engineering (the time required by a vendor to set the system up so that all of the hardware and software is working properly), on-site warranty, twenty-four-hour help line, and other extras, the generic system costs were much higher! It is also worth mentioning that some of the features peculiar to the brand-name computer were not available in the generic system, period. They were perks and special programming that had been worked up by the manufacturer for its systems alone.

In Chapter 6 we will take a closer look at some of the differences between generic and brand-name systems, to see just how this distinction affects the value of a PC down the road when it's offered in the used marketplace.

PC MARKETING: LAND OF HYPE AND GLORY

It's no wonder so many PC shoppers have unrealistic expectations: skim the computer section of any large-circulation newspaper and you'll find it filled with absolutely fabulous equipment at unbelievably low prices. Unfortunately, that old adage is as accurate in the computer business as in any other: if it seems too good to be true, it probably is. Obvious examples of this are ads proclaiming very low-priced computers which don't even contain essentials such as a hard drive or video card! Certainly, there is nothing wrong with selling parts or even partly assembled systems to shoppers who are fully aware. Problems arise, though, when resellers mislead readers with boldface type and relegate the absent necessities to the fine print. It's rather like a local car dealer shouting, "New car, $2,495!!!" and then whispering, "Doors and wheels extra, of course."

This all really boils down to honesty. If a company is so anxious to grab customers that it engages in misleading advertising, what does that say about its integrity when it comes to dealing with you face to face? An interesting sidelight on the various ethical standards of dealers you may encounter is the fact that the huge demand for certain computer parts (such as RAM and hard drives) has caused some vendors to dump inventory below cost and create planned bankruptcies. In this frightening scenario, partners in what is usually a small, recently formed enterprise get into business quickly and establish lines of credit with as many suppliers as possible. They then sell goods at or below cost and simply keep the money, sometimes fleeing to another country. When this happens, not only are their unlucky suppliers left holding the bag, so are the customers to whom they owe after-sale commitments such as warranties and equipment. It's a horror story all too familiar in a business where vendors are guaranteed to sell commodity-style products if only they price them low enough. The result of this competitiveness and rocky advertising terrain is that many people have unrealistic expectations when they actually set out to purchase a complete computer from a reputable source.

Once you have decided on a vendor who appears to be honest and have reasonable prices, then what? This is when a process sometimes referred to by sales trainers as "reduction" often directs the course of the transaction. This is jargon for reconciling one's desires with one's budget.

When confronted with the total cost of everything he or she needs to buy – computer, operating system, application software, monitor, printer, and applicable taxes – a purchaser must usually decide what to "reduce," what to leave in and what to take out, to keep within his or her budget. Remember this when you examine PC ads. The business is extremely competitive, and every vendor wants you to think he or she is offering the best buy. So make sure when considering a quotation that you have taken into account everything you're going to need.

COMPONENTS AND BALANCE

We will look at typical components and their relative importance to a computer's price and performance in more detail in Chapter 3, but for now let's take note of some basics. Probably the single most important characteristic of any system, whether it is new or used, is the speed of its processor, or CPU (central processing unit). This speed is normally measured in megahertz, or millions of cycles per second. It is the CPU chip which regulates the data pulsing through a computer to and from its subsystems. Certainly, the overall performance of a PC is dependent on all of its characteristics: RAM, cache memory, video memory, and hard drive specifications, to name a few. But the platform on which all of these rest is the CPU. Because the processor is so important, it is essential to purchase the fastest one you can afford, even at the expense of some other subsystems such as the amount of memory or the size of the hard drive. I have heard some PC shoppers say that, really, they don't mind saving money if it just means having to wait a few extra milliseconds during a computing session. A fraction of a second here or there is no big deal, right? Wrong! Speed in the computer world is more than just time. A faster system will run a wider variety of programs farther into the future, which means it will have a longer useful life before it has to be upgraded, sold, or abandoned. So among all the parts of the computer you are thinking of purchasing, go for the fastest processor first, and take advice about the other minimum specs in the PC that will be needed to keep up with it.

From the concept of subsystems working together arises the notion of balance in a microcomputer, the principle that no one component should be too far ahead of, or behind, the others. If you do purchase the fastest processor you can afford, and take care to ensure that all other parts of the system can keep up with it, you will be selecting a computer that will be useful and current as far as possible into the future.

BUILDING PEOPLE POWER

One thing that constantly amazes many of us in the retail part of the computer business is how downright apologetic people often become when purchasing high-tech equipment – new or used. Several times a week, I hear the familiar disclaimer, "I'm so sorry that I don't know as much about this kind of technology as I should . . ." or, "Now please be patient with me, because I'm really not very computer literate . . ." Perhaps this humble attitude has something to do with the intimidating marketing we have all been subjected to for so many years from manufacturers of computer products. Their message is clear: buy the most up-to-date system you can! Don't be left behind! Well, let us not forget, computers were not always the hot topic they are today. There was a time not long ago when they were lumped into the office-equipment pile with typewriters and calculators, about two notches on the sex appeal meter below washing your car.

In 1982, the yellow pages in my city directory were dominated by one or two large computer corporations aiming way above the technical abilities and budgets of ordinary people. In those days IBM PCs cost between $5,000 and $7,000, plus software, printer, and the almost mandatory installation and training fees. Even Apple's friendlier and more affordable IIs and IIes were in the $3,500 to $4,000 range. This situation was a continuation of the thriving mainframe and minicomputer markets of the '60s and '70s. Before the personal computer made its appearance, large manufacturers marketed their products in a highly controlled manner. They enjoyed the privileges of security and stability inherent in a scientific enterprise. In the cold-war era we readily accepted the idea of secluded, buzz-cut technicians working on a common cause for the common good. Public thinking about many things, including computers, has changed a lot since then.

By the end of the '70s, the industry was shaken to its foundations by the appearance of the personal systems worked up by pioneer tinkerers Bill Gates, Steve Wozniak, Paul Allen, and master marketer Steve Jobs. The legacy we have inherited from those innovators is aptly described by the product label itself: the "personal" computer. It's personal alright. That means it's yours to own and control and use however you want. Users should never have any qualms about how much they don't know about their computer, about how to set it up, tear it down, or put it to work. What a refreshing contrast it will be when all of us, manufacturers and users alike, grow to understand this idea fully. Before 1975, even a cheap computer cost hundreds of thousands of dollars and required precise knowledge to use. Now, for less than $2,000 you can buy a system thousands of times more powerful than the room-filling monsters of old. We just don't need to treat these things with the reverence we used to. The novice user is the standard to which tomorrow's systems must aspire. This idea should be publicized as a kind of eleventh commandment, marking a coming of age of the PC. Think of it as user power – the design and marketing of systems so intuitive that anyone can operate them productively without any training at all.

My own interest in computers and technology springs from my family's experience as owners and managers of an office-equipment store for nearly a hundred years. Our company originated with the curiosity of a telegraph operator named J. J. Seitz in Buffalo, New York. On a trip to New York City in the 1890s, he noticed some recently introduced Underwood manual typewriters. An enterprising sort, he brought what surely must have been some of the first machines of their kind into Canada, to Toronto, around 1900. Shortly afterward he started the Underwood Typewriter Company of Canada, selling machines announced as amazing labour-saving devices, in much the same way that the PC was presented about eighty years later.

The new typewriters were reviled by many as instruments of the devil, designed to lure young women into the workforce and away from their proper place at hearth and home. Whatever the social or political significance of these early writing machines, they did serve to provide at first thousands, and later millions, of jobs to women who had previously been allowed to choose from a very limited group of careers. As the typewriter became a standard piece of office equipment and the sales of Underwood Canada grew, Seitz hired my grandfather, who was handy at taking small appliances apart and putting them back together. Not long after this, about 1910, my grandfather was offered the chance to purchase a repair company associated with Underwood Canada, and so assumed ownership of Dominion Typewriter. This business is still operating, and in 1992 was renamed Dominion Business Machines.

In the store we display early newspapers and pictures advertising our buy, sell, and exchange services of the first half of the century. Since then, we have remained more or less on course with developments in office technology, handling in turn typewriters, calculators, fax machines, personal computers, and laser and inkjet printers as they became available. By 1984, we were selling Commodore 8032 desktop computer systems with two 360K floppy drives and an integrated green-on-grey twelve-inch monitor. As a business with a history of new and used office-equipment sales, it wasn't long before we started getting calls for used PCs as well. Before 1985, there was very little available in the used marketplace, but very soon this too would change.

THE RISE OF THE USED PC

So the first commercial microcomputers were introduced to the public around 1982. Supremely innovative, these systems were still pretty difficult to operate – a product line in its infancy. The cryptic commands you had to learn to run programs in those days make today's "intuitive" software seem almost miraculous by comparison. Even the better designed Apples were limited by the primitive programs available to run on them. A few years later, as hardware advancements appeared, the whole computing experience improved, and so followed PC sales.

It was not until the mid-'80s that the character of the used marketplace really began to establish itself. Basically, this was, and still is, a situation of short supply. The term "seller's market" aptly describes this side of the business. The reason is simple, as anyone who has purchased a PC and then tried to resell it can verify. Computers devalue very rapidly. This is chiefly because new products of higher specifications are so quickly and relentlessly introduced. The result is that people and companies don't want to sell their old equipment and endure a heavy loss. This resistance has created a chronically short supply of used computers, which is only partly alleviated by the fact that new systems are appearing so rapidly at lower prices. When Microsoft's Windows first emerged as a widely accepted operating system in the late '80s, easy, powerful, intuitive programs that piggybacked on top of it began to appear in large numbers. It is significant that many of these are just as relevant and effective today as in the year they were introduced. Examples like Microsoft Word, Microsoft Works, WordPerfect for Windows, Lotus for Windows, and Windows for Workgroups were real advances up the ladder of productivity. Suddenly, in the early '90s, no longer was a computer (or its software) difficult to handle simply because it was a few years old. This was an important watershed. As hardware innovations have continued, the prices of easy-to-use systems have fallen within reach of increasing numbers of people. In many cases these are users who would otherwise not have been able to afford a computer at all.

In the '90s, the natural evolution of the microcomputer and the expansion of the used market have altered the perspective formerly held by many on the new side of PC sales, namely, manufacturers' representatives, consultants, and advanced users. People experienced with computers often view used and upgraded systems with a skeptical eye. After all, isn't being "leading-edge" the whole point of the technology business? Not anymore. For a rapidly growing number of people and businesses, a used or upgraded computer is not only an excellent avenue through which to participate in the information revolution, but the only affordable one. From a philosophical as well as an economic point of view, this is indeed what I think the next wave in computer and information technology is all about: accessibility for everyday people.

But the used-computer marketplace does present some special problems. In it, you do not have as much freedom to select a computer with exact specifications as you do when buying a new one. With all of the usual PC purchase factors in mind – your requirements, the decision of whether to buy a brand-name or a generic product, what kind of computing power you need, and, of course, how much money you have to spend – be prepared for a couple of extra hurdles: where to find a good used PC, and how much to pay for it.

If the fundamental challenge of this marketplace is getting your hands on a good system at a reasonable price, how difficult is it to do so? This depends on how up-to-date the computer is that you are looking for. The older a system and the more basic its software, the cheaper and more readily available it will be. As of 1998, newer PCs with Pentium or Power PC level processors are still recent enough to remain highly sought after. Again, this is because of the drastic loss that any owner, whether a single user or a large corporation, has to endure when selling a system at a price competitive to the falling value of new goods.

It is not uncommon for a computer worth $3,000 when bought new to be driven down to a retail value of $1,000 or less by the associated reduction in new machines of the same specs within twelve to eighteen months of its original purchase date. And of course, if the owner decides to trade in or sell the equipment to a dealer, who must then resell it at a profit, this devaluation is even greater.

It is therefore easy to see that the more recent a computer, the less likely it is to be put on the used-market block. Nevertheless, there are still plenty of companies and individuals out there who, for one reason or another, must dispose of equipment whether they like it or not. You can find them if you know where to search. Later, in Chapter 6, we'll look in greater detail at the main tasks in this market: where to find good used PCs, and how to evaluate and purchase them.

THE NEXT WAVE

A good friend of mine, who is happy to admit that he doesn't know much about computers and doesn't want to learn, always delights in telling the same story when we start talking about technology. He has found, he says, the perfect answer to that most vexing of problems, the programming of his VCR. He's simply waiting until he can buy one that will understand him when he shouts at it. Of course, he always adds, this wonderful new model is going to become affordable much sooner than everyone thinks, and of course he is perfectly right.

The next wave in technology is not just going to be about how fast and powerful microprocessors have become, or how much data can be stored in a device the size of a pack of cards. While fundamental, innovations like these by themselves are not going to satisfy the demands of computer users of the future. Instead, technology designers are already fully aware of the bigger issues: how to make computers friendlier, and how to make it easy for ordinary people to use them. It's not as if these goals haven't been pursued in the past. But it's fair to acknowledge that we get closer to them every year. This means, among other things, being able to communicate with computers in our language instead of theirs, without having to learn much about how they actually work. It's perfectly reasonable to resent having to master all kinds of special knowledge when what you really want is to get your own work done. Who wants to have to learn how to take the car apart in order to drive it to the store to get the groceries? With these ideas in mind, I will set out a few guidelines in this book to help people find, evaluate, and purchase PCs so they can use this exciting new technology productively.

2

DECIDING WHAT YOU NEED

FIVE KEY QUESTIONS

From conversations I've had with customers, novice and expert users, and people inside and outside the computer business, I've learned five key questions you should ask yourself to help decide what kind of PC to buy:

- What do I want to use the computer for?
- How much can I afford to spend on it?
- What software do I want the computer to run?
- Will I be able to operate my computer and programs productively?
- How long do I want my computer to remain current?

A little attention to each of these issues can help make the difference between an unproductive, hair-raising purchasing experience and the acquisition of an educational and entertaining tool. It's also an excellent idea to consider these questions *before* you pick up the computer catalogue, buy the high-tech newspaper, or wander into the superstore. Do a little soul-searching before exposing yourself to the marketing tornado.

CREATING A TASK LIST

What do I want to use my computer for?

It seems obvious, but you'd be surprised how many people actually set out to buy a PC without first thinking carefully about this question. The temptation is strong to charge ahead blindly once you've decided to make a purchase. By all means allow yourself to get excited about the prospect of a new system, but be careful not to become enmeshed in technical jargon and advertising promotions too early in the game. Unfortunately, the specifications of the PC you're planning to buy can obscure the bigger issue: what you really want to do with the thing.

Many personal computers are equipped with all sorts of wonderful gadgets which might seem nice to have, but don't forget that these take time to learn and may wind up falling by the wayside. Ask yourself this: are you really going to have the time and energy to learn and use what you are paying good money for? Remember, you can acquire more software and hardware any day of the week, so don't lose sight of your immediate requirements.

Most people setting out to purchase a PC do so because of a mix of circumstances ranging from absolute necessity to simple curiosity. For a college student who has been informed that he must open an email account in order to submit work for a course, there is no alternative. For a retired lawyer who has time on her hands and would like to broaden her horizons, the purchase is purely voluntary. This is not to say, however, that the lawyer is going to find her shopping trip any easier. At least the college student knows exactly what he needs his system for. It's important he doesn't forget this when he walks into the store.

One easy way to remain focused on your goal is to sit down and write yourself a list, in plain English, of the most important duties you want the computer to perform. To keep things manageable, try to limit yourself to ten major tasks. Be sure your entries are short and sweet and describe precise human tasks such as "writing letters and reports" as opposed to vague computer-oriented directions such as "running Windows 95." An exception to this might be the case of a shopper who must operate a specific program, say, to comply with a direction to work on spreadsheets at home. In such a case, this all-important requirement jumps to the top of the list. Also, if your PC is going to have to satisfy the demands of more than one user, create a list for each of the other users too, or ask them to produce lists of their own.

A SAMPLE TASK LIST

Let's consider Christine, a single mother who is an ad salesperson for a small inner-city newspaper. She has a nine-year-old daughter and a brother in a city out west with whom she corresponds regularly. She is only marginally interested in computers and technology but realizes she needs an improved working knowledge of an up-to-date wordprocessing package, to continue growing in her job. She also has a sneaking suspicion that a newer computer might benefit her in other ways, though exactly how, she is not quite sure. She has a limited budget of $1,200 and is graduating from a slow, 486SX system she inherited in 1991, which she has been using for simple wordprocessing. This system has recently begun to show error messages when she turns it on, and last night it wouldn't start at all. Her task list might look something like this:

Christine (Purchaser)
Write articles and letters (less than fifty pages)
Produce promotional documents for work
Send and receive email to my brother via the Internet
Browse the Internet
Run some recreational CDs
Allison (Daughter)
Play games from disks and CDs
Run educational software from disks and CDs
Write stories and papers for school
Learn the Internet and keyboarding skills

These tasks will dictate the specifications of the PC Christine is going to need – and also what she can live without. Though it would be nice, she doesn't have to run out and lay down $3,000. On the other hand, at the very minimum she must find a computer capable of running Windows 95. This operating system will be needed to allow her access to any reasonably current wordprocessing software – the task at the top of her list – as well as permitting other applications involving the Internet and graphics. Microsoft Works, Corel WordPerfect Suite, Claris Works Office, or some similar all-in-one home package might be a good starting point here; these programs are inexpensive and, together with Windows 95, would allow her to create attractive documents using a surprisingly wide variety of fonts (styles of type). The range of these typestyles could be expanded quite inexpensively with font software available in many computer stores and on the Internet. These would help Christine with her promotional endeavours. This combination would also allow her to take graphic files (pictures) she had produced to a service bureau to be printed out – in colour. At this stage, Christine's budget does not really allow her to acquire the full-blown graphics software and laser or high-quality colour ink jet printer she really needs. But they could come later. If possible, she should also make sure her system contains a modem, in order to gain access to the Internet, although this too could wait until after she becomes familiar enough with her setup to perform her most important work-related tasks.

Given these considerations, and the size of her budget, Christine might pursue one of two options:

1. buy a new Pentium 166 or 200 MHz computer, probably one assembled locally, with a CD-ROM, and omit some items such as the modem, sound card, and Internet access as her budget demands, with the idea of acquiring them later;
2. buy a used, less powerful PC, say an older Pentium running at 90–133 MHz, that contains all of the components (CD-ROM, sound card, and modem for the Internet) she needs to perform the tasks on both her own and her daughter's lists.

In 1998, either of these plans could be adopted for well within Christine's budget of $1,200, including 15 percent taxes.

Of course, there are trade-offs associated with either plan. A new, "bare-bones" PC and some general-purpose software will fit the budget and offer maximum potential to add components in the future. But this choice also requires that Christine muster the patience to remain satisfied with only half of the tasks on her and her daughter's lists. On the other hand, a used PC already containing a CD-ROM drive, sound card, and modem is also a compromise. The components in it will be a year or two old and of reduced capability, so she will not be able to run a wide variety of programs as far into the future. How far? This is impossible to say for sure, but two years is a reasonable guess. If Christine is willing to accept these limitations, and hopes to be in a position to purchase a better system in a year or two, the used option is worthwhile.

It's also important to note that these specifications will be greater the longer Christine waits to make her purchase. However, this doesn't mean she should delay the project; for just as she can buy a more powerful PC in the fall of 1998 than she could in the spring, the system purchased later will still be about the same distance behind the "leading edge."

HOW MUCH SHOULD I SPEND ON MY COMPUTER?

Every time I ask people how much they plan to spend on their computer, I get the same answer: "As little as possible!" Whatever was I thinking? While I certainly sympathize, this issue really does demand a bit more thought. Setting the budget is one of the most important parts of the whole exercise of buying a PC. Here are a few tips:

1. Consider just how much money you can afford, at least in approximate terms, before allowing yourself to enter the high-tech bazaar and become hypnotized by the marketing blizzard raging there. Otherwise, you can quickly become convinced that you absolutely can't live without that fabulous $4,500 hot rod that's now on sale just down the street – Hurry! Only three left! – for $4,199.
2. Set a budget that not only is in line with your own financial capabilities but also includes everything you're going to need. And remember, don't be fooled by the ads. Consider the price of the whole purchase, not just what you see in the newspaper. Here's a list of different factors that affect the bottom line:

Hardware Costs

The complete computer system, including all necessary components: CPU, motherboard, hard drive, serial and parallel ports, video card, monitor, mouse, and keyboard. When you're shopping around, be sure to remember the term "complete computer system," and beware of unusually low prices; as mentioned previously, they're a dead giveaway of an incomplete configuration. Other items you'll need are a compact disc player or DVD, sound card, speakers, and probably a modem and printer and printer cable. When accepting a quotation, make sure it includes everything.

Software Costs

Some manufacturers or vendors include the cost of programs with a computer, and some don't. Be sure you know exactly what software comes with your PC and what will cost extra. Take special note of its operating system.

Software Installation Costs

Will the software that comes with your computer be installed and ready to run, or is the supplier planning to give it to you in a box ? If you do ask him or her to install it and assume the responsibility of it running properly, how much will he or she charge?

Component Installation Costs

Suppose you find a complete system which suits you perfectly. Then you decide to add an item such as a modem or scanner. Don't forget to enquire if the price you've been quoted includes its installation. In today's competitive retail environment, many vendors charge extra to install parts that weren't in a system in the first place.

Delivery and On-site Installation Costs

If an advertisement announces that all computers sold by a company will be delivered and set up in your office or home, remember to ask if there's a fee attached to either of these services.

And remember that they are not the same thing. In the first instance, expect a courier to drop the boxes off. In the second, a technician or installer should deliver the equipment, unpack it, and set it up. Be sure both you and your vendor have the same expectations about exactly what is involved.

Financing Costs

We'll deal with computer financing in depth later on, but for now, remember that when you make up your budget you should separate the cash cost of whatever you're buying from any financing or interest you're paying over time. No matter what an advertisement may claim, very few companies are able to offer interest-free loans and stay in business. Also, don't forget to consider all applicable federal and provincial taxes; they can be as much as 18 percent.

So don't omit any of these details when it comes time to request quotations or discuss your purchase with a potential vendor. Make a point of asking whether the system you are considering is complete. Time and again I have heard bitter complaints from buyers who invested precious time and energy researching a computer purchase, only to step up to the cash register or sales desk and find they must pay extra for an essential component. Typical of this is a missing operating system, the basic software "platform" needed by any computer to allow it to run "applications" such as spreadsheets or wordprocessing programs. Windows 95/98 is a good example of an "extra" which is often not included in the published hardware prices of generic or locally assembled systems. So be certain when you are trying to decide just how much your whole PC is going to cost that you are aware of everything you need.

WHAT SOFTWARE DO I WANT MY COMPUTER TO RUN?

People purchasing computers seem to fall into one of two categories when it comes to choosing the programs or applications they want to run: (1) they have specific software requirements; or (2) they have task-oriented software requirements. Let's look at each in turn.

Specific Software Requirements

A shopper with specific software requirements might be an executive who is seeking a system to use at home to work on spreadsheets from her office in Lotus 1-2-3 Version 5.0. The choice here is clear, and to a large degree will direct the rest of her computer purchase. Nowadays, most programs have minimum hardware requirements printed on the box, and these specifications can easily serve as a shopping list to take to a computer store. Of course, if your specific program requires only a rudimentary PC, the danger arises that you will not be able to broaden your horizons later. In that case, you should take the time to research other programs you may want to run and the hardware needed to support them as well.

Task-Oriented Software

Alternatively, a person who has a task-oriented software requirement, such as getting on the Internet or writing a book, has a bigger choice. Without some direction to guide you through this vast field of products, you can find yourself quite confused. Asking a computer salesperson what kind of software you're going to want without anything to guide you is a bit like asking a VCR sales rep what kind of movies you are going to like after you get the thing home and hooked up to your TV. It's pretty hard for a third party to make accurate recommendations without sitting down and talking to you for a while, something sales reps in today's fast-paced retail environment are not likely to want to do. So when it comes to evaluating software, it's a good idea to take a moment away from the hardware end of the purchase and consider information from someone other than the person who is trying to sell you something. Obviously, there are conventional ways to research which programs will do what: computer hardware publications, software magazines and reviews, computer-oriented TV shows, newspapers, and professional consultants. All of these sources can be worthwhile if you are so inclined, but they also pose one of the greatest opportunities for novice and intermediate computer users to get in over their heads and become even more confused than they were in the first place. This is because all publications, shows, reviews, and consultants have to pick a rung on the technical ladder which suits their place in the computer world and appeals to a chosen set of customers.

You may think it's hard to find an information source that's just right for you – one which doesn't use terms and concepts you don't understand and yet offers enough information to be really helpful. Don't be discouraged. If you aren't successful in locating good resource people and publications the first time around, try again. There is quite a wide variety of pre-sale information out there, aimed at users at almost every technical level, including people who have *never* used a computer before. One option to consider if you don't want to dive into the confusing world of software on your own is to seek a trusted friend or associate who is using his or her computer in a similar application. PCs are so common now that most of us know at least one or two people to whom we can turn for some kind of advice. Don't be ashamed to admit to your best friend's kid brother that you're thinking of buying equipment to perform a certain task and you'd like to know what he thinks. Many people are happy to share thoughts about the way they use their systems, and some of them can offer surprisingly valuable information about how a certain combination of hardware and software does or doesn't work. But one thing to remember about advisors is that they're *only* advisors. Beware of allowing a really knowledgeable person to railroad you into a program or computer beyond your budget or abilities. Better to look for people whose application and outlook are similar to yours and then ask precise questions about what they are using and how they like it.

Another good rule for novice users seeking a computer package oriented to a specific task is not to spend too much money. Lots of programs are available when you need them, so start slowly. Look for a system that has a broad range of capabilities, is easy to learn, and fits your budget.

WILL I BE ABLE TO USE MY COMPUTER AND PROGRAMS EFFECTIVELY?

Why is it, exactly, that some people seem to become computer wizards, while others spend half their lives researching the PC market, consulting experts, family, and friends, only to wind up with a big credit card bill and an expensive paperweight?

Just as there are signposts to watch for on the path toward a successful computer purchase, there are obstacles to avoid. To keep these in mind is to take a step toward the goal of having a system that does more or less what you purchased it for without breaking your bank account in two. A bonus will follow if the PC also offers some new insight into your life or your work. So take two sides of your personality – your heart and your head – into account.

FOLLOW YOUR HEART

As in many other pursuits, the more you like the idea of acquiring a new computer in the first place, the greater the chance you will be happy with the thing in the long run. To buy or upgrade your system just because someone else says you should is a good recipe for trouble. How many times have you heard about the small-business owner who was badgered into new technology by an advisor, only to lay out a lot of money and wind up right back in his old accounting routines a few months later? Or what about the elderly grandmother whose kids think that her life would be somehow enriched if only she had access to the Internet? Neither of these people should worry too much about buying a PC until *they* really want one. Sure, there are times when people get pushed into buying computer technology, but if that appears to be your situation, first make sure your advisors are telling you the truth. If they are, then your only alternative is to get into the project and try to concentrate on the ways it's supposed to benefit you.

FOLLOW YOUR HEAD

Which is to say, don't put too much stock in the ideas in somebody else's head! By all means, get as much information in advance as you can. Talk to co-workers. Pick up a few magazines. Read them in the bedroom if the technical terms scare you. Look at the pictures and don't try to understand everything at once. Talk to people who are reasonably close to you in outlook and expertise, and pick their brains. But don't be bullied. And if you choose to buy from a store, it's not a bad idea to attend the place on your own as opposed to taking your trusty consultant, at least on the first visit. It might be a bit more daunting, but it allows you to work up a more accurate feel for the place. Scout it out, talk to a sales rep, and absolutely do not fear anything he or she might say. Sales reps are there for your information and convenience. If they project any other countenance, especially a condescending one, go elsewhere. Life is too short, and there are many other places selling this kind of equipment which will appreciate your business and treat you properly.

Finally, if the whole project of buying a computer seems like it's growing out of control, take a break from it. Talk to a close friend or family member about the philosophy of having it in your life, as opposed to having further discussions about the merits of different specifications. Take in the big picture, and, even if you are under a tight deadline, give yourself as much room to breathe as you can before making your decision.

HOW LONG DO I WANT TO KEEP MY COMPUTER?

Probably the most frightening issue confronting a person shopping for new or used computer equipment is the fear of its impending obsolescence. On one hand, you are preparing to invest money and days or even weeks of research and shopping time in the acquisition of an important and expensive item. On the other, you are acutely aware that your beautiful new equipment will probably devalue faster than any other object you will ever purchase, except maybe for fruit and vegetables in the fridge. This is an unavoidable problem facing everyone who shops for a PC, new or used, big or small. What is there to do about it? Not much. One way of approaching the question is to treat the system as a throwaway item and buy the cheapest one you can find that will get your job done. Here are a couple of additional observations:

Remain calm. Whatever it is you purchase will become yesterday's computer sooner than you expect, so accept this and get over it as soon as you can. Be prepared for the reality that your hard-earned investment is about to devalue by about 50 percent per year, and get on with your life. No point worrying about things you can't change, and the ever-evolving world of technology is not going to stop for you any more than it will for the president of IBM. And don't make the simplistic mistake of thinking that if you wait until next year the whole situation will somehow be different. New technology will be causing obsolescence then just as it is today, just as it did five years ago. So when you're ready to swim, hold your nose and jump into the pool. Don't forget, we're all in this water together.

Aim high. Try to purchase the fastest computer you can afford so it will see you as far into the future as possible. For most people, a PC purchase is a process in reduction; you start out with an ideal configuration which gradually gets trimmed to fit your budget. This is OK. Almost everyone approaches this exercise with fixed resources, and although all systems become outdated sooner or later, they can and should remain productive for many years.

And by the way, if you think there might be some kind of conspiracy among resellers or manufacturers in the computer industry, think again. The future for them is a lot scarier than it is for you. Imagine how the problem of obsolescence looks to a buyer who has to purchase quantities of these things every week! Imagine having to invest hundreds of thousands of dollars and man hours in an inventory which you know is going to remain current about as long as a truckload of toaster waffles. Most computers become virtually worthless on company books in three or four years. So no, there's no grand scheme on the part of the manufacturers to manipulate the market. Neat new stuff simply appears so fast that no standard ever remains current for long, and the forces causing this are extremely diverse. Of course, there are some ways in which industry players use predictable devaluation to their advantage, but as a fact of life that is known to just about everyone, obsolescence is usually much more of a risk to computer companies than it is an opportunity for profit.

3

Inside Out

The purpose of this chapter is to introduce you as gently as possible to the main components of a personal computer: what they do, how they work, how they're measured, and what those measurements can mean to a system's performance and price. It is not to provide an in-depth discussion of PC design, or to burden you with more technical terms than you are likely to need.

You may feel an immediate and uncontrollable urge to skip this section, and I must say that I wouldn't blame you one bit. But remember, avoiding all knowledge of computer terms when setting out to purchase one is a bit like trying to buy a car without taking the trouble to learn a steering wheel from a transmission. It simply increases your chances of winding up with the wrong thing. Certainly it's a pain to have to learn concepts that might not seem necessary, but this section is a good place to start if you'd like a basic introduction to the terms flying around in the marketing whirlwind.

THE SUBSYSTEMS OF A PC

I remember reading about a student at the Massachusetts Institute of Technology who actually built a primitive computer out of Lego blocks and other wooden parts that would have been available to anyone in the nineteenth century. He did this to illustrate the way a computer works. How far is that model from the systems we are familiar with in

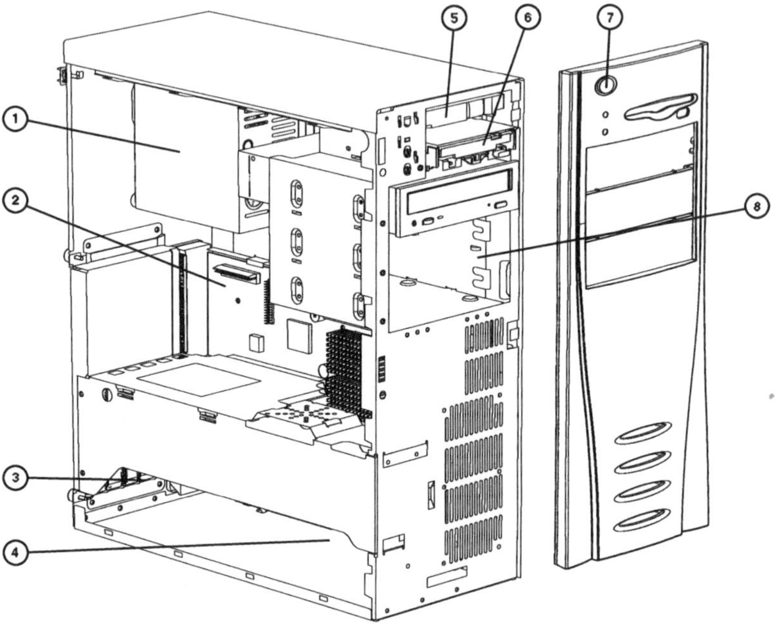

1. 185-Watt Power Supply
2. System Board
3. Expansion Slots (two PCI, two ISA, and one shared)
4. Memory Expansion Sockets
5. SMART EIDE Hard Drive
6. 1.44-MB Diskette Drive
7. Power Switch
8. User-Accessible Expansion Bays

FIGURE 3A

A multimedia minitower computer exploded

the late '90s? From an overall perspective, any computer – a personal system (powerful), a minicomputer (more powerful), or a mainframe (very powerful) – is a collection of switches that work in concert, exchanging information on directions from the user and a program. It is composed of subsystems which manipulate very small amounts of electricity, tiny positive and negative charges which make up the famous bits and bytes. These enable a computer to make logical "if/then" decisions and display the results. It's worth remembering these basic concepts when considering PCs, otherwise they can assume magical, mystical qualities that make them abstract and frustrating.

When considering the subsystems of a PC, it is probably best to start

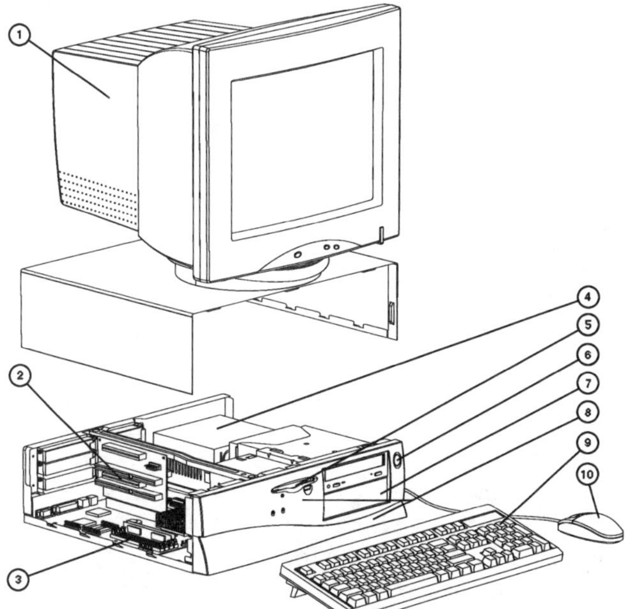

1. V 70 Colour Monitor (Optional)
2. Expansion Slots (two PCI, two ISA, and one shared)
3. System Board
4. 145-Watt Power Supply
5. 1.44-MB Diskette Drive
6. Power Switch
7. Expansion Bays
8. SMART EIDE Hard Drive
9. Keyboard
10. Mouse

FIGURE 3B

A multimedia desktop computer exploded

with a picture. If you are not used to seeing a computer with its hat off, Figures 3A and 3B offer a visual idea of a couple of different designs. It's pretty easy to spot the main components you will commonly hear about from manufacturers and salespeople. How do all of these subsystems work together to perform computing tasks? Let's look at them one at a time.

THE CPU

One of the most important and miraculous parts of any microcomputer is its CPU, or central processing unit, a microchip normally plugged into a computer's motherboard (see page 39), or, in some cases, into a card connected to the motherboard. The CPU is sometimes called a system's "heart" or "brain," and indeed these terms reflect its importance. Physically the CPU chip is small, an inch or two square, although the new Intel Pentium II chips are a bit larger. A CPU is a bit like a computer within a computer, an assembly of "on" and "off" switches connected by their own circuits and controlled by their own special set of instructions. The CPU's lot in life is to regulate the speed and flow of data constantly moving around the other parts of the PC. At a very basic level, it does this by assigning a 0 or 1 value to a high or low level of voltage and then making logical conclusions about combinations of the results.

It's worth noting that the instructions that control a CPU chip are similar to, but separate from, the software programs you run during an ordinary computing session. So think of a CPU's instruction set as a computer's "higher power." It enables this all-important chip to accept data from one part of a system, such as its keyboard or hard drive, send it to the RAM (memory) to be sorted and counted, then back to other components such as the monitor or printer. Quite a lot of responsi-bility for such a little device. It's no wonder that CPU chips and their characteristics occupy such an important place in discussions of PCs and their prices. CPUs are the juice; or more accurately, they control the juice. They do it quickly too. They're measured in megahertz – a frequency of millions of cycles per second – the speed at which a CPU's internal clock ticks. So this subsystem is a fundamental part of a PC, ticking super-fast, performing the following data management tasks:

1. The CPU controls and directs data traffic within itself and throughout the computer.
2. It makes its own arithmetic calculations for use internally and in any programs the system runs.
3. It tracks the processing of data in its "registers."
4. It provides its own "bus," or pathway, for data to move around inside itself.
5. It provides its own "cache," or bin, for data waiting to be passed through it, so it doesn't run out of things to do and slow the whole system down.
6. It provides calculations of "floating-point" decimal numbers, and in the case of newer chips such as Intel's Pentium MMX and Pentium II processors, manages the flow of sound and video data and other repetitive tasks.

Not all CPUs contain all of these features; like other computer components, these chips have been constantly improved and redesigned over the years. Nor are the processors in mini- and mainframe computers the same as those in PCs. But the newest issues in the microcomputer marketplace are absolute marvels of engineering.

Let's look at how CPU chips are measured, and what you should watch for in a computer you are thinking of purchasing.

CPU Types

Throughout the years, successive issues of CPUs have been manufactured by major builders such as Intel, IBM, Motorola, Cyrix, American Micro Devices, and Texas Instruments. We have seen steady increases in the number of bits in a chip's bus – that is, how much data it can grab and move around inside itself in one processing cycle. The wider its bus, the more information a CPU can handle in a given time. Early processors – the 8086s in IBM's original PCs – were 8-bit chips. Current Pentium and Pentium II issues have 32- and 64-bit architectures, a significant increase over products of fifteen years ago.

Each generation of CPUs is commonly known by the last three numbers in its formal name: 80286 chips as 286s, 80486s as 486s, and so on, with variations occurring in Motorola's line of products for Apple PCs. However, when Intel, the chief innovator in CPU manufacture and design, reached the 80586 threshold in 1992, it introduced the name Pentium, because the number 586 was not eligible for copyright. This did not stop its competitors from producing products with names like the K5 or the Nx586. Intel's original Pentiums, running at 60 to 133 MHz, have undergone marked improvements over the past three years, with new versions available at 450 MHz. Pentiums have been available in five main design types up to our date of publication: the original Pentium, the Pentium MMX, the Pentium Pro, the Pentium II, and the new Celeron series. New issues are sure to follow. For more information on these processors – their physical sizes, internal speeds, voltages, and other properties, see the CPU Characteristics section below.

CPU Speed

As mentioned above, CPU speed is measured in megahertz and is arguably the most important specification in a PC. It's important to understand, though, that each generation of CPU is not tied to a specific speed. Instead, processors have been issued in ranges (see Figure 3C). For example, 386s fell between 16 and 40 MHz, 486s between 25 and 133 MHz, and Pentiums between 60 and 300 (and climbing) MHz.

Muddying the waters further, CPU chips of the same speed do not necessarily perform equally; that is, they don't always run the same programs at the same speed. As we have seen, processors contain several different systems, just like the computers they're part of. So comparing them by considering one specification and forgetting about the others is simply not sensible. Acceptable MHz levels in new PCs for general use are now at 200- to 233-MHz minimums. For used PCs, shoot for 100–166 MHz, depending on the software you plan to run. These numbers will of course continue to increase over time as new processors, and programs written for them, appear.

CPU Characteristics

It's important to understand that not all CPUs of the same generation are designed the same way. There can be big differences in the characteristics, performance, and price of processors of the same generation. For example, 486s were issued by Intel in several different designs and speeds, two notable categories being those that contained a floating-point decimal calculator (486DX series) and those that did not (486SX series). In Intel's Pentium processor series, we have seen five main versions appear during the '90s: the original Pentium, the Pentium MMX, the Pentium Pro, the Pentium II, and Pentium overdrive processors, intended for insertion into older 486 motherboards.

The original Pentium CPUs, introduced around 1993, are obsolete in new computers in 1998. They were improvements on 486 processor technology, containing an internal 32-bit bus, over 3.1 million transistors, and the ability to address 4 gigabytes (4,000 MB) of memory.

The Pentium Pro, which appeared around 1995, was Intel's improved version of its original. Among other enhancements, it offered a group of features called "dynamic execution" to predict processing, and was optimized to run 32-bit operating systems common in network environments. It too has been displaced from the market by subsequent CPU issues.

The Pentium MMX (formally labelled the "Intel Pentium Processor with Multimedia Extension") is an original Pentium with nearly sixty extra instructions in its preprogrammed command set allowing it to process sound and moving pictures (multimedia) more quickly and efficiently. Still available in 1998, it too appears ready for obsolescence in the shadow of the Pentium II.

The Pentium II incorporates the features of the Pentium Pro and the Pentium MMX CPUs – it is optimized to handle 16- and 32-bit software, contains dynamic execution processing techniques, dual independent bus architecture, and multimedia extension. It contains improved cached memory, and the power of more than seven million transistors to provide for visually based applications such as digital still photography and video editing and transmission.

Each of these chips contains other specific characteristics in terms of size, electrical requirements (voltage), internal speed, and clock speed. These are especially important for anyone considering upgrading a late-issue 486 or older Pentium computer.

CPU Manufacturers

A pretty hot debate rages about the relative merits of third-party, or "reverse-engineered," chips. Are they as good as the originals? Are they worth the savings? These are difficult questions because many factors apply. A reverse-engineered processor is really just an attempt by one company to copy another company's success. Sometimes cloned CPUs are made by taking an original apart right down to the molecular level, then redesigning it with enough differences to be manufactured and sold legally under a new name. A good clone will perform all of the tasks of the original and will usually cost less – that's the whole idea. When reverse engineering was a new concept, however, many CPU copies simply did not work. Back in those days, the mid- to late '80s, the issue of compatibility, that is, whether a copied chip would run all the programs designed for the original, was a big concern.

Today, in non-networked computing environments where you are planning to run off-the-shelf programs, it's probably riskless to accept a generic, or cloned, CPU. Be aware, though, that it may be slower. Other characteristics built into it (or left out) mean that its megahertz speed is not the only thing to consider. The overall performance of some 233-MHz processors is not equal to that of some others. Furthermore, some CPU manufacturers have gone so far as to identify their processors with a number that is not even accurate to their internal clock speeds. So the megahertz speeds of two CPUs is an important comparison only when their other characteristics are the same; and be sure the number on a chip really does describe its internal clock. Different generations of processors you will encounter are shown in Figure 3C.

How do all of these CPU features affect your choice of a new or used computer? Given the rate at which new programs tailored to run on faster processors appear, most purchasers won't want to be left out in the cold. So aim for the highest-performance CPU you can afford,

COMMON MICROCOMPUTER PROCESSORS AND THEIR CLOCK SPEEDS

PROCESSOR	CLOCK SPEED (MHz)
Intel 8088	4.7 to 8 MHz
Intel 80286	8 to 20 MHz
Intel 80386	16 to 40 MHz
Motorola 68030	8 to 26 MHz
Intel 80486SX	25 to 50 MHz
Intel 80486DX	25 to 133 MHz
AMD Am486	66 to 120 MHz
AMD K5	75 to 166 MHz
AMD Am5x86	133 MHz
IBM/Cyrix 6x86	100 to 133 MHz
AMD K6x86	100 to 150 MHz
AMD K6x86 MMX	233 to 266 MHz
Intel Pentium	60 to 200 MHz
Motorola Power PC Series	60 to 300+ MHz
Intel Pentium with MMX	133 to 266 MHz
Intel Pentium Pro	133 to 266 MHz
Intel Pentium II/Celeron	233 to 450 MHz
Motorola G3 Series	233 to 300+ MHz

FIGURE 3C

Note: The Motorola 68000 series, Power PC series, and G3 series have properties that make them faster than other CPUs of the same MHz ranges.

even if you have to skimp on other, more easily upgradable components. And be sure you're able to remove the CPU from the motherboard of the computer you buy and reinsert a better chip later. CPU apertures in motherboards which allow this are known as ZIF (zero insertion force) sockets; you can simply pull a chip out of a ZIF socket and push in a new one.

The form of a ZIF socket and the size and voltage of the processor in a computer you may already own will determine whether you can upgrade it this way. In most current (two years old and newer) motherboards, ZIFs are described by the terms "Socket 4," "Socket 5," and "Socket 7." Early Intel Pentium 60 MHz and 66 MHz CPUs were 5-volt chips requiring a Socket 4. Newer Pentium MMX 133s and 200s require 3.3-volt Socket 5s or Socket 7s. Some motherboards offer dual voltage ZIFs, making them more upgradable than others. Pentium II processors require a motherboard with a single edge contact (SEC) connector, so these CPUs cannot normally be retrofitted onto older motherboards.

As far as CPU manufacturers are concerned, the decision whether to purchase an Intel chip or one of its competitor's products is less straightforward. It's difficult to lay down hard and fast rules about different kinds of processors because the market is changing so rapidly. Just be sure that when you compare products you enquire about true performance rather than just looking at a single number.

Finally, here's a Lemon-Aid tip on CPUs: Higher-megahertz chips may actually be inferior in some situations, or simply not as fast. Be sure to raise this issue with your vendor when considering different PCs.

MOTHERBOARDS

As their name implies, motherboards are a major component in conventional personal computers. They have been designed in many shapes and sizes over the years, some of which are "proprietary" – they are intended for specific makes and models of PCs – while others are "generic" – they can easily be taken out of one computer and put into another.

A typical PC motherboard is a large composite plastic card about 8" x 8" in size and covered with printed circuits. It has a number of receptacles into which various microchips and other parts of the computer can be connected, either directly or by the use of controller cards. So this main circuit board holds the whole show together, acting as the physical base by which subsystems are connected and providing for the transfer of data to and from them. It accepts the plug from the keyboard, for example, provides connectors for the hard drive and video card, and has special places for the RAM memory chips and the all-important CPU chip. It even has its own little battery, which helps it retain information about the system even when the system is turned off.

Two important features of a motherboard which help any computer retain its identity are the CMOS and BIOS. Similar enough to be confusing, these are small but important reservoirs of information any PC needs to run properly.

As its name implies, the more basic of these sets is the BIOS, or basic input/output system. This is a table of values, normally stored in ROM ("read only memory"), which enables a motherboard to move data from one part of itself to another.

Similarly, the CMOS (complementary metal oxide semiconductor) is a low maintenance memory chip which holds a wider set of parameters: information about a PC's peripheral systems and environment such as its hard drive type and the date and time. All common PC motherboards contain both CMOS and BIOS information.

As you can imagine, with all of these characteristics, different motherboard designs have appeared over the years. Soon after IBM's first PCs arrived and were recognized as conglomerations of components which could be manufactured by different companies, a variety of motherboards began to appear, as well as different products to plug into them. Today, two of the main features of a motherboard's design are its physical layout and the characteristics of its connections.

The basic "pathway" on a motherboard through which data flow to and from the processor is known as its expansion bus. This is the path connecting the processor to the motherboard's expansion slots, physical apertures into which you can plug devices like video cards and modems.

Motherboards and the devices they accept are often categorized by the types of expansion slots they offer, though it is not uncommon for a motherboard to contain expansion slots of different types. But interface cards that can be plugged into one type of slot will not usually fit into another. From the beginning, it was essential for manufacturers of computer parts to build similar products, so that their hard drives and video controllers, for example, would work together properly. As a result, various standards of expansion slots on motherboards have arisen throughout the past fifteen years, each one defined by an acronym (what else?) and established by manufacturers or groups of manufacturers who collaborated on the design.

No matter how exotic or technical they may sound, these acronyms simply represent different computer card types, rather like the VHS and BETA standards in the video business. Here is a list of expansion slot standards you're likely to encounter when considering motherboards built in the last ten years:

ISA – Industry Standard Architecture
EISA – Enhanced Industry Standard Architecture
MCA – Microchannel Architecture
VESA (Local Bus) – Video Enhanced Standards Association
PCI (Local Bus) – Peripheral Component Interconnect

ISA (Industry Standard Architecture)

A standard which appeared in IBM's original PC and AT computers more than fifteen years ago, this design has endured. Many current IBM-compatible PCs have at least one or two refined versions of the

ISA slots IBM developed, which means that you can still purchase and connect ISA components today. Motherboards limited to this standard, however, are obviously out of date: the originals were slow and unable to accept new generations of controller cards. The ISA expansion bus allows a transfer rate of only 8 or 16 bits of data per processing cycle.

MCA (Microchannel Architecture)

Here is an excellent example of the treacherous waters at the manufacturing end of the computer business. In the mid-'80s, it became apparent to IBM, as well as other companies, that certain features associated with ISA motherboards should be changed. Drawing on its extensive knowledge of larger systems and some new research, IBM announced in 1987 a whole new design standard for its PCs: microchannel architecture. This move may be seen as a major corporation's response to the large-scale copying of its premier product by many imitators.

And there was no doubt about it, the new PS/2 computers containing this design really were an improvement. They were faster – data flowed from their motherboards to other components through a wider 32-bit bus – and they allowed the use of "smarter" controller cards because of a feature called "bus mastering." In essence, this meant that subsystems in the computer such as its hard drive or video controllers were able to help manage their own operations instead of requiring the main CPU chip to do it all for them. This was definitely more efficient. Nevertheless, with the introduction of this technology and its subsequent decline, a major point was reaffirmed to IBM and everyone else regarding PC hardware and software: if a product is too proprietary, or "closed," for other companies to manufacture parts for it, build on it, upgrade it, or repair it, its chances of long-term survival are compromised. If there has appeared one constant in personal computer manufacturing, this is it. Even today, Apple is reaping the bitter rewards of the proprietary nature of its products established years ago. In the same way, the microchannel standard was born, blossomed with promise in the late '80s, then died in the early '90s from lack of attention and support by manufacturers and users of more "open" PCs.

EISA (Enhanced Industry Standard Architecture)

A response by a group of manufacturers to IBM's ill-fated attempt to dominate motherboard design when it introduced the MCA standard, extended industry standard architecture might be thought of as a triumph of the common computer user over one company's effort to capture the market. Like several other computer-design examples

(MPEG and PCMCIA), EISA motherboards were the result of several major companies (nine in this case) collaborating to establish a playing field they all could live with. In simple terms, they took several of the features missing from the old ISA design standard – notably the features being offered by IBM in its proprietary MCA design – and added some further advantages. Some EISA features are interrupt sharing, a 32-bit architecture, a higher-speed transfer rate (33 MB/sec versus about 8 MB/sec for ISA), and some other automated functions.

With these extras, EISA motherboards also enjoyed success in the late '80s and early '90s, but have since been relegated to the "where are they now?" pile, along with great old TV shows like *Honey West*. Remember, a motherboard designed to a certain standard must handle conforming controller cards, so compatibility is important. While EISA systems outperformed their older ISA relatives and could communicate with ISA components, they too have become obsolete.

VESA (Video Electronic Standards Association)

In the tradition of the EISA design, the VESA standard also issued from a collaborative environment. If it sometimes seems to you that the computer-manufacturing business is being run by committee, you're not far off. Creating a successfully designed anything in the PC world is almost certainly a group effort today. There are simply too many people, companies, and applications to consider for any one manufacturer to treat its competitors only as competitors.

In the early '90s, a group of companies agreed on a third improved version of the old ISA design. In essence, improvements in these VESA motherboards provided extra connections in their expansion slots to allow faster transfer of data. This was added to allow information to flow directly from the controller card to the CPU using the new motherboard's "local bus" rather than its slower "expansion bus." This innovation went hand in hand with the faster, newly developed 486 CPUs of the day, which could handle several conversations with different subsystems of a computer at one time.

Pioneered by companies in the video card part of the computer business, VESA motherboards soon caught on, and manufacturers of all kinds of controller cards and other pluggable devices jumped on the bandwagon. A distinct advantage of the VESA standard was that motherboards with these slots also accepted standard, old-fashioned ISA cards, a VESA slot being the same as an ISA slot except with a few connectors added to talk to the local bus.

Alas, this design too is now out of date. One of its chief drawbacks was a limitation on the number of local bus devices a PC could handle effectively: any more than two and the CPUs of the day would start creaking and groaning and slowing the system down. Other data flowing around a PC use its local bus as well. Still, with its flexibility (the ability to accept old ISA cards), increased performance, and popularity, the VESA standard remains in use in 486 computers in the used marketplace. It's also still common to see a couple of VESA slots on new PCI motherboards in Pentium-level computers.

PCI (Peripheral Component Interconnect)

Developed in 1992 by Intel and other hardware manufacturers, this expansion slot design has become standard in Pentium-level PCs. In general terms, it improved on the principle of the local bus by adding a new set of chips to help manage the direct flow of information to and from the processor. This enables data to flow out of the expansion slots at the same time that the CPU is working on other tasks, allowing greater efficiency. These chipsets – sometimes called "logic sets" – affect when and how fast PCI components talk to the CPU. They also affect the system and cache memories as well as directing other traffic.

As PCI motherboards have evolved, so have the chipsets they use. This in turn has created opportunities for misinterpretation and misrepresentation. Originally, Intel created the Triton chipset for PCI motherboards, but abandoned this name in 1996 even though other companies issued products called Triton II and Triton III. Intel's chipsets have been renamed the 430 FX, VX, HX, MX, and TX, with the 440 FX PCIset designation applying to the Pentium II systems as of publication. This is an area ripe for aspiring manufacturers who want to ride on the coattails of Intel's success. It's a good idea to confirm that Intel's name appears on the chipset in any computer you purchase, unless you can get confirmation that an alternative manufacturer's product will perform as well.

Other important characteristics of PCI motherboards are the memory sockets and CPU sockets they present and the "form factor" they meet – a term describing a board's physical design as well as some of its internal features. Intel Pentium MMX motherboards will generally allow the insertion of a 3.3-volt processor into a Socket 7 receptacle, as well as the use of SDRAM (synchronous dynamic random-access memory). Pentium II motherboards offer a single edge contact (SEC) connector. In addition to the size of the processor, the type of chipset, and the design of memory chips they accept, PCI motherboards in Pentium MMX and Pentium II PCs also define a system's compliance with certain case sizes, as well as containing sensors to keep you informed of internal conditions like the operation of the cooling fan, the temperature and voltage of the motherboard, and the presence of viruses.

Recommending a particular motherboard manufacturer to computer shoppers is problematic. This is one of the fastest-changing markets in the PC world. When you purchase a system from a large company such NEC, AST, Dell, or IBM, you place your trust in the manufacturer to select a high-quality, up-to-date product for you. In locally assembled computers, the motherboard is one of the most difficult components to evaluate, which is why you must choose your assembler with care when shopping in this end of the market.

Among well-known motherboard manufacturers are Acer, American Megatrends, Asus, Biostar, Computrend, Dataexpert, Genoa, Gigabyte, Microstar, Nexgen, and Pine Technology, although this is by no means a complete or recommended list. Excellent information on motherboards and motherboard types is available on the Internet at several sites including the following:

http://www.motherboards.org
http://www.sysopt.com/mboard.html
http://www.tomshardware.com/mainboard.html

A browse through the PC hardware section of any well-established search engine such as Yahoo or AltaVista will yield a host of other sites describing up-to-the-minute motherboard and chipset technologies.

RAM

Of all of the components in a personal computer, memory is one of the most difficult to understand and describe. Perhaps this is because it spans the range between a system's identity as a machine and its unique ability to make logical, almost human, choices. In addition to this spooky identity, RAM comes in a bewildering array of shapes, sizes, and speeds, and is used in different parts of a computer for different tasks. In this section, the objective is to present basic concepts of PC memory for referral when reading advertisements or listening to salespeople or consultants.

All kinds of in-depth technical information is available on the topic, although really accurate and up-to-date facts are hard to find. If you feel like venturing farther into the technical jungle, one of the best places to start is the Internet. Sites are maintained by manufacturers and academic and scholarly publications, and there are even some surprisingly good ones posted by interested individuals.

A few I have found of interest are shown below. They vary from presenting facts about different kinds of RAM to offering new and used chips at discount prices.

http://www.accessmicro.com
http://www.sysdoc.pair.com
http://www.micron.com

Most people are at least familiar with the concept of random-access memory chips. After all, these devices are present now in everything from alarm clocks to automobiles to those little electronic pets for kids. Classically described as "volatile" memory, RAM stores information in a PC temporarily, for use only when a system is operating. This is different from the concept of "storage" on a hard drive, which, confusingly, has been measured in the same increment: megabytes. Current hard drives are now large enough to be measured in gigabytes – a gigabyte being approximately 1,000 megabytes – so the confusion between storage and volatile memory in PCs is disappearing.

To help novice purchasers with the distinction between RAM and hard drive storage, I sometimes use the analogy of a teacher sitting inside the front door of a library. Think of RAM as the information she has learned – the facts that are stored in her head. If you ask her a question to which she knows the answer, she will respond quickly and efficiently. If not, she will have to go back to the book stacks (think of them as a PC's hard drive) and look it up. At the end of the day, when the teacher locks up and goes home (when a computing session is ended and the system is turned off), her learned information (RAM) is not available anymore.

We have already seen that data flow through a computer in the form of very small electrical pulses. The processor assigns each positive or negative "bit" a numeric 0 or 1 value which can be manipulated according to predetermined rules to cause specific results: show a certain letter on a screen, instruct a modem to start dialling, or write a series of characters on a hard drive. These controlling properties mean that RAM chips get used in different locations in a PC, which is one of the reasons why discussions of them can quickly become confusing. Usual RAM locations in a computer are its main memory, cache memory, video memory, and device memory. Chips intended for these tasks come in different designs and behave in various ways.

Over the years, main memory, or DRAM (dynamic random-access memory), chips have undergone several changes in order to keep up with increasingly fast computers. These are the chips most often mentioned in advertisements and by salespeople. They normally fit into slots on a motherboard, and along with a PC's processor, largely define its overall performance: which operating system and applications the computer can handle, and how fast it does so. Current motherboards designed for Pentium MMX or Pentium II processors usually present four slots to accommodate a combination of chips totalling 32 or 64 megabytes of RAM with a possible maximum of 128 MB, 256 MB, or more. In addition to defining software capabilities, this main memory affects almost every other component in a PC, so it's important to have enough. All kinds of problems arise when you don't.

Here is a list of the major classes of DRAM chips used in the main memory of personal computers:

FPM (Fast Page Memory)
The oldest type of RAM chip, and rapidly falling out of the mainstream market, these "standard" DRAM chips run at 60 to 100 nanoseconds (meaning it takes them from 60 to 100 nanoseconds to access a single piece of information and make it available for processing) and were common in 386, 486, and some early Pentium-level systems.

EDO (Extended Data Out)
A current standard, but losing ground to newer designs, EDO DRAM chips enjoyed peak popularity in 1996–97. They are similar to FPM (standard) DRAM, but use the timing of a system's processor more efficiently, to crank out data faster. Most popular in 50-, 60-, and 70-nanosecond issues, they have given way to SDRAM because of the demands of faster CPUs and motherboards.

BEDO (Burst Extended Data Out)
A refinement of the EDO design, these DRAM chips process data in chunks, or "bursts," which makes them faster than their predecessors. Running at the same 50- to 70-nanosecond levels, BEDO DRAM was also common in systems of 1996 and early 1997 but has lost ground because of its inability to handle processors with bus speeds over 66 MHz.

SDRAM (Synchronous Dynamic RAM)
As their name suggests, these chips are directly synchronized to the processor in a PC and so are better able to keep up. Wait states –

the periods when a CPU is able to process data but doesn't have any – are virtually eliminated, and the control of data flowing in and out of SDRAM memory is greatly simplified. These are most common now in the main memories of Pentium II PCs.

Physical Properties

DRAM chips have appeared in different designs over the years. They are usually about 2" to 4" long and 0.5" wide, presenting 30- or 72-pin metal (usually gold, tin, or, in newer chips, copper) connectors or pins to a motherboard. Note that the actual form of a RAM chip is not necessarily an indication of its type. Different physical designs are a further alphabet jumble, the most common form factor today being the 72-pin DIMM (dual in-line memory module) or 72-pin SIMM (single in-line memory module). Macintosh PCs have been using DIMMs for several years.

Other types of DRAM chips were used in 286, 386, and 486 PCs of old, and I note these more for computer enthusiasts than for people researching a computer purchase. They are the SIPP (single in-line pin package) and the DIP (dual in-line pin). In some cases, these old chips were soldered right into a motherboard, making a system impossible to upgrade. They laboured along at 90, 100, or 120 nanoseconds, while current chips are pushing the 40-nanosecond barrier.

Cache Memory

As noted earlier in this chapter, one of the fundamental problems of computer design is the difficulty of keeping various subsystems working together with no one of them lagging behind or surging ahead. This problem is especially important in the marriage of RAM and CPU, and has resulted in the development of cache RAM – a small amount of very fast memory designed to keep data always ready for the processor. Sometimes known as "level 2," or "external" (external to the processor), cache, these chips have appeared in three major flavours: asynchronous burst SRAM, synchronous burst SRAM, and pipeline burst SRAM (PB-SRAM).

By the standards used to assess main memory, all of these chips are quick – in the 10- to 20-nanosecond range. (Remember, that's ten to twenty *billionths* of a second!) As a result, cache RAM is expensive and must be purchased with care. SRAM chips are also often peculiar to certain types of motherboards, and cannot be mixed or matched. Current PB-SRAM chips are able to keep up with bus speeds of up to 133 MHz, and process data at 4 to 8 nanoseconds. Wow! As of publication, new Pentium motherboards using the VIA chipset will support over 2 megabytes of this kind of memory. How new operating systems will use it, however, remains a matter of debate. If you are purchasing a PC in 1998, aim for at least 512K of pipeline burst cache to keep your Pentium 233-MHz or faster CPU filled with data.

Video Memory

This type of memory affects the performance of a personal computer by controlling the amount of information that can be displayed on a monitor at one time, as well as the speed at which that information can be changed. The appearance of any picture on a PC display is a direct result of the amount of data that can be offered to it by the system at a given time. This raises the issues of resolution and colour, both of which are affected by video card memory.

A picture displayed on a computer monitor is composed of several lines of tiny coloured dots, or "pixels," which are constantly being changed, or "refreshed." The number of these across by the number down is known as resolution. In current systems this is usually 640 x 480, 800 x 600, or 1024 x 768. The higher the resolution, the greater the amount of information needed from the video card.

In addition to satisfying the demands of resolution, the video card must manage the information needed to define the number of colours a PC uses when drawing an image. This is usually set at 16,000, or 256,000, or sometimes more. As you might imagine, the greater the available palette, the more lifelike the image. For more information on these concepts, take a look at the video card and monitor sections elsewhere in this chapter; I mention these concepts now because they are the chief performance results of video card RAM.

In general, there are two types of memory chips on video cards: DRAM and VRAM (video random-access memory). Although their names are similar, these chips are quite different. Video card DRAM works the same way as the DRAM used in a PC's main memory, but is physically smaller. VRAM chips, however, are differently designed inside and out. They are faster because they allow data to flow right through them – in one side and out the other. As a result, they are sometimes called "dual port" chips. Video cards containing VRAM, which was once expensive and unusual, have now become commonplace in order to keep up with Pentium and Power PC processors and other fast system components today, although they still cost a bit more. It is also worth noting that in the past two years, VRAM chips have been refined by some video card manufacturers seeking a market edge.

As a result, this kind of memory is now available in such exotic forms as SGRAM (synchronous graphic random-access memory) and WRAM (Windows random-access memory), the latter being common in cards from Matrox Corporation.

When considering the amount of memory on a video card in 1998, keep in mind that 2 megabytes of DRAM is an absolute minimum, and 2–4 megabytes of VRAM is recommended.

Device Memory

Another place you will find memory in a personal computer is inside individual components such as its hard drive, sound card, or modem. In most cases, these chips are intended solely to enhance the performance of the device, are proprietary, and are not removable or upgradable. Because of these limiting properties, they are seldom mentioned in general descriptions of a PC, and are usually the subject of discussions at the component level. If you are interested in learning more about hard drive caching or sound card chipsets, there is plenty of information available directly from manufacturers and on the World Wide Web.

HARD DRIVES

As the part of the computer in which your programs, your personal files, and your PC's system files are stored, your hard drive is a very important subsystem. Like other computer parts, hard drives have undergone major changes since their appearance in the early '80s. Alternatively known as fixed disks, internal disks, or hard disks, hard drives are usually palm-sized devices into which are sealed one or more circular platters which permanently store information in the form of magnetic codes. Data can be written to and erased from them. They are usually only taken out of a PC when being repaired or replaced, although some removable varieties are available.

A point of confusion among novice computer purchasers used to arise from the fact that hard drive storage capacities were commonly measured in megabytes – the same unit of measurement used to describe a PC's random-access memory. While RAM is also a memory subsystem, it's quite different from permanent, hard drive information storage. In the current computer market, hard drives have become large enough to hold several thousand megabytes, and are now measured in gigabytes – one gigabyte being about 1,000 megabytes. This, as well as an increased awareness among computer buyers in general, is helping to separate these two memory concepts.

In the early days of computing, when data and programs were written, stored, and retrieved by more rudimentary programs than we're used to today, a 10- or 20-megabyte hard drive seemed astonishingly large. After all, if created with an old, "character-based" wordprocessing program, this whole book would easily fill less than two megabytes. But hard drives are an excellent example of the symbiotic relationship between PC hardware and software. New, larger capacity models have appeared hand in hand with larger applications that take advantage of their increased characteristics. Today's programs require space that was unheard of ten years ago. In 1998, PCs normally come equipped with hard drives in the 2- to 8-gigabyte (2,000- to 8,000-megabyte) range, a size you can expect to see increase by about 2 gigabytes every six or eight months. Certainly, larger hard drives are always available, but the most common models seem to be determined by the specifications that manufacturers can build into models selling in the $250 to $600 retail range. Anything over these values calls into question the balance of other components in a normal home or business microcomputer.

Data are normally stored on a hard drive the way sound is arrayed on the tracks of an old phonograph record. The primary unit of storage is called a "sector." Sectors are arranged into clusters, which in turn are arranged into tracks. In the past the size of these units was more standardized than in today's larger drives. Functionally, hard drives contain a read/write "head" which transfers information in the form of magnetic codes to and from the platters. These platters are sealed inside a housing along with a motor to spin the disks at very high speeds, and a circuit, or "logic," board, which manages the reading, writing, and transfer of data.

Other characteristics besides capacity affect a hard drive's performance and price. The first of these is its type. Early models required a separate controller card, which plugged into an expansion slot on a PC's motherboard. These controllers were peculiar to the drives they liked. Most hard drives now have controlling devices built in, and are directly connected to a compatible motherboard with a ribbon cable.

Since 1983, hard drives for personal computers have appeared in a variety of standards, most of these established by groups of manufacturers who agreed on a certain design. As usual, these standards present an alphabet soup of acronyms: MFM (modulation frequency modulation), RLL (run length limited), ESDI (enhanced small device interface), MCA (microchannel architecture), SCSI (small computer system interface), IDE (integrated drive electronics), EIDE (enhanced integrated drive electronics), and UDMA (ultra direct memory access). Of these types, the three most common today are enhanced IDE, SCSI (pronounced "scuzzy"), and UDMA (an EIDE refinement), because of their performance and acceptance in the marketplace. SCSI drives require a SCSI controller card, while the prevailing standard, enhanced IDE and UDMA drives, are now connected directly. It is usually not worth paying the extra money for a SCSI hard drive and controller card in stand-alone computer systems. Less expensive EIDE and UDMA drives are close enough in performance. UDMA drives are a recent addition to the conventional hard drive market. Utilizing a transfer process that places minimal demands on the CPU of a system, they are more than twice as fast as regular, enhanced IDE hard drives.

A second element affecting the price of a hard drive is its speed. Oddly, larger hard drives are usually faster. They are normally measured in milliseconds (ms). When a computer gives an instruction to a hard drive, the drive must find the data and then physically move its read/write head into place. The time taken to find a location on a platter is known as a drive's "seek time." The time taken getting to that location is known as its "latency."

There are different methods of rating hard drives, some more telling than others. These include:

Data Transfer Rate
Measured in MBps (megabytes per second) or KBps (kilobytes per second), this is an important figure. It is sometimes hard to learn, however, because it is also dependent on the computer and controller to which the drive is connected. The data transfer rate is a measurement of how much data flows from a specific hard drive to a specific computer in a given time. Look for EIDE transfer rates of between 10 and 25 MBps.

Average Access Time
Measured in milliseconds, this is the most common way of comparing hard drives, even though it may not be the truest. This is because it doesn't allow for influences from the outside world. It's a measure of the amount of time a drive takes to access a given number of randomly selected tracks. Usual ms rates in hard drives at the time of publication are in the 8- to 12-millisecond range.

Average Seek Time
Similar to access time, seek time is also measured in milliseconds but refers to the time taken for a drive's read/write head to move from one track to an adjacent one.

Drive Cache, or Buffer
Similar in concept to the cache inside a processor or in a system's RAM, hard drive cache is a small amount of fast memory that keeps some data always ready for processing, to minimize the times the device will be idle. Hard drive caches of 256K are common in current products. The hardware cache in a drive can be augmented by the creation of a software cache, using the RAM of a PC.

Mean Time Between Failure
This is a measurement, in hours, of a drive's likelihood of failure. It's a prediction, mind you, not the result of real-time tests. This is because some MTBFs (200,000 hours, or more than twenty years) are longer than the drives have even been in existence! This is not to say the measurement is useless, but remember that it's a highly researched, statistical guess.

With all of these measurements in mind, choose the largest, fastest drive you can afford, from a reputable builder such as Seagate, Western Digital, Maxtor, or IBM.

VIDEO CARDS AND MONITORS

As the saying "Beauty is in the eye of the beholder" suggests, the visual subsystem in any PC is important not only to the way it works but to how it looks. No matter how fast and wonderful all the other parts of a computer might be, you interact with them by sight.

A video card is normally plugged into one of the expansion slots on a PC's motherboard and supplies information to its monitor – the screen on which you watch everything happen. Because the video card manages all data flowing to the display, it must be able to keep up with everything else going on under the hood. There is no point in paying all that money for a superfast processor and oodles of RAM just to have them dragged down by a video card bottleneck. And remember, everything on your screen has to go through this important card.

Throughout the years, various monitor and corresponding video card standards have appeared; Super VGA (video graphics array) is still most common. Super VGA (S/VGA) video cards are of a physical design that presents a small, fifteen-hole (15-pin) outlet to the exterior of a system, into which a Super VGA colour monitor will plug. Your monitor connector may not actually have all fifteen pins, but it will accommodate this pattern. The Super VGA standard refers to the number of pixels a monitor is able to display: technically 800 x 600 (800 across by 600 down), although now commonly assumed to be 1,024 x 768. So what is this, a design standard that isn't really standard? Exactly.

Before we go any further, note that in the video end of the computer business, even accepted industry terms can mean different things to different people. When this is combined with the different terms and numbers used to describe video card and monitor technology, an understanding of these subsystems can become elusive indeed. Figure 3D shows major classes of video cards that have appeared since the early '80s:

VIDEO DISPLAY STANDARDS AND PROPERTIES

NAME	ABBR.	COMMON BUS TYPES	ONSCREEN COLOURS	MAXIMUM RESOLUTION
Monochrome Display Adapter	MDA	ISA/EISA	Green or amber	600 X 400
Colour Graphics Adapter	CGA	ISA/EISA	8 colours	640 X 200
Enhanced Graphics Adapter	EGA	ISA/EISA/MCA	16 colours	640 X 250
Professional Graphics Adapter	PGA	ISA/EISA/MCA	16 colours	640 X 480
Video Graphics Array	VGA	ISA/EISA/MCA/PCI	64 colours	640 X 480
Super Video Graphics Array	S/VGA	ISA/EISA/MCA/PCI	256 colours+	800 X 600; 1,024 X 768+

FIGURE 3D

Instead of labouring over the various properties of older video cards, let's concentrate on the current Super VGA standard, for this is most common in current computers. Most S/VGA cards are now separate devices, about 3" in height and of varying lengths known as 1/2 length, 3/4 length, and full size. They can be plugged into, or removed from, a motherboard as necessary, which makes them a favourite upgrade item.

Some motherboards have their video subsystem and monitor port built right into them, but these are much less popular today. Like other controller devices that plug into the expansion slots of a motherboard, video cards have appeared in different bus widths: 8-bit, 16-bit, and 32-bit. This is the "size of the pipe" bringing data to and from the card and is important in determining the speed at which the card handles data. Most current computers will accept a 32-bit video card.

A related property in a video card is its bus type: which type of motherboard expansion slot the card is made to fit. Cards have been developed for all of the standard bus designs: ISA, MCA, EISA, VESA, and PCI. PCI video cards are most popular today, in line with motherboards in Pentium MMX and Pentium II computers. These cards are definitely an improvement over all of the older designs.

A third property important to the performance and price of a video card is the size of its memory. When a PCI Super VGA card tells a monitor to draw an image, the quality of the picture is dependent not only on the characteristics of the monitor itself but also on the amount of information displayed in each "frame" of the picture. This in turn is dependent on the memory of the card. Now, here is where discussion of video cards and monitors becomes obscure. Performance results – how many colours are shown – can also vary according to the resolution of the monitor.

One megabyte of video card memory, for example, is able to manage 256 colours on a monitor that displays 1,024 pixels across by 768 pixels down. The number of pixels a monitor displays readably is dependent on its size. Most 14" and 15" monitors look best when presenting 800 x 600 pixels only. While these monitors are capable of showing a resolution of 1,024 x 768, this higher standard would make everything on the screen a little smaller. With this in mind, 1,024 x 768 and higher resolutions are still the domain of monitors 17" and larger in diagonal.

Separate from the RAM on the motherboard of a PC, video card memory comes in two general types: DRAM (dynamic random-access memory) and VRAM (video random-access memory). The practical difference between these kinds of chips is their speed. DRAM, which is of the same design but physically smaller than the DRAM chips on a motherboard, accepts and receives data through one pathway. VRAM presents two paths by which data come and go, so it's faster. It's also more expensive. In the past year, different variations of VRAM, including WRAM and SGRAM, have appeared, developed by video card manufacturers to work with specific cards.

RAM is not, however, the only specification that determines a video card's speed and colour capabilities. Many recent models contain their own little processor, sometimes called a graphics coprocessor, which is able to help out with the management of data to and from a monitor. Video cards are also compared in terms of their refresh rate, which is the number of times each second that the screen is redrawn.

With the proliferation of graphically oriented applications today, it's essential that you have the maximum amount of video memory you can afford. Two to 4 megabytes of DRAM on a video card are minimum, and 4 to 8 megabytes of VRAM (or a comparable memory product) are minimum for visually oriented tasks such as image scanning and reproduction, photograph retouching, video editing, computer-aided design/computer-aided manufacturing (CAD/CAM), animation, or other kinds of graphics and drawing.

One other property worth noting in any consideration of a video card is its ability to handle multimedia. For more information on the other parts of a PC that support the display of video pictures and accompanying sound, see the Multimedia section later in this chapter. Two terms you will hear used to describe the multimedia capabilities of video cards common in computer systems today are: MPEG (Motion Picture Experts Group) and MPEG-2.

Each of these acronyms refers to a transmission standard in which data are compressed to speed things up. These standards are *supposed* to enable manufacturers to produce hardware and software that work together. Alas, like many "rules" that have appeared in the computer business, different products claimed to be compatible in the past sometimes let us down. By 1998, however, MPEG and newer MPEG-2 compliant video cards have achieved a reliable level of stability. Now it does not make sense to purchase any video card, whether separately as an upgrade or contained in a new PC, that cannot handle MPEG-2 multimedia data. Also, if you are having a PC assembled for you with a DVD (digital video disc drive) in it be sure to confirm that the system will be capable of displaying full DVD multimedia, assuming that is one of the reasons you asked for the drive in the first place. As of publication, the inclusion of a DVD in a generic PC did not necessarily mean its other components could handle the full motion data being delivered; in some cases a separate DVD "video decoder" card is required to assist the video card. The need for these "add on" cards will likely decrease throughout 1998 as DVDs become more popular and mainstream video cards equipped to deal with them appear.

NTSC is an acronym describing the playback standard used in television and videotape recording in North America. Video cards with connectors that accept input from a coaxial TV cable or VCR (also known as TV tuner cards) have the ability to display regular television, VCR, or video camera images on a computer monitor, and allow you to capture them frame by frame. More expensive video-editing cards allow the same thing for strings of images (video clips), opening the door to video playback and editing. A word of warning though if you are considering an NTSC input/output card that offers video editing. Make sure you have a fast computer (Pentium 233 MMX minimum), a big fat hard drive (4 gigabytes), and some kind of external storage device – a Zip drive or tape backup. At thirty frames per second, a short "full motion" video can soak up computer resources and storage space mighty fast.

As far as monitors are concerned, the main characteristics to consider are size, resolution, dot pitch, and refresh (or vertical scan) rate. There are other details to watch for, such as radiation emission, control panel type, and overall design, but the most important aspects of any computer's display relate to the way it looks. Before considering these measurements in any detail, note that this is one part of your PC you pretty much have to get right when you purchase it: you can't change it, so if you decide you want a better one later, your only recourse is to trade in the unwanted piece or sell it privately. Both scenarios are better avoided, because of the continually falling prices of new products. So when purchasing a PC, even a used one, rank the monitor right up there with the processor on your priority list.

Probably the most important element of any monitor's attractiveness is its size – and the bigger the better. Monitors are usually measured by their diagonal (the length between opposite corners of the screen). Hence the standards: 14", 15", 17", 20", and 21". As with many other component measurements, the integrity of these numbers has taken a bit of a beating, and rightly so. A normal 14" monitor has a viewable area, or viewable-in-picture measurement (VIP), of about 12.5", a 15" diagonal has a VIP of about 13", and a 17" has a VIP of about 15.5" to 16". These figures may vary according to which manufacturer you consider and how the screen is designed – whether it's flat (desirable) or slightly curved (not as good).

Over the years, monitors have remained a bit more stable than other computer components in terms of pricing and specifications. This is not to say they do not cost less today than they used to, but their prices have not dropped as dramatically in the past five years as those of hard drives or processors. The current minimum market standard is fast evolving from 14" up to 15". If you can afford one of them, 17" models are now available starting around $500, with high-performance products at about $1,000. It is interesting to note that in 1998, 17" displays are predicted to outsell 14" models, accounting for more than 25 percent of the market in North America. Fifteen-inch monitors are expected to remain at the top of the pyramid at 45 percent of all units sold.

A second important measurement of any monitor is its resolution, which is also sometimes referred to as its frequency. Because a display's vertical refresh rate is sometimes called its vertical frequency, we'll stick with the term resolution to avoid confusion. As mentioned in the section on video cards, resolution describes the number of pixels (tiny dots which make up a picture) a monitor can support, measured in sets of two numbers such as 640 across by 480 down.

Since the beginning of personal computing, several monitor and video card standards have appeared, each one characterized by, among other properties, a resolution range. Look back at Figure 3D in the video card section to get a quick idea of these levels.

As we have seen, the latest monitor and video card standard is Super VGA, which refers to a resolution of 800 x 600 or 1,024 x 768. But just because you buy a Super VGA monitor and video card does not necessarily mean you will be looking at information at the higher level. In fact, 14" and 15" S/VGA monitors are often throttled back to even 640 x 480 pixels for normal use. Why? There are practical differences between these settings related to monitor size. At higher resolutions, information on a display is more finely drawn by a larger number of pixels, so it's clearer. The bad news is that at higher resolutions, objects also become smaller. At 800 x 600 on a 15" monitor, I find the icons in Windows 95 markedly easier to read than at 1,024 x 768. The higher resolution is best used on monitors 17" in diagonal and larger.

Hand in hand with any consideration of monitor resolution comes the concept of dot pitch. This is determined by the holes or apertures in a monitor's shadow mask, or slot mask, the matrix through which it fires beams at the screen to create colours. These beams result in a mixture of red, green, and blue dots which make up each pixel. The smaller a monitor's dots, the clearer will be its image, no matter what its resolution. A monitor's dot pitch is not the actual size of the dots it uses to compose each pixel, but the distance between any two dots of the same colour. Measured as fractions of a millimetre, acceptable dot pitches fall in the .26- to .28-mm (still the most common) or .24- to .25-mm (more expensive and unusual) ranges. By comparison, monitors a few years ago were common in the .41 and even .51 classes. With any dot pitch over .28 you can expect your eyes to be doing a little polka all by themselves.

So a monitor may display over a thousand lines of picture elements across, and hundreds of them down, several times each second. Its vertical scan rate – the number of times it redraws these pixels – is also known as its refresh rate. This frequency, measured in hertz, should be higher than 70 Hz in a quality monitor in 1998. Anything lower means that the picture won't be redrawn often enough and may flicker and cause eye strain. A related monitor characteristic affecting stability is the property of interlacing. It's worth taking note of this term as it's sometimes mentioned in advertisements and used to portray inferior products in a better light. Here's how: when a monitor produces a picture it does so by drawing lines of pixels at a certain rate. This is repeated back and forth, from top to bottom, until the screen is complete. Interlacing occurs when a monitor cannot manage to draw a complete picture in one pass; it must draw every other line, then start back at the top and "interlace," or fill in the gaps, to make a complete image. The result? Flicker and eye strain.

Confusion surrounding the interlaced and non-interlaced labels is possible because this property is tied not only to the monitor you buy but to the resolution at which it runs. Even the cheapest low-performance dud will be non-interlaced at a resolution of 640 x 480. But what happens when you run the thing at 800 x 600 or 1,024 x 768? Will it start to flicker? In the marketplace today, "non-interlaced" has come to mean "non-interlaced at a resolution of 1,024 x 768," but be sure to confirm this when making a purchase. Otherwise, the term on its own does not necessarily mean you are buying an acceptable product.

A final note when considering monitors and monitor technology is the issue of radiation. Without making any claim to in-depth knowledge of scientific studies or experiments on the topic, I am of the opinion that you should make this a factor when considering one model against another. Remember the technology: three guns shoot electrons out of the device and into your face every second you sit in front of it. That energy doesn't stop at the screen. Even though ELF (exteremely low frequency) and VLF (very low frequency) levels fall off sharply about three feet away from a PC display, who doesn't sit close enough to be concerned? Over the past ten years, the Swedish government has endorsed various guidelines about monitor emissions. Their current standard is known as MPR II, sometimes called the Swedac MPR. This term refers to acceptable levels of ELF and VLF energy emanating from a screen. If you have the choice, make adherence to this emission level a prerequisite in any monitor you consider.

In summary, here are some common characteristics to look for when purchasing a Super VGA colour monitor:

1. The largest size you can afford (15" diagonal if possible)
2. A large viewable-in-picture measurement
3. A low dot pitch (nothing higher than .28 mm, and .26 or .25 if possible)
4. A fast vertical refresh rate (nothing lower than 68 or 70 Hz)
5. A high resolution capability (at least 1,024 x 768)
6. The ability to produce a non-interlaced image at 1,024 x 768

7. Adherence to MPR II or the similar Low Radiation Emissions standard

MULTIMEDIA

As you might imagine, the term "multimedia" refers to a combination of computer components working together to present different kinds of information: sound and pictures at the same time. While we're all a little jaded about moving pictures after years of being exposed to television, computer designers know well the challenge this task presents a PC. When watching TV, we're used to seeing a ton of information pouring from the screen in a very short period. Normal "full-motion" (NTSC) video pictures appear at thirty frames per second, each one, of course, accompanied by sound. When you consider the time some computers need to prepare and draw even one or two screens of data, you can see that multimedia applications place scary demands on a system's resources.

Your television is able to manage audiovisual information quickly because it deals with incoming data in analogue form, which is to say, it doesn't have to go through the same kinds of conversion processes necessary in a digital PC. But we all know that computer capacities are growing in leaps and bounds, and only recently have we begun to see personal systems capable of handling true multimedia without coughing, sputtering, and making us wait.

The computer parts usually involved in the multimedia process are a compact disc (CD-ROM) or digital video disc (DVD) drive, a sound card, and speakers. Let's examine each in turn.

CD-ROM (Compact Disc Read-Only Memory)

One of the most important components in a computer's multimedia subsystem is its CD-ROM (or DVD) player. Available in internal and external models, CD-ROM drives allow your PC to read any kind of digital information from a 5 1/4" compact disc. This includes regular audio CDs you may be used to playing in your home stereo as well as computer games or other programs which in days of old used to come on 3 1/2", 1.44-megabyte floppies. CD-ROM drives come in two basic flavours (IDE and SCSI) and several different speeds. They now all read the same sized discs, which contain approximately 500 to 700 megabytes of data. In practical terms, this means lots of room for computer programs. (Remember the bad old days when software came on two, three, or even fifteen or twenty floppies?) But in their present format, compact discs still do not have enough room for even a half-hour of full-motion video and sound.

Unlike the read/write head in a hard drive, a CD-ROM's laser does not float over data on a disc to find what it wants. Instead, it must start from the beginning or the end of the whole data track and spiral through it each time you search for new information. Not only that, once it gets where it's going, it often must slow down to do its reading. These factors made early CDs a poor second in speed comparisons to the hard drive technology everyone was used to. So manufacturers invented the "x" measurement standard. This speed, or "spin rate," specification is the most common way of comparing one CD-ROM to another. Today's products fall into the 16x to 32x range. Alas, this is yet another part of the PC business where marketing has overridden the real world in order to make a component appear more attractive. The "x" or "times" measurement included in this description implies that a drive actually transfers data 12, 16, or 24 times faster than the original 1x CD-ROM drives of old, which delivered about 150 kilobytes per second. By that logic, a 24x CD should deliver 3,600 kilobytes per second. In fact it does not. Instead, the "times" measurement is a description of the maximum rotation speed of the outer edge of a disc in a drive – a measurement which makes these components seem faster in comparison to the original than they really are. So even though this has become a standard in the CD-drive world which allows comparison of different products, it is, in essence, an inflated measurement.

There are other ways to evaluate CD-ROM performance, particularly in terms of actual data transfer – in kilobytes per second (KBps). This is also known as a drive's throughput, but as is the case with hard drives, while this measurement is more accurate, it is not as well publicized. When purchasing a CD-ROM, if you really want to be precise, don't just rely on its 20x or 24x rating. Try to find out how fast it sends and receives data. One last point: don't forget that fast CD-ROMs are of advantage only when dealing with multimedia applications: games with full-motion video, or CDs with video clips, such as a multimedia encyclopedia. To read audio data, a CD-ROM drive actually has to slow down considerably.

DVD (Digital Video Disc)

Probably the most important product to hit the world of multimedia computing in 1997 is the digital video disc. Think of this as a super-CD-ROM; DVDs are several times faster than conventional CD drives and will hold more than seven times the data on one disc. That's a whopping 3,500 to 4,000 megabytes (4 gigabytes). Not only that, they're being designed to accommodate higher storage standards in the future: 10 gigabytes and beyond! Current models also meet the AC-3, or Dolby Digital, sound standard, which is better quality than offered by audio CDs today.

By featuring this kind of speed and storage, these drives open the door to really high-grade audio and video in ways that may soon alter even established home entertainment technologies such as your VCR and television. DVD drives are catching on about as fast as any PC product ever. It's easy to see why. In addition to their own advanced properties, they're also downwardly compatible, being able to read regular compact discs as well.

Sound Cards and Speakers

Important parts of a PC's multimedia system, sound cards and speakers have come a long way in the past five years. Once a novelty, computer audio systems have now become powerful and sophisticated, offering features from voice recognition to musical instrument interfaces to the ability to read a document aloud to you right off the screen.

In the beginning, sound cards were rudimentary in function and design. Early issues were made to fit an 8-bit expansion slot and presented a jack to the exterior of the system into which a headphone or speakers could be plugged. These cards worked with some programs and not others, and the noise they produced was more akin to the output of a tinny PC speaker than a CD stereo. But things have changed.

Before we look at features in current sound cards, note the way these devices handle information. Sound coming from a computer is stored and transferred in digital form – as 0s and 1s coming from a hard drive, a compact disc, or other source such as the Internet. This data is passed by the PC to its sound card, which contains a digital-to-analogue converter, a little device which changes the bits to a "wave" signal, which in turn vibrates external or headphone speakers, which vibrate the air, which vibrates your eardrum.

All of this means that sound cards are about conversion, the reproduction of mathematical bits in a familiar, listenable format. How do they work? The main principle they employ is a process called sampling. The card takes a "look" at data coming into it and reproduces sound based on that information. The more often it performs this cycle, the truer to the original the result will be. Current cards sample in the 25- to 50-MHz range; that is, 25,000 to 50,000 times each second.

Other factors affect a sound card's ability to "hear" and "play" information coming from a CD or hard drive. These are its "bit depth" – the number of bits it uses to describe a sound over a given period – and enhancement features such as "wave table synthesis." Bit depth, as described by the numbers 8 or 16, does *not* describe the expansion bus slot into which the card fits. Rather, this is the number of bits the card uses to describe a sound in one sample. Once again confusion arises, because the same numbers are used to measure completely different computer standards.

It's also confusing when parts manufacturers come up with advertisements that imply their products are more sophisticated than they really are. That is exactly what has happened in the sound card end of the PC business. While early audio cards were labelled as 8 and 16 bit depth products in reference to the way they sampled and described sounds, some current models bear names using the numbers 32 and 64. Unfortunately, these refer to the number of "voices" on the cards, quite a different characteristic from an ability to sample sounds in increments of 32 or 64 bits. If they did have that ability, they would require a heap of on-board processing power, produce an extremely rich spectrum of sounds, and undoubtedly cost a lot more money. This is not to say the new multivoice cards are not exciting products. But it would be a lot less confusing if their manufacturers had named them differently.

Wave table cards have a built-in library of real sounds in digital form, so when they "hear" an instruction, they locate the real thing (or the closest sound they can) in memory, and play it. Higher-grade cards also contain features such as pitch and timbre controls, different kinds of filters, vibrato, tremolo, reverb, decay, sustain, and other musical attributes.

Many cards accept data directly from a musical instrument or other sampling device via a MIDI (musical instrument digital interface) port designed for this purpose. MIDI ports open the door to all sorts of musical explorations: plug in a keyboard and have the notes you play recorded and mixed, moved from one key to another, played back along with other instruments, even scored automatically by the computer and printed out. In addition to a MIDI interface and wave table library, a good sound card will provide ample connections to headphones *and* speakers and will come with software that is easy to install and run.

Several compatibility standards have arisen in the sound card market which affect a product's ability to work with different programs and especially games. Two common types are Adlib and Creative Labs Sound Blaster. These have evolved because of the pre-eminence of both companies. It's a good idea to be sure that anything you buy is compatible with one of these standards, or at least another well-known sound card manufacturer, otherwise you may find yourself tearing out some hair after trying all night to get Revenge of the Graveyard Computer Nerd running for your nine-year-old hacker in training.

Two newer features making waves in the multimedia market are voice read and voice recognition. In the first of these operations, a specially equipped sound card and program allow you to highlight text in a document and have the PC "read" it back to you. The products I have played with offer several male and female voices, all of which are customizable in terms of speed, pitch, timbre, and a couple of other qualities. It still sounds like a computer talking, but it's safe to say these voices are going to become more lifelike as the products evolve. I have even started recognizing some of the voices from the Sound Blaster AWE 64 on television and radio.

Another sound card application catching fire is voice recognition. IBM has ventured into this in a significant way, offering entry-level software for less than $150. To use one version I played with, you had to speak slowly, pausing between each word. But newer products are available which take advantage of faster computers and allow you to talk normally. You must "train" voice recognition programs to the sound and rhythms of your speech, but once this is accomplished, you can create text much faster and more easily than by mucking around with a keyboard. Marry this to the grammar and spellcheck features in a good word processor, and you have a whole new writing scenario.

In summary, when considering a sound card, watch for the following features: compatibility with an established standard, 32- or 64-bit depth, ample headphone and microphone connections, wave table library, and if you're interested in music and special effects, MIDI interface and musical effects. Also, don't forget proper installation software, including "drivers," and any other special programs required to implement all the features of the card.

PC Speakers

Riding the multimedia wave along with sound cards and compact disc drives, PC speakers have enjoyed a huge increase in popularity and diversity in the past few years. Early versions were dinky little things that sounded about as good as they looked. They reminded me of the 16-transistor radio I won selling Peewee hockey tickets back in the '60s. But computer users have grown sophisticated. We're now used to listening to music CDs while surfing the Net or doing home office work, and we've become accustomed to stereo, full base, and surround sound to accompany games and recreational programs.

Speakers can plug into two different places on a PC: directly into the compact disc player or, more commonly, into the sound card on the external back panel to take full advantage of a system's ability to manage music and sound. But if we all expect a lot more than the tinny little products of yesteryear, what are the internal characteristics of good PC speakers? Just as the product lines have improved, they've become more complicated to consider.

At the very bottom of the ladder is the set you get when you purchase that $129 complete multimedia package (CD-ROM and sound card with speakers included) from a discount parts supplier. These will be small (three or four inches high) and lack any enhancements. They will accept data from a sound card or CD and do their best with it, but that's about all. Forget any extras. Unless you want speakers for the most rudimentary purposes, these are not the way to go. Why hobble a $2,000 system with a component that cheap? For not much extra money (under $50), you can at least purchase speakers that have their own power adapter, contain two or three cones per box, and provide a minimum level of excitement when the Winged Warrior zaps the Caped Crusader. These will be rated at 25 to 50 watts, which raises an important issue about PC sound systems: advertised power. Wattage is one of the most outrageously exaggerated measurements in computer marketing.

Ever wonder how that little set of speakers you saw advertised at $39.95 can produce 200 watts of power? They probably can't. The best way to see through this kind of hype is to understand a couple of concepts, the most important being the industry standard measurement of (Nerd Alert!) root mean standard (RMS) watts per channel. This is a measurement of the power that a single channel can *sustain* when a speaker is operating. It is not the same as the maximum power a single channel can handle, or the total power produced from two, three, or four satellite speakers.

Different manufacturers and vendors have come up with some very creative ways of describing their products, including advertising the peak power of each channel (the peak power output [PPO]) and the total maximum power output (the peak music power output [PMPO]). PPO is misleading because it implies that a speaker continuously devotes 20 watts of power to production, which it does not. PMPO is misleading because it implies that all of the parts of a speaker system will work together to produce a better sound, which is not true either. Even a whole group of weak, tiny little speakers does not equal the quality and richness of two good big ones.

Transcending the small desktop speakers sometimes bundled with PCs are the subwoofer sets from companies such as Yamaha and Altech Lansing. These products add significant amplification to the sound from a computer, and provide a high-end solution to anyone who is serious about sound.

Finally, a subjective piece of advice: if you can possibly afford to spend a bit more for a good set of speakers with subwoofer and real power and quality, it's worth it. This is especially true if you are musically inclined or if children are part of your PC scenario. The increased excitement of a high-grade subwoofer system will really enhance the multimedia programs and games now available.

PRINTERS

There are three major types of printer technology common in the personal computer market in 1998: dot matrix, ink jet, and laser. A few years ago, this list would also have included daisy wheel printers, but these have become obsolete. Other special-purpose designs are also available, including bar code and colour dye sublimation printers, but are known as niche-market or specialty-market products.

Each of the main printer groups has advantages, disadvantages, and intended uses. All can be characterized by their design, print speed, print quality, colour capability, impact, price, cost per page, and paper handling. While these are not the only attributes to consider when judging a printer, they're the most important.

As far as market mix is concerned, dot matrix products are rapidly falling into a narrow box. Ink jet printers have enjoyed a tremendous increase during the past five years, and laser printers have remained about even. Let's look at each of these technologies in turn.

Dot Matrix Printers

Developed back in the age of the mighty mainframe – the 1960s – dot matrix printers survived the appearance of the personal computer about twenty years ago and have remained in common, though declining, use ever since. While they have become faster, quieter, and colour capable, and while the quality of their text has improved, they remain unchanged in the way they print. They present a small (about 1/8" square) flat panel to a ribbon which is held by a guide in front of the page. Inside this panel are usually nine or twenty-four holes which contain tiny pins. Each pin can be instructed to slide forward and back by a minute jolt of electricity. Working together, the pins strike the pattern of a desired character, hammering the ribbon to leave a precise mark on the page. The panel containing these pins is usually encased in a housing – the whole assembly being known as the print head. In turn, this is positioned on a rail and slides back and forth to print each line.

Dot matrix printers offer advantages and disadvantages. Of all PC print technologies today, they produce the crudest work. This is because the pins, when striking an inked ribbon, do not leave a clean impression; there can be variations among the dots used to assemble each character. Also, since matrix printer ribbons are normally fibrous and soaked with ink, they gradually dry as they're used. This does not allow consistent quality. So while these printers are simple, fast, and time tested, they are least desired in terms of the clarity of the image they produce. Since this has become an overriding concern in the printer market, matrix printers have all but disappeared from use in new computer configurations in home and office.

Dot matrix printers remain in demand, however, in the production of multipart forms: shipping documents, invoices, and the like. This use alone has kept them from dying out. Because of the "impact" nature of their design, they can hammer through three, four, or more pieces of paper, a feat neither ink jets nor lasers can match. Dot matrix printers are also fast, with some models printing up to 500 or more characters per second. They are also inexpensive to operate because they use ribbons instead of toners, ink cartridges, or drums.

In keeping with their primary function, these printers are almost always equipped with tractor feeders – little spiked wheels which hold continuous, linked sheets of paper. There was a time when cut-sheet feeders for dot matrix printers were common. They accommodated stacks of letterhead or regular paper but, except for special applications, they became obsolete with the appearance of laser and ink jet printers in the late '80s.

Ink Jet Printers

Following the graphics boom that has accompanied faster computers and the growth of the Internet in the past three years, ink jet printers have become a favourite in 1997–98. One or two years ago there was a marked difference in the quality of work these products produced in comparison to the longtime leader in high-grade printing, the laser. Now it's getting difficult to distinguish between the outputs of the two. Add to this the ink jets' new ability to print photographic-quality pictures, as well as their low purchase price (starting below $250) and reasonable cost per page, and you have an attractive group of products indeed.

Several ink jet printing technologies have been developed since 1990, because this marketplace has been targeted by manufacturers as a growth industry. Inexpensive, fast, clear colour printing offers opportunity and profit in the vast fax and copier markets as well.

Like their dot matrix cousins, most ink jet and bubble jet printers present a "head" which slides back and forth in front of the page. While different manufacturers have introduced their own variations of this technology, the general idea of ink jet printing is that a series of (typically between twenty-four and sixty-four) holes, or nozzles, each containing a tiny drop of ink and a small conductor, is activated by a signal from the PC. On command, the conductor in each chamber heats the ink, which expands and shoots (or in some cases "bubbles") onto the page. Thus each little "gun" is able to issue a dot to form part of a desired character or image.

As a result of this technology, ink jet and bubble jet printers present a unique set of characteristics. First, as noted earlier, recent refinements have enabled them to produce text which is very close to the quality of a laser – up to 600 x 600 dots per square inch (dpi). But the way these printers work also makes them sensitive to the type of paper used. On some parchments and fibrous stocks, especially those costing more money because of a higher cloth content, ink can bleed from fibre to fibre, causing edges of an image or character to appear ragged. Most ink jet manufacturers issue special paper designed for their lineups, sometimes even for specific models. If you're serious about graphics, these paper stocks are a must. They vary widely in price, from $1.00 to $3.00 per sheet. For text printing, do a little testing before rushing out and ordering 5,000 sheets of letterhead. I have found that inexpensive copier paper which presents a flat, treated face to the printer usually does not allow ink to bleed as much, even though it can take a little longer to dry. (You usually have to take care handling these sheets right after printing; wait a minute or two or they can smudge.) Nor is shiny stock as formal and luxurious to handle as the expensive stuff. The only way to find a suitable balance is to try different grades of paper and play with the settings in the software that accompanies most ink jet printers today. You can usually switch from draft to high-grade to photo output to improve the look of a document.

Other considerations when evaluating ink jet printers are resolution and speed. In 1998, all of the major manufacturers in Canada – Canon, Epson, Hewlett-Packard, and Lexmark – offer mainstream products ranging from a little over $200 up to $1,000 or more. Higher-end issues (those over $600) produce astonishingly clear colour pictures and very crisp text, and come with drivers and software which enable you to manipulate images or work in tandem with well-known graphics packages such as Corel Draw. All produce basic text at four to eight pages per minute, although a single high-resolution, page-sized picture may take as long as five minutes to print.

For reference, readable text resolution is 300 x 300 dots per square inch, and excellent resolution is 600 x 600. Clear colour pictures start at about 400 x 400 dots per inch, while sharp, presentation-quality graphics start at 600 x 600 and go up from there. Variations of these measurements are offered by some printers, such as Hewlett-Packard's Deskjet 722, which boasts 400 x 600 dpi and printing speeds of up to six pages per minute for text. Don't forget, though, that at higher resolutions, both in text and graphics documents, printers use up ink at a much faster rate. (See the section on consumables, below.) All in all, the combination of reasonably fast printing, good text and colour output, and prices starting at under $300 have catapulted ink jets and bubble jets into the top slot in the home and small-business printer markets.

Laser Printers

The development of the personal laser printer has sometimes been linked with the success of the Apple PC, especially the Mac and Mac Plus, back in the '80s. First appearing around 1984 from industry pioneer Hewlett-Packard, these were the first printers to allow home and small-business computer users to produce truly excellent, typeset-quality documents. They took full advantage of Apple's graphical user interface (GUI) and mouse, to enable users to compose and print documents containing several different fonts, or styles of type, and use enhancements such as italics, boldface, and bordering. While we now take these features for granted when writing and printing with PCs, ten years ago they were revolutionary indeed.

Although the laser printer was the undisputed king of the market in the '80s and early '90s, it has recently lost ground to ink jets because of their increased print quality and lower price. Still, lasers continue to be the product of choice in applications requiring the very best possible text on different types of paper. Current home products in the $500 to

$800 range print at from 600 x 600 to 1,200 x 1,200 dots per inch at speeds of six to eight pages per minute. Mid-range issues fall into the $1,000 to $1,500 price bracket and offer greater speed, better paper handling, a longer consumable cycle, and extras such as infrared, or cordless, connection. Major builders include Hewlett-Packard, NEC, Lexmark, Brother, Okidata, and Panasonic. It is worth noting that this group of products has posed some confusion because of different kinds of "laser-like" printing technology, although the majority today do indeed contain a laser and fully merit the name.

Personal laser printers work on the principle of photostatic transfer. Remember those magic iron filings you were able to control by moving a magnet around underneath a sheet of paper in the fourth grade? Laser printing works a bit the same way, using a process quite different from ink jet and dot matrix systems. When a print job is sent from a computer, each page is assembled in the memory of the printer, which then directs the laser, or a set of light-emitting diodes (LEDs) in the case of "laser-like" products, to reproduce the image on a photosensitive drum using a system of mirrors. As this is achieved, the drum revolves and is exposed to toner, a very fine black powder which adheres to the pattern because of electrostatic attraction. On the next rotation, the toner is transferred to the paper and baked onto it by a heating element. The result is a very clear, finely described image which is not particularly sensitive to different types of paper or subject to smudging.

Laser printers offer advantages and disadvantages. Even home and small office models are reasonably fast, able to produce six to eight pages of normal text in a minute, with higher-end network-ready products performing in the 12- to 20-ppm range. Like ink jets, and unlike dot matrix printers, lasers require regular care and feeding: the purchase of toners, drums, and sometimes other consumables such as corona wires, fusers, and developers. They have no capability to produce two or more copies of a document at one pass, and because of their design, they must "draw" each page before printing it. They do this using their own memory, which is more or less independent of the computer sending the print job, and this is a feature important in pricing and selection. Memory in lasers makes them susceptible to RAM shortages; a high-quality graphic, even though it is composed of shades of black and white, may require more resources than a printer has to offer. In such a case, you can find the top half of that great picture of a girl's face printed on page one, and the lower half, from the tip of her nose to the bottom of her chin, on page two. Most manufacturers now offer one or two megabytes of RAM to avoid this situation, with empty sockets to accept more. Hewlett-Packard also advertises a memory swapping feature (RAM enhancement) designed to allow its printers to use RAM more effectively. It's important to find out whether a laser printer will accept conventional 72-pin SIMMs (single inline memory modules) before buying it, or whether you will have to purchase expensive, harder to find, proprietary RAM if you want to improve it later.

Printer Consumables

As far as consumables are concerned, ink jets and laser printers vary in terms of ongoing costs, although a rule of thumb for ordinary text is between one and three cents per page. It's worth looking at this in some detail, because several factors apply. First, remember that the actual cost of a consumable – a pot of ink, a toner, or a drum for a laser – is not the real issue, any more than a monthly payment is a measure of a mortgage. It is the combination of coverage (the amount of ink or toner used on one page) and the number of pages yielded by the cost of *all* consumables which determines the bottom-line. If, for example, a Canon Bubble Jet BJ 260 replacement cartridge costs $40 and yields 500 pages of text at 30 percent coverage, the per page cost is a little less than a dime. If the same printer is used to print pictures at 60 percent coverage, the yield of 500 will obviously go down and the cost per page will double.

To avoid overcomplicating this equation, remember to compare text output with text output, and total consumable costs, including drums and other long-term replacements, when evaluating a product. If you have trouble with the promises of a salesperson or advertisement, call a manufacturer. They can generally be relied upon to issue accurate maintenance estimates. The questions to ask are, what consumables will you have to purchase as you use the printer over a long period? How much does each one cost, and how many pages of normal text should you expect it to produce?

It's also a good idea to find out how long a product has been on the market, and whether other printers can use the same kinds of consumables (the more the better, for third-party toners then become an option). Try to locate stores in your area that carry them. When you do find a supplier who sells consumables for your printer at a competitive price, let me offer one last bit of advice: *buy an extra!* The havoc, parking tickets, frazzled nerves, missed deadlines, and other general destruction I have seen caused by last-minute searches for toners and cartridges you would not believe. This is a bit like advising you to change the oil in the family wagon, I know, but do it. It may save you one day.

MODEMS

One of the fastest-growing collections of products in the PC market in the past five years has been communication and networking components. In the forefront of this group are modems, internal or external devices which allow a system to send and receive data across a telephone line. The two basic jobs modems perform are

1. connecting your system to another computer so the two can exchange data, thus opening the door to the Internet and other computer networks;
2. sending and receiving faxes directly to and from other computers or fax machines.

Back in the '80s, modems were a lot slower and less versatile than they are today. Early models were limited by slow transmission rates, and it wasn't until 1989 or 1990 that competitively priced models gained the ability to communicate with fax machines.

The name "modem" is an abbreviation of the words *mo*dulation and *dem*odulation, describing the way these devices take digital data from one PC and modulate (change) it, so it can be sent in analogue form over a telephone line. At the other end, another modem demodulates the data back to digital form for use in the other computer.

And how do these components actually understand each other? There is, in fact, a regulatory body in the modem world, known as the CCITT (International Telephone and Telegraph Consultative Committee), which governs transmission standards. Throughout the years, as faster products have emerged, the CCITT has established rules to govern such things as speed, data compression, and error correction. A list of these standards is shown below:

MODEM STANDARDS AND SPEEDS

MODULATION	STANDARD SPEED	APPROX. TIME FOR 100K FILE TRANSFER
V.22	1,200 bps	14 minutes
V.22bis	2,400 bps	7 minutes
V.32	9.6 Kbps	2 minutes
V.32bis	14.4 Kbps	1 minute
V.34	28.8 Kbps	30 seconds

MODEM STANDARDS AND SPEEDS cont'd

MODULATION	STANDARD SPEED	APPROX. TIME FOR 100K FILE TRANSFER
V.42/V.42bis	33.6 Kbps	26 seconds
V.42/V.42bis	56 Kbps*	15 seconds

FIGURE 3E

* Downloading at 46 Kbps

One of the most important elements of a modem is its transmission speed, and as usual, there is room for confusion. A common concept in the marketplace is a product's baud rate, which, in strict terms, is a measurement of the number of any frequency or signal changes per second. In fact, modems are now described in terms of kilobits per second (Kbps), a similar but different way of describing data flow. In 1998, 56 Kbps is the speed to watch for, although 33.6K products are still being sold.

While 56K modems are *capable* of sending and receiving data this fast, they really don't – at least not yet. They're limited by law to the amount of electricity they can present to the telephone system, which means they actually run only at about 40K to 46K, and that's on a good day. When connecting to the Internet, they can achieve this level only under certain conditions, and must be speaking to a server computer that supports one of two 56K standards: US Robotics x2 or Rockwell/ Lucent K56flex. There is more information on these standards in the modem section of Chapter 9. Also, transmission at 40 to 46 Kbps only happens in one direction – when you are downloading data from an Internet service provider (ISP) – and is subject to environmental conditions such as traffic on the phone lines.

Physically, modems are available in three forms: internal, external, and PCMCIA (sometimes known as "PC Card"). Most common and least expensive, internal modems drive the market. A typical example is about 4" x 3" (a "1/3 length" card), and plugs into an expansion slot on a motherboard. The modem presents two jacks to the rear exterior of the system. Into one of these fits a standard telephone cable, which at the other end is plugged into the familiar box on the wall. Into the other jack can be plugged a second device, normally a desktop telephone, which you can continue to use whether your PC is on or off. Of course, when a system is using its modem, other calls coming in will get a busy signal, and if you pick up the handset you'll hear the machine in the middle of its conversation – that high static that sounds like an old home-built radio searching for its mate out there in deep space.

Internal modems are approximately $50 to $100 cheaper than their external counterparts, and are usually available for $100 to $200, depending on properties such as the stature of the manufacturer and included extras such as voice mail and bundled software.

A disadvantage to internal modems is that they're more difficult to install, requiring you or a technician to take a computer's hat off to insert one. After that, the system must be "configured" – told what kind of modem it is speaking to and which communication, or "com," port it's going to use. This process has become a lot easier with the introduction of "plug-and-play" technology, which means your computer *should* recognize and configure the device automatically. But when this does not happen (sometimes because of conflicts with other components vying for the same ports), internal modem installations can become tricky. Besides being physically easier to install, external modems can be moved quickly and easily from one PC to another, or taken to a service depot or Internet service provider for diagnostics and service. However, external modems require their own power source, more space, and (not to be forgotten when purchasing one) a cable to connect to an external serial port (usually a 25-pin male) on the back of a PC.

No mention of external modems would be complete without taking note of the different types of serial ports to which these devices connect. The speed with which a port handles data is controlled by a (Nerd Alert!) universal asynchronous receiver/transmitter, known as a UART chip. These have appeared in different designs over the years, the current standards being 16550 or 16550AFN UARTs. In simple terms, these provide a bit of buffer memory for increased efficiency. Although any new computer in 1998 should at least contain UART serial ports, it's not a bad idea to confirm this feature before buying.

A new type of connection which is poised to take over serial interface device design is called the universal serial bus, or USB. Different in both form and function from older connections, USBs offer a lot of advantages and will likely become standard in new PCs before the end of 1998. USB ports permit two-way data flow between a device and a computer, and they are "hot swappable," allowing you to plug peripherals such as joysticks and scanners into them without having to turn a computer off or reconfigure it. These connectors promise a whole new level of communication between parts of a system, providing for automatic voice and fax message management, and the development of "intelligent" digital cameras, gaming products, and speakers. So watch for a USB in any new computer you purchase in 1998.

PCMCIA Modems

Sometimes known as "credit card" or "PC Card" modems, these are the portable members of the family. The name arises from yet another manufacturer group: The Personal Computer Memory Card International Association. Measuring about 1 1/2" x 3", these wafer-thin cards plug into a specially designed port in current notebook PCs. One edge of the device protrudes from the system to accept a telephone line. Some PCMCIA modems require a special connector cable (a "dongle"), which plugs into the card on one end and accepts a familiar RJ-11 telephone connector from the wall on the other. Others have a receptacle which pops out to accept the telephone plug directly. These "X-Jack" modems are definitely superior. Connecting cables for non-X-Jack products are usually proprietary (you must buy a specific cable for a specific modem), easy to lose, and small and fragile enough to be subject to problems. A strong jerk from a pet can send you running all over for that little piece of the puzzle needed to get back on line. PCMCIA modems usually run $100 to $200 more than their internal counterparts.

Some PCMCIA modems are also capable of working with cellular phones. A word of warning, though, when purchasing a cellular PC Card modem: be sure to check its compatibility with the manufacturer of your portable phone and your cellular service provider. Not all modems work with all phones, and at $250 to $400 plus installation, this is not a purchase you'll want to get wrong.

ISDN Lines

Another development which has affected the modem market in recent years is the appearance of specialty telephone lines. The most common of these are known as ISDN (integrated service digital network) lines. That's really just a big mouthful to say that they're fast. How fast? They come in two speeds, 64K and 128K, available from most phone companies at a rate starting from about $60 per month. Remember, you can use an ISDN line to handle your regular telephones in a home or office, so the price should be considered as a total telephone bill, not as an addition to what you're paying already. To take advantage of increased ISDN speed, your PC will have to contain a modem specially designed for this environment. These are available from companies such as Motorola and US Robotics, at press time in the $400 (internal) to $500 (external) range. Your Internet service company must also be equipped for ISDN service, an investment that many smaller providers simply don't offer. Be sure to find out whether you'll have to switch ISPs, if you are thinking about migrating to this higher level of Internet service.

KEYBOARDS

In our company's antique typewriter collection, we are lucky to have some great old machines dating back to the turn of the century. One of the most interesting characteristics of these early models is their keyboards. A keyboard is an intimate part of any communications device because you touch it during every session. Of course, this may become a process of the past as voice recognition improves. In the meantime, however, we're stuck with the keyboard in its various forms. Over the years, I have seen typewriter and computer users become devoted to certain kinds because of their layout and touch. The QWERTY design has endured, an excellent example of backward logic that perpetuated itself. Originally developed to slow typists down so their mechanical typewriters wouldn't jam, QWERTY became a keyboard standard by default. Its competitor, the Dvorak layout, was designed later to make typing more efficient, but never caught on. If you are determined to become a Dvorak user, these keyboards are available if you hunt for one, or you can program a QWERTY model to respond to the Dvorak design.

Even within the QWERTY group, several variations of computer keyboards have appeared. Some of these have extra ALT and FUNCTION keys, fat RETURNs (a favourite with writers), BACKSPACE keys, and even new keys designed for specific programs. Other keyboard developments have been the inclusion of trackballs or trackpoint pegs in substitution of a mouse, altered articulation to ease repetitive strain injury (Microsoft's Natural Keyboard), and exotic additions such as microphones and scanners, the latter being offered as part of Compaq's Presario series in 1996/97, without that much success. (As sometimes happens with bundled hardware, users did not like being tied to one kind of product when purchasing another.)

Underneath a keyboard's buttons are printed circuits which are connected every time you hit a desired character. A variety of assemblies have been designed to accomplish this: conductive, mechanical, capacitive, and membrane. All of these join two contact points in different ways, although the differences are not necessarily identifiable by physical feel. When a key is hit, a message is sent to a little buffer (typically 16K or 32K) in the PC, where it may or may not have to wait to be processed. This, and not the mechanics of the keyboard itself, is what accounts for different response speeds. You can change the way many computers handle keyboard data by altering the setup section of the Bios or, as in Windows 95/98, by changing the keyboard speed settings or keyboard type.

As far as connecting cords are concerned, the keyboard plugs which attach them to the system unit come in two forms: 5-pin DIN (a 1/2"-diameter, 5-connector, enclosed male plug) and 6-pin Mini DIN (a 1/4"-diameter, 6-pin version). The smaller, 6-pin design is becoming standard, although adaptors to convert either type are readily available. Another development in both keyboard and mouse design is the appearance of infrared connections, allowing cordless freedom. If you purchase one of these, be aware that you'll have to keep buying batteries, and make sure you keep some spares on hand. If this essential part of your PC runs out of power in the middle of the night, you don't want to be driving around in the rain.

MICE

For many people, I suspect that one of the most magical things about using a PC remains the ability to move a mouse around on top of a desk and have the cursor on the screen immediately respond. Mice have been in common use for many years now, and in that time they have become a favourite part of PC culture. Just how, exactly, do mice translate the movements of your hand on a desktop onto a screen? Like many enduring inventions, they're brilliantly simple.

Developed in the '60s by Douglas Englehart at the Stanford Research Institute, the mouse was originally called an "XY position indicator." Different types have been introduced over the years, but variations on the common "optimechanical" design still work on the inventor's original principles. That shell which fits so conveniently under your palm houses a little ball which rotates as it's moved around on top of the desk. Inside the shell and tight against the ball are two small cylinders, each one on its own little shaft. These cylinders are connected in turn to tiny wheels with holes in them. As the ball turns, each wheel spins.

And now for the really ingenious part. Positioned next to each perforated wheel is a little light source (think of a tiny flashlight) aimed through holes at a sensor. As the mouse moves and the wheels turn, the light source is cut into pulses which are sent to the computer. These pulses are then interpreted as co-ordinates which tell the system where to position the cursor on your screen. In recent years, improvements on this original design have included alterations in the way the pulses are measured and translated.

In order to track the movements of a mouse successfully, a PC has to have a little program, known as a "mouse driver," installed, so it

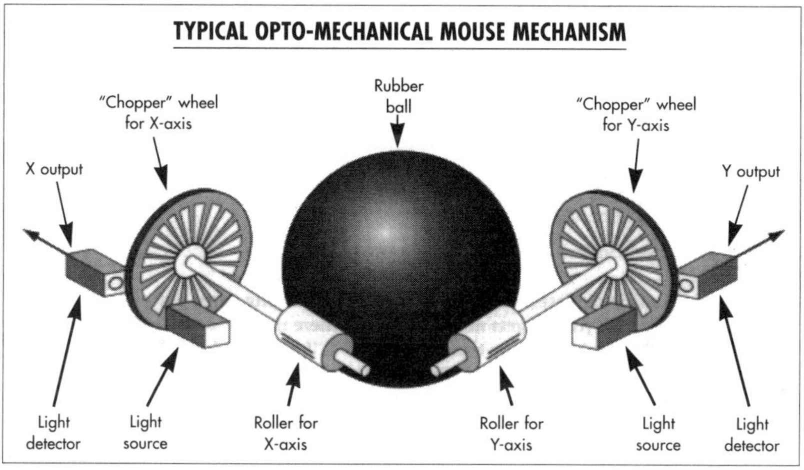

FIGURE 3F

has a starting point on which to base the position of the cursor in the first place.

Variations on the external design of mice have appeared over the years. These include trackballs, mouse pens, trackpoints, touchpads, cordless models, and specially featured versions such as Microsoft's Intellimouse, which has scroll bar control built in. Trackballs are basically an upside-down version of the old standby and work the same way, except that you spin the ball instead of moving its shell. If you're considering one of these, be sure to get a model that is responsive enough, otherwise it can be tedious moving the cursor from one point on the screen to another. Trackpoints, often built into notebook computers, are little posts you move around with the tip of your finger. Touchpads track the pressure or heat of your finger as you slide it around on a small silicon or plastic pad. Cordless mice send pulses via radio signals to a little box plugged into your computer from up to ten feet away.

With all of these pointing products available, what's the preferred design? Still the original, according to Logitech Corporation, one of the world's leading manufacturers of mouse and trackball technology. Price and market acceptance probably have a lot to do with this; the conventional design is still produced in the largest quantities. This in turn keeps its price low – a simple economy of scale. Or it could be that people just continue to like an original that works well.

4

SOFTWARE BASICS

ASSESSING YOUR SOFTWARE REQUIREMENTS

You need a new computer, right? What kind? Well, you're not exactly sure; it depends on the software you want to run. And what kind of software do you want? Well, you're not exactly sure; that depends on the hardware you can afford . . . Is this a chicken-and-egg question or what?

Actually, there are some rules you can apply to the tricky business of choosing software. They depend on asking yourself pointed questions before entering the marketing arena and being confronted with thousands of products which, according to their manufacturers, you absolutely *must* have, can't live without, would be a fool to turn down. What are these questions? They are very similar to the questions in Chapter 2 dealing with your choice of computer hardware:

- What do I want the program to do and will it do it?
- Am I buying, or do I own, a PC to powerful enough to run it?
- Can I afford it?
- Can I learn it?
- Can I get training, support, and custom programming for it?
- Can I upgrade or change it later?

Of all these issues, the first is the most important. I have often been asked whether a particular piece of software is suited to a particular job, and as I have noted earlier in this book, getting advice from your hardware dealer about software is rather like asking the guy selling you a VCR what movies you're going to like. Perhaps this analogy is a little over the top, but it points out that you really should do a bit of research, or at least some soul-searching, before deciding on a program.

Good sources of reliable software advice are people or companies who are (a) not trying to sell you something and (b) performing the same kinds of tasks. If you can find a third party off of whom to bounce some questions about a product you are considering, you are already in a much better position.

A second tip to keep in mind is not to purchase too much too soon. It's a good rule of thumb to err on the side of caution upon hearing that you might need a $2,000 package that someone says you'd be crazy not to buy. Low-cost "over the counter" programs have become powerful and plentiful in the past few years, so be wary of specialty software which may be medicine in search of a cure. The more obscure a program, the more difficult and limited are likely to be its training, upgrade, troubleshooting, and compatibility properties.

Try to find accurate, up-to-date information, and get an opinion from an impartial source about any product you're considering. Ask about its limitations. Will the information it manipulates be compatible with other, similar programs? Find out if there's any way you can get your hands on a trial or "demo" copy to see if you'll like the program when it comes time to use it. Many software manufacturers offer testing options or lenient money-back guarantees. Finally, try to determine how difficult the program is going to be to learn. If you can satisfy even a majority of these questions, you will protect yourself against spending too much on an unknown quantity.

BUYING SOFTWARE: WHAT (AND WHAT NOT) TO EXPECT

One of the prime areas of difficulty in a computer purchase concerns misunderstandings surrounding software. It's easy to see why. On the one hand, we have all been subjected to advertising and hype, truthful or otherwise, involving famous personalities and attractive people using their computers perfectly and living happily ever after. Let's face it, there are some major expectations being generated here. On the other hand, the vendor and manufacturer, part of what is known as the "marketing channel," are trying to make a profit. No matter where your reseller sits in the food chain, he will probably be selling his products on a margin of 5 to 15 percent if he is competitive. If he's a mainstream dealer, he has access to perhaps 5,000 different programs, 200 of which he is lucky to have a passing acquaintance with. He and his staff may have in-depth knowledge of twenty or twenty-five.

This situation is not unique to the software business. In the '70s, when scientific calculators became popular, office equipment companies were confronted with products so complex they could take a salesperson hours to demonstrate, and a user more hours to learn. Yet these were products being given away in cereal boxes! On a good day, a vendor could make five or ten dollars when selling one. Who ultimately got hurt? Some dealers, of course, but in the long run, it was the purchasers. This is because they were dealing with a very complicated product which no one – neither manufacturer nor vendor – could afford to explain.

Mainstream software sales are close to this dynamic, so be sure you're honest with yourself about how much time and effort a new program is going to take to learn, and how much money proper assistance with it is going to cost. Don't assume *anything* unless you get it in writing from a manufacturer or the vendor. Today, even wealthy software developers are distancing themselves from the after-sale market because of the competitive margins in the business.

This issue of support also points to the difference between retail and OEM (original equipment manufacturer) versions of some programs. Ever wonder how a product such as Microsoft Office can cost $795 at one place and $395 at another? Are we missing something here? It's the OEM difference. In the computer industry, the term OEM is commonly used to describe different sides of a manufacturing scenario in which one company makes a product and then sells it to another which in turn remarkets the item under its own name or as part of a package. The term is sometimes used in connection with the original manufacturer, and sometimes in connection with the remarketer.

OEM AND RETAIL

So, like the "white box" computer hardware components we take note of in Chapter 8, OEM software is offered in the PC business as a family of generic products at reduced prices. It is usually, though not always, sold on condition that it be packaged with a new PC or some other hardware. Most major manufacturers – Microsoft, Corel, and Lotus Development, for example – offer programs in this form.

What are the implications of purchasing something that is so much cheaper? OEM software versions vary. In general, expect the same product you get when buying "full retail," only with limited packing, smaller or absent documentation, and – here is a major snag – limited support. It has not taken software manufacturers long to learn the bitter lessons of the after-sale equation: a low-margin item must produce high volume and carry minimal post-purchase obligations. So that $395 price tag for OEM Office, compared to its $795 retail counterpart, enables Microsoft to refer you to the place you purchased the software when you call with questions. Or, of course, you can buy support separately. This is offered in various forms, from pay-per-call to annual subscriptions for assistance and upgrades.

But what if you don't want to pay any more money to learn about the program you just bought? Your dealer is about as capable of spending after-sale hours with you as he is of purchasing control of Microsoft. If he thinks he has the time, and continues this way for long, he'll be out of business. So when you do choose to purchase OEM or bundled software, particularly if it's an application for which you feel you'll need assistance, be aware that you'll likely be asked to pay to have your questions answered after the sale. Also be warned that a high percentage of pirated programs are issued as "OEM" products.

Note, however, that OEM software is not always to be avoided. It is indeed an excellent way to save money, as long as you have support alternatives in place. There are plenty of books, courses, and videos available, as well as all kinds of instructors and specialty programmers (sometimes known as "contractors") ready to help if a manufacturer won't.

SOFTWARE VERSIONS

It's important to keep in mind the various incarnations in which different programs are now available. This knowledge can save you hundreds of dollars. Take a good look at the different issues of a program you're thinking of buying. Think about these as you would about the differences between flying full fare, taking a bare charter, and going on a packaged tour. Almost all major programs, suites included, are now available in several versions:

1. Full retail: The full product, at the full price.
2. OEM: Usually, though not always, the same product with reduced manufacturer support, packaging, and manuals. Sometimes this version can be purchased only with a new PC.
3. Educational or academic: These too may be feature-reduced programs, and available to qualified students or teachers who meet

criteria designed by the manufacturer to ensure that the software is being used in an educational environment.
4. Upgrade: You must be a licensed user of another product (not always from the same manufacturer) to qualify for a reduced price.
5. License-only: You purchase a piece of paper (a licence) from a software manufacturer and are thereby authorized to make a legal copy and use the product on a PC.

Often you can save hundreds of dollars when purchasing one version of a program instead of another. A good example of this is Microsoft Word. Available at a street price of $359 to $399, a fully featured upgrade of this product is contained in Microsoft's "Home Essentials," a bundle which also includes Microsoft Works, Microsoft Encarta, Microsoft Money, and a few other perks. The catch, of course, is that you must first have an eligible product in your PC to support the upgrade. This is easily arranged. Shop around and purchase an early version of MS Works (or one of the other low-priced upgrade platforms described on the box) for under $100. Then buy the upgrade at $129. You now have MS Word for a total cost of $229, a little over half the price of the full retail version.

Also, take note of the different media on which computer programs are now offered. In earlier days, you paid your money and received one, two, three, maybe even ten or fifteen 1.44-MB floppy disks. One by one you copied these onto your hard drive and away you went. Now, two major developments have transformed the process of software delivery: compact discs and the Internet.

With storage capacities in excess of 500 MB (think of 400 or so 3.5" floppies), CD-ROMs have opened the door for manufacturers wanting to produce bigger, more comprehensive programs, although this doesn't necessarily mean they work any better. This development has made the inclusion of a CD-ROM drive an absolute necessity in any PC. You simply must have one in order to be able to load and use current programs.

A second development in the software delivery business is the Internet. Still evolving, the World Wide Web has become an excellent tool through which a manufacturer can offer its wares. Increasingly, you can log onto a website, make whatever financial arrangements are necessary – from cybercash to credit card to prepaid cheque via post – and then download a program. Some pretty substantial players in the computer industry are counting on this kind of commerce to support a lot of PCs and new software editions in the future.

SOFTWARE TRAINING AND INSTRUCTION

What happens if you fall into the "needful user" category and have to pay someone for assistance? There are a few points to remember when arranging a successful instruction session on a PC. The most important element is communication, *in advance*. This means writing down the things you want to be taught and making that list available to the instructor well ahead of time. This way, both of you can be sure that the training you're paying for will actually be of some benefit. I shudder to imagine the unfortunate novice who purchased his new PC with its twenty different programs, and after two hours of unstructured tutoring still hasn't learned how to turn the thing off.

Here are the key training issues:

- Do both the instructor and you know what is supposed to be taught?
- Is the instructor qualified to teach it?
- Do you know how much the instruction will cost?
- Do you know approximately how long it will take to cover the things you want to learn?

SOFTWARE LEMON-AID

Let's suppose you have carefully researched what you need, read all the blurbs, consulted with your consultants, and taken the plunge. You have installed your new software exactly as instructed and are using it on recommended hardware for the recommended tasks. You have even paid some pointy-headed character with a pen protector in her shirt pocket to show how it'll wash the dishes and make you a billionaire. And guess what? You still hate it! This is probably where many software manufacturers outclass hardware manufacturers by offering more after-sale options.

The first order of business when you find yourself the owner of an unwanted, ineffective program is to catalogue your dissatisfactions very carefully, and then make them known to the vendor from whom you made the purchase. This may produce anything from an instant refund, to an offer of credit for goods of equal value, to a shrug and a denial. If you don't get anywhere at this level, approach the manufacturer. As companies which pride themselves on being progressive, software houses almost universally offer return guarantees within a reasonable period. It has been my experience that these companies are fairly generous with their return policies.

So have your objections carefully organized and written down, and then be prepared for a proposal of some kind of credit through one of the manufacturer's dealers, as opposed to an out and out refund. This is, of course, unless a money-back guarantee is explicitly offered as part of a product's after-sale support. In anticipation, you might want to research an alternative program ahead of time (even if it's completely different), or you can insist on getting your money back. The chances of this are actually pretty good if you return the unwanted item in its original packing, with its manuals and a written list of your objections.

PIRATED SOFTWARE

Illegally copied software is an interesting phenomenon: a group of products which collectively are worth a lot of money, and yet are easy to duplicate. Billions of dollars are spent on software each year. In most cases, a user doesn't actually "buy" a product in the true sense of the term. Rather, a program is generally licensed from the company or individual who wrote it.

At least half of the people I talk to, before they learn I'm in the computer business, seem to take a nudge-nudge, wink-wink attitude toward copying computer programs. What is it about these products that make them such attractive targets for theft? First, as I've said, they're easy to duplicate. "Copy protection" is a feature which seems to come and go in software design, never showing very much success. Various security features have been introduced over the years, but not one of them is completely foolproof. Protection attempts have included "counters" which allow a limited number of reproductions of a program, hardware fixes such as special keys or cables which a program has to "find" before it will run, and other checks which cause copies to self-destruct or which prevent their duplication after a certain date.

For the average, honest computer user, I suspect that any one of these is more than enough. The problem is that it takes only one perpetrator to duplicate something illegally. Then wham! A pirated program can become global in a minute with the assistance of the greatest copying machine the world has ever known: the Internet.

A second consideration is that this crime is often seen as "victimless." "Are they going to break down my front door and bust me for copying software? Will they scoop up my videotapes too?" Not only is it easy to make a copy of a desired program, it's hard to see who is really getting hurt by it. Don't Mr. Gates and his associates already have enough money?

Third, pirating is ambiguous. Does anyone really read those licensing agreements when they get their new stuff home from the store and tear it open to see how it works? Isn't it OK to make a copy of the program your nephew is using in his office downtown? Can't the computer store load an update of the software that was on the PC you bought from Uncle Joe last year?

For these, and many other reasons, it may seem easy, harmless, convenient, and above all, inexpensive to break the terms of a software licence. But there really is another side to this story and, believe me, it's ugly. If you could sit on the technician's side of a PC service counter for a day or two, you'd see the grief and trouble that illegally copied software causes. In addition to the ethical problems, the practical difficulties are formidable. I can't speak for other businesses, but at least a quarter of the service issues we encounter have something to do with illegal, improperly copied software. So resist the temptation: don't do it.

When is it proper and legal to make a copy of a program? Have a good look at a couple of relevant clauses from the licensing agreement for InContext Spider, a web home-page design program:

> 1. LICENSE: InContext Corporation grants You the non-exclusive right to use the enclosed program(s). The program(s) may be used only on the number of computer systems equal to the total number of licenses purchased. You may physically transfer the program(s) from one computer to another, or electronically transfer them over a network, provided that the total number of programs in use at any given time does not exceed the total number of licenses purchased from InContext. You may not distribute copies of the program(s) or documentation to others. You may not modify or translate the program(s) or related documentation without the prior written consent of InContext. YOU MAY NOT USE, COPY, MODIFY, OR TRANSFER THE PROGRAM(S) OR DOCUMENTATION, OR ANY COPY, EXCEPT AS EXPRESSLY PROVIDED IN THIS AGREEMENT.
>
> . . .
>
> 3. BACKUP: You may make copies of the program(s) solely for backup purposes. You must reproduce and include the copyright notice on the backup copies.
>
> 4. COPYRIGHT: The program(s) and related documentation are copyrighted. You may not copy the program(s) or documentation except for backup purposes and to load the program(s) into

the computer as part of executing the program(s). All other copies of the program(s) and documentation are in violation of this agreement.

In general, it is not proper to copy, give away, or use a program:

1. when it has been included at no cost with a rental PC;
2. when purchasing a new PC and not paying for or receiving an authentic licence from the manufacturer;
3. when purchasing a used PC which contains unlicensed software left over from its previous owner; or
4. under any other circumstance which violates a manufacturer's stated copyright.

So if you are in doubt about what you're doing with a program, the answer is simple: call the manufacturer. If you are supposed to purchase the software, by all means do so.

APPS AND OPS

One of the first things to understand about the way a personal computer and its software work is the difference between an operating system and an application. Think of a PC's operating system as its "cup of coffee" – something it needs to get out of bed in the morning, wake up, and say, "OK, I'm ready, now let's get to work."

In the beginning, operating systems did little more than that: they enabled a PC to "boot," or recognize its subsystems and make them available for use. Examples of major operating systems developed for personal computers since 1980 are Microsoft DOS, Microsoft Windows, IBM's OS2, and Apple's OS.X.

As operating systems evolved and were realized to be fundamental to every PC, it wasn't long before manufacturers – IBM and Microsoft for example – started enhancing their early issues to make them more attractive. They soon gave operating systems new ways of waking a computer up, recognizing its hard drive and other devices, and presenting its programs. They built in all kinds of extras, commonly known as utilities, which made it easier to perform routine maintenance tasks such as copying files or disks, manipulating information on a hard drive, and checking to see what is in a PC. They even added sections to allow you to perform human-oriented tasks such as writing documents or reading the files of another computer connected by a network cable or modem.

Currently, the definitive operating systems in the PC environment are still Windows 95, Windows NT, and the soon expected Windows 98, which was originally codenamed Memphis after the city in which it was developed. Apple's PCs now rely on OS Version 8, designed specifically for them. Certainly all kinds of other platforms, or operating system environments, have appeared, from large, well-known offerings such as IBM's WARP to smaller specialty operating systems such as Linux.

Following are the main points to remember about an operating system:

1. It lives in your computer and may be thought of as an accompaniment to the actual programs (or applications) you use to perform specific tasks such as drawing or wordprocessing.
2. It defines the family of programs you're able to run in your computer, so there is a definite advantage in picking the most popular operating system available. Doing so simply means you'll be compatible with a larger number of applications.
3. It affects the hardware you're going to purchase; operating systems are made for computers of certain specifications. In the stand-alone PCs used in most home and office environments, Windows 95/98 are still clear choices simply because of their popularity. A more network-oriented version of these platforms, Windows NT, is a close second.

One of the most advertised features of Windows 95 when it appeared in its year of release was its "intelligent" ability to detect types and specifications of hardware in a computer: its video card, CD-ROM, modem, or hard drive. This gave rise to a generation of products known as "plug-and-play" devices. In the early days of this operating system's release this standard came to be known in the industry as "plug and pray." This derision arose from the realization that the much-hyped standard advertised by Microsoft and many parts manufacturers was really not all that helpful. Some early "plug-and-play" products were actually harder to install than their predecessors.

Now, however, hardware and software that like to cohabit with Windows 95 have very much stabilized. Let's hope that any new operating system that becomes widely accepted, whether it's issued from Microsoft or not, will cause as few incompatibilities as possible. If you do plan on changing your operating system, perhaps migrating to Windows 98 from Windows 95, keep in mind the following:

- Make sure you have enough hardware to support the new system; this means not just meeting its minimum requirements, but having enough memory and hard drive space to be practical.
- Ask yourself why you are making the change. If it is just because the new operating system is available, consider staying right where you are until a more substantial reason for disturbing your current platform comes along.

In the more distant future, we may see the emergence of radically new operating systems that are dependent on the Internet or other networking situations, and that live in one form during the short time they stay in your computer and then "die." They may be highly sensitive to the particular system in which they run, aware of the person operating them during a specific computing session, and able to alter themselves automatically as their environments change.

THE YEAR 2000 PROBLEM

The Year 2000 problem has received increased attention from computer users and manufacturers throughout 1997 and 1998, and will undoubtedly continue to grow in importance as we approach the end of this century. Simply put, this term refers to miscalculations expected in computers that now store calendar information in a DD/MM/YY format, with only two digits describing a date's year.

Originally established in the name of programming simplicity and storage economy, this date format now poses the threat of disrupting computer systems around the world by making them unable to distinguish between the years 1900 and 2000, producing inaccuracies of all kinds. When you stop to think about the many aspects of our lives, from our telephone bills to our traffic lights, that are affected by computer calculations, it is indeed likely that this problem will cause damage and confusion, not to mention financial losses, though it is a matter of some debate just how serious the situation really will be.

It's a temptation to assume that this problem may only be important to companies that store and use data on which other people depend, but your personal files are not immune. When purchasing a new PC or buying software, choose an operating system and applications that will handle a four-digit year date. New Year's Eve 1999 is approaching quickly so be sure that you and your computer are prepared for it!

5

Personal Computer Applications

"POWER USERS": LOVE YOUR PC

Did you ever notice that some people seem to possess an aptitude for computers and technology, while others are unable to understand anything more complicated than an old rotary dial telephone? I have often considered this question when I've been called upon to hire technicians and salespeople. From my side of the desk, an applicant's ability to one day qualify as an expert, or even become a moderately successful technician, is determined in part by their education and training, but also depends on something more difficult to identify. Perhaps the best way to describe this is as an excitement about technology. Some people just seem to like computers, and are more impressed than others by what they do. I think these are the people who are likely to become most productive with them.

Is there a way to cultivate this kind of interest, to develop it in yourself? I am certain there is. Time and again I have seen complete novices nervously purchase their first PC and printer – equipment about which they know very little – only to return a few weeks or months later with new skills and perspectives. Some users will have followed a certain path – trying this program or that, rearranging their systems a certain way – and reaching a plateau of expertise and productivity with which they are satisfied, and which they can maintain. Others go on to become technology junkies who purchase several systems, take them apart, customize them, network them, and end up teaching us things we otherwise would never have taken the time to learn. As you spend time with a new computer, you'll become aware of its quirks, its strengths, and its weaknesses. With even a little curiosity, you can go a long way toward becoming comfortable around PCs, and that will help increase your effective use of them.

With these hopeful thoughts in mind, let's look at some of the most common tasks for which people and businesses use personal computers, and the kinds of hardware and software necessary to perform them. Many tasks for which we use computers, such as accessing the Internet, merit examination from the *human* point of view; they cannot be handled effectively by a single piece of software. Other tasks can be accomplished by a range of different programs. The simple act of keeping a diary, for example, can be achieved with specialized software such as a PIM (personal information manager) or Sales Tracker, or with wordprocessing software or the Notepad feature of an operating system.

WORDPROCESSING AND DESKTOP PUBLISHING

One of the major applications which helped the personal computer catch fire in the early '80s was wordprocessing – the writing, storing, editing, and printing of documents. As a result of my family's involvement in the typewriter business, the evolution of this process is something we have been watching for some time. Throughout the twentieth century, the typewriter reigned as the supreme business communi- cation tool. Even today a surprising number of people are more comfortable around typewriters than computers. This is not to say the typewriter has much of a future. It is rapidly achieving "cult" or "antique" status. By the late '70s and early '80s, even though many typewriters included wordprocessing capabilities, writing, storing, and retrieving documents were usually done with dedicated systems. These were not quite computers, but workstations whose sole function was wordprocessing. They were offered by companies like Wang, AES, and of course, IBM, which launched the popular Displaywriter series. These behemoths were expensive, and sometimes quirky, designed primarily for corporate and institutional use. Some had networking capabilities (the ability to share documents), while others came with built-in printers. Needless to say, this family of items was hard hit when everyone discovered that a little desktop PC would accomplish the same tasks at a fraction of the price.

What are the main features of a wordprocessing PC? Hundreds of different programs have become available over the years, but they all share some common characteristics.

For hardware, you need a computer on which to run an operating system such as DOS, Windows, or the Macintosh OS; some kind of wordprocessing program, or application, such Corel WordPerfect or Microsoft Word; and a printer to print what you've written.

Regardless of cost, computing power requirements, or added frills, wordprocessing programs all perform the same basic functions: they display text on a screen for you, then allow you to store it on a disk, recall it, make changes to it, and print it out.

These basic steps – write, store, recall, edit, and print – are the foundations of the task, and they can actually be performed with very inexpensive equipment. Beyond these features, many wordprocessing packages now include the more advanced abilities to enhance a document which, in the past, were included in desktop publishing programs.

Originally, desktop publishing was treated as a separate application in the computer world because it required much more computer power and more expensive, more complicated programs. The main advantage desktop publishing software offered was that it allowed a user to create typeset-style work. When a document is typeset, wide letters such as Ms and Ws are allowed more room than narrow Is and Js. When text is printed this way, it takes on a "bookish" feel, as opposed to work that has been typed on a typewriter, in which all characters, wide or narrow, are allowed the same amount of space. The term "pitch" refers to the number of characters per inch – 10 pitch means there are ten typewritten characters per inch.

A second "extra" available in desktop publishing programs, but absent from early wordprocessing software, is the ability to alter the "point size" of a character. Also a publishing term, the "point" measurement refers to the height of a letter in increments of 1/72nd of an inch. Hence the designations 18-point or 24-point type. Figure 5A shows different styles of type and different pitches and point sizes.

Typestyles in desktop publishing and current wordprocessing programs are given names such as 20-point Helvetica, or 10-point Times Roman. Notice that neither of these names includes mention of the pitch because, as proportional typestyles, the number of characters in an inch of type varies. Since the introduction of Microsoft Windows and the Macintosh OS, wordprocessing programs have crossed into the desktop publishing domain. These new-generation programs are generally known as *graphical* wordprocessors because they create a graphic image of each character on the screen with a series of small dots. A user can change the size and look of the type and see the resulting changes quite easily. This characteristic gave rise to the whimsical acronym

SAMPLES OF DIFFERENT TYPESTYLES AND POINT SIZES

UNIVERSE	12 POINT
COURIER	12 POINT
TIMES NEW ROMAN	12 POINT
BANK GOTHIC	12 POINT
BERNHARD MODERN	12 POINT

SIXTEEN POINT TYPE

TWENTY-FOUR PT TYPE

FIGURE 5A

WYSIWYG (What You See Is What You Get), indicating that text is drawn on the screen exactly as it will appear on the page.

Older, less flexible, wordprocessing packages are known as character-based programs – when you type a character, you get the same old letter every time, and can't change it much for desired effects. Current packages such as Corel WordPerfect and Microsoft Word allow you to perform most of the functions contained in early desktop publishing issues. Even with an entry-level computer and relatively inexpensive software, it's possible to produce a stunning document, complete with different fonts and point sizes, columns, graphics, and drawings. Many programs also offer the ability to create HTML (hypertext markup language) documents and post them directly to the World Wide Web.

FEATURES COMMON IN WORDPROCESSING PROGRAMS

Input from/output to multiple text file formats
Multiple fonts, pitches, point sizes
Drawing layering (graphics overlay to create graphics directly on top of text)
Colour gradient to fill shapes or patterns
Automatically changing property bars
Document print preview
Table enhancements to size and arrange rows in table, join and split cells
View, delete, and edit embedded text codes
Undo/redo to correct editing and formatting changes
Application bar to switch between several wordprocessing documents
Recognize and repeat often-used abbreviations
Automatic creation of hyperlinks

FIGURE 5B

DRAWING AND GRAPHICS

A friend of mine recently told me about his mentally and physically challenged grandson who, at the age of twelve, is still trying to learn to walk. Despite his difficulties, the boy seems to be able to learn certain physical activities by emulation. My friend explained to me that he would like to take some still pictures of his grandson crawling, and then animate the pictures with a computer to illustrate the various stages of learning to walk. This project might seem ambitious, but it's exactly the kind of graphics job you can achieve with what is now a medium-range computer, a little perseverance and ingenuity, and appropriate software. Several packages that allow you to manipulate images in all sorts of ways are now available.

Today, with more or less ordinary desktop computer hardware and software, it's possible to perform artistic feats that only a few years ago were exclusive to professionals with expensive equipment. A computer user can easily put together a system that can scan colour photographs or drawings, alter them in any way imaginable, print them in colour, email them, fax them, place them in a newsletter or poster, and even animate them. A few add-ons can turn a three- to five-thousand-dollar PC into a virtual movie studio able to play and record video clips from a standard video camera, capture individual frames from television broadcasts or videotape, alter and blend pictures together seamlessly, and publish them on the Internet.

FEATURES COMMON IN DESKTOP PUBLISHING PROGRAMS
Full colour library
Output to multiple graphics file formats
Trapping and separation for precise colour printing
Print fit view (preview and print on specific paper sizes)
Print reader view (preview and print two facing pages)
Printers' marks (provides use of printers' marks within text)
Automatic HTML conversion (formatting of text for use on the Internet)
Multiple master page layouts in a single document
Grouping and ungrouping of automatically needed marks or data
Object masking for use with graphics programs
Rotation and skewing (manipulate text or images in .01-degree increments)
Storyboarding
Magnification up to 800 percent
Cropping of text, graphics, and images into polygons, ovals, and other shapes
Auto table creation
Professional typographic controls: point-sized tracking, kerning

FEATURES COMMON IN DESKTOP PUBLISHING PROGRAMS cont'd
Object locking
Preview and print selected portions of a single page
Automatic tables of contents and indexes
Layering page on page to preview effects
Automatic object and text alignment

FIGURE 5C

In the beginning, graphics programs were limited by the usual factors: slow hardware and rudimentary features. But even then it was a thrill to sit in front of a blank screen and be able to draw anything you wanted and then save your artwork on a disk. Early in the game, and fundamental to the whole concept of computer drawing, was the introduction of the mouse. Invented by Douglas Englebart of Stanford University in 1964, and pioneered at the Xerox Corporation's PARC Labs in 1964, this ingenious device relied then, as most do today, on the revolutions of a little ball under a shell in your hand on the desk.

Steven Jobs, co-founder of Apple Computer, was quick to grasp the significance of this different way of communicating instructions to a computer. The concept of the mouse was key to the building of his empire. Because of Apple's early adoption of the mouse, many graphics-related programs were designed for its Macintosh computers first, making them the computer of choice among artists and designers. See the illustration of a typical mechanism on page 77.

Today's graphics packages offer designers some amazing creative possibilities. See below and page 95 for some examples of a graphic which has been scanned and altered in different ways using Adobe Photoshop.

A Basic Photograph

Adjusted Levels

Imperfections Retouched or "Cloned Out"

Reversed Picture

FIGURE 5D

CAD/CAM

Professional cousins of common graphics packages such as Corel Draw and Adobe Photoshop are the family of computer programs known as CAD or CAD/CAM applications. Those terms are acronyms for Computer-Assisted Design and Computer-Assisted Modelling. CAD packages have followed the lead of the most common AutoCAD series, which was released by the Autodesk Corporation in the mid '80s, and as of spring 1998 had progressed all the way to Release 14.

A flock of related programs has followed AutoCAD, from personal products to a variety of home design, drafting, and blueprint-producing products.

As with much professional software, the distribution of fully featured CAD/CAM packages is more tightly controlled than common household programs, and has remained commensurately higher in price. At the time of publication, an authorized AutoCAD reseller quoted me a price of over $4,000.

Also, conventional drawing programs are becoming more sophisticated. Most household and small business graphics jobs are more than adequately served by the likes of Corel Draw, Photoshop, and PhotoStudio. What kind of a computer system is recommended for CAD and graphics? The most powerful one you can get your hands on. These applications soak up a PC's resources voraciously. That's because the human eye is a very critical piece of machinery. People instinctively want the brightest colours, the sharpest definition of shapes, the fastest rendering of a changed image. These demands mean lots of RAM (64 megabytes), a large hard drive (8 gigabytes), a fast processor (266 MHz) and, perhaps most important, the best 17" monitor you can afford. When shopping for a monitor, look for a low dot pitch, which means the dots that make up the picture are close together (.26 DP), a fast monitor refresh rate (at least 72 Hz), and a video card with some memory of its own (say, 4, 8, or 16 MB of VRAM or WRAM) to help speed up the show. For more information on video cards and other monitor characteristics, refer to Chapter 3.

DATABASES AND SPREADSHEETS

Two of the best-known personal computer business applications are databases and spreadsheets. Databases are programs which enable you to store, retrieve, and standardize information. They do this by allowing you to design a "screen," or record, on which you can enter data in designated places (usually known as fields), then perform tasks such as searching all of the records by a given combination of characters. They also allow you to create and alphabetize lists, merge one group of records into another, and print out selected information in almost any form to your screen, printer, or another computer. All records of a common design are usually stored in groups, known as files, which can be accessed, updated, copied, and changed.

Databases are commonly used to keep track of customers and inventory, print out invoices and delivery forms, and manage information on demand. Many computer programmers build entire careers around database design. Some will learn a certain program, such as Microsoft Access, so well that they can resell their expertise to businesses who need software tailored to suit their needs.

There are two general types of databases used in home and small business computers: "relational" and "flat file" products. The former are most common and powerful, allowing more flexibility in the way they manage and share data. Unfortunately, because of their many features, they can also be difficult to learn for an ordinary computer user. Common databases now on the market include Microsoft Access, Borland Paradox, and Claris FileMaker Pro. Almost all integrated "office" software bundles include a database program of some type. If you're planning to purchase a PC package for your business or a home office, it's essential that it contain a database program.

Because they're flexible and can be customized in many ways, databases can also do some of the jobs of other applications, such as spreadsheets – to array numbers in columns, as on a page in a ledger, or make automatic calculations. Similarly, you can keep records and print alphabetized lists and special forms from information in a spreadsheet. Spreadsheets were also developed early in the PC's history and at one time were seen as a "killer app" – a main reason to buy a PC. You're probably familiar with the way spreadsheets present information on a "screen" or "sheet," which is sectioned into small boxes or "cells." Data typed into each cell can be manipulated by the computer and the results shown in other cells according to your instructions.

With the appearance of VisiCalc and its successors, particularly Lotus 1-2-3, in the early '80s, it became apparent that all kinds of business functions relating to numbers could be easily automated: account ledgers, forecasting, profit and loss, and the manipulation of scientific data and statistics.

Spreadsheets are now also seen as such an essential home computing application that it's rare to find a "suite" – a package of different programs – that doesn't contain one.

OFFICE SUITES

One of the most important trends in the home and small office software markets in recent years has been the emergence of the suite: a package of several programs, usually from the same manufacturer, sold together at a lower price than if they were sold separately.

On the plus side, these packages really do give good value if – and this is an important condition – you want the applications included, either now or later. A suite offers a shotgun approach that enables you to be prepared for a whole range of tasks with one purchase. Also, the programs included in a suite are made to work together. They look and work similarly, minimizing the shock of evaluating and learning products from different manufacturers. But should you spend the extra money for software you really might not need?

Suites and bundles force you to gaze into your crystal ball and predict whether all of the programs you're getting will be useful to you. Suppose, for example, you're buying a new PC and, after researching the choices carefully, you've decided on Microsoft Word as your word-processing software. Perhaps you already know and like it. On its own, the retail version costs $395. But vendors are telling you that you need Microsoft Office. Sure it's $400 more, they say, but look at the extras included! Spreadsheets! An organizer! Web page creation!

Now is the time to take a critical look at your requirements, and at yourself as a computer user. Are you a novice, intermediate, or expert? Are you using this software in your home, or in a business? Are you likely to grow into the extra applications in the bundle, or is this a "need" being imposed upon you? Finally, of course, can you afford the price?

I often recommend that people purchase programs as they need them. Especially when it's included as part of a new computer purchase, too much software can be overwhelming. The key to making a good decision when looking at a suite is to take careful note of just how many of the individual applications are going to be of use to you. Then add up the prices of buying them separately, and ask:

- Are they programs you really want? (Perhaps you want one manufacturer's spreadsheet, and another's graphics package.)
- If not right away, will you need them in the future? How soon?
- Do you have the expertise and time to learn them? Don't forget that, while the extra programs in a suite almost always come from the same manufacturer, they are indeed separate entities.

If you've answered yes to these questions, a suite may be the most economical solution to your software needs. If not, don't be railroaded into purchasing something you don't want.

UTILITIES AND TOOLS

Trying to describe the huge number of software utilities, or "tools," now available in a short overview is a bit like fitting a tour of the Louvre into a Saturday afternoon. But it's worth taking note of some of the "nuts and bolts" products out there. If you're so inclined, you can do further research on your own.

In the PC world, the term "utility" is a catchall title used to describe programs, or parts of programs, that perform workmanlike duties: copying files or data, diagnosing your PC when it's not feeling well, or protecting it against viruses.

This is a rapidly changing group of applications, to be sure. They move in very close concert with new developments in hardware and, for developers, the financial stakes in this market are quite high. Whenever a routine computer operation that everyone needs comes along (and these appear rapidly as PCs evolve), it can generate a tremendous market – and corresponding amounts of money. Two such recent developments are the remarkable growth of virus detection programs and Internet browsers. Even if a successful utility does not itself become a household name, at least it offers its inventor the prospect of a sale to a larger company, which, in turn, may integrate the product into one of its existing offerings, or simply sit on it to control competition.

Examples of utility applications are: diagnostic programs, which tell you what's inside your computer; file management and conversion programs, which allow you to move, convert, and automatically back up files one by one or in groups; and memory management programs, which allow you to customize the way your PC uses its memory, hard drive, and other subsystems.

Programs peripheral to this market include programming languages, reference and information software, menus and organizers, voice recognition, virus protection, and security packages.

If you're purchasing a new PC, many of the utilities you'll need should already be included in its operating system or in an accompanying suite. In addition, if you buy a special device – say, a Zip drive designed to allow easy backups or a fax/modem – make sure it comes with the software needed to manage it. If it does, have a good look at what you've already paid for before grabbing additional, and possibly unnecessary, programs off the shelf.

At the very least, be sure you're not without an up-to-date anti-virus package, particularly if you plan to use the Internet or frequently share files with other computer users. This probably applies to more than 90 percent of all buyers of new PCs in 1998. Otherwise, buy utility programs when and as you need them; seek advice from your consultant or dealer, depending on how you plan to use, customize, and alter your PC.

One last word of warning: many utilities, whether you purchase them separately or find them included with a new computer, allow you to alter a PC's system files and other basic properties, perhaps disabling it. If you're about to get into the nuts and bolts of your computer's setup, be sure you know:

1. why you're changing it in the first place;
2. that you have a good knowledge of what you are doing. (Read the manual!);
3. that you have a good backup of the file(s) you are altering if they are fundamental to your system's setup.

NETWORKING

One of the most rapidly expanding and exciting areas of software development in the late '90s, communication and networking programs have exploded with the popularity of the Internet and the sharing of information. Some predict this trend will alter the design of personal computers in an unprecedented way, paving the way for the Internet "toaster" or "appliance" PCs already being sold by Oracle, IBM, and Apple, among others. These systems are designed primarily to connect to the Internet, and run programs managed by more powerful, remote systems usually known as "servers" in local area networks.

If you read computer publications you'll know that a lot of analysts argue that these new products are either going to take over the computing world or shoot, fizzle, then die. Most probably they'll assume a niche in the marketplace and evolve from there. But whatever the future of networking hardware, it's clear that communication software is a growth industry.

In the '80s computer networks were chiefly the province of large corporations which had the money to set them up. They required uncommonly powerful hardware and special software, and specially trained people to implement and maintain them. Now, thanks to the increased strength of over-the-counter PCs, and the friendlier programs they can handle, internal networks or LANs (local area networks) have become common in most companies that own more than three or four systems.

LANs basically come in two flavours: peer-to-peer, in which all systems are of equal importance and can read from, and write to, each other, and client/server, in which a central computer (the server) manages the activities of its workstations (the clients) more completely. Like a lot of other computer concepts, these network types are flexible and can mean different things to different people. A peer-to-peer network, for example, can be set up to behave like a client/server network, and vice versa.

All kinds of LAN software is available, from dedicated products such as Novell and Lantastic, to the networking capabilities built into operating systems such as Windows 95/98, Windows NT, and UNIX. Very common now are peer-to-peer setups which utilize the communications properties of Windows 95/98 – an attractive option for small companies who don't want to spend extra money on network software when they already own the capability.

A network program, or an operating system which supports networking, is required to allow one PC to recognize another and exchange data with it. Of course, the involved computers must also have some form of connective hardware in place. Most common are network cards, which fit into an expansion slot on a motherboard and have a jack, or connector, into which the cable to other PCs can be plugged. There are different standards of plugs and cables, the most common in use in homes and small businesses now being known as ethernet-compatible network cards, which accept 10 Base or 100 Base T connectors on the ends of a twisted-pair cable. These cables and connectors look like, but are internally different from, those which connect your telephone's handset to the junction box. Network cards may be purchased for $50 to $200, depending on their speed, the type of motherboard they're designed for, their manufacturer, and the included items such as manuals, software, and support. If you are thinking of networking two or more PCs, it's a good idea to start small. This is an endeavour that can soak up time and money quickly, and one that is particularly vulnerable to misunderstanding between service providers and users.

If you do enlist an outside company or consultant to help set up a local area network, remember the following points:

1. Consider why you want to network your computers in the first place, especially what applications you want to run once they are connected.

2. Get written quotations from at least three companies that have set up the kind of network you are considering. Make sure the one you choose knows exactly what programs and files you want to share, and how you want to share them after the network is up and running.
3. Be sure the quotes you get are detailed. Is the company offering a complete solution, or selling hardware only? How much training and special programming is included, if any? How much will they charge to return should you need them? (You probably will.) Are there elements of the network setup they're not qualified to handle, and if so, who will help them see the project through to completion?
4. Will they provide references of other similar network setups they have installed? Be sure to follow these up. Ask the previous customers if the work was completed on time and within budget, if they are happy with the overall results, and if they would use the provider again.

SETTING UP A HOME OFFICE

As fax, modem, and Internet communications have become more accessible, and corporations continue to downsize and lay off employees, more and more people are choosing to work at home. Here is a list of the hardware, software, and other services needed to set up a typical workstation:

Computer
Software
Printer
Fax machine
Telephone line
Answering service
Internet access

Computer and Software

There are all kinds of things to consider when shopping for a personal computer to use in a home office. First, buy the fastest processor you can afford. Second, make sure you get a price for a complete system: the computer and all of its necessary parts, including monitor and operating system. Be clear about the obligations of your vendor. Is this a cash-and-carry purchase? Do you need extra services like delivery, setup, and training? Try to create an alliance with someone, whether with your vendor, a separate consultant, or even just a knowledgeable friend to whom you can turn for advice.

Sample specifications needed in a typical home office PC are an Intel Pentium 200-MHz processor or equivalent, 32 megabytes of memory, a 2-gigabyte or larger hard drive, CD-ROM, sound card and speakers, 56K modem, 15" monitor, keyboard, mouse, operating system, and printer. Although it has some disadvantages, Microsoft Windows 95 has become standard, so it's easiest to find support and software for PCs running that system. If your business and clients demand Apple compatibility, then take that into account.

A Used Computer

You can also look for a used home office computer at a lower price. It's still important to purchase the fastest processor your budget will allow, but if you only have $500 or $1,000 for this part of your setup, don't panic; used 486 and early Pentium systems are available in your price range. If you aren't a computer whiz, you might want to buy one from a store. You'll pay more than if you were buying privately, but at least you'll get pre-sale assistance, help with software, and a warranty, even if it's only thirty days. On the other hand, if you're familiar with computers and have the time to spend hunting for a bargain, tackle the classifieds.

Printer

For a home office printer, look carefully at the new colour ink jets. Their ability to produce near photographic pictures is impressive. They also produce text that is close to the quality of a laser, though if you are really particular about this, a laser is still the way to go. Either of these types of printers requires regular care and feeding. Expect a cost of two to four cents per page, with special photo paper for ink jets costing up to $2.00 a sheet and sometimes more. As far as the new multifunction, all-in-one printer/fax/scanners are concerned, make sure you really like the way the one you buy performs *all* of its functions. If you do you can save money; otherwise you're better off buying exactly what you want separately.

Software

Don't go overboard on software. Remember, programs take time to learn, and you can always buy new ones as you need them. A good place to start is an integrated package that performs several tasks, such as Microsoft Office, Corel WordPerfect Office, or Lotus SmartSuite. In a typical home office you'll need:

- a wordprocessor to create documents
- a spreadsheet for accounting, budgets, or scientific calculations
- a database for customer records, inventory, and mailing lists
- an Internet browser to navigate the World Wide Web
- an accounting package for bookkeeping and invoicing

In addition to these essentials, you may want to add:

- a graphics program to create and manipulate photographs and pictures for promotion, marketing, and the Internet
- a fax program to allow you to send and receive documents
- a virus protection program to guard against foreign invaders
- a contact management program to create customer lists and manage other day-to-day information
- any other specialty software which pertains to your business

Notebook or Desktop

The ability to take your computer with you whenever and wherever you want is indeed attractive, but comes with disadvantages. In comparison to ordinary PCs, notebooks are more difficult to upgrade and repair, have smaller keyboards and displays, and, feature for feature, can cost up to 50 percent more. If you can overlook these drawbacks and concentrate on the freedom a portable system buys you, then go for it. Otherwise, get a desktop.

Fax Machines and Fax/Modems

Even though a PC will be able to send and receive documents with its fax/modem, it's worth considering a separate fax machine for your home office. Remember, to receive a fax with a personal computer, the system has to be on and the fax software enabled. You then have to take extra steps to view the message and print it out. Also, with a fax/modem, anything you send must somehow first be scanned into your computer.

Telephone Line/Telephone Answering Service

To get your home office hardware connected to the outside world, the best bet is a separate telephone line. Whether you can justify this extra expense will depend on how often you need to talk to your customers and clients, send and receive faxes, and use the Internet, but if you can afford it, a dedicated line is recommended. Variations such as distinctive rings for different types of incoming calls are also available. And don't forget that incoming calls are the lifeblood of most small businesses – get an automatic answering system, whether it's mechanical or a service from your phone company.

Internet Service/Email

In addition to telephone hardware, you'll need an email address and an Internet connection providing access to the World Wide Web. Internet service providers, or ISPs, come in all shapes and sizes. When choosing one, be aware of all the rules: how many hours per month you are buying, how long your contract is, your options to quit if you are not satisfied, the circumstances of setup and training, and methods of payment. Many ISPs offer specials such as home page creation to small businesses. For more information on choosing ISPs, see the later section, "Communications and the Internet."

Home Office Costs

Here are some sample costs involved with setting up a home office*:

HIGH-END HOME OFFICE	
Computer	$3,500
Software	1,000
Printer	700
Fax machine	600
Two telephone lines (six months @ $40)	240
Answering service (six months @ $5)	30
Internet service (six months @ $25)	150
Accessories	700
TOTAL	**$6,920**

MID-RANGE HOME OFFICE	
Computer	$2,000
Software	200
Printer	400
Fax machine	350
One telephone line (six months @ $20)	120
Answering service (six months @ $5)	30
Internet service (six months @ $15)	90
Accessories	500
TOTAL	**$3,690**

* Prices do not include applicable taxes

BASIC HOME OFFICE

Computer	$750
Software	100
Printer	250
Fax machine	200
One telephone line (six months @ $20)	120
Answering service (six months @ $5)	30
Internet service (six months @ $15)	90
Accessories	250
TOTAL	**$1,790**

* Prices do not include applicable taxes

FIGURE 5E

Location

Finally, a word about the location of your home office. People vary in the ways they like to work, and one of the advantages of setting up your own space is that you get to control this. But any place of business should be well organized and separated from the traffic in other parts of your living space. Take into account the nature of your work. If you'll be entertaining clients often, or shipping out goods, locate your workstation appropriately.

COMMUNICATIONS AND THE INTERNET

The Internet is one of the highest profile and most exciting developments ever to hit personal computing. A global collection of linked computers and computer networks, the Net can be difficult for novice computer users to comprehend because of its enormous size and complexity. It can perform a myriad of tasks involving combinations of computer hardware and software, and increasingly includes information from telephones, cameras, and even radio and TV broadcasting systems. It is actually getting difficult to find communications machinery that isn't connected to the Net. But in simple terms, the Internet is just a big network that allows the computers connected to it to exchange information. How does it do this?

A good place to start when trying to grasp the idea of the Internet is a communications network more familiar to most of us – the telephone system. Instead of the handset sitting on a desk in your home or office, imagine a personal computer connected to the box on the wall.

With some special software and a modem, a PC can dial a telephone number and be connected to an Internet "gateway" maintained by an

Internet service provider, or ISP. When the service provider's computer, sometimes known as a "server," answers your PC's call, it verifies your identity and in turn enables you to send and receive data to and from computers connected to other service providers around the world. If you're thinking that sounds like a heck of a lot of systems exchanging a heck of a lot of information, you're right! Various estimates put the number of PCs accessing the Internet at anywhere from thirty to forty million, and growing.

Your ISP provides its services for a fee. Expect to pay between $10 and $40 per month for the hours you are connected. All kinds of variations on this scenario are possible of course, from large companies using their own private setups (sometimes known as intranets) to access the Internet in a controlled way, to special group and community service providers, to Freenets and tiny enterprises running in basements. As far as the phone company is concerned, the call placed by your computer to a service provider is normally a local one, so it is subject to the same charges that would apply if you were talking on a handset. Of course, having seen the explosion of Internet use in the past few years, virtually all telephone carriers have also become Internet service providers.

As well as referring to a large and mixed group of computers and computer network hardware, the term Internet has come to include the several kinds of communications programs it supports, each of which can perform different kinds of data transfers between participating PCs. Some of these you may have seen and be familiar with, others are more obscure. Common communications applications supported by the Internet are the World Wide Web, email, Gopher, FTP, Telnet, and Archie. For an in-depth description of the last four of these less common applications, several excellent books are available, perhaps the best known in Canada being *The Canadian Internet Handbook*, by J. Carroll and R. Broadhead. On the topic of the most popular applications, the World Wide Web and email, here is a quick overview.

Email and the World Wide Web

Not even ten years old in its current form, the World Wide Web is the most exciting and information-intensive part of the Internet. It is the network to which any person, company, or organization can add a "home page" or "web page" containing information of almost any kind. It is from this idea of the "signpost" that the term "information highway" has arisen. In order to access the World Wide Web, your computer must be connected to an Internet service provider, and then you normally must run a program called an Internet browser. Microsoft Internet Explorer and Netscape Navigator are most common, and while they are designed primarily with web presentation in mind, they support other Internet applications as well, particularly email.

Email is a generic term that has come to mean the sending and receiving of information files from one computer to another.

This most popular and useful Internet application has done much to change business and personal communication in the past few years. Of course, it is no longer exclusive to the Net, as many local area networks, both large and small, offer email in one form or another.

In a conventional email Internet scenario, a computer running an email program presents you with a blank "notepad," or wordprocessor-style screen. You type the text of a message, and then enter in designated fields at the top of the screen the email address of the intended recipient. You can also select files written previously and stored on the hard drive of your PC and include them as "attachments." Once you have prepared the message and any attendant files, perhaps pictures or other wordprocessing documents, you execute a "send" command with your mouse or keyboard. At this point, the message files do not actually leave your computer. Rather, copies of them are forwarded instantly to your ISP's computer (your "server") which in turn forwards them to the server of your intended recipient. There they will be stored until the recipient logs onto the Internet and learns there is a message waiting. Either automatically or on command, the email files are then downloaded from the server into the recipient's email program, where they can be read, stored, or deleted. Email has become such a popular computer application that many new wordprocessors contain special features designed to make composing, sending, and receiving messages even easier. Some hardware, notably printers, also come with email-specific features designed to make reading and printing email simpler.

An Internet Setup — Necessary Hardware and Software

When tackling the question of what hardware and software are needed to get connected to the Net, several combinations are possible, but remember that because of its increasing graphics content, the World Wide Web demands firepower.

As an absolute minimum, you need a computer containing a 486 DX–level processor, running at 66 MHz or faster, with 16 megabytes of RAM and about 200 megabytes of free hard drive space. In addition, you need a 28.8 Kbps (kilobits per second) modem and some Internet software.

Certainly you can access the Net and send and receive email with a system of these lower specifications, but this is not really advisable. You'll find browsing the World Wide Web frustratingly slow.

To take better advantage of all that information out there, a more current setup is in order. This could be a Pentium MMX or Pentium II–level computer running at 200 MHz, 233 MHz, or 266 MHz, with 32 or 64 megabytes of RAM, a 4-gigabyte hard drive, and a 56K modem. These specifications are common in personal computers in 1998 at $2,000 or less.

In addition to appropriate hardware and a browser program such as Netscape Navigator or Microsoft Internet Explorer, you need to choose an access path to the World Wide Web – an Internet service provider. Evaluating ISPs can be one of the most difficult and confusing parts in the whole process of purchasing a PC. This is chiefly because Internet access is an overheated and competitive marketplace in which some players are trying to carve a niche by offering prices they can't sustain. As is the case when evaluating other computer hardware, software, and service, it is not always a good idea to choose the most inexpensive supplier, particularly for an Internet subscription that you hope won't have to be disturbed any sooner than necessary.

Internet service providers offer large and small packages, with various connection plans and degrees of support. Some things to consider when choosing one are:

1. How many lines per customer does the service provider maintain? A supplier with a large number of lines but many times that number of customers presents a greater chance of a busy signal when you try to connect.
2. What kind of technical support do they offer, what are their support charges, and in what situations can you expect to have to pay for information? How available are their support personnel? Nine to five? Seven to seven? Around the clock?
3. How long have they been in business, and what services do they offer? Training? Setup? Special Internet services such as home-page creation and assistance in registering a domain?
4. Do their prices compare to their real competitors in the ISP market? Are they out of line – either higher or lower – than other providers of similar size and stature? If so it's a good idea to find out why.
5. Do you understand their operation policies? When they sell you "unlimited" access to the Net each month, do they really mean a

fixed number of hours? Most ISPs impose a "time-out" policy which automatically disconnects an unused computer after a certain period; otherwise a subscriber who forgets about his connected PC and drives to Florida could tie up a line for a month. But too short a time-out can be irritating and may even interfere with the downloading of large files.

6. Finally, do you understand their payment policies? Before handing a credit card number to an ISP, have a close look at their contract. Are you signing up for a certain period no matter what, or can the agreement be cancelled? If so is there a fee? What are your options if there are disputes about payments automatically charged to your card? All of these issues should be considered when using a credit card to pay for any ongoing service, but they are especially important when considering an Internet service provider.

6

FINDING AND BUYING A USED PC

The process of buying a used computer is really not much different from buying a new one: you have to know what you want and what you want to do with it, then negotiate the best price you possibly can, and make sure you get everything you paid for. However, the purchase of used high-tech equipment does pose some special problems.

THE USED-PC MARKETPLACE

Perhaps the toughest difficulty to overcome in the marketplace is finding up-to-date equipment at a reasonable price in the first place. While almost everyone today knows that the price of technology is continually falling, few buyers, I suspect, actually realize how fast this happens. There is simply a chronic shortage of current used PCs available at competitive prices. It's hard to convince the owner of a system which cost say, $3,000 to $3,500 a couple of years ago that it's only worth $600 or $700 today. Ouch! That's a walloping drop of 80 percent! By those standards, computer resales make even the used-car market look like the gold standard.

Another hurdle is deciding, usually all by yourself, what kind of equipment you need, then making sure that you actually get what you paid for and that it's functioning the way it should. "Let the buyer beware" has never been truer than in the used-PC market. Nevertheless, there are lots of honest companies and individuals out there who are selling systems for a variety of reasons – downsizing, trade-ups, expired leases, and of course, the plain old need for ready cash.

When shopping for a used PC, you should be prepared to make an opportunistic purchase; that is, to move quickly and decisively. Like all private markets in high-profile consumer items – cars and appliances, for example – the better the bargain, the quicker you must act. At least in the new-PC marketplace, once you've decided on a specific model, or at least narrowed your choice, you can take a little time to cogitate and compare.

Finally, in the used market, it's an almost certain bet that vendors, particularly if you are buying privately, will assume that their equipment is worth a lot more than it really is, because they have not taken the trouble to keep up with the prices of new, competitive goods.

So there are some rather daunting considerations here: it's a big, technical purchase, you may not have any sales assistance, you may not be able to verify what you're buying until after you've bought it, you may not have any recourse if you are sold inferior goods, and you may be forced by a potentially uninformed vendor to make a decision before you're ready. But before you skip the rest of this chapter and concentrate on buying something new, take heart. Despite these pitfalls, there are all sorts of bargains to be had in the used-PC marketplace.

WHAT'S AVAILABLE

For many people and businesses the only way to acquire useful technology is to find it at an affordable price. This is when used and upgraded PCs become attractive. An older, cheaper system might be just the element required to power a fledgling company down the runway and into the air. Even though it may not have as long and useful a life as a new, more powerful computer, it could be just the right tool to get the job done at the right time.

Used PCs are suitable for a variety of small business and home office scenarios: people setting up bulletin boards, working on the Internet, or developing limited applications or software-specific networks for small businesses. All of these interesting projects are placed within reach of more people because of the lower cost and increased power and availability of used computers.

From a technical point of view, there are definite advantages which apply to used electronic, as opposed to mechanical, equipment. A high percentage of the components in an ordinary computer have no moving parts. Exceptions to this are isolated mechanical assemblies in things like the keyboard, hard drive, and the power supply, which is usually cooled by some kind of fan. As a result, most PCs fall into disuse because of obsolescence rather than mechanical failure.

So from the broad perspective – an increased ability to run more productive applications, reasonably low rates of failure, and reduced pricing – a used computer can be pretty attractive. It might just enable you to set up a small office network, or start a business in your basement that will move you into a higher tax bracket next year.

USED PCs: SHOULD YOU OR SHOULDN'T YOU?

Before actually setting off to shop, it's wise to consider different classes of used PCs. Starting at the bottom, if you just need a basic wordprocessing station, a trusty old 386 might well serve your purpose. Plenty of these can still be found on either side of the $100 mark, depending on the monitor, hard drive size, and general condition. Of course, this processing level is sure to generate a major league guffaw from anyone who has even a vague acquaintance with the word "computer," so don't consider one if you think you'll ever want to perform tasks other than wordprocessing and very simple record keeping. Buying a system with these built-in limitations is a bit like purchasing a car and saying to yourself, "I promise I'll never drive it more than three blocks from home." Most people, whether they admit it to themselves or not, need a computer with at least some growth potential, in which case a 386, and in most cases even a 486, will simply not do.

For Windows 3.x you need a minimum of 4 or 8 megabytes of RAM and an 80–120 MB hard drive. In the Apple group you need a 68030 processor (roughly 386 equivalent) or 68040 (roughly 486 equivalent) and 4 or 8 megabytes of RAM to run operating system 7. Even at these levels, you're scraping the bottom of the barrel and can expect to run out of power and space in pretty short order. Some situations may dictate that you buy something new. You may have an advanced application in mind that requires state-of-the-art power and specifications. For example, you might be setting up a local area network (LAN), a wide area network (WAN), or an intranet (a LAN with Internet access); running computer-assisted drafting and design (CADD) software; or working on a project involving more than one computer or demanding lots of power. A new PC will be ready when you are, with warranty and technical support available, in most cases, from vendor *and* manufacturer.

Let's look at a specific example:

> Suppose you run a small business with eight employees and four networked personal computers. Happily, you've just been awarded a contract which requires you to increase productivity and hire two new people immediately. Your expansion plans include upgrading your old DOS-based network software and database, and buying two additional workstations. Under these circumstances, you are almost certainly better off to seek two new computers. Why? For starters, you are using this opportunity to upgrade your network and that's an excellent idea. It's better not to dump too much development time and money on the shoulders of that outdated DOS-based software. But the network part of the equation presents special considerations. It may be difficult to introduce a new network card to a used computer that will likely come without adequate documentation. Who will you call for support? And trying to find a used PC with a compatible network card already installed is also risky.
>
> You might overcome some of these difficulties by approaching a used-computer dealer who can provide you with a system close to your specifications and offer support. But by the time your vendor finds the right equipment and provides proper assistance, you may find you've paid the price of a new PC.

Most up-to-date in today's used-computer marketplace are the 586, 686, and Pentium-level PCs that were selling for $500 to $1,000 in early 1998. These computers put you in striking distance of more current operating systems and applications: Windows 95, Macintosh OS8, and accessing the Internet. The first order of business, of course, is where to find them. For the sake of simplicity I have broken the used-computer marketplace into five sections. Each one has its advantages and disadvantages, its difficulties and strengths.

THE PRIVATE MARKET

The private market is a natural place to look for a used PC. It may seem daunting if you're not overflowing with technical confidence, but by planning a strategy you may turn up a surprising number of opportunities. Start with the obvious places – the classified ads in your local papers, or computer trade or exchange magazines. Check the "For Sale" notices in your local supermarket. Talk to co-workers (the ones with the plastic pen protectors in their pockets of course), and make it known to one and all that you are in the market for a good used PC at a rock-bottom price. As simple as these approaches may seem, they may be all you need to dig up a great buy.

If you feel confident, you may want to get a little more sophisticated. Range around on the Internet if you can, or access a local bulletin board. Have a look at the section on used PCs on the World Wide Web later in this chapter. Though this approach will certainly consume valuable time and energy, you might just find a hidden gem at half the market price.

But the private side of the market offers special pitfalls. Without benefit of a middleman or dealer, you must rely on your own knowledge of what you need and be prepared to trust the seller's claim that the system you're considering actually meets those needs. Other key elements to look for are a trademark from a recognized international manufacturer, or, if it's a privately assembled system, top-quality components – though such systems are not always easy to find at a reasonable price. Generic, or locally assembled, PCs offer more firepower for the dollar and easier repair and upgrade possibilities, but are notorious for unknown components and lack of third-party support. On the other hand, a well-known manufacturer's warranty may have ceased to become a consideration in the used marketplace long before you entered the picture anyway.

Once you've found a private seller with a computer that interests you, then what? Now is the time for a reliable third-party evaluation, or, if that is not possible, some investigation on your own. There are several diagnostic programs available which will tell you about the specifications of a PC. Touchstone and Checkit are good examples. But even without a special program you can "look inside" most computers using software already in them. In the Mac world you can select "About this Macintosh" from the Apple menu; in older DOS/Windows systems you can run Microsoft Diagnostics (type MSD at the C> prompt), or you can click on the "My Computer" icon in Windows 95 systems.

If you do purchase a system privately, do your absolute utmost to obtain correct documentation, even if this means approaching a manufacturer or store and buying or copying the appropriate manuals if the previous owner has lost or misplaced them. This step can mean the difference later between being able to find a quick fix or having to junk some components (sometimes a complete system) if they fail.

LEASING AND FINANCE COMPANIES

But suppose you've scoured the countryside, the trade mags, the neighbourhood, cyberspace, and beyond, and still not been able to find that perfect little minitower and just-right keyboard? Time to get creative. In these days of economic uncertainty, alternative sources of good used computer equipment are leasing and financing companies. Often, current systems are available from these kinds of companies at considerable savings. Keep in mind, though, that these enterprises are in the business of lending money, so they usually acquire equipment in one of two ways: by repossession or by buying it back at the end of a loan.

Repossession occurs when a customer for whom a leasing company has bought equipment is no longer able to make the payments each month, and so surrenders the goods. The company will then sell the PC and keep the money. The lessor may or may not apply this money to the debt owed by the unfortunate lessee.

In a second, happier scenario, the lessee has made all his payments and agreed to start a whole new contract on newer equipment. Usually, the lessee will have paid the complete worth of the old computer and will elect to keep it rather than give it back to the leasing company. But not always: sometimes large companies will, for tax, budgetary, or other reasons, allow their computers to revert to the leasing company.

In either of these cases, the lessor suddenly finds itself in the computer business. It's no secret that most financing companies that acquire goods in quantity already have established business contacts through which they dispose of them. If you cold-call a leasing company and they won't sell to you direct, don't forget to ask how they do get rid of their equipment and whether they can refer you to that company or individual. You might be surprised at the reciprocal arrangements some leasing companies have with suppliers. In any event, the chief advantage here is that you can sometimes track down a very late model computer at a very good price. In these situations companies or people have to part with their goods because they can't pay for them, so the equipment is thrown onto the block as quickly as possible. And because they will likely have had to dispose of used computer equipment before, leasing and finance companies may be less inclined to overvalue it than individuals selling privately.

If you decide to purchase from a leasing or financing company, don't forget to ask about the legal status of what you are buying, and be prepared to perform your own diagnostics before taking possession. Warranties, technical assistance, and product information are not available from this group of vendors.

SELL-OFFS AND AUCTIONS

These are two of the riskiest purchasing options, particularly auctions. Standing before the block, bidders are usually expected to purchase equipment with one non-refundable, secured payment (a money order, certified cheque, or cash) in an open environment with little or no opportunity to even turn a system on before taking the plunge. Under these circumstances, even the most seasoned purchaser stands an excellent chance of winding up with a hard drive that doesn't spin, or a motherboard that just will not get out of bed. The excitement of the bid is fun I guess, but how practical is this as a way of buying something as complicated as a PC?

USED-COMPUTER DEALERS

A more stable and perhaps friendlier purchase option for the used-computer buyer is to consider a dealer. Novice users may want the market and equipment explained to them by a solicitous salesperson. A dealer might also be a better choice if time is important. But don't expect an especially wide or deep selection at the average used-computer outlet. The vast majority of them work in the same opportunistic fashion that drives the purchaser's side of the market; the used-computer business simply moves so fast that whatever a company can buy for resale on a particular day or week is what they'll have to sell.

Used-computer outlets are subject to the same general constraints as the rest of the retail marketplace. Every time new computers gain in power or price-to-performance ratio, a fresh wave of old systems becomes more widely and reliably available at the commercial level. Expect to pay 15 to 35 percent over private market prices for a normal home or small business PC when buying from a known reseller. But insist on certain conditions for the extra money.

Number one on the list, of course, is warranty. It stands to reason that if you pay more for a used system from a commercial establishment, the store should darn well offer competent sales help and a guarantee, even if only for thirty days. Three-, six-, or twelve-month warranties are also common. While shopping, take the time to ask the usual questions of the salesperson, and evaluate the place just as you would with any establishment with whom you might do business:

- How good is the store's technical support?
- Does it offer any sort of refund or exchange policy?
- What kind of financing options are offered?

- What, exactly, are the terms of its warranties?
- Do they offer on-site repairs?
- Will they configure your peripherals? If so, for how much?
- Do they take trade-ins?
- How long have they been in business?

Most used-computer stores are known by their reputations, and can be rated pretty accurately by their customers. Don't be afraid to ask for references; even if another customer purchased different equipment, you can get an idea of a reseller's response time and technical expertise by asking a few pointed questions.

DISTRIBUTORS AND WHOLESALERS

Like a lot of other consumer products, PCs are usually moved through a marketing chain from manufacturers, to distributors, and finally to dealers. Each handler is supposed to add value to the distribution, and in return, take a profit. There are variations on this marketing theme, with some manufacturers selling directly to the public, others employing their own special set of dealers, and so forth. For the most part, distributors are large enterprises capable of turning over thousands of items in a single day. They are also subject to the vagaries and quick changes of high technology. Imagine having to keep fuel in that kind of a pipeline! So, while a distributor's mandate is to move large amounts of equipment fast, there is no way it can always do this perfectly; sooner or later there is going to be a surplus of out-of-date, repaired, or returned stock on which it couldn't get credit from a manufacturer. These companies sometimes offer this equipment below market prices. One of the first obstacles you'll encounter when approaching a distributor, however, is that they prefer not to deal with end users. This is understandable. With markups of as little as 3 or 5 percent, these enterprises provide a minimum of pre- and post-sale support. Some have no technical support departments at all! Distributors may, however, make available their end-of-line, or "seconds," list through a co-operative reseller. If a dealer is unfamiliar with this list you can mention that the products on it might enable him to offer competitively priced computers to his other customers, too. This may take some selling on your part, but these items might just present a good bargain. If you are able to find a PC through a distributor's list, be sure to get the terms of payment and warranty straight before actually pulling the trigger. Here is where you may find that after-sale support is thinner than from other, more conventional sources of pre-owned PCs.

MANUFACTURER SECONDS AND END-OF-LINES

A close cousin to the returned products at the distribution level of the PC business are items which, for various reasons, can become available directly from a manufacturer. This situation usually only arises when a company is unable to rotate components from a returned PC back into stock. Though they try to avoid this, computer builders and assemblers can and do wind up with systems which are not current, cannot be sold as new or complete computers, and so must be sold at whatever price the market will bear. Is there a good time to approach a builder? Enquire when you're ready to buy. And as is the case when approaching a distributor, don't feel bad if you are rebuffed – ask for a further referral. Make it clear you're looking for something outside the usual retail channel, that you're willing to wait for it and to make some effort to acquire it, that you're flexible about what you'll accept, and that you're willing to talk to whomever you must to find out about it. Depending on the company, if they're at all used to selling direct, you'll find yourself transferred to the new-PC sales team faster than you can say William Gates. On the other hand, the corporation may have flexible policies governing the disposal of end-of-line or repaired items. Again, the same cautions apply as when approaching distributors. If you are allowed to purchase equipment which came from a manufacturer's repair department, at least ask about the PC's history and make sure you know the terms of the warranty. One company I know of had an arrangement with a representative who sold notebook PCs coming from the repair department of a major manufacturer in the Far East. The company was able to retail the PCs as used products with a limited warranty at a pretty good profit. It was a happy situation until the systems started flooding back. The obvious question arose: "Were the things even fixed properly in the first place?"

THE INTERNET

No discussion of the used-computer market would be complete without mention of the Internet. Here are some sites, mostly Canadian, that turned up in a casual search:

www.b&bsolutions.com
Fill in a form to request an online quotation.

www.interlog.com/~afford
Toronto outlet with sections for used, new, and notebook computers, current specials, and a "wanted" section.

www.remarketing.com
General listing of different dealers and brokers on the Net. U.S.-based but has some Canadian connections.

www.123computer.com
Buy, sell, and rent new and used computer systems, including PCs or Macs.

www.microtrader.mb.ca
Winnipeg-based site featuring general market information and information on inventory, accessories, and service.

www.dominiondigital.com
Home page of Dominion Business Machines, a Toronto retail store managed by the author. Features Canadian used-computer price index and links to manufacturers.

www.cpused.com
A Toronto-based dealer in new and used Macs. Price list updated daily with computers, monitors, modems, removable drives. Also provides links to various sources of technical support.

www.nacomex.com
One of the best used-PC resources on the Web; U.S. based. General overview of the used-computer market with some twists. Provides the business perspective: appraisals, forecasting, hardware research, brokerage, a stolen computer registry, and other services.

The Internet is not limited to product research. You can also purchase a PC and pay for it with a credit card in what is advertised as a secure transaction. I harbour some skepticism about buying something as complex as a PC over the Net. Think of the usual contingencies: do you really know what you are buying, and who you're buying it from? What are your options if you don't like what you get, or it doesn't work, or it isn't what was represented? Can you get help with the computer after the sale if it fails? If you are reasonably sure about these issues, or if you're prepared to sacrifice them in the interests of the convenience and novelty of purchasing a PC via the Net, go ahead. Personally, I would like to see this side of the market evolve a little more before using it to purchase a used computer.

7

FINDING AND BUYING A NEW PC

HELP — I NEED A COMPUTER!

I have seen all kinds of people shop for computer equipment: novices, small-business owners, professionals such as doctors and engineers, even computer experts from large corporations. Each customer usually has his or her own idea about how to research the equipment they're thinking of buying. Most go about the purchase in a predictable way: they have their own requirements, they've heard advice from friends or associates they consider knowledgeable, or they've read something in the newspaper or a buyer's guide. Many take the extra steps of calling a manufacturer or surfing the Internet for technical information. In almost all of these cases, I believe that purchasers, novice and expert alike, find buying computer equipment a daunting task. PCs are complex and usually described in abstract, technical language. They're expensive and important, and they're cloaked in mystery to those who are not used to dealing with them. It's a natural reaction to seek help. This can come in many flavours. Here are a few notes on the various sources of assistance I've seen customers use when buying a computer, and some of the experiences I've had with them from the sales side of the counter.

Guide Books

Is it really OK to talk about guide books in a guide book? Let's assume so. First, try to choose one that has the right technical voice. I talked to one shopper who told me that before doing any reading or research, he'd started out with a pretty clear idea of what he wanted, how much he wanted to spend, and where he wanted to buy. Unfortunately, after reading a well-meaning but technically challenging "how-to" volume, he became so confused by the terms in it and frightened by its dire predictions of obsolescence that he abandoned the idea of buying a computer altogether! So try to find a book you can understand, that's up to date, and contains the information you want. Keep your own technical level in mind and seek a guide that suits you.

Also don't forget that you don't have to master all of the technical information in it – don't be afraid to skip a few sections and read it for the information you want. If it's not helping you, give it to someone it will help.

An excellent source of information available to people researching a computer purchase are industry and market publications – magazines with titles like *Today's Notebooks* or *The Computer Printer Guide.* Some are one-time publications, designed to take an up-to-date snapshot of a fast-changing market. They can be very valuable. Also worth reading are computer industry publications such as *PC World* or *Macworld.* They offer information not only about computer products, but the computer business itself. To a novice, though, some PC publications can be intimidating. Some of them assume a high level of technical expertise, or are soaked with what a musician friend of mine refers to as "attitude." "I wish they'd stop pushing all this technology at me," one customer told me recently, "and just let me get into it at my own speed!" It's a valid concern.

One advantage of product review magazines and industry publications is their pictures. With an illustrated guide, at least you can see for yourself the difference between a PCMCIA modem (a little credit card–shaped device used primarily in notebook computers) and an external modem (a small box which sits on a desktop PC).

Another important thing to remember about computer guides is to look for one containing information about products available in your area. It's not uncommon for manufacturers to issue different lines of equipment in different parts of the world. The product review book you bought at the airport in Miami will not necessarily show the goods and prices available when you get off the plane in Montreal.

Industry Information

A heart surgeon came to me not long ago and said he was about to retire and wanted to purchase a state-of-the-art system. His goal, besides common tasks such as wordprocessing and email, was to learn about computers in general. He had become interested in technology and saw its study as an endeavour that might ease him out of his professional life and occupy his still-impressive mind and energy.

When he first came to me, I could see he was just learning about PCs. He had more or less made up his mind about the major elements of the purchase, including which manufacturer he liked, so after telling him all I knew about the line he was interested in, I referred him with his many questions to the builder. He spoke to them several times and got all kinds of information which, as a busy salesperson who juggles several lines of computer equipment, I was simply not able to provide. Not long after this, his concerns addressed, he proceeded with the purchase and was happy with his choice. Looking back, it's easy to see that this was a situation where assistance from a manufacturer was a big plus for all.

While things do not always turn out so amicably, the advantage of approaching a manufacturer for technical information before deciding whether to buy one of its computers is that you can be reasonably assured of getting accurate and up-to-date information. Even though you must remember that it's coming from the sales side of the company, manufacturers are one of the best sources of technical details. Certainly they would like you to buy one of their products, but they are also able to answer a wide range of questions. Computer retailing has evolved into a cash-and-carry business. A vendor's sales staff often can't afford the time to research answers to questions arising from different combinations of PCs, software, and their peripherals.

An exception to this rule might be the purchase of a computer from what is known as a value-added reseller or value-added dealer. These vendors become knowledgeable about a specific combination of hardware and software designed for a particular task, hence they have special knowledge about the equipment they're selling. Examples of applications targeted by these kinds of vendors are point-of-sale retail systems; hardware and software setups intended for professionals such as architects, engineers, or lawyers; or integrated systems for particular businesses, such as copy centres, sporting goods stores, or leasing companies.

Unless you're dealing with a special vendor, it's a good idea to contact a manufacturer with in-depth questions when evaluating a product. This can also apply if you simply want to verify some of the facts thrown at you by an eager salesperson. If a manufacturer is directly involved in the sale (and more and more manufacturers are selling direct these days), you can also approach the company's technical support people.

Finally, in any discussion of pre-sale evaluations, it's worth taking note of the issue of referrals. They're a great idea, especially if you're thinking of buying more than one computer or using a system for an unusual task. In either case you'll want to know as much as you can from previous customers about what you're buying, how it works, and who you're buying it from.

Both the vendor and manufacturer of the equipment you're considering should be comfortable supplying you with information about other customers who have bought the same thing. Be aware, though, that putting a sales rep through this process communicates a strong buying signal. You're not obligated to anything by asking for references, of course, but be prepared for a sales pitch if you do.

Advisors and Friends

One of the most common sources of information about computer equipment is advice from a friend, associate, or family member. It's an easy scenario. You just get them to come to the computer store or read the catalogues with you, then they'll tell you what you should buy, right? Well, sort of. At the best of times, a good advisor can indeed make the purchase a lot easier. But he or she can also make the process more difficult. It's worthwhile to keep a couple of things in mind when choosing an advisor.

Retain Control

Make absolutely sure they know that you are the purchaser, not them. Without getting the authority issue straight, the sale can get away from you, and you can wind up with a system you neither want, need, nor can afford.

Communicate

Make sure your advisor knows why you want to buy the computer, the tasks you want it to perform, and how much you can afford to spend on it. And try to get your stories straight before a salesperson enters the picture.

A common scenario involves the novice who enlists the aid of a knowledgeable friend. Without much forethought or discussion, they present themselves to a competitive, commissioned sales rep. Soon the specifications and prices start flying, and you can guess in which direction – up!

Intimidated, or, at the very least, eager to listen and learn, the purchaser remains quiet as a mouse while advisor and sales rep engage in a friendly game of technical one-upmanship, until all are standing in front of the cash register. Then the fur starts to fly.

To help avoid this unfortunate situation, be sure that you and your advisor are not only on the same team, but shooting at the same goal. Take time to discuss how much you have to spend, what you want the system to do, and when you want to buy it.

CHOOSING A COMPUTER

How can you judge a computer system accurately? You can't exactly kick its tires or learn much about how it feels to use it. You can type on its keyboard, play with its mouse, and look at its monitor in the store, which are about the only physical points of interaction you'll ever have with the thing anyway. But how can you tell if you'll like the way it operates once you get it home, set it up, and engage in the tasks you need it for?

In fact, evaluating the long-term usefulness of computer equipment is very difficult. The best defence you can throw at this problem is to go through a process such as the one outlined in Chapter 2, aimed at helping you decide what you need. Ask yourself:

- What do you want to use the computer for?
- How much can you afford to spend on it?
- What software do you want it to run?
- Will you be able to operate it productively?
- How long do you want it to remain current?

Two other issues specific to the purchase of computer hardware are:

1. Should you buy a Mac or Windows–based PC?
2. Should you buy a brand-name PC from a large manufacturer or a generic system from a smaller company?

MAC OR WINDOWS?

Since the beginning of personal computing, purchasers have been confronted with the choice between Apple and IBM-compatible (or DOS-based) systems. Even in today's market, this decision remains an issue. Across the board, Apple's products still cost more for the power they deliver. But they are also able to run programs their

Windows 95–based competitors can't. And since new Apples can also run Windows programs, they are the more flexible of the two groups.

But the market has simply overwhelmed Apple in recent years, shrinking its share to less than 10 percent of all Canadian personal computer purchases. Unfortunately, this slide means less competition, higher prices, and fewer sources from which to obtain service and software. If you are a committed Apple user and can justify these disadvantages, or you are driven to a Power Mac by a specific application such as graphics or music, your decision is easy. But when it comes to mainstream personal computing, the Apple family simply does not enjoy the stature it had in the '80s.

BRAND-NAME OR GENERIC?

The distinction between generic and brand-name PCs is one of the most important distinctions in the personal computer marketplace, and one of the toughest to understand. In basic terms, brand-name computers are those that have been assembled in a standardized environment by a large corporation, and are backed by a warranty from the manufacturer.

Generic, or locally assembled, systems are built to order out of compatible "third-party" components, usually by smaller companies. They are typically less expensive than brand-name PCs, contain parts which are more up to date, and are easy to upgrade and repair because of their mix-and-match design. On the other hand, they are less reliable (at least they are only as reliable as the company that builds them) and are supported by the limited resources of the smaller assembler.

It's important to remember that these brand-name and generic labels are not necessarily distinct. Several manufacturers might be thought of in both ways. Dell and NEC, for example, are large corporations which will, much like a local assembler, build a system more or less to order. Other "generic" PCs from smaller international companies such as Hewitt Rand are hard to distinguish from brand-name products.

To help you with this choice, remember that if you choose a local assembler, do some homework. Find out as much as you can about their reputation, products, and policies. And resist the temptation to purchase the cheapest generic PC you can find – it's simply too dangerous. A locally assembled computer is a good choice for a purchaser who knows about computer equipment – parts and software – and can work with a vendor to make sure he will get the right thing. A brand-name system is a good bet for a person or company concerned about reliability and support, or who may want the bundle of programs that come with many of these computers.

Once you've considered these issues, it's time to start shopping.

MANUFACTURERS, MODELS, AND COMPONENTS

Your choice of manufacturers almost certainly affects factors such as how and where you purchase a PC, its availability (that is, how soon you can get your hands on it), and whether you have to deal with a salesperson or you can buy over the phone. Take some time with this, and try to find out about different builders – large and small, international, national, and local – who offer systems meeting your specifications.

Several agencies who advise large corporations and organizations evaluate major computer manufacturers according to their size, market share, and other characteristics. Computer companies are sometimes assigned to "tiers" in the marketplace. Loosely described, tier one systems are those from established manufacturers such as IBM and Compaq, tier two systems are from companies not quite as well known and well supported, and tier three systems are from other players in the international market. These classes are subject to change at the discretion of various companies who issue market reports.

But when you are shopping for a single PC, the evaluation process will lead you from the outside to the inside of the system, and will bring you face to face with common terms by which computers are described.

Here is where it's easy to become discouraged, but don't be. Learn what you can. The alternative is to buy something about which you know very little, which increases the possibility that you'll wind up with something you don't want. For a description of different kinds of computer parts, how they're measured, and what tasks they perform, take a look at Chapter 3, if you haven't already trekked through that territory. Assuming you've gained a grasp of the differences between a motherboard, video card, hard drive, and DVD or CD-ROM – which is to say, you at least know what these things are – it is possible to judge the makers of parts in a computer you're thinking of purchasing.

An obvious place to start when looking at components in a system you are thinking of buying is the name, size, and reputation of their manufacturer. This is particularly important when shopping for a locally assembled PC.

Reputation
Are the parts from large, recognizable companies? Are they internationally, or at least nationally, known?

Compatibility
Does the company building the computer have experience with the parts it will be putting in yours? Can they guarantee they'll all work together? If you've insisted on a special item that was recommended by an advisor, think twice. Locate a builder who has experience with the kind of parts you want included, or allow the vendor to put in parts he knows and recommends.

Allowing your vendor to suggest components, particularly those going into a locally assembled PC, carries advantages. They'll have experience making them all work together, and will be able to troubleshoot and replace a failed part faster and more easily than if they'd bought something exotic just for you.

Warranty
Who will take responsibility if two manufacturers claim their products are working perfectly and it's the other guy's component causing the trouble? This is one of the most common causes of stress and difficulty in warranty situations. It's also when your vendor can become an indispensable aid.

BUYING FROM A DEALER

Since the dawn of PC retailing almost twenty years ago, the computer business has undergone several revolutions, from the introduction of the first stores actually selling small systems to the public (quite a retailing innovation in their time), to the appearance of electronic super centres which offer all kinds of high-tech gear via various marketing plans.

Is any one of these outlets clearly better than the others? Actually, there are advantages and disadvantages associated with each one. Figure 7A summarizes the different sources of computers in terms of four major elements important to a shopper: price, selection, informed sales help, and after-sale support.

NEW COMPUTER RETAIL SOURCES: ADVANTAGES AND DISADVANTAGES

SOURCE	PRICE	SELECTION	SUPPORT	PRODUCT KNOWLEDGE
High-tech superstores	Best	Medium	Worst	Medium
Department stores	Medium	Medium	Worst	Worst
Computer and office equipment stores	Medium	Medium	Best	Medium
Manufacturer direct	Medium	Worst	Medium	Best
Mail-order and catalogue stores	Best	Best	Medium	Medium
Trade shows	Best	Medium	Worst	Worst
The Internet	Best	Medium	Worst	Worst
Value-added dealers and resellers	Worst	Worst	Best	Best

FIGURE 7A

HIGH-TECH SUPERSTORES

The most recent addition to the world of personal computer shopping, and the category with the highest profile, huge warehouse outlets are part of a trend that has rocked every retail marketplace in North America since about 1980. You're familiar with the format: a big building filled with boxes and boxes of goods, sometimes arrayed without much attention to presentation, but a wide selection, usually at very competitive prices. Often these stores are owned by national or multinational corporations and adhere to carefully determined policies on everything from delivery to methods of payment to product returns. Conspicuous advertisers with lots of buying clout, big chains will sometimes purchase large quantities of a specific model. These might be advance or end-of-line products from a manufacturer who wants to sell its goods quickly and easily to one customer. Sometimes they are "exclusive" to a particular chain, or to the superstore category in general. This can make it difficult to compare a certain product in a chain's lineup against competitive goods in other sectors of the marketplace.

This happened in Canada in 1997 when Future Shop, a high-tech mass marketer, became the retail source of the Hewlett-Packard Series 682C printer before the product was made available to traditional retail outlets. Shoppers were confronted with a choice between the older 680C printer, which had slightly lower specifications, and a newer model for a little more money. This special issue was exclusive to superstores for a few months before being released to other retailers. While in this case the product offering was a benefit to chain store customers, sometimes exclusive products become a disadvantage. This can happen when a chain finds itself overstocked with a certain line and offers old product without reducing the price.

In addition to specially issued or "private" lines of computer products, large outlets also offer easy access, lots of parking, long hours, and sometimes, an atmosphere in which a shopper who knows little about computers can grab something off a shelf with a minimum of interaction with intimidating salespeople.

On the other hand, in this retail environment, floor staff are usually paid completely or largely on commission, which cannot help but affect how they deal with the public. They may or may not have the product knowledge and patient manner many shoppers want. And many chains make a point of concentrating on goods which are supported directly by the manufacturer. It's worth investigating any store's warranty policy before deciding to buy.

INDEPENDENT COMPUTER AND OFFICE EQUIPMENT STORES

The wide variety of small, medium, and large computer and office equipment companies that have appeared since the dawn of PC retailing is difficult to categorize. There are, however, some observations that help compare these outlets to alternative PC sources.

It's more probable that you have a small specialty store located close to you than any other type of computer outlet – there are simply more of them around. Of course, not all neighbourhood retailers are necessarily competent and competitive, but when they are, this more intimate atmosphere is attractive to some people. Proximity can also be a plus if your computer breaks down, whether or not it's under warranty.

It may also be that your local retailer has a preferred group of products in which it specializes. If it does indeed have a focus on the hardware or software you're considering, you can benefit greatly from this expertise, both before the sale, when trying to decide what to buy, and later, when you need technical advice.

On the other hand, specialty outlets should be expected to offer fewer demonstration systems, and have fewer items in stock that you can cart away if you need something in a hurry. Chances are your neighbourhood outlet will have to order an unusual product from a distributor. This can be a benefit: they may be able to offer you a more current, lower price than a warehouse giant which has been carrying an item in inventory for three months. But it may also mean your local store will have to pay top dollar and be susceptible to supply problems: if systems are out of stock at distribution, then everybody's unhappy.

You are also more likely to be exposed to arbitrary return and financing policies when dealing with an independent. This can affect everything from methods of acceptable payment to making a warranty claim.

DEPARTMENT AND CHAIN STORES

It wasn't long ago that the computer business was the exclusive domain of technically savvy sales and support people employed by large manufacturers, or companies associated with the defence and academic communities. A common theme from these organizations was that they didn't "just sell boxes," they also sold pre-sale consultation, training, software, warranty, and maintenance.

But in the '80s, some informed observers of the personal computer marketplace began to assert that a plain box with an easy-to-use computer in it was exactly what a lot of people really wanted! And as computer manufacturers began to recognize that demand, the PC was transformed from a high-tech, specialty product to a household, consumer item. Enter the department store.

Buying from a department store can have its ups and downs. On one hand, your sales rep (if you can find one in the downsized '90s) might know all about personal computers. On the other, he might just have strayed over from the shoe department.

Nonetheless, department stores have become a force to be reckoned with in PC retailing. Their sheer marketing power, through advertising and catalogues, guarantees a presence in the industry, and, usually, competitive pricing. They follow much the same model as their cousins, the high-tech mass marketers. On a good day, you can find an incredible deal; on a bad one, outdated stock at inflated prices. Department stores are a good choice of vendor if you know something about what you're buying. Unfortunately, though, I suspect that many of their customers are novice users drawn by the decidedly non-threatening atmosphere they offer.

Typically, department stores sell out-of-the-box, home-oriented products such as Packard Bell's Multimedia series. Don't expect to have a custom hot rod put together to meet your specifications. On the positive side, department stores are known for liberal return and financing policies, and they are more likely to add services like free delivery, or allow you a return for a full refund after you've opened the box, looked inside, and decided you don't like what you bought. Alternatively, don't look for much expertise before the sale; more likely, expect the whole purchase to be a do-it-yourself affair: walk in the front door, get your cart, take the big boxes off the shelf, pay your money, and load your car.

PHONE AND MAIL-ORDER VENDORS

In the late '80s, Dell Computer Corporation became the first of the order-by-phone vendors, and it was followed quickly by companies such as Gateway, Zeos, and, later, NEC. Now, in the late '90s, the direct sales market has been entered by such crossover catalogue enterprises as Sears, who offer chain-store selection, prices, and policies, as well as the convenience of shopping by phone.

The most notable characteristic of buying a PC by phone is that a purchaser is able to remain in control and avoid having to listen to a pitch or run the risk of feeling inadequate or uninformed. These are undeniable attractions. Another important advantage is that a phone purchase is physically easy. And, since most enterprises playing in the game are large, their prices are usually quite competitive. If you have the forethought to make a few enquiries about the market and current prices, ordering by phone can be an excellent way to get your hands on equipment quickly and easily.

On the other hand, the idea of buying something you can't see and touch simply sticks in some people's throats. In a mail order purchase, obviously, a demonstration session isn't an option.

Also, think about what might happen if you don't get what you wanted, or if the equipment doesn't work when you unpack it and turn it on. Some remote vendors may respond more quickly than the understaffed store across the street, or the superstore that doesn't have any technical support people on hand period, but remember, in the remote marketplace, your vendor is just that – remote.

Finally, for all their futuristic marketing, packing, and quality control, PCs are still complex, delicate, valuable pieces of equipment. Therefore, they are risky to transport. They can accidentally be dropped, frozen, baked, or soaked. Worse, they can find their way into the wrong hands. Insurance and guarantees from reputable remote vendors – and their associated shipping companies – cover problems like these, but take a moment to imagine in practical terms what any one of these slip-ups can mean.

First, a physical fault will have to be verified by the vendor or manufacturer, or both. Next, responsibility will have to be assigned. Third, the damaged goods will have to be returned. Fourth, replacement goods will have to be prepared, then shipped, perhaps via the same channel as before.

These steps can prove trying to a company or individual who is counting on receiving a new PC on schedule.

VALUE-ADDED RESELLERS AND VALUE-ADDED DEALERS

"Value-Added Reseller" (VAR) is a designation which originated in the marketing plans of IBM, Hewlett-Packard, and other large computer manufacturers in the 1980s, when companies who were authorized to sell personal computer products were more strictly controlled than they are today.

The term referred to an enterprise that would "add value" to a PC by selling it as part of a package – say, with software, a printer, and specialized support – rather than over the counter in competition with the manufacturer's own sales reps. Manufacturers saw VARs and their cousin VADs (value-added distributors, who do the same thing as VARs, but in greater quantities) as a way to increase total sales, rather than segment the fledgling retail market. VARs and VADs still sell computer equipment today. An example might be a small company which has worked up a piece of software designed for a particular business. Or it might be a neighbourhood whiz who assembles PCs in his basement and is willing to install a favourite program and offer support to go along with it. Vendors like these are not as common as they used to be, now that a wider variety of off-the-shelf computers and programs have become available.

It's still quite reasonable, however, to approach a reseller who is considered expert in a specific field to help you select, purchase, and integrate a computer into your life or business. The advantages of such a personalized approach are obvious, especially if you are planning to use your PC in an application such as networking or point-of-sale, or to run a special graphics program.

But, don't expect a wide selection of products or the best pricing from a VAR. By their nature, these resellers offer limited hardware and software choices – those with which they're familiar – and they usually charge accordingly for extra service. You must also be prepared to trust their expertise, their integrity, and their product choices more completely than other, conventional outlets.

Also, if your VAR goes out of business or moves away, you might wish you had chosen an alternate source. It can be difficult for a new support person to pick up where a specialty vendor left off. Still, when VARs are good, they can be very good. Some of the happiest computer users I have known are those who dealt with VARs. These were purchasers who had specific needs and were willing to pay extra for increased attention before and after the sale.

TRADE SHOWS

An increasingly popular way of buying everything from boats to cars to household furnishings is to attend a trade show with money in your pocket. These range from big, information-oriented expositions aimed at computer professionals, to local events where a few retailers try to drum up extra business. Trade shows can be a good place to find well-priced computer equipment, though you have to be prepared to wait for the event to be held. For vendors, trade shows are usually a fiercely competitive environment. It's hard to hang that $499 price tag on a printer when it's sitting on your neighbour's table for $450. Also, there's often a good mix of products on display, depending on the size of the show and the resources of its participants. You might even see some specialty applications which have been worked up by a vendor targeting a corner of the market that interests you – say, video conferencing.

Take some precautions, however, especially if you're purchasing a locally assembled PC in this environment, to make sure you'll have someone to talk to if the deal goes sour. If you purchase a peripheral such as a printer or scanner made by a well-known manufacturer, your liability is lessened somewhat. Still, know what you're getting into when buying at a show.

Anyone can throw a sheet over a table, hawk a few PCs or components for a fast profit, and be gone tomorrow. Nevertheless, trade shows provide good opportunities to acquaint yourself with prices and products. If there is a retail-oriented exposition in your neighbourhood around the time you're thinking of making a purchase, I would highly recommend taking a Saturday afternoon to pay it a visit.

THE INTERNET AS A NEW-PC SOURCE

The Internet has had as exciting an effect on retailing as it has on personal computing. With their obvious relevance, computers are among the most well represented of products being sold on the Net. The

World Wide Web is an unprecedented compendium of product information, third-party reviews, buying guides, discussion groups, and all sorts of other perspectives. It can tell you a lot about a PC, the company that manufactured it, and even the company selling it before you have to spend money and learn the hard way.

If you have questions about a particular component – RAM, for example – you can easily find up-to-date information, provided you know where to look. Before the Web became popular, this was a difficult task. You must not forget, however, that with its size, complexity, and open access, the Internet does not always offer accuracy. Anyone can post "facts," truthful or otherwise, for public consumption.

A good place to start is a search program (or "engine") such as Alta Vista, Yahoo, HotBot, or Lycos. Any one of these, when queried for "computer hardware," will cough up thousands of sites, from the excellent to the mediocre to the waste of time. With this kind of choice, it's easy to get caught in the "virtual labyrinth" and wander around aimlessly before finding what you really want. So it's best to approach the Web jungle with some kind of plan. Be specific when you search. Two good rules to remember are:

1. If you are looking for a manufacturer, try going directly to their website by using their name followed by the letters .com or .ca (i.e., http://www.samsung.com or http://www.dell.ca). This is an easy way to get up-to-date information on new products from almost every major manufacturer.
2. If you are looking for a retailer or retail information, check out the Canadian version of Yahoo and follow the links through "computers" to "retail." This approach will yield several screens of pages from large and small retailers. There are also several magazines, both in print and on line, dealing with computer information and product reviews; again, a search through the Canadian section of any recognized search engine will produce good results.

Here are some examples of Canadian computer sites on line as of publication:

http://www.canadacomputes.com
http://www.tcp.ca
http://www.p3p.com
http://www.compucentre.ca
http://www.shift.com

http://www.ifmagazine.com
http://www.monitor.ca

For retail information, try contacting these sites:

http://www.microtrader.mb.ca
http://www.123compute.com
http://www.interlog.com/~afford
http://www.dominiondigital.com
http://www.computerliquidationctr.com
http://www.fastekk.com

EVALUATING A VENDOR

Computer shoppers choose their vendors for a variety of reasons, but let's assume you have enough time and money to consider three or four different PC outlets – what should you look for?

I have tried to group the following criteria in a rough order of importance, based on what I have seen and heard from my own customers over the past several years:

- *Do you like the store?* Are you comfortable with its people, its selection and display of merchandise, its appearance, and its niche in the market? Whether upscale or street level, service-oriented or mass marketer, does the place suit you?
- *Do you like the people in the store?* Let's face it: you're going to have to deal with these people and be able to communicate with them accurately and pleasantly. Are you more or less happy about this? Is this feeling reciprocated?
- *Do they have what you want?* Does the store usually stock the equipment you are looking for, or is your PC a special order? Have they any experience with it, and will it take them long to get it? What will happen if they're not able to fill your order in a reasonable time?
- *Are their prices competitive?* Be sure to judge a vendor's pricing on the specific products you're looking for. Competitiveness can vary from one computer to another because of the volatile nature of high-tech goods. One store with low prices on printer toners may not offer the best deal on the printers themselves. Compare prices of the goods you're shopping for, at the time you really want to buy them, then choose accordingly.

- *Are they far away?* These days, distance means less in the choice of a retail outlet than ever before, but shouldn't be ignored. What if you have a problem at 8:47 on the night before you have to turn in a big presentation? Can you run across the street and get it solved? Or do you have to put your computer in your car and drive for fifty minutes through snow and sleet and wind and hail?
- *Are they likely to be in business next year?* "I'm sorry, but the number you have dialled is no longer in service . . ." There are few words more likely to strike terror into the heart of a computer user when trying to call his vendor three months after a purchase. Of course, computer retailing is an unpredictable business, and these are uncertain economic times, so there is no sure way anyone can protect himself completely against "vendor failure." Still, if a place has been open for a long time (anything over five years is an achievement in the world of computer sales), it should gain a point or two over the competition.

Six Questions to Ask Your Vendor

Once you've searched the neighbourhood, the city, or even the whole country and decided on a PC outlet, there are six questions you can, and should, ask about your choice:

- What are their purchase policies?
- What are their delivery policies?
- What are their return of goods policies?
- What are their technical capabilities?
- What are their warranty policies?
- What are their service policies?

Purchase Policies

Just what exactly do you have to do to buy a computer from these guys? It's not always as easy as paying money and walking away with the goods. Does the PC have to be prepared or is it available off the shelf? Do you have to leave a deposit? Is the deposit refundable if you don't have the equipment within a specified time? Are there forms of payment – certain credit cards, personal cheques, or banking cards – they don't accept? Do they require full payment in advance? Finally, are you being charged extra for the way in which your payment is being made?

Delivery Policies

Are the goods you are buying in stock? And when they do become available, how will you get them home? The average computer monitor box is 2' x 2' x 2' and weighs about twenty-five pounds. If you can't struggle with the thing on public transit, will your vendor deliver it? If so, for how much? And what, exactly, does that term mean anyway? Some purchasers assume "delivery" means a technician will bring equipment to their home or office, unpack it, set it up, and instruct them on how to use it. While installation is a service commonly offered by companies selling computer equipment, don't assume it is included in a delivery price. Expect instead that a non-technical person who is probably in a hurry to get to his next call will drop some boxes on your doorstep, ask for a signature and perhaps some money, then rush away.

Return of Goods Policies

Of all the issues over which retailers and customers are likely to clash, the return of goods is easily the leader. Many shoppers assume that a major purchase carries a responsibility on the part of a vendor to take back an unsatisfactory item. But for resellers, a fiercely competitive marketplace makes it all but impossible to absorb expenses associated with returned goods: selling them again at a reduced price, or returning them by courier to a supplier.

In most Canadian provinces and U.S. states, consumer laws are specific about a vendor's obligations. Educate yourself about the rules of retail in your area. In some locations, for example, any vendor of equipment over a certain value *must* provide a full refund within a specified time, provided the goods are returned in their original condition. But be aware that rules like these may not apply to certain products – to used items, or goods being financed and paid for over time. In all cases, the best assumption for a computer purchaser is that whatever you buy becomes yours once you pay and take possession, and a vendor or manufacturer has no explicit responsibility to take it back. What parties in any sale *are* required to do, however, is live up to the terms of any contract or undertaking which accompanies the equipment.

Technical Capabilities

This is probably the toughest thing to determine about any computer vendor. Beyond asking a few questions and keeping your eyes and ears open when you're at the vendor's place of business, there's not much you can do except rely on his reputation. Of course, if you are planning to purchase a PC made by a large company such as Compaq or IBM, which offer their own support and warranty network, this becomes less important.

But if you are planning to buy a used computer or a new generic system, it's perfectly reasonable to request the names of two or three recent customers to whom the company has supplied equipment. If you have the time to call them, be friendly, non-aggressive, and forthright. Ask them:

1. How long ago did they buy their system from the supplier?
2. Was the equipment ready on schedule and on budget?
3. Has the equipment worked well – have there been any problems?
4. Has the vendor fielded after-sale calls satisfactorily?
5. Did they feel the vendor's prices were competitive?
6. How long was the guarantee?
7. Would they buy from the vendor again?

Even if you don't get wildly enthusiastic answers to all of these questions from all references, make sure that the main issues (price competitiveness, after-sale support, willingness to use the same vendor again) come up positive. If they do, and you are happy with the other elements of your chosen PC source, forge ahead.

Warranty Policies

Because of the varied and sometimes complicated nature of computer equipment guarantees, there is a separate section in this guide on the subject of warranties and service contracts. Most important, however, are the policies a company offers, and which one in particular (if any) is included in the price of the system you are planning to buy. Will the vendor actually participate in the warranty or support scenario at all? If so, to what level? Would you be better off approaching the manufacturer yourself? Make sure you choose a vendor who is able to offer the right combination of support and price to suit your after-sale requirements, and that you understand what warranty jobs he will – and, more importantly will not – perform.

Service Policies

Related to, but different from, warranty policies, service policies determine what, exactly, will happen if and when the store undertakes to fix a malfunctioning system *after* its warranty has expired. Will the supplier attend a service call on site (at your location), or will you have to transport it to his location? How long do repairs usually take, and what are his rates? Obviously, any vendor known to offer prompt service has an advantage over one who does not.

What to Avoid

Vendors you don't get along with – Are you happy with the store and the people you're dealing with? If not, it's pretty certain you shouldn't buy a computer from them just because their price is low, or they're located nearby. If you can't get along with a store's staff in the beginning, the relationship will probably only get worse. If a sales or technical person is condescending, or difficult to deal with for any other reason, stay away.

Dishonest vendors – I happen to believe that this problem goes hand in hand with the one above. What kinds of products does the store have on its shelves? Are they marked for resale only with a new PC, and being offered separately at a discount? Does the rep ask if you'd like a copy of Microsoft Office on your new hard drive to help close a hardware sale? Does she suddenly offer to waive the taxes if you pay cash? If a vendor reveals that he has no problem cheating his software suppliers or the tax man, what makes you think he's not going to cheat you?

Unreliable vendors – It's not the end of the world if a vendor makes an error or has to delay a shipment, either because they can't solve a tough technical problem or they get caught in supply circumstances beyond their control. But if a store or individual shows inherent clumsiness, if there is inadequate paperwork, or you have a bad feeling about the competence of the people you are dealing with, go elsewhere.

FINANCING

To Buy or Not to Buy — That Is the Question

You've spent several weeks wandering through the high-tech marketplace, studying specifications, sifting through advice from salespeople, consultants, family, and friends. You've finally decided on a system you can't live without and have found a place to buy it. Should you purchase it outright or finance the deal over twelve months? Should you lease over three years with an option to buy? What the heck is the difference, anyway? What about renting something similar for a month or two to see how you like it? The best choice depends on a range of factors: your tax bracket, your ready cash, even how soon you think your new equipment is going to become obsolete, at which time you'll probably have to go through the whole trying process again. Don't you just wish they'd stop inventing new stuff so you could simply buy something and use it happily ever after? In a world of high-tech finance characterized by certified cheques, conditional sales contracts, and rentals with option to buy, there is perhaps *too* much to consider. Here are some suggestions.

Cash Is King

Lord Byron's observation that "ready cash is Aladdin's lamp" is as true today as ever. The most obvious advantage to buying any item with a "secure payment" (cash, certified cheque, or money order) is the position of power it imparts to you, the purchaser. If you know exactly what you want, and you can pay for it immediately, in cash, you can demand maximum attention and minimum price. A cash offer also enables you to be precise about other circumstances of the transaction. If you plan to finance, lease, or rent a computer or other electronic gear, you may have to accept a different package than that fabulous deal you saw advertised in the high-tech section of the newspaper. Extras such as software configuration or on-site installation are easier to negotiate when you are able to pay in cash. In today's highly competitive retail environment, vendors will often insist on cash for certain "blow out" packages; otherwise they have no choice but to pass additional costs to the customer: insurance to guarantee a personal cheque; business and collection costs involved in managing a receivable; and fees deducted by a credit card company. Shopping with cash also enables you to compare products and services easily. High-tech purchases are difficult enough without having to account for competing financing rates, possible buy-backs, or amounts that may or may not be credited to you under rental agreements or other financing plans. With payment in hand, you can shop the same hardware, software and service package to several vendors and choose accordingly. And once you have made your purchase, there are no hidden clauses, no further payments, no extra worries.

Or are there? Believe it or not, there can be disadvantages to purchasing high-tech gear outright. When you've bought a computer system, for example, paid for it in full and completed the deal, your options of recourse are limited.

An entire sum paid before you have actually had time to see a system in action means it's important that you buy carefully. Horror stories abound of shoppers who paid in full for equipment that doesn't work, only to return it and be rebuffed – or worse, to find the supplier unreachable or out of business. At least when you finance your purchase, even by using a credit card, you have some options if it was, for example, misrepresented.

There are other disadvantages to paying with cash. From an accounting point of view, an immediate outlay for computer or other business equipment is not always a good idea. It ties up precious working capital, and does not provide the income tax deductions offered by lease or rental payments. In a profitable company, equipment purchases are a capital investment that can only be depreciated at a small percentage per year, so in many cases it makes more sense to lease goods and use the payments on them to reduce taxable income. Buying outright may also limit you to a less powerful system. A new desktop or notebook PC is likely to devalue faster than almost anything else on Earth. By choosing to lease or rent, or even stretch its purchase payments over time, you may be able to afford a more powerful system that will be more valuable and flexible in years to come.

Lease Now, Pay Later

Leases and conditional sales contracts allow you to carry equipment home after signing a promise to make regular payments over time. Throughout the industry, a lease is recognized as a contract between a lessor who owns the equipment and a lessee who makes payments for its use. Title of ownership normally stays with the lessor (usually a finance company), who registers this fact with the government, just in case a dispute should arise.

This retention of ownership is one of the chief differences between a lease and a conditional sale. It is usual in computer leases for retailers to handle the preparation and delivery of equipment, and then be paid in full by a leasing company or agent within five to thirty days of the date the user takes delivery. You should be aware, however, that in most cases it will be a third party to whom you must make lease payments – not the vendor from whom you got the goods. If you intend to keep your computer after a lease is finished, be sure your leasing or sales representative specifies how much you will have to pay for this "purchase option."

You don't have to be a financial expert to realize that leased equipment usually costs more in the long run than if you purchase it with one payment – leaving aside any other tax or budgetary advantages. The cost of different leases will vary, so be sure to find out all financing charges up front. Remember, leasing can be a more expensive financing option than a simple bank loan.

But leasing has its advantages. By borrowing money to purchase equipment, or by financing it through a supplier, you are still not eligible, in most cases, to write the payments off as an expense. A lease conserves your borrowing power for other business uses or the purchase of other goods. And in larger companies, leases are valuable to maintain budgetary levels which can be renewed from year to year without a board of directors or decision-maker having to authorize a capital expenditure.

Conditional sales contracts are close cousins to lease agreements, but there are differences: a conditional contract is simply a note which states that you promise to pay $XX over YY period during which ownership of the goods stays with the user. These agreements offer slightly different repayment options than a lease; normally you'll be accepted more quickly, and there is no extra money to pay to buy the goods at the end of the term.

Resource people in both the financial and retail sectors of the technology industry strongly advise that you read all documents thoroughly before signing, and ask a lawyer or other professional to verify your position if you are unclear about anything. Try to separate the cost of financing from the cost of the equipment, and compare this with any tax or other savings that may be provided.

Remember, when you sign a lease or finance agreement you are doing more than just buying equipment – you are borrowing money to do it.

Rent It — Like It — Buy It

In cases where a lease or outright purchase is not an option because of credit or cash flow problems, or if you do not actually need to own equipment after having used it for a time, consider renting. Perhaps you need a system for a specific task during a short period – say, a demonstration or conference. In the rental scenario, the advantages are obvious. You actually get to test drive your dream system for a fraction of its retail cost.

Many rental outlets will allow at least some of your payments to be put toward the purchase of the rental equipment. Even better, until you've actually decided to buy, your rental payments can usually be written off – just like those in a lease. A word of warning, though: rental payments claimed as an expense on equipment which is later purchased may or may not be legitimate income tax deductions;

consult an accountant or tax expert before claiming these on your return.

Other advantages to the rental scenario are flexibility – you can return the equipment whenever you want – and support – most rental houses include some kind of on-site or replacement guarantee in their price. But before picking up the phone and calling every rental establishment in the city, consider other factors as well.

First, remember that if you buy equipment after renting it, you have added a considerable surcharge to what might have been a straightforward purchase. The monthly rental of a current (486 or Pentium-level) computer, for example, can be as much as $300 to $400. If you purchase this equipment at full price after two months, you are paying well above the market price for what may not even be a new system. That trial period you enjoyed has suddenly become mighty expensive. So be certain what percentage of your rental payments may be applied to the purchase price. If none at all, as is the policy of some establishments, remember that you will be back at square one at the end of the term! In general, rental payments are higher than lease or financing installments because rental houses must recoup their costs quickly for equipment that devalues so fast.

Secondly, remember that when renting, your choice of product may be limited. You will probably be asked to accept stock from the equipment "pool" of a supplier, in which case you will be evaluating products of different specifications than you had originally wanted, or a system that might not run the software you wanted to test in the first place.

Where to Sign?

So the decision whether to purchase outright, lease, rent, or finance equipment depends upon your situation. How much ready money do you have? How important is a tax write-off? Do you think you'll want to trade in the system or relinquish it entirely after a defined period?

For certain companies, leasing is the only way they can get a decision to acquire equipment without putting a politically charged proposal in front of a board of directors. Their credit is well established, they have a history of leasing other goods with a specific company, so the choice is clear.

Individuals who have done their research and want a specific system, and are definite about wishing to own it in the long run, should usually choose a good vendor and negotiate the best possible cash price. They will likely save money.

The owners of a cash-starved small business might consider a financing plan that allows them to pay for equipment over time, but still gains them equity in a system which is powerful enough to see them well into the future.

And for a company or user who is unsure about whether they need a computer at all, or who wants a system for a specific task over a short period, renting is an attractive option.

Whatever course of acquisition you choose, don't be afraid to ask for references and demand the best price available for both products and financial services. It is a challenge to find the perfect deal, but it will be very satisfying when you do.

THE DEMO

Once you've gathered information about the manufacturer, components, and the vendor of the computer system you're considering, what about a test drive?

There are some things to watch for when you're listening to a salesperson trying to sell you a PC. The first is attitude. A good salesperson shouldn't be hurried, pushy, judgmental, or condescending.

It can be a complicated business shopping for a computer – one-third show biz, one-third education, one-third business – so look for accurate and honest communication. A good demo should be a positive presentation of goods you're actually trying to buy. One of the biggest problems facing high-tech vendors is keeping their shelves stocked with current products. Don't feel shy about asking to see the exact model you're thinking of purchasing. If it's not available right away, no problem. Give a place a day or so to get their act together, if you can afford to wait. If you can't, move on.

If it turns out for some reason that a demo system is impossible for the store to put together, a helpful salesperson should at least try to arrange a show-and-tell off site, say, at a manufacturer's location.

BARGAINING AND NEGOTIATION

Few people really like the whole idea of bargaining and negotiation, and no wonder – this is a confrontational part of any transaction which contains strong potential for disagreement and difficulty. Still, it has been my experience that most purchasers are just not comfortable spending the substantial amount of money needed for a new, or up-to-date used, computer without some kind of comparison shopping.

Usually this leads to discussion about goods, services, and of course a competitive price. If you don't feel comfortable confronting a sales rep with the bad news that his price is too high, then shop around via phone or fax and migrate quietly to a more competitive supplier. If you are inclined toward a little haggling, here are some observations.

First, establish with your sales rep whether it's even possible for him or her to move on the price. Most establishments have flexible prices, but a few do not, particularly value-added retailers because of their special talents and services.

Even if a vendor says his numbers are indeed fixed, let your salesperson know that you're shopping around and that best price is going to remain a factor. This may open the door for him to be creative with other concessions such as delivery, extra goods, or extended warranty, in order not to lose the sale.

But what if your vendor is eager and enthusiastic to bargain? Well, don't just sit there, make an offer! Whether formally stated or not, your proposition might consist of the following elements:

- Exact description of the goods and services you want to buy
- The price
- When you will pay
- How you will pay
- How and when you will take possession
- Whether you have a trade-in
- How long the offer remains in effect

These elements should all be considered when you are really serious about buying a specific PC. They all make a difference to the cost of the sale from your supplier's point of view.

Many combinations of these factors are possible, so look at them one by one and decide where you can be flexible. Suppose, for example, you can afford a definite price for your new PC and not a penny more. You have the money readily available though, and can pay by cash or certified cheque. This makes your offer more attractive. On the other hand, if you know you're not going to have the money until the end of the month and you need to use a credit card, you should mention that, too.

You may be able to bend on the actual goods or services you need, or you may offer to buy the computer quickly, like today, right now, or even within a certain period. A salesperson will watch for any of these because they increase his chances of closing the deal. And until you have actually bought your system, that's the all-important issue.

An experienced sales rep is also more apt to be circumspect about offering a lower price to a purchaser he knows will need a great deal of technical support. If you can communicate that after-sale effort will be minimal in your case, you may well be able to negotiate a better deal. But a word of warning: be sure not to misrepresent this. If you are indeed a novice or are migrating to equipment with which you're unfamiliar, say so. Don't expect to have it both ways. Whatever you're buying, be truthful, and get any agreements in writing.

Be Truthful

When you prepare an offer, be sure you are truthful about what you do and don't want. Nothing invites argument and dissatisfaction more than bargaining in bad faith. This isn't to say that a deal can't change. In fact, most PC purchases do as people talk to advisors, rethink their needs, and just plain change their minds. They end up wanting different equipment and services at a different price. That's OK. A good sales rep will have the patience to roll with the changes and finally provide you with what you want.

Get It in Writing

After you've communicated all of your desires to your vendor, and offered him a price you can live with, you've decided to think about the whole endeavour for a day or two. Now there's another detail to remember: his quotation to you. Do your best to get the main elements of your computer deal in writing. Quotations can assume many forms. They can be as informal as jots on the back of a business card, or, in corporate submissions involving hundreds of systems, they can be complex documents many pages long. At the very least, a quotation should be similar to a final bill of sale. It should outline:

- The vendor's name and the quotation date
- The goods and services being offered
- Payment details – how much, how, and when
- The warranty
- The date the quotation expires
- Any special conditions attached to the sale

With a written record of this information you are protected if you have to deal with a different sales rep, or if the one you originally dealt with forgets his offer. Finally, a couple of additional thoughts about bargaining and negotiation:

1. Don't make or consider ridiculous offers. Computer sellers normally deal on 10- to 20-percent margins. If you counter a slightly high $2,000 price with a $1,400 reply you're probably wandering over to Never Never Land. Work in increments of 3 percent or so unless you have lower quotations from a competitor to back yourself up. If you sense a rep or store is overcharging, walk away. It's the best and most final statement you can make.
2. Finally, don't forget the goal of the whole exercise: to get yourself a good computer at a good price, not to beat someone else at negotiating so you can feel like a winner. The best deals are those in which both buyer and seller feel they are getting a good bargain.

TAKING POSSESSION

When you take possession of your new computer system, be sure to go over it very carefully. If a courier drops off three boxes and asks you to sign for them, note that you've signed for three boxes. Then open them up, set up the equipment, and check everything carefully against your invoice or spec sheet. This might seem obvious, but it's an important and often overlooked part of many PC purchases. Check all physical components – cables, software, device drivers, CDs, and manuals. Watch your PC carefully during "power-up." Any error messages? Go into its operating system and check its main memory, video card memory, modem speed and type, and other components. In Windows 95, you can do this by clicking on the "My Computer" icon. Use the Apple System Profiler or "About this Macintosh" to find out about a Mac. Don't feel shy about loosening a few screws, taking the case off and peering inside, although be very careful that the system is turned off and that you don't touch anything while you're in there. Everything look shiny and new?

Run any included programs and look for problems, because this is the very best time to discover them. If you do find an irregularity – a missing part, or a malfunction – *don't panic.* Make a careful note of the trouble, check any applicable documentation, then contact your supplier. If a short shipment was a legitimate back order, get a firm date by which the situation will be resolved. This is the time to be precise about what you bought, what you got, and the difference between legitimate oversight and deliberate misrepresentation.

8

AFTER THE SALE: PC LEMON-AID

EVERYBODY HAPPY?

It's extremely satisfying to buy a complex new piece of equipment like a personal computer, bring it home, set it up, and get it running successfully. But what if this doesn't happen? What if the thing breaks down before you even get a chance to use it, or if the place you bought it from won't even talk to you? What if you feel you were cheated – perhaps sold inferior goods, or feel you never even got what you paid for in the first place? That's what this chapter is all about.

As a person who has bought and sold PCs for many years, I've seen problems, scams, arguments, difficulties, and misunderstandings of almost every description. I've seen resellers come and go, and smooth operators swindle unsuspecting customers one month, declare bankruptcy the next, and reopen under another name the next. I've also seen customers behave badly, unfairly, even dishonestly, though much more often, I have profited from the knowledge, energy, and goodwill of computer users of all kinds, from novices to experts.

Of all the manufacturers, vendors, support people, technicians, and customers I have dealt with, I have found the honest, open, positive-minded people to be the ones most likely to get a problem sorted out with a minimum of stress. Accidents happen, people and companies make mistakes. PC support is all about overcoming these challenges. This means, first and foremost, working together: communicating in two directions, being fair, patient, and above all, honest. What happens when these elements fall out of the service equation? Let's look at some of the problems that can crop up after you've bought a PC.

MY COMPUTER DOESN'T WORK!

So the nice, neat, fantastic PC you just bought is not working. Just how much trouble is this going to cause? How angry should you let yourself get?

The first order of business is to look at all of the circumstances surrounding this unhappy situation. You've been presented with what may turn out to be a complex problem, so it's not a bad idea to break it down. How much, if anything, is this likely to cost? How long is it going to take to get fixed? Will you be without the thing for a long time? If there is a warranty involved, is there likely to be trouble invoking it?

Can you beg or borrow a replacement to buy yourself some time? Evaluate the whole situation from afar, and consider your position with your service provider. Is this a warranty job? Have you got an on-site contract so you can expect the cavalry over the hill in the morning? Are you going to have to ship the PC to the factory if you bought it by phone?

If you're planning to make a warranty or service claim, assume that most computer companies – vendors and manufacturers – are going to make you follow rigid rules before even allowing you access to a qualified technician. Of course, these rules will vary from company to company.

So prepare yourself. Get out the paperwork, especially your bill of sale, and any other documentation which describes your warranty, and what is required to invoke it. Also, once you see your PC starting to act up, report the problem promptly to your service provider! You are in a much stronger position to make a service claim if you are within the specified time frame. Showing up on month fourteen of a twelve-month guarantee and claiming the problem started back in month eight is definitely not advisable.

IDENTIFYING AND COMMUNICATING THE PROBLEM

Once you've got an idea of what to expect from your support people, what they expect of you, whether you're inside or outside any warranty opportunity, and whether you're likely to be without your computer for the next few hours, days, or weeks, you're ready to carry it down to the depot or call the hotline.

Here are some questions support people will ask themselves when you finally get the opportunity to describe your computer's problem:

- Is this is a hardware, software, or human problem?
- Can the problem be reliably reproduced?
- What subsystem of the PC appears to be involved?
- What costs are involved, and who will absorb them? (Is this a warranty obligation or a paid repair?)
- What will be involved in replacing or repairing the failed component, or resetting the malfunctioning software?
- How difficult will it be to communicate to the user that everything is OK but they simply don't like how it works?
- How difficult will it be to schedule this repair? Where will it be performed, and how much time will be allowed to finish it?
- What is involved in getting appropriate replacement parts?

Think ahead by asking yourself these questions, and be ready with as much information as you can provide.

Also be sure to satisfy yourself that the person to whom you are describing the problem is qualified to solve it or, at least, to pass the information accurately to someone who is. If you are unsure about this, don't go any further until you feel you are talking to the right rep. An inexperienced "front man" who miscommunicates the trouble is a common cause of disputes in the repair business.

For your own protection, write down the specifics of the difficulty: when the problem first appeared, what you were doing with the PC, how often it has reappeared since then (not once, often, every time you use the system), does it always appear under the same circumstances? If you try, can you re-create the problem? It's also important to remain open to the possibility, especially with software-related problems, that the product is not all you expected.

In the event of obvious hardware failures, it's often easier to pinpoint the events that led up to them than to isolate the failure. If you've jotted these down, perhaps you can fax them to the tech support rep. After you've described the trouble, don't forget to confirm any potential charges, the length of time the service might take, and the results you expect after the job is completed. Will you, for example, be given back your PC with a new or reformatted hard drive that has no programs on it? How about the operating system?

As far as scheduling is concerned, a service provider should be able to complete a very high percentage of their jobs in five business days.

Custom configuring a system – putting your software back together – or other special circumstances may add to this, but with their modular design, most PCs can be taken apart and reassembled pretty fast. With the right components and experience, a good technician can build a brand-new one inside an hour. If a job takes longer than a week, it's your right to know exactly why. If you're happy with the explanation, OK – unforeseen things can happen, people can make mistakes. Remember, though, that you are the customer. This is your PC. Too many pleas for extra time should alert you that it's time to consider other options.

IT'S *STILL* NOT FIXED!

So your PC's broken, the technicians have had it for three weeks, and it's still not fixed! Or worse, they returned it and the thing is a bigger headache than before! What can you do when you encounter really tough problems with a service or warranty provider?

Now, more than ever, is when you need to rely on a written description of your difficulties: not only the problem, but the machine's repair or replacement history, and any ongoing failures. This should include details on the original problem, names of technicians who serviced it, when they serviced it, and any recurrences. Once you have all this ammo, what should you do with it? How do you communicate to a manufacturer or vendor that they have not behaved properly and must change their tune?

Before going further on this topic, it's worth noting how the computer service business has evolved. Each year PCs grow more powerful and can run a wider variety of programs. This technology explosion has pushed the people who build and support computers into a constant race to keep up with new products while developing viable ways to explain and fix them and stay in business. Intense price competition has squeezed profit margins to a fraction of what they were a few years ago.

Some companies, overwhelmed by all of this, have simply given up. Others have developed ingenious new responses to requests for information and service, most of them, unfortunately, at the expense of the customer. There are now fewer technicians per user, and they often specialize in certain subsystems of a PC or its software. Getting help requires formal procedures which take longer and cost more money. "Free" support services that once were bundled with the more profitable computers of the past have been cut back.

All of these factors mean that it's imperative when seeking assistance to get to the right person, and to present the right information to them as clearly, quickly, and precisely as possible. But what can you do to get your service provider's attention if they don't seem to be living up to their commitments? It's important to remember that most computer companies are quite protective of their reputations. If you have an unresolved issue with a PC you purchased, let both vendor and manufacturer know very clearly that this has become for them not only a technical matter, but one of customer satisfaction.

This may mean going beyond the usual avenues of support, to the people at the top of the service department, or even in other parts of the company. If you're dealing with a chain or a franchise, deal directly with the head office. If the PC was purchased recently, another place to seek assistance is the sales rep from whom you bought it. If no response is forthcoming, or the company simply reaffirms a position you feel is unfair, you may wish to seek a third opinion. This does not necessarily have to cost money.

Often, companies and individuals bring equipment to our store for evaluations and written service reports. Occasionally, we are presented with them by our own customers. A reasonable vendor should look at a third-party evaluation of a problem and learn from it if he can.

One of the best sources of information about PC failures and components are manufacturers. Unlike some other products, PCs are mostly composed of parts from several different manufacturers, and, of course, they run programs from still others. An enquiry to a manufacturer, say, of video cards, may shed light on why the picture on your monitor is unsatisfactory when you run a certain application. This can provide a context in which to present the case to the technical people originally involved. However, when seeking the opinion of a third party, it's best not to betray your interest in the outcome of the enterprise. You are seeking technical information about a combination of products – leave it at that. Are there known faults or incompatibilities? What are the details? When confronted with hard evidence from a reliable third party, a service provider or manufacturer is at least compelled to acknowledge a problem, and may even learn something about solving it.

THE VENDOR FROM HECK: MISREPRESENTATION

One of the most frightening possibilities you face when purchasing a PC is the spectre of being deliberately misled – told something by a vendor that isn't true, or sold something and not receiving it. Of all the elements that can go wrong in a sale or service transaction, this is about the worst. It means your supplier or manufacturer can't be trusted, and your relationship may move quickly into the realm of stress and legal action. What are the main risks of misrepresentation in the PC business? Unfortunately, as in other human endeavours, the possibilities for cheating are endless. While some misrepresentation scenarios are familiar old retail saws, others are peculiar to the world of high technology.

Misleading Advertising

Certainly the introduction to all kinds of problems, this is one of the most difficult misrepresentations to overcome when shopping for a new or used computer, simply because it's so common. It ranges from "incomplete" advertisements promising low-priced systems without all the necessary components, to promises which are baldly false. Very common are variations on the "bait and switch" technique: a vendor advertises products he doesn't have, then tries to sell you something else on which he makes more profit. Refined versions of this practice involve advertising a "basic" system, then overcharging on other parts of the sale: the monitor, the printer, software, or warranty. It's probably safe to say that advertising problems like these are more common in the locally assembled side of the business where smaller companies are trying hard to distinguish themselves from the competition. Unfortunately, in doing so, they do more harm to their reputations than good.

Inferior, Missing, or Used Components

This sort of misrepresentation is one of the most difficult to spot. It too is more likely to happen when you purchase a generic, or locally assembled, PC from a small company living (and perhaps dying) by its own rules. The modular nature of generic PCs, and the fact that packaging for them is usually opened so the system can be customized, and then resealed, makes them an easy target for a vendor wishing to unload old, used, or otherwise inferior components. But brand-name computers are not immune. Packard Bell was sued by Compaq in 1996 over the issue of shipping used parts in some of its new PCs. The case was settled out of court.

The trademark and technical integrity of PCs from large corporations can also easily be compromised by a nefarious reseller. So how can you protect yourself against this kind of dishonesty? It's very difficult to insulate yourself completely from fraud if you choose a dishonest vendor. If your chosen reseller's prices seem way below everyone else's, ask yourself why. Don't be shy about requesting references.

Look at how long the company has been in business, and use your intuition about a supplier's integrity. In addition, gently confirm with your rep that it's important to you that all components in the PC or other equipment you are buying are exactly as they were represented, and if they're not, you expect to be consulted in advance. Presented properly, this idea shouldn't ruffle an honest reseller at all.

Particularly when purchasing a locally assembled computer, find out what kind of packing, manuals, and software you should expect. Verify that the components you're getting are what you ordered, and are indeed new if they're supposed to be. The main components you are buying should be accompanied by documentation, software, and, as possible, original packing:

Monitor	Manuals and Software and Packing
Keyboard and Mouse	Manuals and Software and Packing
Motherboard	Manuals and Software
Hard Drive	Manuals and Software
Video Card	Manuals and Software
Sound Card	Manuals and Software
Speakers	Manuals and Packing
Software	Manuals and Packing and Disks or Licence

Once you have the PC, watch carefully for two other elements: an accurate, written document showing everything you have purchased – what it is, how and when you paid for it, and how long it is guaranteed; and don't be afraid, once you have your new PC home, to take a very careful look at it. If you're so inclined, take the system's cover off and examine it inside. If you have any questions, now is the time for them; that's what your PC support team is for.

Copied Software

One of the most pervasive and damaging misrepresentations in the world of PC retailing is the practice of copying software in order to entice a purchaser to buy goods. The Canadian Alliance Against Software Theft (CAAST) says that software manufacturers are defrauded of millions of dollars each year because of this practice in Canada alone. For more details about different forms of applications and operating systems and the implications of copying them in different circumstances, refer to Chapter 4. Where your vendor stands on this issue speaks volumes about their reliability on other fronts. Even though improvements have been made in the areas of copy protection and software licensing in the past few years, it's still a quick, easy process to load an illegal product onto five, ten, or even fifty or more PCs.

Also, illegal software copying by a vendor sometimes happens because it's actually requested by a purchaser.

But any justification a retailer or user offers for stealing something is rubbish. People and companies are either honest or they are not. If a vendor offers to sell you a computer and cheat his software supplier at the same time, it's a clear indication that you should choose an alternate computer source.

THE EVIDENCE, PLEASE

What happens when you're confronted with hard evidence of these or similar problems impugning your supplier's integrity? First, make sure the information you have is accurate. Does your friend suspect your vendor on a hunch or did you open up the PC yourself and realize it was missing a hard drive? Is the evaluation software that reported your processor to be slower than advertised recent enough to recognize the new one that's installed? Is the opinion that you bought a bad PC coming from a person who is hoping to sell you a replacement?

Everyone's perception of buyers and sellers in the retail environment is somewhat different. I am sure some purchasers must regard all PC vendors as antagonists who are out to swindle their ways to fame and fortune. However, I suggest an even view when you're confronted with the possibility of deliberate misrepresentation. Be suspicious, but don't jump to conclusions. Contact the appropriate people in the company quickly – that is, as soon as you discover the problem – and describe it thoroughly. If a satisfactory explanation is not immediately forthcoming, watch very carefully for the following warning signs:

1. No timely response to your initial enquiry
2. No immediate explanation of the evidence you provide
3. Absence of a firm pledge to investigate and solve the problem quickly and to your satisfaction
4. Absence of continued action to solve the problem
5. Conflicting opinions from different people in the company
6. Inability or reluctance to commit to solving the problem in writing

Any vendor or manufacturer that cares about its customers will be eager and quick to deal with each of the steps above. If it is not, it's a clear signal of dishonesty.

LEGAL ACTION

In Canada, most legal actions to resolve disputes in the $3,000 to $6,000 range – and the majority of single PC purchases fall into this category – are resolved in small claims court. The law assumes you'll be able to purchase replacement goods to your liking, so it offers financial satisfaction as opposed to compelling a person or company to provide a specific service or piece of equipment.

A first step when such action becomes necessary is to make it known that you are indeed entering the legal arena. While this is not always a good idea, it may help to avoid further travel down a road that can become difficult and expensive. Make any communication brief, free of rancour, and to the point. State who you are, what happened, and how you want the situation resolved. Say what you think you should receive in the way of goods or payment, what action you plan to take, and when.

SAMPLE LETTER

The Date

The Manager
A Computer Company
Ontario, Canada

RE: COMPUTER PURCHASE

Dear Sir or Ms:

Please be advised that on Saturday, May 8, 1997, I paid $2,395 plus taxes (copies of my cancelled cheque and invoice are enclosed) for a personal computer from your company. The system was not functioning when I received it, and I returned it to you for replacement or repair under the terms of your warranty.

Despite several calls to your company, more than two months later I still have not received what I paid for. Please be advised that, unless my computer is returned in completely functional condition, or a suitable replacement is supplied, or a refund of my payment including taxes is issued within five business days, I will pursue the matter in provincial court.

Please contact me immediately to resolve this situation.

Sincerely,

It certainly doesn't hurt to have a lawyer begin advising you at this early stage, though it is not always necessary. You can issue a letter such as this yourself, and give the company or person time to respond. If nothing happens, or if the reply is unsatisfactory, move to stage 2.

SMALL CLAIMS COURT

While the general principles of small-claims actions are the same throughout Canada – a complainant seeking compensation pursues a defendant – details vary in different jurisdictions. In the Toronto area, for example, any claim under $6,000 is eligible, while actions for more money must be pursued in the Ontario Court, General Division. In other parts of the country this ceiling can be higher or lower. Still, since most single computer purchases fall under $5,000, lawsuits concerning them will be dealt with in the small-claims forum. This is fortunate; actions requiring the attention of higher courts almost always require more time, money, and legal expertise.

To start a small-claims action, visit the court office and fill out a statement of claim. In Ontario, this costs $50. Information booklets on how to do this are available in Toronto from an information hotline. It's a good idea to make a call to the court office in your area before presenting yourself in person. That way you'll have some idea of the steps involved and the information and documents required. Once you're sure you want to proceed, and your statement of claim is filed, the door opens for your adversary to file a defence. From here the process can vary, but major milestones include: serving the defendant with notice that an action has been started, attending the court or a hearing before a mediator (an appointed court official), receiving a judgment, and enforcing the finding. Here are a few notes to remember along the way:

- When preparing your statement don't forget to separate the amount of the claim from any interest or other costs. If a matter takes a long time to settle, these can add up. Extra costs do not normally affect your case's eligibility to be heard by a small claims court.
- Be very particular about getting the proper name of the person or company you pursue. A trade style may be owned by another entity, say, XYZXYZ Ontario Limited, operating as "Jack's Electronics." The recommended way to confirm this is to conduct a search of corporate trade styles, usually through a branch of the appropriate ministry in your province. This is not as complicated

as it may sound. It can be done in person or by mail, and in most cases costs less than $100. The results will show whether or not "Jack's Electronics" is part of another business entity, enabling you to pursue them with accuracy.

- Find out as much as you can about the time involved in the small-claims process: how long the whole action might take (three to five months is common), how many times and what time of day (day or night court) you may be asked to appear, and when you can expect satisfaction after a judgment is handed down. While court officials are not empowered to offer legal advice, they can often provide information about the steps in the process.
- Pay attention to your liabilities. Is your adversary likely to file a counterclaim? Will you run into rough terrain requiring a lawyer? If your opponent hires a lawyer or other assistance, what are your risks if you have to pay costs? What are the filing and other fees you'll encounter along the way?
- Finally, remember that you probably have choices about which small claims court to use. These include, but are not limited to, the jurisdiction in which the defendant conducts business, where the disputed transaction took place, or where the defendant resides. This choice can affect your eligibility for a small-claims hearing in the first place due to different maximums in different areas. Better to file a small-claims suit for $5,500 in one jurisdiction than to pursue the same matter in the more costly higher court of another.

YOU DON'T LIKE WHAT YOU BOUGHT

So your new PC is home from the store, all set up, plugged in, working the way it should, and guess what? You hate it! It's terrible! You'd really rather not have bought the thing in the first place. Perhaps the system is too slow and won't run the software you thought. Perhaps the software it does run is poorly designed and was horribly exaggerated. Perhaps the computer itself is poorly designed, or you feel it was slapped together cheaply, even though you're hard pressed to say exactly how and why. Perhaps now that you've tried the whole high-tech experience you've decided you'd rather not have anything more to do with computers and technology. Is there any way you can pick up the pieces of this mess?

Of all of the after-sale predicaments and pitfalls, this one is the most dependent on your vendor. To a secondary, though rare, extent, a manufacturer may also become involved. If you're the kind of individual who likes the ability to change his or her mind after a major purchase, take this into consideration before buying a PC! There are indeed computer outlets out there that will allow you blanket return options after a sale, sometimes with no questions asked.

On the other hand, most computer stores, large and small, have carefully thought-out return policies from which they usually will not deviate without a major fight. But let's suppose you didn't take this into account when you bought your PC, and now you'd like your money back.

There is nothing to prevent you from simply requesting a refund. It may even be a legal responsibility of the store in some cases. If it is not, companies can and do make exceptions to their policies when customer satisfaction is at stake. Needless to say, your chances of success in this situation are greatly enhanced if you alert them to your dissatisfaction soon after the sale – say, within ten days – and if you can convince or demonstrate to them that, even though it's been opened and slightly used, the equipment is as good as new and complete with all packing and manuals.

Second, you may be able to seek satisfaction from the manufacturer of the specific component with which you're unhappy. While they may not provide a flat refund, they might help rectify your original objections in a way you did not think possible, or provide you with a replacement you might find acceptable.

A last remedy in this situation is the substitution of goods by the vendor. Remember that when a store sells you something, they have marked it up and made a profit. If they have to provide a cash refund, not only are they getting back goods they may or may not be able to return to a distributor for credit – and cannot sell to someone else as new – they're also giving up the original sale. If you allow them to substitute other equipment – perhaps not even a computer system – you at least provide them with the opportunity to retain the profit of the original transaction. It's worth pointing this out to a vendor who does not appear willing to allow any after-sale redress.

YOU PAID TOO MUCH MONEY

Everyone always seems to think they paid too much money for a PC. As I've said elsewhere in this guide, new products appear in the high-tech marketplace faster and more regularly than most people realize – almost every week – which means the price of this equipment declines quickly indeed.

But how cheap is cheap? When is it appropriate to contact your vendor with the news that you saw the same thing at his competitor's store down the street at a much lower price?

This problem has been targeted by many stores who offer what is becoming an industry standard: the "best price" policy. This is designed as a selling tool to show that the advertised price of a store is the best available – it is not intended to protect you against the falling prices of computer equipment. In general, the policies work this way: a store advertises,

> **"Buy a computer from our place! Lowest Prices Guaranteed!"**
> The fine print reads, "We guarantee to beat any advertised competitor's price for the same equipment by 50 percent of the difference up to $50. Price guarantee does not apply to demo stock, special orders, or in-store promotions. Please see in store for details."

Well, at least they've taken the trouble to lay out some kind of policy toward their competitors, which is more than some outlets in the computer business can even manage. But remember, the competitor's price has to be advertised – that means proven in writing. Don't just walk into your supplier and tell them you saw the same thing cheaper down the street. Get a competitor's written quotation or published advertisement and go over it with a fine-tooth comb – your original supplier certainly will. Are the cheaper goods you saw really comparable?

And make sure you are invoking the price warranty on an eligible product – one that was not a demo, special order, or in-store promotion. There is leeway here, even after the sale, as to which products qualify, though we'll assume your original supplier clearly assigned these labels to their products because of their price guarantee in the first place. Finally, what about those worrisome in-store details? Most of these promises are good only during a specific period, anywhere from seven to thirty days after the sale. Obviously, no retailer can offer a price refund on PCs it sold a long time ago.

So what happens once all of these conditions have been satisfied? If you're at all interested in fine print, you'll have noticed that your supplier's maximum liability in this promise is only $50. It may be minimal protection, but you have to give your vendor credit for offering a best price policy at all. Not all computer suppliers do.

What if you have purchased a PC from a supplier that does not have a published policy on this issue? Is there any hope? No harm in asking.

Impose the same conditions you see offered by other pricing warranties: get written confirmation from the competition, present it quickly after the sale, and see what happens. Unless stated otherwise, your vendor is under no obligation to honour someone else's price, but in order to retain you as a customer, he very well might.

I'M SORRY, THAT NUMBER IS NO LONGER IN SERVICE

When your computer is acting up, or you just want advice from the guy who sold it to you, there is no more harrowing answer to your call for help than the famous: "I'm sorry, but the number you have dialled is no longer in service . . ."

Actually, of all after-sale possibilities this is not necessarily the worst, unless an outlet still owes you equipment, money, or service. In these cases, it's apparent that you're on your own. Legal pursuit of a disappearing vendor is a possibility which must be weighed against the importance of your unfinished business. But if his account with you is clear, many other support contingencies can be handled, particularly if the equipment you bought came from a third party. If the local computer store or high-tech franchise has gone belly-up and you've got a brand-name PC, your warranty and other after-sale issues can likely be addressed by the manufacturer. Approach them directly, first by phone (the situation may well be known to them), or, if need be, in writing, and request a recommendation to alternative authorized service providers. Expect the manufacturer and its new representatives to honour any remaining warranty and assist with out-of-warranty questions on operations or upgrades.

In the generic, or locally assembled, PC market, if the company that built and sold a system goes out of business, there is usually not much you can do. Your position is improved slightly if the components in your generic PC come from nationally recognized manufacturers. They might assist you, but OEM (Original Equipment Manufacturer) products commonly used in locally assembled PCs can be difficult to identify, even though they may have come from a major company. Where did those guys get that weird modem, anyway? If you can, you might find some warranty or support, or, at the very least, obtain a referral to a service provider who can help. Otherwise, be aware that the disappearance of your vendor is one of the prime risks involved in purchasing generic, or locally assembled, PCs. Insist on components from national or international manufacturers when you're wandering through this marketplace.

9

Your Existing Computer: What to Do with It

SHOULD YOU UPGRADE OR NOT?

There really are no hard-and-fast rules about how and when you should add to, or subtract from, your personal computer. All I can offer are observations about which parts will and won't fit together, when it makes sense to change them, and what to expect when you do.

First, if your system is running well and doing its job properly, may I suggest leaving it alone? Just because somebody invents a new computer part doesn't mean you have to buy it. New PC technology appears so often and is marketed so skillfully that it's easy to become convinced you just can't live without the latest hardware or software. Unfortunately, this overselling has set up many a purchaser for disappointment, and tarnished, to some degree, the reputation of the computer business.

On the other hand, people's requirements change, their skill levels increase, and they become acquisitive and curious. They want faster, more powerful equipment. If you already own one of the more than two hundred million PCs in use around the world in 1998, you've probably given some thought to improving it. Here are a few basic questions to consider.

1. *Why are you upgrading?* Take a good hard look at the reasons for changing your computer.
2. *What do you want the upgraded system to do?* Let the tasks you want

your improved PC to perform govern the money and components you put into it. Most important, will it really do what you want after you've finished?

3. *Is your system new enough to justify upgrading it?* If you get reasonable, reliable advice that your PC is too old to enhance, don't do it. At the time of publication, it's simply not practical to try to improve any XT, 286, 386, and, with a few exceptions now, 486 level computers. Macs with 68000, 68020, 68030, and even 68040 processors also fall into this category.
4. *Who will perform the upgrade work?* Decide at the beginning whether you are going to perform this surgery yourself. If you are, get all the necessary manuals, parts, and tools. Identify a support person to whom you can turn if your efforts are unsuccessful. Also, be sure to allow yourself a reasonable amount of time to complete the job.
5. *Have you considered your budget?* Remember that one of the primary goals of the upgrade scenario, in addition to winding up with a better computer, is to save money. But on any given day you can buy a one- or two-year-old used PC for $700 to $1,000, or a basic new one for $1,100 to $1,400. If your parts and labour costs come close to these figures, think about replacing what you've got.

Remember the different possibilities. You can upgrade what you have, you can sell what you have privately and reinvest the money in another system, or you can trade in what you have on something better. More often than not, the age and design of your existing PC will dictate whether upgrading is even a possibility, making your decision that much easier. But when you do have the option of upgrading, here are some other things to consider:

- Selling your computer privately takes work, but should net you more money. Take special note of its resale value, and what a replacement will cost. Is the difference more or less than it would cost to improve the old one?
- Trading in your computer on a better model is easier than flogging the old warhorse yourself. But your reseller is only going to allow you its wholesale value – 25 percent or perhaps 50 percent less than you might expect if you sell it yourself. Is the reduced effort worth the smaller reward?

If you weigh these concepts and realize your system is indeed new enough to be improved, and that the upgraded result will satisfy your requirements, the next step is to determine exactly what parts should be enhanced. This means analyzing its subsystems one by one.

CPU AND OVERDRIVE CHIPS

As the shoulders on which the speed of the subsystems in your PC rest, your computer's processor is one of the most likely places to look when considering how to improve its performance. In the easiest cases, a CPU chip can simply be removed and replaced with a faster one. CPU receptacles which allow this are referred to as ZIF (zero insertion force) sockets. In some motherboards there may be a separate socket to accept the faster chip, which, when installed, should disable the original.

If you can't remove your old CPU and have no place to add a new one, you'll need to replace the motherboard as well – an expense which means you must reevaluate the upgrade.

Consider upgrading your CPU only when you have a 486 or a Pentium. If you have a slower 486 (50 MHz or less) PC that will accept a faster CPU, the situation may be workable, provided that after the improvement you'll be satisfied with a system that is still out of date. Common 486 upgrades involve replacing a DX/25- or 33-MHz CPU with so-called replacements that speed up the system to 75 to 133 MHz. More rarely, 486 motherboards, particularly those manufactured in the year before Intel introduced its Pentium CPUs in 1993, have a socket capable of accepting a Pentium processor or 686 equivalent. For the most part, these sockets did not accept the whole range of Pentium CPUs – they were limited to special issues that went for more than $300 – and offer not all that much of an improvement in performance by today's standards. This "Pentium-upgradeable" feature in some 486s was as much a marketing tool as a viable upgrade. Indeed, in some cases the special Pentium upgrade chips that were supposed to become available for certain motherboards never even appeared.

In any event, improvements to a 486 today are reasonable only if you need a system for a utilitarian purpose – for an isolated task which is never going to change. Otherwise, you are not even going to be within shouting distance of the programs, components, and Internet features most users want today.

When upgrading the CPU in a Pentium PC, the main features to look for are the generation of the processor and the socket on the motherboard into which it fits. Intel alone has produced four families of CPUs (Pentium, Pentium Pro, Pentium with MMX, and Pentium II). Alternatively, a recent PC might contain a CPU from a third-party processor manufacturer such as AMD (American Micro Devices). Each class of CPU has physical features peculiar to it, and these determine how it can be replaced. They relate to a processor's size and the voltage it requires. The oldest classic Pentium CPUs, for example, fit into an aperture design known as a Socket 5. Newer classic Pentiums (120 MHz and faster) and Pentium MMX CPUs require a Socket 7, though MMXs require a slightly different voltage. The socket type on your old Pentium motherboard will determine whether it will accept a new Pentium MMX 233 CPU.

The newest Pentium II processors require yet a third class of socket, being larger than their earlier counterparts. They fit into a single edge contact (SEC) connector simply not found on Pentium MMX and Classic Pentium PCs. So to upgrade to this highest level of processor you'll have to change your motherboard.

The only way to be really sure about your CPU upgrade options is to study your motherboard's manuals, or, of course, get assistance from a professional. For a more in-depth look at the features of different kinds of processors and how they can be upgraded in certain systems, Myles White's book *How to Avoid Buying a New Computer* (McClelland and Stewart, 1997) is an excellent reference.

CHANGING YOUR MOTHERBOARD

Like CPU chips, motherboards have been issued in several designs. This is important if you're thinking of changing the one you own now. First, the replacement must physically be able to fit into the case you have and must be able to support all of the subsystems the old one did. Either that or you must be prepared to replace such components as the video card or the hard drive controller. Again, the total cost must be kept in mind. A motherboard swap that makes you buy too many accompanying parts may not be worth it. In addition to size (form factor) and expansion bus design, other features to consider when looking at old and new motherboards are the kinds of CPUs, the RAM chips, logic chipsets, and cache chips they support. All of these are important when examining your old setup to see what you can keep and what you must throw away.

As with processor upgrades, if you have anything slower than a late-issue 486 computer, it's probably not worth replacing your motherboard at all. Too many other parts of the system will either have to be changed or, if left in, will slow it down, defeating the purpose of the project.

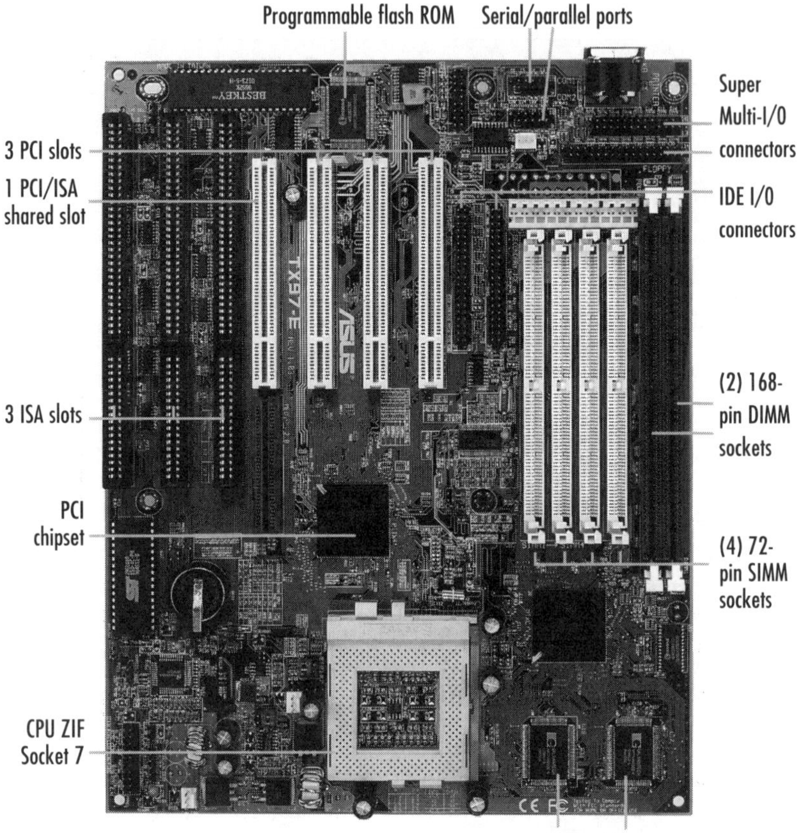

FIGURE 9A

Parts of a typical motherboard

If you are replacing a motherboard in a Pentium-level PC it is probably because you can't simply swap the CPU. Some features – RAM types and logic chipsets, for example – common to Pentium and Pentium MMX motherboards are interchangeable, but can't be accommodated by motherboards used in Pentium IIs.

You may now own an original Intel Pentium, or a newer Pentium MMX–compatible motherboard, and want to move up. It is important to note that computers powered by all four of the Pentium processor groups – the original Pentium (sometimes called a Pentium Classic), Pentium MMX, Pentium Pro, and Pentium II – can contain a variety of motherboards. It's difficult to outline rules about when you can and can't change them without referring directly to your motherboard manual.

Some motherboards are upgradeable in certain ways and not in others. Major characteristics to look at when changing them are:

1. The processor socket: The voltage supplied to, and size of, a motherboard's processor aperture are important in determining which CPU you can put in your upgraded computer. Original Pentium processors needed a 3.3-volt socket. Some boards containing these also offer an overdrive socket for a second CPU. Pentium MMX processors need a 2.7-volt socket. Some motherboards contain variable or dual-voltage processor sockets. Pentium II CPUs require a special SEC connector.
2. The logic chipset and BIOS: Some motherboards in original Pentium computers contain logic chips and a BIOS (basic input output system) which support newer MMX processors, while others do not. Early Pentium PC motherboards will not support the newest Pentium II processors. The chipset and BIOS must support the processor in any upgraded system.
3. The RAM chips: Older, classic Pentium motherboards normally accept 72-pin SIMMs (single in-line memory modules). Motherboards in the newest Pentium II–level PCs usually accept SDRAM (synchronous dynamic random-access memory) only. Some Pentium MMX PC motherboards will accept both.
4. The form factor: This is the aspect of a motherboard's design that makes it physically compatible with the case and other subsystems in one computer, and not in another. Classic Pentium and Pentium MMX motherboards are typically described as being of the "AT form factor"; Pentium II motherboards are of the "ATX form factor."

So to improve your system, choose a motherboard with the fastest processor you can afford. Determine whether your computer can accommodate a Pentium MMX– or Pentium II–compatible board, as they're different. In either case, be sure you can remove and replace the CPU later. Look for an up-to-date logic chipset and BIOS, with at least 32, and preferably 64, megabytes of SDRAM. You'll need seven or eight expansion slots to accommodate PCI and ISA connector cards, and 512K cache.

In practical terms, once you have decided on a new motherboard, your PC will have to be torn down and reassembled from scratch. This is a fascinating and instructive exercise, recommended to anyone interested in microelectronics and computers. By the end of it all, you'll know a lot more about your PC than when you started. But if you're in doubt about the process, hire help. Have a look at the end of this chapter for more information about the choice of upgrading your own PC as opposed to having someone do it for you.

ADDING AND CHANGING RAM

One of the easiest and most cost-effective ways to improve the performance of a PC is to increase its memory. As we saw in Chapter 3 there are different kinds of memory chips in personal computer systems. Three that often figure in the upgrade scenario are:

1) The main memory. On the motherboard, this is usually known simply as a PC's RAM.
2) The cache. This is known as cache RAM or, less commonly, as Level 2 memory.
3) The video memory. Known simply as video memory, it may come in the forms DRAM, VRAM, WRAM, and SGRAM.

RAM: Main Memory Upgrades

A chief target of envy, discussion, and endless speculation among computer users of all levels, a PC's random-access memory ranks with its processor and motherboard in determining overall performance. But unlike the other two components, RAM is usually easy and inexpensive to add or replace, so it's a favourite target of improvement. In most 486 and Pentium PCs today, RAM chips meet design standards which make it possible for even inexperienced users to change them. Still the most common of these are 72-pin SIMMs (single in-line memory modules), running at speeds of 70 or 80 nanoseconds. SDRAM (synchronous dynamic random-access memory) is newer, and it has remarkable abilities to perform floating-point calculations and remember commonly used data paths. Both of these kinds of memory chips are available in forms that allow you to plug them into a recent motherboard. Removing chips can be a little trickier. It's easy to bend one of the tiny prongs, or leads, on the piece when taking these small components out. A tool called a chip fork has been designed for this task – it's like a small pair of tweezers with a spring between the tongs which allows you to grasp the memory module and pull it out evenly.

If you're thinking about upgrading your RAM, the same criteria apply as to any other improvement: value, compatibility, performance, and balance. On a pre-486 system which might be used for a specific task, RAM is about the only thing you should consider upgrading. The ability to run a particular program may justify the investment. The saving grace is that memory for some old PCs can be quite cheap.

Without offering a detailed discussion of sizes and standards of memory in pre-486 systems, these PCs could usually be improved by adding 30-pin modules in different combinations of 1, 2, 4, 8, or 16 megabytes. There were a few exotic types of chips prominent in those days, such as SIPPs. If you can find them, and you're not worried about putting money into an old-timer, these upgrades can still serve a limited purpose in some situations.

Next generation RAM chips appeared in the 72-pin design, running at speeds of 70 and 80 nanoseconds (billionths of a second), and usually assembled in groups of 4, 8, 16, 32, and 64 megabytes. These are common in 486, classic Pentium, and Pentium MMX systems. Mac standards are 72-pin SIMMs for 68K (non-Power PC) CPUs, and 168-pin DIMMs (dual in-line memory module) for Power PCs. These too run at 70 and 80 nanoseconds.

In Windows-based computers, most current motherboards require that you install RAM modules in pairs – two 16-MB SIMMs to add 32 MB to your system, two 32-MB SIMMs to total 64 MB, and so on. There can be a mix of different sizes of memory on these boards, as long as each two-chip set is of the same size, speed, and type.

Since 1996, two new memory standards have become popular: EDO (extended data out) SIMMs, and SDRAM. You can't mix EDO and non-EDO SIMMs or EDO and SDRAM. This is important if you are adding RAM to a PC.

One approach to this compatibility problem is to remove all memory from your computer and start anew, in which case the type of motherboard you have becomes an issue, as does the trade-in value of the memory you have removed. Your motherboard will determine what kind of SIMMs you can throw at it, so it's essential to know. Verify this by looking at the chips yourself, or removing them and taking them to a dealer so they can be matched. Alternatively, you can read your motherboard manual, which should state explicitly the type of chips it will accept.

Once you've stuck the extra memory into your PC, you shouldn't need to do anything else – the system should recognize them automatically. As when upgrading a system's motherboard or CPU, you'll see an almost universal improvement, no matter what computing task you attempt.

Cache

This more obscure upgrade path can in fact improve the performance of a PC significantly. As described in Chapter 3, cache is a small amount of high-speed (15- to 20-nanosecond) memory which makes sure there is always some data ready to be handled by the processor. A PC's cache acts as a buffer between the processor and the system's RAM, thereby increasing overall efficiency. Some motherboards – early 486s and older – had little or no capacity for cache RAM at all. Others were limited to 8K, 64K, or 256K maximums. Pentium-level motherboards usually have 256K or 512K, and 1- and 2-megabyte cache standards are on the way. Like system memory, cache is user-installable, provided you're able to buy the correct chips in the first place. Again, it's not worth spending money upgrading the cache RAM of an older 486 motherboard.

Cache chips have to match the speed and form of a motherboard. They have appeared in different types over the years, with 32-pin DIMMs (dual in-line memory modules) being common. They are usually sold in sets, plugged into six or eight special slots, and accompanied by a specific cache controller chip. Some Pentium-level motherboards will also accept a new form of cache memory known as "cache on a stick," or COAST. These allow up to 1 megabyte, and will provide a significant improvement in a system's performance.

Video RAM

Improvements to the memory on the video card in your PC may or may not significantly improve its performance, depending on the applications you run.

In older systems, video cards were controlled by the CPU. In most Pentium-based computers, these cards play a more active role in the processing of data passing through them. So by increasing the video memory in your PC you can realize tremendous gains if you run graphics-based applications – viewing drawings, retouching photographs, or running picture-oriented games from the Internet or CD-ROMs. If you are performing tasks such as video editing, lots of video RAM is a must. It is secondary to the importance of the CPU and the PC's main RAM, but lack of it can slow down a computer considerably. It's also worth noting that memory in a video subsystem can be peculiar to the video card you have, so we now see product-specific upgrades. Some common video card memory types are DRAM, VRAM, SGRAM, and WRAM. Most older video cards will require 25- to 30-nanosecond DRAM, or dynamic random-access memory, which is a speedier, smaller version of the chips in the main memory of the motherboard. More recent cards – those most likely to be found in Pentium-level PCs – may accept VRAM (video random-access memory), or a manufacturer-specific equivalent.

The chief advantage of faster VRAM chips is their design: they have the ability to process data both coming and going, instead of bringing it in, clocking it, then sending it back out.

Apart from increasing the speed of your PC, more RAM on the video card allows your monitor to show more colours at higher resolutions. This will allow your picture to appear finer, although the objects being displayed will be smaller. Higher resolutions are usually best viewed on a larger (17-inch or larger) monitor. More memory on a video card also helps your PC draw larger numbers of colours at a faster speed. There's a trade-off when you set a monitor to a higher resolution without video RAM: your monitor won't be able to show as many colours. Video memory never used to matter much in the text-based DOS world, but in today's graphical environment, your computer is always drawing things. The strength of its video card can have a lot to do with how realistic a photo looks, or how quickly a video clip plays.

So think about the kinds of applications you run, and how fast the other components in your computer are. If you have anything less than a 75-MHz Pentium CPU with 16 MB of RAM on a reasonably recent (less than two years old) motherboard, you should probably consider putting your money into other, more fundamental components – a better CPU, more RAM, a new motherboard, or even a more fully featured video card.

If you do own a relatively recent PC and decide to improve its video card memory, be sure to purchase the right type. Upgrading from 2 to 4 MB of DRAM is of questionable value. If your card will accept the change, you might consider removing all of the old DRAM and converting to VRAM. You'll see a marked increase in performance if you do.

Finally, how much is all of this going to cost? The good news is that video card DRAM is normally inexpensive, ranging from $15 to $20 per megabyte at the time of publication. Faster, more desirable VRAM, SGRAM, and WRAM can range from $25 to $40 per megabyte. At these prices, while extra memory for your video card may not be at the top of your upgrade list, it can be an inexpensive and easy way to improve the performance of your PC.

VIDEO CARD UPGRADES AND MONITORS

It may be worth a look back at Chapter 3 to refresh your memory about the ins and outs of video cards, video RAM, and monitors before proceeding any further.

As we have seen, there are three elements in your computer's video system which are to be considered in the upgrade scenario, all of which affect the speed and clarity of the images it can display. These are the video card or adapter; the amount of memory it has; and, of course, the monitor itself. Is it possible to upgrade a monitor? Sure – just buy a new one, and give the old one away! Seriously, your monitor is one of the parts of a PC that you really have to get right on the day you purchase it, because you'll be stuck with it until it gives out. You can, I suppose, trade it in for a better one at a store which allows this, but unless you already have a recent 15- or 17-inch display, don't expect much more than a few bucks.

As we saw in Chapter 3, your video card plugs into a slot on your motherboard (into the expansion bus). I should note that in the past some PCs came with what are known as VGA adapters, not cards. The difference is that a card is removable, while an adapter is physically part of a motherboard – the video circuitry and VGA port, or opening, into which you plug in your monitor is integrated into the main board's design. It's possible in most of these cases to disable the video adapter and add a new, better video card, but check with the motherboard's manufacturer before going ahead. If your system has an integrated VGA adapter, chances are it's so old you shouldn't bother to upgrade it anyway.

When is it a good idea to change your video card? Look at your PC as a whole, again keeping the issue of balance in mind. Are you thinking of putting a fast, expensive video card on a slow, outdated motherboard, or matching it with a CPU that really should be replaced instead? Only late-model 486 and Pentium PCs are reasonable candidates for these kinds of improvements.

If you can't simply add or replace the chips on your existing video card to improve its performance, the whole thing has to go. Be sure you know a few things about your system when planning the switch.

First, you'll need a new card which is compatible with your motherboard. That means matching a PCI, VESA, or ISA expansion slot. Note that PCI is the dominant standard in 1998; it doesn't make much sense to purchase an upgraded VESA video card, though they're still available.

Things to watch for in a video card are its transmission characteristics; the amount, type, and maximum levels of its memory; whether it supports MPEG, MPEG-2, or other multimedia transmissions; and any other special features, such as the ability to accept data from a TV cable or VCR.

Common characteristics of major video card types are shown in the table below, which gives an idea of the wide variety of products that have appeared since 1980.

If you're going to the trouble of making this kind of upgrade, try to pick one from a major manufacturer: ATI, Trident, Matrox, or Diamond are all well known. Seek a minimum of 2 megabytes of VRAM, with a maximum of 8, to allow you room to grow. You'll need it – applications keep getting more and more graphics intensive. Finally, insist on a card capable of the MPEG-2 (Motion Picture Experts Group) transmission protocol. This is a software and hardware data transmission standard which allows the smooth display of sound and video – a must when you are using new CD-ROMs and digital video discs (DVDs) that contain video clips. When purchasing a DVD and video card

SAMPLE VIDEO CARD CHARACTERISTICS

CARD TYPE	RESOLUTION	COLOURS
MDA (Monochrome Display Adapter)	720 by 350	2
	600 by 400	2
CGA (Colour Graphics Adapter)	640 by 200	8
	320 by 240	8
	320 by 200	8
EGA (Enhanced Graphics Adapter)	640 by 350	16
	640 by 200	16
	320 by 200	16
VGA (Video Graphics Array)	640 by 480	16
	320 by 200	256+
S/VGA (Super Video Graphics Array)	800 by 600	16
	1,024 by 768	256+
	1,280 by 1,024	256+
	1,600 by 1,200	256+
8514/A	1,024 by 768	256+
XGA (Extended Graphics Array)	640 by 480	256+
	1,024 by 768	256+
TI 34010	1,024 by 768	256+

FIGURE 9B

together, be sure to check that the card can handle the full-motion video images the drive sends to it. It if can't, you'll have to buy a separate card to help the system display movies from the DVD.

Demand for extra video support is no longer limited to games. Even the most serious office and business software contains multimedia. The video capabilities of your PC can no longer be ignored.

ADDING AND CHANGING A HARD DRIVE

If you like to collect things, you probably turned to this upgrade section first. Even if you're a fastidious computer user, various files, programs, Internet plug-ins, and other shreds of data can accumulate in your PC faster than you can say Steve Jobs. It then becomes tempting to run out and buy new hardware to accommodate all the information you've saved, rather than get out your broom and clean house. So a replaced or added hard drive is a very common upgrade path.

One of the first things to consider is what to do with your old drive – remove it completely, or leave it in and simply add a new one. Factors affecting this decision are the size of your existing hard drive, the design of your computer (whether it will physically accommodate an additional drive), and, of course, whether you actually need the extra storage in the first place.

You shouldn't consider adding or replacing a hard drive in a system with a 386 or earlier processor except under very special circumstances. Even in a 486 running at 66 MHz or less, it's hard to justify the upgrade unless you have a specific computing task in mind. In Pentium-level systems, it begins to make sense. You simply get more closet space. What a new hard drive won't do is increase the speed of your PC.

If you do have a recent system which will benefit from increased storage, the next step is to determine the size and type of the new drive you need, and how you're going to get it in the PC.

For a discussion of different hard drive types, their controlling devices and performances, have a look at Chapter 3. As far as installing a new one is concerned, this is a task that's about two-thirds of the way up the difficulty scale. A proper "kit" purchased from a parts vendor should include not only the drive itself, but also any "rails" – mounting hardware – proper cables, and screws that may be necessary. And don't forget documentation. Even with these aids, this is an upgrade best handled by a technician.

The following steps are generally necessary to the successful installation of a new or replacement hard drive: first, the new drive must be connected to the motherboard inside the PC by an appropriate cable. Next, the computer must be configured – that is, it must be made aware of the new device attached to it. In most cases, the drive then has to be formatted, or prepared to receive data, and, at some point, physically mounted inside the PC.

Experienced tinkerers reading this description will probably be quick to notice four or five other steps left out of the drive installation procedure. I intended to give only a basic account of the mechanics of the process, to allow a person without technical experience to determine whether he or she is interested in taking on the task in the first place.

Add or Replace?

As I have already pointed out, you can remove your old drive and replace it, or you can keep it and add a new one. In most cases the second option is simpler. You buy the piece, bolt it in (or have it done for you), tell the system it's there, and start working. But, the presence of two storage reservoirs can present problems and the extra physical space the new drive occupies may be an issue. Most PCs today, however, allow for the inclusion of several 3.5 format internal devices, so it's not likely that you'll actually run out of room.

Perhaps the main drawback to the replacement scenario is getting your data from the old device onto the new one. Back in the days before Microsoft Windows 95, and even before Windows 3.1, dumping programs and files from directory to directory was easier than it is today. Current applications like to insinuate themselves into various subdirectories which are not necessarily straightforward to copy, regardless of whether you are transferring data from one drive to another in the same system, or between two separate PCs with a program such as Laplink.

This is not to say that data transfers are impossible, or even that they should always be avoided. But they can be tricky.

In some cases the easiest way to reconstruct a hard drive is to reload the operating system and all your applications. But weren't we doing all this because we had so much stuff in the darned computer in the first place? So this is a dilemma. At the very least, before attempting a data transfer or having someone do it for you, follow two rules: back up and clean up. Back up so you can avoid seeing your irreplaceable data erased in a second or two of absentmindedness. And clean up your drive by going through all files and applications carefully, deleting anything you don't want, or storing on external media the information you don't use very often. A warning though: when meandering through your system looking for data to erase, be careful! If you're in doubt about a file, leave it alone.

As far as price is concerned, hard drives are one of the most relentlessly devaluing computer components available. A 1.2-gigabyte model you paid about $300 for when you bought your system in 1997 isn't even on the market in 1998. The good news is that you can buy a 4- to 6-gigabyte replacement for almost the same money. So this is a good upgrade to consider.

MULTIMEDIA: CD, SOUND, AND SPEAKERS

Multimedia – playing sound clips or showing moving pictures – is a capability most of us have come to expect in computers today. To perform these tasks, you need a sound card, CD-ROM drive or DVD, and speakers. If your system doesn't already contain them, the first question to ask is whether the PC can support them and perform well with them installed.

Again the cut-off point is a late-model 486 (66 MHz or faster) system. Many computers below this level can accept and manage a CD-ROM and sound card, but they'll operate them at a crawl.

If you choose to add multimedia to a PC that doesn't already have them, you've got two further decisions: should you buy the components separately and figure the puzzle out yourself, or buy a kit from a company like Creative Labs or Hewlett-Packard? With a kit, everything comes in one package – the CD-ROM drive, sound card, speakers, and necessary installation hardware and software. The drawback is that you have to accept all the stuff the company's marketing department thinks you'll want. Usually, too, these packages cost more money. (At the time of publication the 24x CD multimedia kit from Creative Labs – a leader in the field of pre-packaged multimedia – retailed at about $399.) Still, if you're thinking of doing this upgrade yourself, these kits are a good bet. They're better supported and less prone to incompatibilities than a set of devices you bought à la carte.

A second route is to take your PC to a vendor who will sell you the components and install them for you. In this scenario, even when you ask for parts from recognized manufacturers – and you should – you will probably not get all of the extras included in a retail package. Most computer service stores assume that you'll be happy with OEM (original equipment manufacturer) components. These come with minimal packaging, skimpy or non-existent documentation, and, in some cases, reduced warranty and support. Ask about all of these things if you're having a PC upgraded for multimedia. On the plus side, buying "white box," or OEM, parts will probably save you a little cash, but insist that the equipment be tested in your presence before you carry it away. Listen to the speakers (make sure they're plugged into the sound card, not just into the CD-ROM drive). Watch a demonstration of the system playing a video. Make sure that all multimedia properties are working before accepting it. Otherwise, it's all too easy for a vendor to claim that your system was altered after it left their possession. They may then charge to perform a configuration that should have been done properly in the first place.

To be fair to the service provider, you wouldn't believe the ways in which people can take a properly configured PC and trash it. Still, after a computer has left the store, it's one party's word against another's, and this can lead to disagreement and trouble. Make sure everything works before bringing it home.

DVDs

As an alternative to adding a CD-ROM drive or replacing your old one, consider upgrading to a digital video disc, or DVD, drive. With the capacity to hold more than four times as much information as conventional 630-megabyte CDs, digital video discs are rapidly becoming the storage medium of choice for both home computers and televisions; in fact, with their better image quality and other advantages such as digital zoom, picture in picture, and high-definition slow motion, they stand poised to surpass even videotape cassettes in popularity.

As with most emerging communications technologies, however, questions have arisen regarding standards: which DVD drive will work in which computing environment, and what components must be present if full performance is to be expected? For example, many video cards are not yet equipped to handle the increased throughput of multimedia data delivered by DVDs without assistance from an expensive multimedia DVD adapter, or "decoder card," which is specially designed to allow the smooth playback of movies – surely one of a DVD drive's greatest attractions. DVDs also offer zoom, freeze-frame, and other manipulations of high-quality video images on demand. Without extra components, a DVD will perform conventional CD-ROM functions.

Undoubtedly this technology will stabilize during 1998, pressured as it is from both the computer and consumer electronics industries. In the meantime, it's important to enquire about all necessary hardware and software when considering this upgrade, and to be sure that your new, enhanced system will be compatible with emerging standards.

MODEMS AND THE INTERNET

One of the most common improvements people want to make to PCs is to add or replace a modem. The explosion of the Internet has made it imperative to have the fastest possible means of sending and receiving data. Other applications involving modems are the new host/remote programs that allow you to use one computer to call another and run a program over the phone. Symantec PC Anywhere and Norton Lambert Close-Up are good examples of these. They allow you freedom to move, and access to your PC at the same time.

So a modem makes it possible for your system to deal with the outside world, and its speed is critical. Modems have evolved over the years from the snail-paced 300 baud products of the early '80s up to the 56 Kbps (kilobits per second) and faster ISDN (integrated service digital network) issues of today.

A word about the two physical types of modems – internal and external. The obvious difference here is that an external modem is a separate box that sits on top of a PC and plugs into its serial port. These are easier to add if you plan to take the project on yourself. Be sure when you buy one that the right cable is included. You should be able to plug this in, run the software it came with, and get connected. One possible wrinkle in this scenario is the old modem which may already be in your PC. In Windows 95/98, or even 3.x versions, you should be able to disable this easily.

An internal modem is a card about four inches by three. It fits into one of the expansion slots inside your PC, and has two telephone jacks – one coming in from the wall, one going out to your telephone set, so you can still have a phone on your desk.

You can try installing or changing an internal modem yourself, especially if you're interested in the process and you're not under a deadline. Your system should have at least a 486 CPU running at 66 MHz or faster and your new modem should be a 56K model. It's not advisable to surf the Internet with anything slower, although sending and receiving email can be done with a 386 PC and 9,600-baud or 14.4 Kbps modem.

If you are considering an email-only setup, check with your Internet service provider. Many of them have a minimum allowable modem speed, because slow transmissions tie up their lines. If you buy any kind of used modem, be sure to get proper manuals – they're critical.

Apart from adding a modem to a computer which doesn't have one, most modem upgrades involve moving from the 14.4, 28.8, or 33.6

Kbps product up to the new "56K" standard. What is this new speed all about, anyway?

56K Yin, 56K Yang

At the time this guide was published, data transmission from the Internet at 56 Kbps was being offered in two competing, but incompatible, modem standards, each hoping to gain the upper hand.

First off the mark in early 1997 were the new "x2" 56K products from US Robotics, the world's largest manufacturer of consumer modems. A few months later, competing modems from Rockwell International, in association with Motorola and Lucent Technologies (formerly Bell Labs), appeared.

Soon after the competing standards appeared, communications giant 3Com, which was already allied with the Rockwell/Lucent group, purchased a major stake in US Robotics. 3Com found itself backing both sides, so it would appear that a single 56K standard will soon be established.

In the meantime, differences in the designs of these two groups of products may not mean all that much to consumers – since both make claims to equivalent speeds – but Internet service providers have a dilemma. ISPs have had to decide whether to invest in equipment that complies with the USR technology, or the Rockwell/Lucent standard, which is now known as 56K Flex. Some large providers, including Compuserve and Netcom, decided early in the fray on x2. To date, according to USR, thousands of other ISPs have followed suit, though it is still not clear which standard will prevail.

To further strengthen its position, USR licensed its x2 design to modem manufacturers Logicode and Cardinal Technologies, as well as offering free upgrades to some of its existing Courier V.x and Sportster 33.6 models. Eligible users can log onto the USR website, (x2.usr.com/news/ships.html), download the appropriate software, and run it to modify the modem already in their PCs.

So regardless of the type of 56K product you purchase, remember it has to match your service provider's choice – even then, you'll be able to achieve high transfer speeds during downloading only. Still, when surfing the Net, this is the direction that counts. For the time being, when talking back to your server you have to be content with 28.8 and 33.6 Kbps, though this too will undoubtedly change.

Also, note that while the new hardware is capable of supporting 56 Kbps, existing phone lines don't. They top out at about 53 Kbps because of practical and legal limits on the power a modem can present to the telephone system. A review of USR's x2 technology in *PC Magazine* reported downloads in the 40–50 Kbps range – still pretty impressive.

All of this is to advise you that you shouldn't buy a new modem before checking with your Internet service provider to see which standard it supports. Also, be sure the make and model of the modem you purchase are current. As of March 1998, 56K products had been on the market for over a year. As one Internet service provider recently warned me, if you buy a K56 Flex product that's more than six months old, it's almost certain to require an updated chipset or software tweak in order to work with ISP technology today. The x2 products suffer less from these incompatibilities.

ISDN Modems

No discussion of modem upgrades would be complete without mention of ISDN products. Once the domain of corporations who could afford these "specialty" connections, most phone companies offer this wider pipeline at prices at lot of people can now afford, on average $50 to $75 per month. ISDN service offers two-way transmission at either 64 Kbps or, for a little more money, 128 Kbps. You need a special ISDN modem to handle this speed; these are available from most major manufacturers and at the time of publication cost anywhere from $250 to $600.

SOME NUTS AND BOLTS

Finally a note or two about upgrades in general. When considering enhancing any PC, don't be afraid to ask a dealer or consultant for a third-party opinion about what components you need and the time required to install them. Don't forget to consider the software on your upgraded computer – are you purchasing a new operating system or other programs? Who is going to reload your old programs and files if this is necessary? How long will all of this take? Lastly, as I have advised elsewhere in this chapter, be sure to compare the total cost of your upgraded PC against what it would cost to sell your current system privately or trade it in, and buy a replacement. If the difference is less than $250, consider the replacement.

10

Selling Your Computer System

WHAT ARE YOU SELLING?

The first order of salesmanship is: know exactly what you have to offer. So spend a little time on this by creating an accurate description of your PC and all of its components. Find your old bill of sale if you can, and any records or documents pertaining to your PC's upgrades and peripherals. You should be readily able to describe your PC's manufacturer and specifications in a positive way.

If your computer was assembled locally you should be able to tell a possible buyer where it came from and when you purchased it. If you have a system from a recognized builder such as IBM, NEC, AST, or Compaq, so much the better. You undoubtedly paid more for the quality control and after-sale security these companies offer in the first place, so it's perfectly reasonable to ask a bit more when you sell. Below is a list of the main elements that fix the value of a personal computer in today's marketplace. Even though you need not put all of this information in your advertisements, you should do your best to be able to answer questions about these items should a customer ask. If you need help understanding what some of the terms mean, turn to Chapter 3 or the glossary for explanation.

- Processor level: 386/486/586/686/Pentium/Pentium MMX/Pentium II, Apple 68030/68040, Power PC 601/603e/604e?
- Processor speed: how many megahertz?

- RAM: how many megabytes, what kind of RAM, its speed in nanoseconds?
- Hard drive: manufacturer, seek time, size in megabytes or gigabytes?
- Video card characteristics: manufacturer, type and amount of video memory?
- Monitor: screen size (diagonal), monitor type, dot pitch, manufacturer, refresh rate?
- Printer: manufacturer, printer speed (pages per minute), general condition, status of consumables (toner, drum, ribbon, etc.), amount of RAM if it's a laser or LED, paper-handling capabilities (sheet-feed or tractor)?
- Additional special system features:
  Compact disc: manufacturer, speed (4x, 8x, 24x, 32x)?
  Sound card: manufacturer, special characteristics?
  Modem: manufacturer, speed, fax capabilities, software?
- Other special peripherals: tape backup system, special keyboard, DVD, scanner?

YOUR TARGET MARKET

Now it's time to consider different sections of the computer market from a seller's perspective. All kinds of businesses and individuals are interested in used PCs, of course, but try to imagine who among them might want to buy yours: a specific company? a student who is primarily interested in wordprocessing? a tinkerer who might want to cannibalize your system for its parts? a professional who wants to run the same specialized programs that you do?

The specifications of your computer are a good base from which to determine who might want to buy it. What are you using the system for now? Assuming it is in working condition, there is probably someone out there who can make use of it in the same way you are – there's your buyer.

There is still one other decision to make: whether to sell your computer to a dealer or a user. This will determine, in most cases, how much money you'll get, and how much work and aggravation you should expect before and after the sale.

Selling to a Dealer

The first thing to remember when you approach a dealer about selling your computer is that they're going to view it as a commodity. The main issue in their equation is to make money, so be prepared to have any sentimental and aesthetic attachments to your computer immediately swept aside. When you take a PC to most vendors, or resellers, they will attempt to acquire your computer at the lowest possible price, so they can resell it for maximum profit. This raises the important issue of the difference between wholesale and retail prices. Many people seem to forget this when they try to sell their equipment to a dealer. Buying computers below the normal market price is the dealer's aim, so when selling to one, be prepared to settle for as much as 10 to 40 percent less than you might expect from a user.

You should also keep in mind that a dealer will likely want to see some proof of ownership and identification to verify that he is not accepting stolen property, and will also probably want to keep your computer for a day or two to evaluate it. Before taking a system to a store, remove your personal files and programs from it. No responsible reseller will assume liability for data or software in a computer they are evaluating.

What are the advantages of selling to a dealer? Time and energy. As with any transaction, price is only one of the elements that make it a success or failure. Perhaps you have an unusual piece which you've tried to unload privately without success. Perhaps you have been operating in a vacuum and had it priced too high. Perhaps your situation demands that you get the system sold in very short order. In any of these circumstances, you're perfectly justified to go to a reseller who will be able to evaluate your computer quickly and pay a fair wholesale price for it on demand.

If you are unhappy with the money a dealer offers after his testing has been completed, you might suggest a consignment arrangement. Not all resellers will allow this, but when they do there can be advantages to both parties. Consignment allows a dealer to fill his showroom with inventory that costs nothing until it's been sold. It also allows him to probe the market and try to find exactly the right customer for a specific piece, rather than having to sell it quickly to avoid depreciation. This scenario can mean more money to you at the wholesale level.

On the other hand, there's risk involved in any consignment arrangement, most of it borne by you, the owner. You're giving up the use of your system in the hope it will be sold at a pre-authorized price, but there's no guarantee. And suppose you get it back, only to discover it's not working the way it used to? Under the terms of most consignment agreements, you probably won't have any recourse. So while your chances of realizing a larger sum for the system are increased, you also have to assume some liabilities. If you do have to entrust your PC to someone else while they try to sell it, you must do your best to be sure they are reputable and reliable before handing it over to them.

Selling Your Computer Privately

But suppose you don't have to sell your system in the next forty-eight hours and you feel you have a pretty good shot at advertising it, demonstrating it, and selling it successfully yourself? By all means, forge ahead – you're almost certain to get a higher price.

The first step before announcing you intend to sell anything is to research your competitors. Know what they're selling and how much they're charging. A few phone calls and a study of the newspaper classifieds are a good start. Why not contact two or three used-PC dealers and ask how much they would charge for a system comparable to yours? But don't forget to be brutally honest about your system's specifications when judging the competition.

Check the local computer buy-and-sell publications and price out similar systems there. Be careful, though. Newspaper want ads will almost certainly list prices that are out of line because advertisers have priced them according to what they paid, rather than current market value. This is less likely to happen in computer publications. Stay away from advisors unless you are absolutely sure they have their fingers on the pulse of the used-computer business. If Uncle Joe sold his computer system effortlessly two years ago for a really fantastic price, it means absolutely nothing today. Even if your PC is exactly the same as his was, this market evolves so fast that it's even hard for salespeople in daily contact with it to be current. Do your own research, find out what to expect for your PC, and do your best to sell it without becoming unduly influenced by those who may have misconceptions. Market research, advertising, and price negotiation are best carried out when there is only one voice in the chorus – make sure it's yours.

Setting the Price

I know it sounds heartless, but try to forget how much you paid for your computer when setting its selling price. Its cost to you two or three years ago has about as much to do with anything today as the price of eggs. Your system is only worth what someone will pay for it now, and not a dollar more. Take for granted that you'll have to accept a lot less than you bought it for, have a good cry if it makes you feel any better, then get on with the business at hand.

What is a fair price to ask? This will depend directly on the price at which people think they can buy new or comparable used equipment from your competitors. And please take special note of the word *think* in that last sentence. Be prepared to have your perfectly good, carefully priced, nicely advertised PC compared quite unfairly to wild and sometimes misleading ads in the local media.

Be prepared to meet purchasers who are dead certain they can buy an unbelievable system – brand new and much better than yours – for next to nothing. Never mind the fact that they haven't taken the time to read the fine print and realize that the $499 price tag on that new Pentium MMX doesn't include a hard drive or monitor. Be ready for shoppers who'll listen to your sales pitch and price, only to tell you that you're wildly out of line.

But is there actually a formula by which you can arrive at a fair and competitive asking price? Pinning down prices in the used-PC market is a bit like trying to grab a slippery trout flopping around in the bottom of the boat on a rainy day, but the two most reliable indicators are dealers and other private sellers who have equipment similar to yours. If your computer is recent enough, you can also compare against prices of new goods.

In the first instance, take the price a dealer is asking (and don't forget to sample at least two or three) and stay within 10 percent – provided you have compared the two systems thoroughly and accurately. Expect that local dealers will be able to command a little more for their wares, but their prices are at least a good place to start. You can always come down. And you can always verify whether a vendor is out of line by checking private sale prices, although, as I mentioned earlier, these are more likely to be unrealistic.

If you call a person or company selling their PC privately for a price check, don't forget to ask how long they've had it for sale. If it's been available at the same figure for longer than thirty days, chances are they're asking too much.

If your computer is still young enough to be available in the new marketplace, you have an even clearer baseline from which to start pitching. Look in the paper and price out systems close in origin (brand-name or locally assembled) and specifications to the one you hope to sell. Take the lowest price, always remembering to be sure the ad you are using is not a misleading one, and knock off about 25 percent. This is not an infallible rule, just a reasonable place to start. If your PC is currently being advertised new at $1,500, try to start the bidding for it around $1,095. If you feel that special circumstances give you an advantage over competitors – geography, for example – keep your price a little higher, because you never know . . .

Time is another factor that can affect how you set your price when selling a PC. If you absolutely have to move it within a definite period, the writing's on the wall. Do the market research anyway, but sharpen your pencil that much more. Take 30 or even 50 percent off the baseline price of an equivalent new PC, or undercut the prices of used systems advertised by competitors by $100 or even $200.

HOW AND WHERE TO ADVERTISE

To paraphrase the author of a popular marketing strategy book, the most successful advertisements are those that get the right information across to the right people at the right time. So when marketing your PC, consider carefully, and ask yourself honestly who might like to buy it. Once you have done this, target your advertising specifically to them.

Try to tailor the look of the information you're presenting to the medium. If you've got a whole page or more to paste up on a bulletin board, it might even be worth trying to come up with some kind of eye-popping graphic. Otherwise, be catchy and brief. The more space you have, the more you must be careful about which specifications you choose to include.

At a very minimum, be prepared to include the processor level, RAM, hard drive size, monitor size, and name and manufacturer of any significant peripherals such as a scanner or tape backup. There is no real need to mention the age of your system – unless it's less than a year old – or too many technical details such as the speed and type of its RAM chips, the manufacturer of its motherboard, or the specifications of its power supply.

Being concise will help keep your ad costs to a minimum if you have to pay for space. Any amount you spend on marketing detracts from the proceeds of the sale. Here are some examples of common and inexpensive advertising venues available to anyone trying to sell a computer privately.

Posters and Flyers

Cheap and very effective, a well-worded, attractive poster tacked up in a local supermarket or meeting place might be all you need. Use some kind of tear system or small pre-cut sheets with your phone number on them – don't depend on prospective customers to stop and write down the information they'll need to contact you later.

With a little imagination you can probably make up a sheet that will do double duty as a flyer and bulletin board poster. Apart from costing very little (you can get a thousand sheets printed for well under $15), these allow a lot of space in which to describe your system and its attributes. Pass 'em out and stick 'em up!

Local Papers
Everyone has their own theory about newspaper advertising – my favourites are smaller, local publications. Their rates are usually low, and their readers are likely to live close by. And though I can't prove it, I also think readers believe they stand a better chance of getting a good buy in the little papers. Maybe it's better to be one of a few fish in a smaller pond than to be thrown into the deep water beside all of your competitors in a large-circulation daily. Don't forget to include the minimum information: processor type and class, speed in megahertz, amount of RAM, hard drive size, and monitor type and size. After this information you are only limited by your creativity; and, of course, your ad budget. It's not a bad idea to have a more detailed spec sheet ready for the day your phone starts to ring, so you can simply read off your pitch, or even fax it to potential buyers.

The Internet
If you're thinking of advertising on the Net, apply the same principles that you would to a locally posted ad. Make your presentation accurate, brief, and attractive. Make it easy for potential purchasers to respond, and try to stress something about your deal that makes it stand out. One big consideration when dealing with the Web, of course, is the international makeup of its users. Don't be surprised if you start getting email from all over the place as a result of a good ad campaign. So be sure not to set out on this road without first thinking carefully about how you're going to respond to interested parties, and physically get them together with the goods.

Companies
I include companies as a separate category in the advertising source list because they may not be a venue everyone thinks about when looking for places to sell a PC. But anywhere you can reach a large group of people is a reasonable place to consider advertising your computer. Even if you don't work for a corporation yourself, you might know someone who does. Almost every large company has a bulletin board over the water cooler or in the lunch room. And here is where you can

be specific in your marketing. Perhaps you can choose a company that has employees that are in some way more disposed than the general population to buy your computer.

Word of Mouth

Hand in hand with any of the advertising strategies listed above is the option of being your own best promoter – talk your system up! Tell everyone you can that you really would like to sell your computer.

Remember all gathering places and groups with which you have any connection: schools, churches, drop-in centres – and make it known to one and all that you are offering a great buy on a fabulous PC.

DEMONSTRATING YOUR COMPUTER

Now you've made your list, checked it twice, you've advertised the wonderful, fantastic system you're trying to sell on the bulletin board of the local supermarket, and your phone is starting to ring – now what? Get it sold, that's what! The first order of business is to get your goods and your customer together. In almost all cases, the person purchasing your system is going to want to see it, touch it, and watch it perform at least one or two tasks successfully before laying down his or her hard-earned money. With this in mind, be sure to have the PC in a place where prospective purchasers can do all of these things easily and without interruption.

This might even mean moving it to a location which is more suited to selling it than to using it for day-to-day work. And take a hard look at your PC with an unbiased eye. Is it clean? Is the desk it's sitting on reasonably well organized? Take the vacuum cleaner and Windex to the thing and make it as shiny and appealing as you possibly can. As any showroom professional will tell you, appearances matter a great deal – the presentation environment, the salesperson (yes, this means you), and, of course, the item itself. Clean it all up! It means more money in your pocket.

Not far behind the appearance of your PC and the way you present it is its actual fitness. Does everything work? Does the "U" key skip sometimes from that nasty coffee spill last fall? If any parts of the system don't work quite as they should, do your best to remedy them. If there are a whole lot of programs you don't use anymore on the hard drive, get rid of them. Arrange your files and go over the operating system or welcome screen so it looks organized and easy to use. And after you've made any changes, don't forget to run the remaining programs to verify they're still OK.

Once you've got your system tidied up inside and out, and you've verified that everything is working more or less as it should, it's time to consider what you're going to say to prospective customers and how you're going to demonstrate the little animal.

Pick a task with which you're familiar, and which shows the customer how the system works. Scan something with the scanner. Create a new wordprocessing document and print it on the printer. Practise the demo so it will go smoothly. Nothing is quite as embarrassing as sitting in front of a PC, trying to figure out why it won't work, while a customer looks skeptically over your shoulder. Prepare a sample page in advance that takes advantage of your printer's capabilities – why not use the flyer that you created to advertise the system in the first place? You can give it to your customers to take away should they want to think further about the purchase before taking the plunge. When a customer arrives, greet him in a friendly manner, take him directly to the PC without distraction, show it to him, and describe it briefly and positively. And don't say anything negative, such as: "Oh, I'm selling this to buy a new one because it's just too slow." Be positive!

Conduct your demo as quickly and smoothly as you can, and then encourage your customer to sit down at the keyboard and type something. In the office equipment business it has long been accepted that an important watershed in a sale has been passed when a customer actually touches the equipment he's thinking of buying. Answer any questions your customer poses to the best of your ability – but take care not to misrepresent anything, and don't guess at something you don't know. If a purchaser starts throwing difficult technical questions at you, don't be afraid to admit that you don't know an answer. In some cases, you may want to offer to find out something for a customer, or you can suggest that he call a local computer store or a manufacturer for information.

If a customer makes finding the answer to a certain technical question a condition of the sale, think twice before starting out on what could be a wild goose chase. Is your prospect really serious when he says he'll buy the system once he receives satisfactory information, or is he just using this as a stalling or avoidance tactic? Perhaps he has raised a complicated issue just to show that he knows a lot about computers – this is actually fairly common. So do your best to stay in control of the demonstration, no matter how technically advanced a buyer appears to be, and don't be drawn into a game of one-upmanship, or worry about how much you know about computers. Present your system as honestly and accurately as you can.

If a purchaser says your PC is too expensive compared to the prices of new or comparable used goods, tell him about your market research. If you are indeed working with up-to-date information, it will be easy to justify your price.

CLOSING THE SALE

With all of the books and guides and videos available on selling everything from cars to houses, this is not the right place to delve too deeply into the subtle and complicated business of closing a computer sale. For most people, selling their PC is a one-time endeavour performed under limited financial, time, and energy requirements. So we'll leave the professional selling advice to the professionals, except to say that there are accepted elements to closing a sale successfully. These are, as follows:

- Demonstrating the product
- Asking the customer for the order
- Taking a deposit or payment in full
- Making out a bill of sale
- Releasing the goods

After you've done your shtick (try to keep the presentation short, please) and it seems that a customer is interested, don't be afraid to ask clearly if he would like to buy. That's why we're all here, isn't it? He's taken the time and trouble to come and see the system and watch you demonstrate it. Unless he's told you specifically that it's not what he wants, he won't be offended if you ask how he likes it, and whether he'd like to take it.

If he would like to buy, it would be a rare occasion if he simply accepted your price without question. Especially when dealing with used goods in a private sale, expect a little haggling. With this in mind, don't set your price too low in the first place.

Sales negotiations can be as varied and unpredictable as purchasers themselves, but no matter how persuasive the person sitting across the table may be, don't make a deal you are going to regret. If a negotiating session grows rough, take a break from it. A little extra time often allows buyer and seller to come up with a compromise, and if not, either of you will be able to pull out more easily. Just remember, for a sale to be truly successful, both parties must come away feeling they have made a good deal.

Some other observations about private sales: A sale is not over until the goods have been paid for in full and are in the hands of the purchaser, but once these conditions have been met a private sale is, to all legal intents and purposes, concluded and is difficult to undo. There are, of course, ways for a purchaser or vendor to kill a deal after the fact, but these are waters to avoid. For goods of the value of a used personal computer (almost always under $2,000), it's debatable whether it's worth the time and effort to pursue the legal means to compel a refund, or to repossess equipment if payments have gone bad.

Litigants can and often do sue over these issues, but I have a feeling that when all is said and done, the driving forces behind these actions are personal more than financial. When you look carefully at the energy and expenses of gaining complete satisfaction in court, the prospect of a legal action over a used PC is not an attractive one.

BILLS OF SALE

You've now demonstrated your PC to an enthralled purchaser, negotiated a price with which you are both reasonably happy, and agreed that your buyer will take the computer then and there. The next order of business – creating a bill of sale – is a tempting one to omit. It's just a detail, right? Wrong! You've probably heard all the reasons why you need a bill of sale before and they apply as much today as they ever did. So write it all down and give a copy to your purchaser. This protects you both. And what is this document supposed to contain?

1. *What you're selling* – An accurate description of the computer: its manufacturer, RAM, hard drive size, and processor speed. Don't forget to include any peripherals such as keyboard, mouse, mouse pad, and other special items such as scanner, tape backup, modem, etc. Use the phrase "all cables included" if that is indeed your intention, and make sure you and your purchaser know what these cables are. Are you including a power bar, for example? This may sound excessive, but a misinterpreted insignificance such as a printer cable can crack the trust of a shaky deal. Even though writing it all down in the first place can cause ripples at the time of the sale, you'll at least be secure (as secure as you can) that you are both doing and getting what you agreed upon.
2. *The vendor and purchaser* – Names, addresses, and especially phone numbers. You may want to get in touch with each other when all of this is over.

3. *The price* – How much you are being paid, how you are being paid, and when you are being paid. Be sure not to write down that you have received any money until it's on the table or in your hand. Don't forget to include any taxes that apply to private sales in your province or state.
4. *Delivery arrangements* – Is the equipment you are selling being taken away immediately? Will you deliver it? Is the purchaser leaving a deposit to hold it until he returns with payment in full?
5. *Warranty or other after-sale conditions* – These are more important to you, as the seller, than they are to the purchaser. It's essential that you have proof of your obligations to your customer in the event of equipment failure. If you don't intend to offer any kind of support after the PC leaves your hands, which would be usual in the private marketplace, state this clearly on the bill. This is a valuable understanding to have if your purchaser calls you a few weeks later with real or imagined difficulties.
6. *Other terms and conditions* – If there are any other special agreements you have made with your customer, put them on the bill of sale as clearly as possible, and draw your customer's attention to them for approval.

DEPOSITS AND PAYMENTS

One of the trickiest parts of completing a computer sale is getting the money and turning over the goods. As soon as a transaction is complicated by outside factors, risks on both sides increase.

A deposit is a customer's way of saying to you, "Yes, I'm committed, I want to buy your computer, so hold it for me until I pick it up and pay the balance." In return for this show of faith, you, as the vendor, should be prepared to reserve the system at the agreed-upon price for a specified period. Be careful, however, to inform your customer if you wish to retain the right to sell the PC to someone else and return his deposit after a certain period has passed. A deposit should not be forever, so give thought to what might happen if a purchaser leaves you a small sum of money, then goes away, never to be seen again.

A more straightforward path is to ask your purchaser to pay for the PC in full. Much easier. Now it's his and he can take it away with his bill of sale, and everyone's happy. Try your best to steer the transaction in this direction. As far as the form of payment is concerned, insist on something secure – cash, a money order, or certified cheque. Any other type of payment – particularly a regular cheque – leaves you, the vendor, open to trouble. No matter how happy and satisfied a customer might seem when he takes your computer away, things may change. Let's go over the top a little: suppose he has a flat tire on the way home. He's late for an important dinner or has to miss his son's appearance in the school play. Tired and out of sorts, he is nevertheless eager to set up his new PC that night, so he lugs it all in from the trunk of his car and doggedly puts it all together – incorrectly. Without another thought, he decides to call his bank and stop payment on his cheque. Through no fault of yours (or your perfectly fine PC's), you are out your money and your computer. If you've happened to hook up with a particularly adversarial character, he might just decide to keep the equipment in addition to stopping his payment. Sound scary? Insist on cash.

AFTER THE SALE

In the world of computer retailing, sales professionals are generally trained in the protocol of after-sale support: their automatic response is to turn a customer with problems over to a technician. That's because pros know first hand that they're at a disadvantage with a user who has a PC that's not working properly. By their nature, microcomputers are prone to after-sale misunderstandings, because they're able to perform such a huge variety of tasks. There is no way any salesperson or customer can anticipate all the circumstances into which a system might be thrown. Here's an example from the private side of the market:

> You've sold your PC to Megan Alexandra Byte – your neighbour down the street. She's always been friendly and cheerful. She saw one of the flyers you posted in the local convenience store advertising your Pentium 133 MHz PC and ink jet printer. You invited her over to look at them, she loved them and paid you $600 cash for the whole show.
>
> She took the equipment home and set it up in her basement. It all worked perfectly until two days later. That's when your phone started ringing. In her wisdom, Meg decided to put a faster modem into the system, and bought one at the local electronic superstore. She pain-stakingly followed all the instructions, installed her new purchase, connected it to the telephone jack on the wall, and guess what? It didn't work! Of course, the superstore that purchased the modem for about $125 and sold it

to Meg for $139 is about as happy to hear from her as it would be to hear from an income tax auditor. The staff have, however, offered to try to help solve her difficulties for a service fee. They have also made some pretty rough remarks about the computer you sold her, implying that there may in fact be something wrong with it and that many of their customers are able to get these peripherals working with hardly any trouble at all. Now, not only does Meg think she has a defective piece of equipment, she feels frustrated as well. It's a classic example of what happens regularly in the computer business. A perfectly functioning PC is altered, with disastrous results. While no individual or company selling PCs is immune to this scenario, you can, as a private seller, protect yourself to some degree. The best way to do this is to define your responsibilities clearly when your computer leaves your possession. Your customer must be made aware that he or she is responsible for any software, hardware, or changes made to the system after it leaves your hands. And there is a happy ending to the story of Meg A. Byte down the street. You happened to have on file the telephone number of the service depot that put a new hard drive in your computer a few months ago. They know your PC well. You gave their number to Meg, and they solved her problem over the phone. Meg is back talking to you over the garden fence, and surfing away in her basement, happily ever after.

11

GETTING IT FIXED: SURVIVING THE BREAKDOWN OF YOUR PC

It's a few minutes after twelve on the night before the biggest presentation of your career. You're just putting the finishing touches on that all-important file in your computer when Pop! With a puff of smoke, your trusty PC picks the absolute worst moment in history to give up the ghost. It's a nightmare, all right, but it's also something that can, and probably will, happen in some variation to all of us as long as we keep using PCs. A whole industry has grown up around what are commonly known as disaster recovery scenarios, but even for the average home or small business computer user it's no longer just sensible to anticipate problems, it's essential.

AN OUNCE OF PREVENTION

There are some simple precautions anyone can take to avoid difficulties when their system fails. These include backing up your data and programs; keeping your manuals safe and handy; storing some basic spare parts (power cord, mouse, printer cable); and developing a plan of action for the times when you encounter equipment failure.

Highest on the list is backing up your files – your wordprocessing documents, pictures, spreadsheets, database files, system files, anything on your hard disk you care about. While almost everything else in your computer can be recovered, your own creations are irreplaceable.

Try to develop a routine which is automatic every time you use your system. There are all sorts of hardware and software solutions to this problem, and frankly, any one of them is fine, as long as you make sure it happens regularly. The simplest backup, of course, is to save your files on removable floppy disks. Don't forget to create a safe place for them – away from the family pet, for example. This labour-intensive approach is only compromised by the fact that it relies on what is by far the most unpredictable part of any personal computer – its human operator. It also limits the size of your backups to the amount of information you can cram onto a single disk – unless you start compressing large files with software such as PKZip, or Stuff It by Aladdin Systems, or even cutting them into pieces. Unfortunately, this extra work reduces the chance that you will make the backups as often or automatically as you should.

A more sophisticated approach is to invest in a device designed for the task, such as an internal or external tape backup, or a removable media drive from a company like Syquest or Iomega. These solutions are favoured by professionals such as graphic artists and musicians who commonly work with large files. The increased popularity of the Internet and of hardware such as scanners and video capture cards, however, has meant that more and more everyday users need larger backups. As a result, there has been a surge in the popularity of these storage systems. Incidentally, they also make it easy to save and restore entire programs, so they pay off doubly if you ever have to reconstruct your computer at two in the morning. Most removable hard drives and tape backups come with software which can be programmed to protect specific files or whole directories automatically. Your computer will probably be a lot more reliable at this than you will.

Another path toward the reconstruction of your hard drive is to reprogram it completely from a backup compact disc containing your original programs, if your computer happened to come with one in the first place, as many do.

In addition to backing up your files and programs to safeguard against the effects of computer failure, you should also be sure to keep all documentation and utility disks related to your PC and its components (printer, modem, video card, etc.) in a safe place. This can make a big difference, whether you try to troubleshoot a problem yourself or ask a service person to get involved.

If you frequently use your computer in deadline situations, it's also not a bad idea to keep extra components on hand – a spare power cord, a mouse, even a keyboard. And finally, if you do nothing else, at least take a couple of minutes to sit down and make up a "What if?" list describing what you would do if your computer failed tomorrow. Does a friend or neighbour have one you can borrow to get out of a jam? Do you know of a reliable service centre nearby? How late are they open? Do they know anything about the kind of computer you own? Do they make house calls? Do they take credit cards?

WHEN LIGHTNING STRIKES

Backups and plans aside, what can you do when your equipment starts acting up?

First, direct your attention to the basic problem. Did your monitor suddenly go blank? Are all of the power lights on but your keyboard is not responding? Did the modem suddenly cut out?

As we've seen in other chapters, PCs are actually groups of subsystems, each with its own task, so employ a little common sense when seeking the origin of the trouble. If a problem happened in the middle of a computing session it's usually, though not always, a good idea to shut the system and all of its peripherals down, then restart them to see if the problem reappears. In a personal computer, data flowing from one component – particularly a printer – to another can sometimes get bottlenecked, or other programming "dead ends" can arise. An exception to this is when a component emits any kind of unusual odour. This may indicate a power malfunction which could seriously damage your PC if it's turned on again. In this case it's definitely time for a trip to the PC doctor.

After restarting your system, try to re-create the failure if it does not happen automatically. Most people would be surprised at the number of times a suspected fault was simply a miscued print job or the result of two pieces of software fighting for a system's resources.

If you do find that a problem is not going away on its own, try a few routine checks before dragging it to a service depot or calling a support hotline.

Do everything you can to check what are known to computer technicians as "environmental" factors – conditions external to a system that may be affecting its performance.

Look carefully at all cable connections, especially those involving a suspected printer, monitor, or power delivery problem. Everything plugged in? All the way? Are all of the appropriate power indicators lit? Is there paper in the printer? Is the "on line" indicator activated? Is the telephone line plugged into the modem? Paid your phone bill?

If everything seems to be exactly as it was when the computer was running perfectly, and the fault persists, it's time for more in-depth action: pull out your manuals and look at the sections on troubleshooting.

If no answer jumps out of your documentation, try a little reduction theory. One at a time, start removing elements (software or hardware) which you suspect are involved in the failure. The object, of course, is to isolate the troublemaker. This is exactly what a professional will do, only in greater depth than you should at home. You may want to draw the line at tampering with anything inside your computer or printer, unless you have some technical experience. After all, you don't want to create more trouble than you've already got. But there are some things you can isolate without too much risk. Does your problem disappear when you unplug the printer? when you disable your modem? when you unplug your keyboard, scanner, or mouse? Try another telephone jack. Listen for the fan present in most power supplies – is it spinning? If you have an Internet connection problem, try dialling an alternate utility or Internet provider. If you can pinpoint the source of the trouble, you are more than halfway toward correcting it – or pointing a professional in the right direction.

Users diagnosing their own problems must not forget to pay special attention to software. Could settings have been changed, even inadvertently, to cause the difficulty? Ask yourself if anything inside or outside the system is different now from when it was working. Could you have contracted a virus when you downloaded that game last night? Does a new combination of programs you're trying to run require more resources than your system has to offer?

If you suspect software even a tiny bit, it's a good idea to reboot (restart your system with an operating system disk in its primary floppy drive), and, if possible, reload and run some test programs which you know to be error free.

A POUND OF CURE

But what if you've checked everything, unplugged and replugged, booted from a certified virus-free disk, tried to run properly configured programs known to work on other computers, consulted all the appropriate manuals, and spent half an hour on the help line, only to find that your computer still doesn't work? Time to bring in a professional.

As in any business, there are good guys and bad guys in the world of computer repairs. Here are a few things to keep in mind when you are dealing with computer service personnel.

- *Be precise.* Do your best to describe the problem as accurately as possible. It's often helpful to prepare a short list of the symptoms, when and how they occurred, and what you have done to try to correct them. This exercise will assist you in being clear about the difficulty, and will tell your repair person what you've already tried.
- *Bring everything involved in the failure.* Even the best technician can't fix your problem if you leave half of the suspected components at home. Don't forget things like software, manuals, sample printouts, special cables, and any other pertinent information. These items can sometimes make the difference between a quick fix and a long wait or even a second trip to the depot for you to complete the picture.
- *Remain calm.* It's easy to get upset when a computer problem has caused you to miss deadlines and thrown your life into chaos, but your PC service person will appreciate an evenhanded description of the difficulty, and your understanding that he or she is there to help you, and not act as an adversary.
- *Expect competence.* You deserve from your service person a willingness to listen, honest and up-front information about all charges and rates, and a professional attitude. Not all jobs can be handled by all service people, so you should also feel assured that if your problem is beyond his or her capabilities you'll hear about it promptly and be released to seek help elsewhere.

Two important elements in the process of having a computer repaired are time and money. Exactly how quickly and cheaply you can get a job done depends on the depot or service bureau you choose, the parts and expertise required, and the complexity of your problem.

A sample of rates in the Toronto area in late 1997 revealed hourly charges ranging from \$25 to \$180 with the average falling somewhere around \$75 to \$125 for depot repairs, and \$75 to \$150 per hour for work performed on site in your home or office. Here are some other important questions to consider when approaching a company or individual for computer service:

- Will they provide a written estimate before starting work?
- How much will the estimate cost and how long will it take?
- How long will they take to complete the repair?
- Is the company or person authorized to work on the type of

equipment you're bringing them?
- Do they guarantee their work? For how long?
- Will they make "best efforts" to save your data and programs?
- Will they reload your software if need be, and if so how much will this service cost?
- Does the repair person have experience with the kind of hardware or software difficulty you have? What is the depot's policy if they're unable to solve your problem?
- Will the person or company provide you with references on request?

In most cases, it's reasonable to expect a problem to be solved quickly, often in a single session, because of the modular nature of most PCs. Once a true hardware failure has been identified, a replacement part can usually be substituted to get you running again in short order. But what happens if things don't turn out this way?

Problems servicing computer equipment usually arise for three reasons:

1. Failure to identify and duplicate a problem quickly and reliably
2. Inability to locate a proper replacement component at a competitive price or in reasonable time
3. Inability to reprogram or reconfigure a system quickly in the absence of proper backups or legally owned programs

It's the mandate of a responsible service provider or manufacturer to watch out for these kinds of circumstances and work with a customer to get around them as painlessly as possible.

An additional problem is that, with the wide variety of components now being used in PCs, it's sometimes hard just to get them all talking to each other. Industry standards are often not as straightforward as manufacturers claim. A device which is perfectly compatible with one set of parts might inexplicably not work with others.

One great new resource many technicians use is the Internet. Most manufacturers of high-tech equipment have websites which not only provide detailed information about their products, but also allow browsers to download drivers and software fixes to an increasing number of problems. Don't forget that these are available to you as well as to computer service professionals.

THE FINE PRINT: SERVICE CONTRACTS AND WARRANTIES

Let's suppose you've good-humouredly endured the whole experience of having your computer fail, you've slugged it down to the repair centre, lived without it for a week, reclaimed and paid for it, and brought it back home. If you're like most of us, you're probably thinking that you never want to have to go through this whole trying process again. So what about some protection – such as a service contract?

Basically, there are four types of computer service agreements. Most of these can be purchased separately, for a computer you already own, or come included with a new system as part of its warranty.

Return to Depot

Most common among generic, or locally assembled, computer systems, carry-in warranties are normally good for one to five years from the date the computer or warranty was purchased. If your equipment fails, you are obligated to return it, at your expense, with a proof of purchase or guarantee certificate, to a designated depot and leave it there while it's being repaired. Variations on this theme include companies who will pay all or part of the transportation costs, who offer multiple service depots across the country or around the world, or who cover parts or labour only for portions of the guarantee period. In an example of this latter circumstance, a user may pay only for the labour needed to install a component covered under warranty, while the part itself is free.

On-Site Guarantees

On-site guarantees are often offered as part of a package by larger brand-name manufacturers when you purchase one of their computers. These are frequently accompanied by access to a telephone help line, which allows users to call for specific information about their systems and any problems they are experiencing. These help lines are a great idea in principle, but are sometimes hard to get through to, or demand a long wait once you're finally connected. Well-managed help lines tell you how long you can expect to wait, which at least presents the option to try again at a better time. In an inventive effort to improve their service, IBM's new Aptiva support plan allows their help line technician to call your computer and run diagnostic checks on it over the phone. While this may not get a hardware problem solved much faster than a traditional on-site warranty, it at least allows them to troubleshoot software difficulties immediately, or confirm the failure of specific components.

Most computer manufacturers or service providers will not authorize a technician to visit you until a support person has gone over your problem carefully on the phone. This is an effort to spare the expense of an on-site call unless it's absolutely necessary.

Enterprises offering this kind of service range from computer-savvy individuals all the way to multinational corporations that view the PC service field as an expanding business opportunity.

Replacement Guarantees

A refinement of the traditional on-site service contract, the replacement guarantee began appearing in the personal computer business in the late '80s. Under the usual terms of one of these agreements, a company – again, usually a large manufacturer or service bureau – obligates itself to solve your computer, monitor, or printer problem by sending you another one by courier within a specified period, say one to three days. You should remember that in these kinds of contracts, the provider will in many cases not send a brand-new replacement, although that is their option. More probably they'll use a component which was previously returned to them, repaired, and thrown back into the "pool." In contracts like these it is more important than ever to keep a backup of your data because the replacement normally arrives with only factory software installed.

Maintenance Warranties

As their name implies, maintenance warranties include an element of ongoing attention which is usually absent from other kinds of guarantees. These typically provide for the scheduled time of a technician, say once or twice a year or more, either on site or at a service bureau, to check a piece of equipment and confirm that it's working properly. This might include cleaning a printer or keyboard, replacing toners or other consumables, or performing regular software checks to be sure the contents of a hard drive are organized, backed up, and virus-free. Agreements of this type used to be more popular when office equipment was more mechanical than it is today, but many companies still offer them, even though the electronic nature of PCs has made them less susceptible to the wear and tear these contracts are designed to relieve. If you buy a maintenance warranty, be sure to get a written list of exactly what is considered maintenance and what isn't. A technician, even by mistake, may charge for work which should have been covered.

Here are some other observations about service contracts and warranties in general:

- *Get it in writing.* The more specific a warranty or contract is, the better. If there are clauses in it you don't understand, or questions in your mind which haven't been dealt with, ask your sales or service rep to explain, and, if possible, write his policies down for you. If you feel an agreement has been made deliberately confusing, and no sincere effort to correct this has been made, seek service elsewhere.
- *Read the fine print.* As with any contract, you should be fully aware of all conditions and terms for which you are paying and to which you agree. Pay special attention to *your* obligations, as well as those of the service provider, before signing on the dotted line. What about things like transportation – who pays if equipment has to be moved? Are there times when a contract or warranty is void? Is the service provider allowed to engage technicians from an outside company to do its work? Will these technicians be authorized to work on your PC? Under what circumstances can you or your provider terminate the agreement?

Finally, be sure not to forget the reputation of the company or person you are dealing with. Remember that any guarantee is only valuable as long as the company issuing it stays solvent. In some instances a shorter warranty from a stable business might be better than a long one from a company that may not be around to honour it later. It's reasonable to assume that the majority of people and companies in the computer service business are honest and reliable. On the other hand, it's always a good idea to be watchful for those who are not.

12

THE FUTURE OF THE PC MARKETPLACE

WHAT'S NEXT?

I guess it's finally time to confess that one of the reasons I wrote this book, in addition to providing information to people who want to find a way through the PC marketing maze, was to be allowed to hazard a few predictions about computers and the future. Finally I get to haul out the crystal ball and make some off-the-cuff, totally unsubstantiated speculations about PCs and the PC marketplace. To be sure, a lot of intelligent individuals and wealthy companies are also pondering this question against the shifting background of innovation.

Probably the most precise look into the next few months of computer design is the PC 98 standard described in late 1997 and early 1998 by Intel, Compaq, and Microsoft. These three companies have produced a set of guidelines with a July 1998 target for implementation. The guidelines are intended to help standardize computer manufacturers and provide a stable platform for the release of Microsoft's Windows 98 and NT Version 5. A basic system meeting these emerging requirements will contain a Pentium 200 MMX processor, 256K level 2 cache, 32 (minimum) or 64 (recommended) megabytes of RAM, a universal serial bus (USB), and an IEEE 1394. With the stature of the players behind these recommendations, and the long time (over a year) they have been forecast, it seems a good bet they will indeed become standard before the end of 1998.

Another, more conceptual influence on the future of the PC is the idea of convergence: the mix of a computer and other information systems, in particular the television and telephone. We all like to see who we are communicating with, and the endpoint of this desire is the amalgamation – or convergence – of communications in a single machine which would allow us to see each other and the rest of the world in ways never before possible. PCs are already available with televisions instead of monitors.

The Internet is rapidly moving toward the ability to download video on demand, even though available bandwidth – the amount of information the Net can handle – remains a big issue.

Perhaps in the more distant future we'll see the World Wide Web, or some high-speed refinement of it, merge with the current television broadcasting system. Perhaps it will "converge" with the telephone system. Perhaps these developments will improve the market share of the "Internet toaster," or "Internet appliance" computers which have been designed solely for network use and are already asserting themselves as a new computer species.

As far as the future of commerce in the PC marketplace is concerned, it seems that the Internet and its related networks are poised to further affect the way we research and execute our purchases, especially the marketing and delivery of software.

Even today you can find a wealth of independent reviews and opinions about products, manufacturers, and vendors on the Web. You can look at different views of a computer, test drive programs, then order and pay for it all by remote control. The Internet is also an unparalleled diagnostic and after-sale support tool. All of these activities are sure to become more popular, even if they only supplement the familiar scenarios of picking up the telephone or visiting a store and making a purchase the old-fashioned way.

A summary of trends for the near future of the personal computer:

- Expect the standardization and acceptance of new hardware developments such as: universal serial ports, IEEE 1394 ports, accelerated graphics ports, and improved chipsets like the 440BX PCI set expected from Intel in mid-1998.
- DVD (digital video disc) should take hold once its standards in the marketplace get ironed out. The impending appearance of digital television should further strengthen the marriage between the computer and the TV.
- Watch for more speed and strength: 266- to 350-MHz (and even faster) processors; more plentiful RAM (with 64- to 128-megabyte

levels becoming common); and affordable hard drives in the 6- to 10-gigabyte range. Also likely is the increased use of faster backup devices such as larger and removable Zip drives.

All in all, the next couple of years in the personal computer industry promise many fascinating new products and possibilities. I hope we can all enjoy them, and the increased productivity, performance, and entertainment they will provide.

PART II

PRODUCT REVIEWS

Introduction

Compiling an accurate, up-to-date catalogue of personal computer equipment is a bit like photographing a speeding train. The best result that can be hoped for is a reasonably clear picture of what was available at the moment, with allowances for new products, falling prices, and discontinued models. On the positive side, many lines of personal computers, especially those from larger manufacturers, have fairly stable histories, so new offerings are often just variations on previous models; thus observations about them – their overall quality and direct competitors – remain useful even if specifications have changed.

There are three types of products reviewed in this section: desktop PCs, printers, and monitors. The characteristics reported on each group are of course different; I have tried to include features that purchasers will want to consider, including a product's name, model, comparative specifications, competitors, manufacturer's list price, and estimated street price.

It is helpful to keep in mind that PCs can be divided into subclasses. When two systems of apparently the same specifications are $600 or $800 apart, you'll undoubtedly be curious about their differences. Personal computers can be grouped loosely into the following categories:

- Generic or locally assembled PCs, which are custom built singly, or in lots, by smaller companies out of diverse components.
- Home package PCs, which are standardized computer systems

from large manufacturers and include a full complement of hardware (modem, CD-ROM or DVD, speakers, and sound card) and a complete group of programs. These systems also often contain proprietary features and parts – components developed by their manufacturer and peculiar to them.
- Business class PCs, which are standardized computers from large companies. They can be customized to specification and may accept third-party parts, but are assembled under more rigorous and stable conditions than generic systems. Intended for business and corporate use, these computers normally, though not always, cost more than locally assembled PCs, should be covered by warranty from the manufacturer as well as the retailer, and should offer certifications – guarantees from networking and software companies that their systems meet established standards.
- Servers, which are faster, more expensive, and better supported than ordinary desktop computer systems, and intended to manage networks of other desktop PCs connected to them. These most expensive computers are intended to be superior in component quality and to offer lower rates of failure. Even though the specifications of a national brand server may look the same as those of a generic PC which costs a lot less, the engineering and certifications it should contain are the reasons for its higher price.

Note that demarcations between these desktop computer groups are subject to interpretation; for example, it is difficult to tell the difference between some national companies assembling generic PCs and multinationals that build systems according to specification. Watch for the size and reputation of the computer's manufacturer, their direct involvement in its warranty, and any certification tests it has passed, to help determine whether it is worth extra money.

WHEN IS A PC A LEMON?

It is worth describing the concept of a "lemon" in the computer business, since this label has acquired such a strong meaning in connection with the automobile industry. There are similarities and differences between the two product groups which can affect interpretation of the term.

It is my opinion that in the personal computer world lemons more often appear because of misleading marketing and advertising, or because of a manufacturer's failure to support a product properly, than because of the deliberate, long-term issue of faulty goods. There have been exceptions to this, of course, and will continue to be, but it is simply not as easy to include malfunctioning parts in a line of PCs over a long period as it is to misrepresent a system which contains inferior or used components at the time of its sale.

Compared to parts in many other common consumer products, electronic components in personal computers more often come from different companies and, for the most part, are easier to evaluate and replace. When a manufacturer is able to identify a faulty piece, a simple fix is to use an alternative, as opposed to having to retool at the manufacturing level.

There are, however, unique problems associated with the computer industry, all of which, when found together in a system, can cause problems indeed. The following are some common characteristics of a lemon PC.

Incompatible Components

Ten perfectly engineered components screwed together do not necessarily make a functioning system, as anyone who has had trouble adding a new hard drive or modem to a PC can verify. Any computer builder, whether small or large, should be responsible for all of the equipment – hardware and software – it sells you. Components in the computer should be optimized and should work together properly.

Inadequate Support

What about the difficulties we often experience when trying to use one of these complicated items after paying all that hard-earned money for it? How much support should you expect, anyway? As a person who has spent time on both sides of the sales counter, I know there are two sides to this story. In today's PC marketplace, no purchaser should realistically expect a vendor or manufacturer to educate him or her about all of the tasks a system can perform. Personal computers have become complex, multifaceted, low-margin items, which means you must be realistic about what to expect from the people who sell them.

On the other hand, a lemon PC is one for which you cannot get the support a manufacturer or vendor has pledged – support you have paid for and deserve. Calling a hotline should not mean a thirty-minute wait. A call to a vendor or manufacturer should be handled promptly and properly. All concerns should be answered to your satisfaction, and a company should be made clearly aware if they are not. Ways of dealing with this are considered in Chapter 8. Be sure to get a precise definition of all after-sale conditions when you purchase a computer, and expect a reseller or manufacturer to live up to them.

Used or Inferior Parts

A third characteristic of a lemon PC is the inclusion of used or inferior parts. If the advantage of easily removable components is the ability to identify and rectify problems quickly, the disadvantage is the easy inclusion of compatible but lower-specification parts. This temptation is not limited to small or local assemblers. In 1996, Compaq, as well as a group of unhappy customers, sued Packard Bell, charging that it put used components in its new systems – a practice the company now says has been discontinued.

NOTICE

Finally, when considering the following section on computers, monitors, and printers, please note that the technical information in it describes equipment that is constantly being updated, and is subject to change without notice. As a result, neither the author nor publisher can assume responsibility for liabilities based on the data it contains. In some cases, product specifications and prices have had to be estimated.

Comments in the review section of the guide are the opinions of the author and are based on published product specifications. They are not intended to be treated as the results of definitive studies or tests. The product specification sheets are intended for general information only, and in all cases it is recommended that buyers research and verify the characteristics of an item for themselves before making a purchase.

Canada Computer Paper (CCP) Test Labs has also assisted with the preparation of technical information in this guide, but it should be noted that the reviews and specification sheets are not official documents from them, or from any computer manufacturer or vendor, nor are they represented to be.

DESKTOP COMPUTERS*

ACER ASPIRE

With North American headquarters in San Jose, California, Acer America is perhaps the least-known large-scale computer manufacturer in the Canadian market. This is not to say the parent company isn't a presence on other continents; Acer is a big outfit, operating in thirty-eight countries, with research and development facilities, a component-level manufacturing section, and strong new alliances in the networking and portable computer fields.

The Acer Aspire series – home and small office PCs in competition with Hewlett-Packard's Pavilions, Compaq's Presarios, IBM's Aptivas, and NEC's Ready PC series – are quite price competitive, reflecting the company's mandate to become better known on this continent and particularly in Canada.

This series comprises a wide range of models, most of them presented in attractive black medium tower cases which come with the extras you'd expect from a big builder: modem, sound, speakers, and bundled programs. The software pack usually includes Microsoft Works, Microsoft Money, Intuit Quicken, Acer Utilities, and some other programs. Priced sharply against the better-recognized Presarios, Readys, and Aptivas, Aspires often appear as mass-market products in technology and department superstores. And, of course, they're available on the Internet.

Acer is large enough to provide the expected trappings of an established multinational: a big website with information and drivers, and carefully thought out support and return policies. It offers a reasonably prompt toll-free help line and has a good reputation for service and support. It is also big enough to build innovations into its systems, placing it on the leading edge along with Compaq, Hewlett-Packard,

* Unless otherwise indicated, the prices shown do not include monitor.

and NEC. On the downside, the Aspire warranty provides service on site only for the first ninety days.

If you can find one of these computers at a price you like, are looking for a home system that isn't priced in the top tier, and are comfortable with a lighter package of included software, the Aspires are a good bet. As with all home packages from big companies, these systems are not easy for you or the local PC guru to take apart and screw back together, but that comes with the territory. If you want flexibility, look for something more generic, but if you are looking for a complete system backed by a big company at a competitive price, the Aspires are worth consideration.

DESKTOP MANUFACTURER: ACER

Model: Aspire 1810M
Physical: White desktop case; switchable power supply
Motherboard and Processor: AMD-K6 200-MHz processor with MMX; 32-MB EDO system memory (expandable to 128 MB)
Cache: 256K pipeline burst cache
Floppy/Hard Drives: 1.44-MB floppy drive; 2.1-GB hard drive
Video: 1-MB EDO video card; MPEG video playback (software)
Multimedia: 24x (max) CD-ROM drive; 16-bit sound card with 3D stereo sound; stereo speakers and microphone
Modem: Internal 33.6-Kbps fax/modem
Bundled Software: Windows 95; Microsoft Works, Money, Encarta; Quicken; Crayola Magic 3D Coloring Book; Acer Utilities; other software included
Warranty: One-year limited manufacturer's warranty (on-site service for the first ninety days); extended warranty can be purchased
Suggested List Price at Publication: $1,799 (Acer monitor included)
Approximate Street Price at Publication: $1,499 (Acer monitor included)
Additions: 104-key PS/2-compatible keyboard; PS/2-compatible mouse; PCI slots, ISA slots

PRINTER MANUFACTURER: ACER

Model: Aspire 1822
Physical: White desktop case; switchable power supply
Motherboard and Processor: AMD-K6 233-MHz processor with

MMX; 16-MB EDO system memory (expandable to 128 MB)
Cache: 256K pipeline burst cache
Floppy/Hard Drives: 1.44-MB floppy drive; 2.1-GB hard drive
Video: 1-MB SGRAM video card; MPEG video playback (software)
Multimedia: 32x (max) CD-ROM drive; 16-bit sound card with 3D stereo sound; Acer monitor (sold separately) has built-in stereo speakers and microphone
Modem: Internal 33.6-Kbps fax/modem
Bundled Software: Windows 95; Microsoft Works, Money, Encarta; Quicken; POD (MMX game); Acer Utilities; other software included
Warranty: One-year limited manufacturer's warranty (on-site service for the first ninety days); extended warranty can be purchased
Suggested List Price at Publication: $1,399 (estimated)
Approximate Street Price at Publication: $1,199
Additions: 104-key PS/2-compatible keyboard; PS/2-compatible mouse; PCI slots, ISA slots

DESKTOP MANUFACTURER: ACER

Model: Aspire 1830/1831
Physical: Charcoal or white minitower; switchable power supply
Motherboard and Processor: AMD-K6 233-MHz Processor with MMX; 32-MB SDRAM system memory (expandable to 128 MB)
Cache: 256K pipeline burst cache
Floppy/Hard Drives: 1.44-MB floppy drive; 4.3-GB hard drive
Video: 1-MB SGRAM video card; MPEG video playback (software)
Multimedia: 24x (max) CD-ROM drive; 16-bit sound card with 3D stereo sound; Acer monitor (sold separately) has built-in stereo speakers and microphone
Modem: Internal 56-Kbps fax/modem
Bundled Software: Windows 95; Microsoft Works, Money, Encarta; Quicken; POD (MMX game); Acer Utilities; other software included
Warranty: One-year limited manufacturer's warranty (on-site service for the first ninety days); extended warranty can be purchased
Suggested List Price at Publication: $1,799 (estimated)
Approximate Street Price at Publication: $1,499
Additions: 104-key PS/2-compatible keyboard; PS/2-compatible mouse; 3 PCI slots open, 2 ISA slots open; 3 open drive bays; 2 USB ports

DESKTOP MANUFACTURER: ACER

Model: Aspire 2850/2863
Physical: Charcoal or white minitower; 200W switchable power supply
Motherboard and Processor: Intel 233-MHz Pentium II processor; 32-MB SDRAM system memory (expandable to 128 MB)
Cache: 512K pipeline burst cache
Floppy/Hard Drives: 1.44-MB floppy drive; 4.3-GB hard drive
Video: 2-MB SGRAM 3D video card (AGP); MPEG video playback (software)
Multimedia: 32x (max) CD-ROM drive; 16-bit sound card with 3D stereo sound; Acer monitor (sold separately) has built-in stereo speakers and microphone
Modem: Internal 56-Kbps fax/modem
Bundled Software: Windows 95; Microsoft Works, Money, Encarta; Quicken; POD (MMX game); Acer Utilities; other software included
Warranty: One-year limited manufacturer's warranty (on-site service for the first ninety days); extended warranty can be purchased
Suggested List Price at Publication: $2,299 (estimated)
Approximate Street Price at Publication: $2,199
Additions: 104-key PS/2-compatible keyboard; PS/2-compatible mouse; 3 PCI slots open, 2 ISA slots open; 3 open drive bays; 2 USB ports

DESKTOP MANUFACTURER: ACER

Model: Aspire 2860/2861
Physical: Charcoal or white minitower; 200W switchable power supply
Motherboard and Processor: Intel 300-MHz Pentium II processor; 32-MB SDRAM system memory (expandable to 128 MB)
Cache: 512K pipeline burst cache
Floppy/Hard Drives: 1.44-MB floppy drive; 6.4-GB hard drive
Video: 4-MB SGRAM AGP video card; MPEG video playback (software)
Multimedia: 32x (max) CD-ROM drive; 16-bit sound card with 3D stereo sound; Acer monitor (sold separately) has built-in stereo speakers and microphone
Modem: Internal 56-Kbps fax/modem
Bundled Software: Windows 95; Microsoft Works, Money, Encarta; Quicken; POD (MMX game); Acer Utilities; other software included

Warranty: One-year limited manufacturer's warranty (on-site service for the first ninety days); extended warranty can be purchased
Suggested List Price at Publication: $2,899 (estimated)
Approximate Street Price at Publication: $2,699 monitor
Additions: 104-key PS/2-compatible keyboard; PS/2-compatible mouse; 3 PCI slots open, 2 ISA slots open; 3 open drive bays; 2 USB ports

ACER ENTRA

Smaller brothers of the Acer Power series, these slimline and minitower desktop PCs are of limited scope and processing power – unless, since the time of publication, Acer has decided to include more resources in them, which wouldn't be a surprise. Often OEM'd (manufactured for other companies which resell PCs under another name), these entry-level business PCs are advertised on the company's website in a basic configuration which needs to be enhanced by items such as a CD-ROM, sound card, and modem. Could it be that they are intended more for remanufacturers than end-users? The features they offer for the price, the necessity to upgrade them at the time of purchase, and their basic warranty make it seem so. All of these systems include a "K" series processor from American Micro Devices. In this price range, a generic computer from a national builder or from a store in your area might be a better bet.

DESKTOP MANUFACTURER: ACER

Model: Acer Entra series
Physical: Slimline and minitower cases; 145W (Slimline) and 200W (minitower) switchable power supply
Motherboard and Processor: AMD-K series processor; 8-, 16-, or 32-MB EDO RAM
Cache: 256K pipeline burst cache
Floppy/Hard Drives: 1.44-MB floppy drive; 1.2- to 4.0-GB and larger enhanced IDE hard drives
Video: 2-MB graphics accelerated video card
Multimedia: Internal CD-ROM, sound card, and speakers available in special "kit" form
Modem: Internal 33.6- or 56-Kbps fax/modem available
Bundled Software: Windows 95; Quicken; McAfee AntiVirus; Lotus

SmartSuite in some models; Acer DMI (desktop management interface) in network models
Warranty: Acer one-year return-to-depot/courier limited warranty
Suggested List Price at Publication: $999 (Acer K233)
Approximate Street Price at Publication: $949 (Acer K233)

ACER POWER

Advertising itself as one of the leading OEM manufacturers in the world, Acer offers the Acer Power series, business class PCs in competition with AST's Bravo series, Dell's OptiPlexes, and NEC's Enterprises, to name a few.

Acer has signed joint venture agreements with National Semiconductor and Texas Instruments and is seeking to strengthen its presence in the North American market. In 1996 it had revenues in the $5.8 billion range worldwide, divided about evenly among North America, Asia, and Europe. In the business PC market, it is hoping to take on IBM, Compaq, and Digital Equipment, but is not quite head to head with these "tier one" manufacturers because of its company profile and prices. In the same way that its Aspire home systems are competitively priced, its business PCs are a consideration for cost-conscious information system managers in small and medium-sized companies. The specifications and three-year warranty with first year on site which these systems offer are attractive. Lotus SmartSuite is bundled with some of them. The company's reputation for support is good, although its marketing presence in the business end of the Canadian marketplace could use increased exposure.

DESKTOP MANUFACTURER: ACER

Model: Acer Power series
Physical: Desktop and minitower cases
Motherboard and Processor: Intel Pentium MMX and Pentium II processors 166–233 and higher MHz; 32-MB EDO RAM
Cache: 512K level 2 cache
Floppy/Hard Drives: 1.44-MB floppy drive; 2.5- to 4.0-GB and larger enhanced IDE and SCSI hard drives
Video: 64-bit accelerated video card
Multimedia: Internal CD-ROM; sound card and speakers in most models
Modem: Optional

Bundled Software: Windows 95 or Windows NT 4.0; Quicken; McAfee AntiVirus; Lotus SmartSuite in some models; Acer DMI (desktop management interface) in network models
Warranty: Acer three-year limited warranty (first year on site)
Suggested List Price at Publication: From $1,199
Approximate Street Price at Publication: From $1,149

AMBRA ISPIRATI

The Ambra series has had uneven support in Canada from Ambra's parent, IBM, since its introduction a few years ago. In distribution, not all models have always been readily available, a situation which has not been without consequences. Originally these were "designer" PCs, in a wider range of models, but as of publication the Ambras have become the company's entry into the low end of the home market.

One of the best places to find information on these systems, or even to purchase one, is the Internet (www.ca.pc.ibm.com/ambra.html). IBM is promoting the Ispirati series for purchase or lease on the World Wide Web. A notable feature of some models is a video card which provides output to a TV, an interesting concept to be sure, but exactly how practical it is remains to be seen. The slimline case, while attractive to users who are space-conscious, is limiting – not a major drawback if you aren't planning to add a lot of internal devices in the future, but the case is a characteristic you can't alter later.

The software complement is pretty good for a PC in this price range, as is the corporate background: IBM's presence behind the Ambra enterprise is reassuring. The express exchange warranty on the keyboard, monitor, and mouse means the company pledges to ship a replacement if the one you bought expires, although you shouldn't assume that the one sent will always be new. It's a replacement – a term that allows a manufacturer to forward someone else's peripheral which it has fixed. Still, this support plan can be a mighty convenient fix. In all, the Ambras are mid- to low-priced bundles with slightly better than average support but less than average accessibility when it comes to seeing, touching, and evaluating one before purchase. Whether IBM will make them more widely available in Canada or relegate them to Internet promotion and sales remains to be seen.

DESKTOP MANUFACTURER: AMBRA

Model: Ispirati series
Physical: Beige or black slimline Ambra desktop case
Motherboard and Processor: Cyrix 150- to 180-MHz and higher; 16- or 32-MB EDO RAM; maximums 96- to 128-MB RAM
Cache: 256K cache
Floppy/Hard Drives: 1.44-MB floppy drive; 1.6- to 4.0-GB enhanced IDE hard drive
Video: Super VGA video adapter with TV screen output
Multimedia: Internal 16x CD-ROM; 16-bit sound card; external speakers
Modem: Internal 33.3-Kbps fax/modem; 56-Kbps in the 243 EX model
Bundled Software: Windows 95; IBM Anti-Virus; Canadian Encyclopedia Plus; Communication Centre; Lotus SmartSuite with Wordpro, Spreadsheet, Lotus Organizer, and Graphics
Warranty: One-year return-to-depot; twenty-four-hour toll-free support; one-year exchange warranty
Suggested List Price at Publication: $999
Approximate Street Price at Publication: From $999

APPLE POWERMAC PCs

While it may be said that Apple's stature in the fierce world of the personal computer business has been reduced to that of just another competitor, the company and its products still stand out as a major force in the marketplace.

With its humble origins and flamboyant founder, Steven Jobs, Apple is still considered by many to be the quintessential counterculture enterprise. The questions facing the company now, however, are: how much extra are people prepared to pay for its reputation and products, and how compatible with third-party hardware and software will its systems become?

Apple has experienced very rocky times in the past five years, but continues to produce attractive PCs that are indeed moving toward what was once the unthinkable – off-the-shelf compatibility with predominant standards. While many observers of the computer business feel that such a move is inevitable, others debate that Apple's differences are still of value.

As of publication of this guide, Apple's PowerMac lineup was divided into five groups, with three or four models available in each one: the 5500 series, the 6500 series, the G3s, the 8600 series, and the 9600 series. A special "Anniversary Mac" is also debuting in 1998.

At the bottom of the pack, the PowerMac 5500s are offered in two all-in-one 603e processor-based systems that have monitor and case attached. These are aimed at the educational market, one of the company's traditional strongholds, and include 32 megabytes of RAM, a 2-gigabyte hard drive, 24x CD-ROM, and integrated sound and speakers. Special multimedia features such as 2-D/3-D graphics acceleration and input from/output to TV (optional on the 225 model) accompany Mac OS 8 and Internet Access software. While the resources in these packages are expandable, the all-in-one design places physical constraints on upgrades and poses potential inconvenience during repairs.

The PowerMac 6500 series is the company's entry into the mainstream home and small office markets, being composed of seven different models targeted variously at small office/home office (SOHO), small businesses, and lower-end graphics designers. Also based on the 603e processor, these systems range from 250 to 300 MHz and include a 24x CD-ROM, stereo and audio input and output, an attractive medium tower case with an ingenious hinged access design, a 56K fax/modem, Mac OS 8, and an Internet software bundle. Some models also include a Zip drive for backup and storage. Bundled software is either the Apple Home Edition or Creative Studio pack – more than fifteen titles including ClarisWorks V 4.0, Grolier Multimedia Encyclopedia, and other programs.

A notch in price and performance above the 6500 series, the PowerMac G3s are based on Motorola's new G3 processor, which, the company's literature says, is optimized for the Mac OS 8 operating system and includes an improved "backcaching" design. Available in four models from 233 to 300 MHz, these systems are configured with 32 to 128 megabytes of RAM, 4- to 6-gigabyte hard drives (the 266-MHz midtower contains a 4-gigabyte ultra wide SCSI), and up to 6 megabytes of SGRAM for fast graphics. With graphics users and medium-sized businesses as their intended market, the G3s come bundled with OS 8 and Internet Setup Assistant, and can also be custom configured.

Based on the 604e RISC processor, PowerMac 8600 PCs are available in three configurations as of early 1998, running at speeds of 250 to 300 MHz. Intended for business design applications and other computing tasks that require power and justify a higher price, the 8600s are expandable (RAM via DIMM sockets and expansion cards via PCI slots), networkable (Ethernet and LocalTalk ports), and come with

4-gigabyte hard drives, full multimedia, and an unusual 1 megabyte of processor cache. There was a "hot rebate" offer associated with these PCs as of early 1998, which calls into question their future, particularly with the appearance of the G3s. In keeping with their intended graphics applications, the 8600s also come with "near broadcast" video in/video out capabilities.

Developed for even more demanding graphics and video-editing tasks than the 8600s, the PowerMac 9600s are also based on Motorola's 604e RISC processor, and occupy the top slot in Apple's desktop computing lineup. They are available in two configurations. Both are 300-MHz systems with 64 megabytes of RAM and 4-gigabyte hard drives, and, as might be expected, they contain lots of video RAM, full multimedia, and flexible networking options. The only apparent difference between the two models is that one comes with a built-in Iomega Zip drive for backup and storage. The 9600s are niche market PCs for professionals who are willing to pay for peak performance.

When considering any of the PowerMacs, the crucial question to ask is whether you wish to pay extra for the duality they offer – the compatibility with Apple- as well as Windows-based hardware and software. There is no doubt that these computers are well designed and well supported. But the two flaws they present are their higher price, and their potential to lead you into a future which is limited by shrinking groups of hardware and software. When compared feature for feature to systems in the Wintel (Windows/Intel) side of the market, they are, in most cases, not price competitive.

DESKTOP MANUFACTURER: APPLE

Model: G3 series, 233/266 MHz
Physical: Midtower case
Motherboard and Processor: PowerPC G3 processor; CPUs available at 233/266+ MHz
Cache: 512K on processor card
Floppy/Hard Drives: 4- to 6-GB hard drive; Apple 3.5" floppy drive
Video: ATI Rage II+ video with 2-MB SGVRAM, 24-bit colour
Multimedia: 24x CD-ROM; 16-bit stereo sound
Modem: Built-in 10 Base-T
Bundled Software: Varies depending on model and age
Warranty: One-year limited warranty

Approximate Street Price at Publication: $2,400 to $2,799 (233-MHz models); $2,799 to $5,199 (266 MHz)
Additions: Revolutionary new processor does things that Pentium II cannot; 32-MB RAM; 3 DIMM slots, up to 384 MB; 1–2 SCSI bays (some models come with a Zip drive); 3 PCI slots, 12"; ships with Mac OS 8

DESKTOP MANUFACTURER: APPLE

Model: Network Server 700/200
Physical: Medium tower; floor tower
Motherboard and Processor: 200-MHz PowerPC 604e with FPU and 64K on-chip cache, processor on removable card
Cache: 64K on CPU, 1-MB level 2 cache
Floppy/Hard Drives: Support for 9 internal SCSI-2 tape backups
Video: S/VGA support up to 1,024 x 768; other video options available
Multimedia: CD-ROM drive; 16-bit stereo sound
Modem: Optional; built-in Ethernet and LocalTalk
Bundled Software: Operating system and network software and utilities
Warranty: One-year warranty
Approximate Street Price at Publication: Contact manufacturer
Additions: 6 PCI slots; support for external SCSI devices; optional RAID controllers

DESKTOP MANUFACTURER: APPLE

Model: PowerMac 5500, 225/250 MHz
Physical: All-in-one design
Motherboard and Processor: 603e PowerPC 225/250 MHz
Cache: 64K cache on-chip
Floppy/Hard Drives: 2-GB hard drive; Apple format 3.5" floppy drive
Video: Onboard 2D/3D graphics accelerator with 24-bit colour
Multimedia: 24x CD-ROM; 16-bit stereo sound
Modem: Built-in 10 Base-T network card
Bundled Software: Variable depending on model; includes Mac OS 8 and "Everything you need to get onto the Internet"
Warranty: One-year parts-and-labour warranty
Approximate Street Price at Publication: Contact manufacturer

Additions: 32-MB RAM; 2 DIMM, up to max 128 MB; has one 7" PCI slot; built-in 10 Base-T
Notes: Meant for educational and home-use markets

DESKTOP MANUFACTURER: APPLE

Model: PowerMac 6500, 225/250/275/300 MHz
Physical: Medium tower
Motherboard and Processor: 603e PowerPC
Cache: 64K on-chip
Floppy/Hard Drives: 2- to 6-GB IDE hard drive; 3.5" Apple floppy drive
Video: ATI Rage II accelerated with 2-MB SGRAM, 24-bit colour
Multimedia: 8x–24x CD-ROM; 16-bit stereo sound
Modem: 56-Kpbs voice
Bundled Software: Variable depending on model; Mac OS 8 and utilities included
Approximate Street Price at Publication: $2,099 (250MHz); $2,499 (275 MHz)
Additions: 2 DIMM slots, RAM up to 128 MB; comes with 16- to 64-MB EDO; 2 PCI 7" slots

DESKTOP MANUFACTURER: APPLE

Model: PowerMac 8600
Physical: Midtower case
Motherboard and Processor: Power PC 604e at 250 and 300 MHz
Cache: 1-MB inline cache
Floppy/Hard Drives: 4-GB hard drive; Apply floppy drive
Video: Scratch video in/out; 24-bit video supports SECAM and PAL
Multimedia: 24x CD-ROM; sound; speakers
Modem: Included
Bundled Software: Mac OS 8/8.1; Apple and networking utilities
Warranty: One-year limited warranty
Approximate Street Price at Publication: $3,699

DESKTOP MANUFACTURER: APPLE

Model: PowerMac 9600/x MP
Physical: Midtower case
Motherboard and Processor: Two xMHz 604e PowerPC chips ("xMP"), one xMHz 604e ("x"); integrated FP multiprocessor machines available 300 to 350 MHz
Cache: 64K on-chip; 512K level 2 external; new models have 1-MB cache on CPU card
Floppy/Hard Drives: 4-GB fast SCSI
Video: 4-MB VRAM, support for up to 1,600 x 1,200, 24-bit colour, 75-Hz max refresh; new models have accelerated "TwinTurbo" video controllers with 8 MB
Multimedia: 12x–24x CD-ROM; 16-bit stereo sound
Modem: 33.6/56-Kbps with voice optional on early models; standard on later models
Bundled Software: System 7.5.5.; Mac OS 8 on later models
Warranty: One-year limited warranty
Approximate Street Price at Publication: $4,699 (300MHz); $5,399 (350 MHz)
Additions: 6 PCI slots; PCI 2.0 compliant; 10 Base-T and Ethernet; later models have 12 DIMM slots with RAM up to 768 MB and 4 SCSI bays

DESKTOP MANUFACTURER: APPLE

Model: Workgroup Server 7350
Physical: Desktop case
Motherboard and Processor: PowerPC 604e RISC with FPU enhancement; 48–MB RAM and higher; PCI slots
Cache: 64K on CPU; 256K level 2 and higher
Floppy/Hard Drives: Internal 4-GB SCSI-2 and higher
Video: video card
Multimedia: CD-ROM drive; multimedia
Modem: Optional built-in Ethernet and LocalTalk
Bundled Software: Appleshare Server Solutions; Apple Net Server Essentials
Approximate Street Price at Publication: Contact manufacturer

AST ADVANTAGE

Established in 1980 by Albert Wong, Safi Qureshey, and Tom Yuen, this Asian company has produced the Advantage series in addition to its servers and business class systems. Bundled with a software package which included Lotus SmartSuite, Advantages were often found on mass-marketer and department store shelves. The deep discounting this series was subjected to in those environments did not make it a favourite among smaller outlets which had to purchase it in small quantities and therefore could not be as competitive. A notch below the IBM Aptivas, Hewlett-Packard Pavilions, NEC Ready PCs, and Compaq Presarios, these computers went head to head with the Packard Bell Multimedia and Legend systems and Acer's Aspires. They were also challenged by smaller manufacturers in Canada such as Patriot and Hewitt Rand, and even IPC, even though AST deserves recognition as a multinational.

AST has experienced such rough times in the past four years that they have recently put the Advantages on hold. The systems are included in this guide for reference, and in anticipation that AST's new partner, Samsung, may revive the series in the future.

An article in *PC World* magazine, entitled "AST's Free Fall," describes how the company has experienced a steady decline in both service and revenue since 1994, scoring a "poor" or "worst" in service categories consistently in 1995 and 1996. According to comments from an AST service executive in that article, a partnership with Korean giant Samsung has injected new life into the company, allowing it to expand its service staff by about 30 percent. The company has renewed its emphasis on quality manufacturing and better support, and in 1998 pledged that its customers would begin to reap the rewards. Unfortunately, as of March 1998, the Canadian division of AST was still clearly in a state of transition and restructuring. Conduct some research into this company's position in Canada before gambling on its ability to reinvent itself. Consider a home package from a competitor such as Acer or NEC, or a generic system built to order.

DESKTOP MANUFACTURER: AST

Model: Advantage 9402
Physical: Beige minitower with AST QuietPC design; 200W power supply
Motherboard and Processor: Intel Pentium MMX processor (430 TX

chipset) 166 or 200 MHz; 32-MB EDO RAM (expandable to 256 MB)
Cache: 256K pipeline burst cache
Floppy/Hard Drives: 1.44-MB floppy drive; 2-GB enhanced IDE hard drive
Video: 3D accelerated MPEG video card with 2-MB DRAM
Multimedia: 16x CD-ROM; 16-bit Sound Blaster–compatible sound card; 3D wave table sound amplified stereo speakers; Microsoft Sidewinder Gamepad
Modem: 33.6-Kbps internal modem/14.4-Kbps fax
Bundled Software: Windows 95; Lotus SmartSuite; Intuit Quicken SE; Systemsoft System Wizard; Sega Virtual Fighter; Sega Bug; Davidson Dimension; 7th Level Helicops; AT&T Watson for Internet Explorer; TV Host; America Online; Compuserve; Prodigy
Warranty: One-year limited warranty; AST Lifeline tech support; System Wizard (Automated Problem Resolution)
Suggested List Price at Publication: Contact manufacturer
Approximate Street Price at Publication: Contact manufacturer
Additions: Windows 95 keyboard with arm rest; Microsoft mouse

AST BRAVO

Positioned slightly downmarket from IBM's business class systems, Compaq's Deskpros, and Dell's Dimensions and OptiPlexes, the AST Bravos are office computers that come bare or minimally configured. They are available in desktop and midtower cases and are generic in design. They will accept third-party components easily, although it's not always a good idea to introduce outside parts to a PC for which you've paid extra because of the stature of its manufacturer. AST has taken a beating recently, and is undergoing unpredictable changes in 1998. You may wish to contact the company directly before deciding on one of its systems, especially if you are looking at a multiple-PC purchase.

One advantage of these systems is their price. They are among the least costly business class systems available from a multinational, although whether AST's new partner, Samsung, will even allow the company's current lines to continue remains to be seen. AST had posted successive losses in recent years, but management and Samsung now assert that they have learned from the past and will make future products and services in Canada more attractive. How successful they will be is a gamble.

The Bravos are a good deal for small or medium-sized businesses that already have networking in place, or have it in mind for the future. If you are thinking about one of these PCs for use at home, be sure that you budget extra for any applications, and check that all multimedia components (sound card and speakers) are included.

DESKTOP MANUFACTURER: AST

Model: Bravo LC series P166, PII 233
Physical: Mid-size case with AST QuietPC and Flex Chassis design; 200W power supply (front panel switch)
Motherboard and Processor: Pentium processors 166, 166 with MMX, or 233 MHz and higher; 16-MB SDRAM expandable to 256 MB
Cache: 256K cache
Floppy/Hard Drives: 1.44-MB floppy drive; 1.6-GB or 2-GB EIDE hard drive (Ultra DMA-33 support, SMART drive technology); total drive bays: 4 (desktop), 6 (minitower)
Video: ATI Mach 64 video card (1-MB SGRAM, upgradable to 4 MB)
Multimedia: 16x (max) CD-ROM drive on some models; ESS 1868 (16-bit stereo, Sound Blaster compatible; headphones with built-in microphone; Spatializer 3D stereo
Modem: K56flex internal modem (some models)
Bundled Software: Windows 95; AST CommandCenter Utilities;
Warranty: One-year on-site warranty
Suggested List Price at Publication: From $1,595
Approximate Street Price At Publication: From $1,495
Additions: Windows 95 keyboard; mouse; 4 expansion slots on desktop models (2 32-bit PCI, 1 16-bit ISA, 1 PCI/ISA shared), 7 expansion slots on minitower models (3 32-bit PCI, 4 16-bit ISA)

DESKTOP MANUFACTURER: AST

Model: Bravo MS series
Physical: Desktop and minitower designs; AST QuietPC and Flex Chassis design; 200W power supply (front panel switch)
Motherboard and Processor: Pentium processors from 166 MMX to PentiumII 200, 233, 266, and 300 MHz; 16- or 32-MB SDRAM (max 256 MB on system board)
Cache: 256–512K cache
Floppy/Hard Drives: 1.44-MB floppy drive; 2-GB or 4-GB EIDE hard

drive (Ultra DMA-33 support, SMART drive technology); total of 4 drive bays
Video: ATI Mach 64 video card (1-MB SGRAM, upgradable to 4 MB)
Multimedia: 16x (max) CD-ROM drive (on some models)
Modem: K56flex DSVD internal modem
Bundled Software: Windows 95; AST CommandCenter Utilities
Warranty: One-year on-site warranty
Suggested List Price at Publication: From $1,899; $2,999 (PII 266)
Approximate Street Price at Publication: From $1,829; $2,795 (PII 266)
Additions: Windows 95 keyboard; mouse; 4 expansion slots (2 32-bit PCI, 1 16-bit ISA, 1 PCI/ISA shared)

AST SERVERS

This family of performance servers is positioned against formidable competitors – Dell, IBM, Digital Equipment, Hewlett-Packard, Compaq, and NEC – which already have a strong hold on the large corporations and mid-sized businesses that dominate this market.

Running at speeds of 200 to 300 megahertz, and available with additions common to these kinds of strong computers – fast, ultra wide SCSI drives and adapters, redundant and independent drives, dual processors, rack-mounted components to ensure stability and a fault-tolerant environment, and premium warranty and support – these servers offer the features necessary to handle medium-sized and large networks.

AST's Premium GS, HS, and KS series servers are priced in the middle of the pack, but the company's recent history and uncertain future have affected its attractiveness in this most sensitive side of the marketplace. It remains to be seen whether its alliance with Samsung and recent pledges to improve will gain it any credibility with the all-important Fortune 1,000 customers in this side of the computer business.

DESKTOP MANUFACTURER: AST

Model: Premium GS
Physical: Medium and floor tower cases; AST Flex Chassis design 200W power supply; rack mount server options available; AST Noise Reduction
Motherboard and Processor: Intel Pentium MMX and Pentium II

processors; 200–266 MHz and higher; 16- and 32-MB EDO or SDRAM
Cache: 256–512K pipeline burst cache
Floppy/Hard Drives: 1.44-MB floppy drive; 2.5- to 4.0-GB and larger enhanced IDE and ultra fast wide hard drives
Video: Accelerated S/VGA video card
Multimedia: Internal CD-ROM; sound optional
Modem: Internal 10 Base-T Ethernet network adapter
Bundled Software: Windows 95 or Windows NT 4.0; AST Network Utilities
Warranty: One-year on-site warranty; toll-free tech support
Suggested List Price at Publication: Contact manufacturer
Approximate Street Price at Publication: Contact manufacturer

DESKTOP MANUFACTURER: AST

Model: Premium HS
Physical: Medium and floor tower cases; AST Flex Chassis design 200W power supply; rack mount server options available; AST Noise Reduction
Motherboard and Processor: Intel Pentium and Pentium II processors; 200–266 MHz and higher; 16- and 32-MB EDO or SDRAM
Cache: 256–512K pipeline burst cache
Floppy/Hard Drives: 1.44-MB floppy drive; 2.5- to 4.0-GB and larger enhanced IDE and ultra fast wide hard drives
Video: Accelerated S/VGA video card
Multimedia: CD-ROM in most models; sound optional
Modem: Internal Ethernet network adapter
Bundled Software: Windows 95 or Windows NT 4.0; AST Network Utilities
Warranty: One-year on-site warranty; toll-free tech support
Suggested List Price at Publication: Contact manufacturer
Approximate Street Price at Publication: Contact manufacturer

DESKTOP MANUFACTURER: AST

Model: Premium KS
Physical: Medium and floor tower cases; AST Flex Chassis design 200W power supply; rack mount server options available; AST Noise Reduction

Motherboard and Processor: Intel Pentium and Pentium II processors; 200–266 MHz and higher; 16- and 32-MB EDO or SDRAM
Cache: 256–512K pipeline burst cache
Floppy/Hard Drives: 1.44 MB floppy drive; 2.5- to 4.0-GB and larger enhanced IDE and ultra fast wide hard drives
Video: Accelerated S/VGA video card
Multimedia: Internal CD-ROM; sound optional
Modem: Internal 10 Base-T Ethernet network adapter
Bundled Software: Windows 95 or Windows NT 4.0; AST Network Utilities
Warranty: One-year limited on-site warranty; toll-free tech support
Suggested List Price at Publication: Contact manufacturer
Approximate Street Price at Publication: Contact manufacturer

DESKTOP MANUFACTURER: AST

Model: Manhattan D
Physical: Medium and floor tower cases; AST Flex Chassis design 200W power supply; rack mount server options available; AST Noise Reduction
Motherboard and Processor: Intel Pentium MMX and Pentium II processors; 200–266 MHz and higher; 16- and 32-MB EDO or SDRAM
Cache: 256–512K pipeline burst cache
Floppy/Hard Drives: 1.44-MB floppy drive; 2.5- to 4.0-GB and larger enhanced IDE and ultra fast wide hard drives
Video: Accelerated S/VGA video card
Multimedia: Internal CD-ROM; sound optional
Modem: Internal 10 Base-T Ethernet network adapter
Bundled Software: Windows 95 or Windows NT 4.0; AST Network Utilities
Warranty: One-year limited on-site warranty; toll-free tech support
Suggested List Price at Publication: Contact manufacturer
Approximate Street Price at Publication: Contact manufacturer

BATRA

A Canadian company started in the early '80s, this assembler of generic systems sells to vendors through distributor Markham Computers; in turn, its PCs are available to the public through an authorized dealer network which includes large and small stores, value-added resellers, and some consultants.

At the time of publication, Batra offered some special bundles and was also custom building computers to specification. Its national warranty is one of the most attractive and least expensive in the business, at $75 to upgrade to three years on site from the one-year return-to-depot guarantee which comes standard. This upgrade covers computers anywhere in Canada, subject to a standard clause stating that you must be within a reasonable distance of a major centre. Together with the Batra toll-free support line, this backup is a notch above most local assemblers and even some multinational manufacturers.

Otherwise, these are generic, standard issue computers, the bundles including basic components which are easy to repair but lacking unusual or innovative features. The power supplies, cases, hard drives, and motherboards in them will be similar to, if not exactly the same as, those in a system built by the store down the street. But that third-party presence and toll-free number, and especially the inexpensive on-site warranty option, are reassuring. The Corel software pack also allows you to get right to work. These are complete PCs, even if they don't include a lot of frills. Priced in the middle of the national generic assemblers, Batra competes with IPC, Bondwell, Pine, and Patriot. Especially for users in outlying areas, these computers are noteworthy for their upgradability and support.

DESKTOP MANUFACTURER: BATRA

Model: B166 MMX Base
Physical: Beige minitower case
Motherboard and Processor: Intel Pentium MMX 166-MHz and higher processor; 16- or 32-MB EDO RAM; or build to order
Cache: 256K external cache
Floppy/Hard Drives: 1.44-MB floppy drive; 2.1-GB enhanced IDE hard drive
Video: ATI 2-MB MPEG Super VGA video card
Multimedia: Available but not included in Base system: internal CD-ROM; sound card; external speakers
Modem: Available but not included in Base system: internal 33.6- or 56-Kbps fax/modem
Bundled Software: Windows 95

Warranty: One-year return-to-depot parts-and-labour warranty; toll-free tech support; three-year labour warranty; on-site warranty upgrade available
Suggested List Price at Publication: From $999
Approximate Street Price at Publication: From $999

DESKTOP MANUFACTURER: BATRA

Model: B233 MMX CV2
Physical: Beige minitower case
Motherboard and Processor: Intel Pentium MMX 233-MHz and higher processor; 32-MB EDO RAM; or build to order
Cache: 256K external cache
Floppy/Hard Drives: 1.44-MB floppy drive; 2.1-GB enhanced IDE hard drive
Video: ATI 2-MB MPEG Super VGA video card
Multimedia: Internal 16x CD-ROM; 16-bit sound card; external speakers
Modem: Internal 33.6- or 56-Kbps fax/modem
Bundled Software: Windows 95; Corel WordPerfect Suite; Grolier's CD bundle including Grolier's Encyclopedia
Warranty: One-year return-to-depot parts-and-labour warranty; toll-free tech support; three-year labour warranty; on-site warranty upgrade available
Approximate Street Price at Publication: From $1,199

DESKTOP MANUFACTURER: BATRA

Model: Pentium II series
Physical: Beige minitower case
Motherboard and Processor: Intel Pentium II processor; 32-MB SDRAM; or build to order
Cache: 512K
Floppy/Hard Drives: 1.44-MB floppy drive; 2.1-GB and higher enhanced IDE hard drive
Video: ATI 2-MB MPEG Super VGA video card
Multimedia: Internal 16x CD-ROM; 16-bit sound card; external speakers
Modem: Internal 33.6- or 56-Kbps fax/modem
Bundled Software: Windows 95; Corel WordPerfect Suite; Grolier's CD bundle including Grolier's Encyclopedia

Warranty: One-year return-to-depot parts-and-labour warranty; toll-free tech support; three-year labour warranty; on-site warranty upgrade available
Suggested List Price at Publication: From $1,895 (estimated)
Approximate Street Price at Publication: From $1,895 (estimated)

BONDWELL

Rated as Editor's Choice in performance by Canda Computer Paper/CCP Labs in 1997, these nationally marketed medium tower systems are quite customizable (at least as far as their processor, RAM, and hard drives are concerned), the manufacturer perhaps having taken note of the success of other companies that offer a nationally distributed product line which is generic and flexible.

In the recent past, Bondwell offered the 150 and 166 series as well, but the lineup as of early 1998 was composed of three packages, one for home, one for office, and one basic system. There is not much material difference between these issues, except in the software bundles. The "Biz" systems come with Microsoft Office, the "Home" PCs with a rudimentary MS Works and Entertainment package, and the BWT 233 with no applications at all.

The pricing of these systems is tightly controlled. Authorized vendors allowed access to the Bondwells have margins more or less dictated to them. The manufacturer sets an advertised retail price which is meant to be extremely competitive – a new twist on the price wars raging in this generic end of the market. While some companies such as Ultinet, Hits, and Just Imagine sell direct, shoulder sales costs, and support themselves, Bondwell, along with Batra and IPC, offers aggressive advertising and a choice of local outlets. There is an advantage here: you can evaluate and test a system from a dealer more easily than you can a directly marketed product. On the downside, that short profit means your vendor will be a lot happier to hear from you before the sale than afterward. Still, Bondwell does maintain its own warranty and support network (two years return to depot from date of purchase), so with this in mind, these computers are not a bad alternative to a system built specifically for you by the local guru. In this lineup, Bondwell's packages seem to be the best bets; those software bundles are a good value precisely because they are part of a complete system.

As a postscript, you might wonder about the 1-MB video card advertised in these PCs in late '97. By the time this guide hits the bookstores, Bondwell will almost certainly have upgraded this to an MPEG-2-compliant, 2-MB or higher specification. If they haven't, they should.

DESKTOP MANUFACTURER: BONDWELL

Model: Biz 200M
Physical: White medium tower
Motherboard and Processor: Intel Pentium MMX 200-MHz; 32-MB EDO RAM; or build to order
Cache: 512K pipeline burst cache
Floppy/Hard Drives: 1.4-MB floppy drive; 2.6-GB enhanced IDE hard drive
Video: 2-MB Rage video card
Multimedia: 16x CD-ROM; Creative Labs Sound Blaster 64 sound card; Zoltrix 75W amplified speakers
Modem: 33.6-Kbps data/fax modem
Bundled Software: Windows 95; Microsoft Office 97, Encarta, Golf, Works, Money; Magic Schoolbus
Warranty: Two-year return-to-depot warranty
Suggested List Price at Publication: Contact manufacturer
Approximate Street Price at Publication: Contact manufacturer
Additions: Microsoft IntelliMouse

DESKTOP MANUFACTURER: BONDWELL

Model: BWT 233
Physical: Beige or charcoal medium tower
Motherboard and Processor: Intel Pentium 233 MMX; 32-MB SDRAM; or build to order
Cache: 512K pipeline burst cache
Floppy/Hard Drives: 1.4-MB floppy drive; 3.2-GB enhanced IDE hard drive
Video: 1-MB ATI video card
Multimedia: 24x CD-ROM; 16-bit sound card; Zoltrix "68" amplified speakers
Modem: 33.6-Kpbs data/fax modem
Bundled Software: Windows 95; Microsoft Plus
Warranty: Two-year return-to-depot warranty

Suggested List Price at Publication: $1,299
Approximate Street Price at Publication: $1,299
Additions: Zoltrix mouse

DESKTOP MANUFACTURER: BONDWELL

Model: Home 166M
Physical: White medium tower
Motherboard and Processor: Intel Pentium 166 MMX; 32-MB SDRAM; or build to order
Cache: 512K pipeline burst cache
Floppy/Hard Drives: 1.44-MB floppy drive; 2.6-GB enhanced IDE hard drive
Video: 1-MB ATI video card
Multimedia: 16x CD-ROM; Creative Labs Sound Blaster 16 sound card; Zoltrix amplified speakers
Modem: 33.6-Kbps data/fax modem
Bundled Software: Windows 95; Microsoft Encarta, Golf, Works, Money; Magic Schoolbus
Warranty: Two-year return-to-depot warranty
Suggested List Price At Publication: $1,029
Approximate Street Price at Publication: $1,029
Additions: Microsoft mouse

COMPAQ DESKPRO

The main lineup of business class computers from Compaq, the Deskpro 2000/4000/6000/8000s replace the company's Prolinea series, which enjoyed success in the early to mid-'90s. These new systems are available in different shapes and configurations, the most common being variations on the slimline desktop, with some models available at a slightly higher price in attractive white medium towers.

Like most other business class PCs, these come bare, all with CD-ROMs now (many did not as recently as a year ago!), and most with some combination of networking hardware and software. Sound, speakers, modem, and applications are, as would be expected, not included. For their intended use in business networking environments, the Deskpros come with extras such as security and diagnostic software, case cover locks, and configuration management utilities.

The Deskpro warranty is three years parts and labour, first year on site, but remember when purchasing to ask if your vendor is authorized to provide Compaq service as well as hardware sales. This is not critical; sometimes you can get a better price when purchasing from a non-servicing vendor. Just remember it so that you aren't surprised if you have to invoke the on-site warranty. Calls should be handled by an authorized Compaq service provider. As far as price is concerned, these systems are very well positioned for the combination of manufacturer, warranty, and firepower they offer. They are not at all intended to compete with the generics – the Ultinets, Batras, or those from even larger national builders such as Hewitt Rand. They are, rather, aimed at the same market as other blue-chip multinationals such as IBM, and fare quite well in that league. Look for a Deskpro, especially the more competitively priced 2000s and 4000s, if you can afford the quality and you plan to see your business and networking requirements grow.

Compaq's recent acquisition of Digital Equipment Corporation has gained it new size and stature in the computer business; it will be interesting to see how this merger will affect its mainstream products such as the Deskpro series in 1998, 1999, and 2000.

DESKTOP MANUFACTURER: COMPAQ

Model: Deskpro 2000 series
Physical: White desktop or medium tower case
Motherboard and Processor: Intel Pentium MMX CPU, 166, 200, or 233 MHz; 16- to 32-MB SDRAM (max 384 MB)
Cache: 256–512K secondary cache
Floppy/Hard Drives: 1.44-MB floppy drive; 2.1- to 3.2-GB EIDE hard drive
Video: S3 Trio 64/G2X embedded with 1-MB SGRAM (upgradable to 2 MB)
Multimedia: 16x CD-ROM drive (IDE); enhanced audio in some systems; systems also available without CD or sound
Modem: Optional
Bundled Software: Windows 95; Insight Personal Edition; compaq setup utilities; Diagnostics for Windows
Warranty: Three-year limited warranty with first year on site; twenty-four-hour toll-free phone support; online support
Suggested List Price at Publication: From $1,456 (166 MHz); $2,031 (233 MHz)

Approximate Street Price at Publication: From $1,299 (166 MHz); $1,849 (233 MHz)

DESKTOP MANUFACTURER: COMPAQ

Model: Deskpro 2000 Pentium II series
Physical: White desktop or medium tower case
Motherboard and Processor: Intel Pentium II CPU, 233 or 266 MHz or higher; 16- or 32-MB SDRAM (max 384 MB)
Cache: 512K cache
Floppy/Hard Drives: 1.44-MB floppy drive; 2.1- to 3.2-GB SMART Ultra ATA hard drive
Video: Matrox MGA 1064/SG with 2-MB SGRAM (upgradable to 4 MB)
Multimedia: 24x CD-ROM drive (IDE); enhanced audio in some systems; systems also available without CD or sound
Modem: Optional
Bundled Software: Windows NT 4.0; Insight Personal Edition; computer setup utility; Compaq Diagnostics
Warranty: Three-year limited warranty with first year on site; twenty-four-hour toll-free phone support; Compaq online support
Suggested List Price at Publication: From $3,156 (266 MHz); from $3,681 (300 MHz)
Approximate Street Price at Publication: From $2,995 (266 MHz); from $3,395 (300 MHz)

DESKTOP MANUFACTURER: COMPAQ

Model: Deskpro 4000
Physical: White desktop or medium tower case; 200W or greater power supply
Motherboard and Processor: Intel Pentium MMX CPU, 166, 200, or 233 MHz; 16- or 32-MB SDRAM (max 384 MB)
Cache: 512K cache
Floppy/Hard Drives: 1.44-MB floppy drive; 2.1- to 3.2-GB SMART Ultra ATA hard drive
Video: S3 Virge/GX enhanced 64-bit graphics card with 2-MB SGRAM (upgradable to 4 MB)

Multimedia: 16x CD-ROM drive (IDE); embedded audio in some systems; systems also available without CD
Modem: Optional; Compaq Netelligent 10/100 TX embedded network interface
Bundled Software: Windows 95; Insight Personal Edition; computer setup utility; Diagnostics for Windows
Warranty: Three-year limited warranty with first year on-site; twenty-four-hour toll-free phone support; Compaq online support
Suggested List Price at Publication: From $1,713 (166 MHz); $2,044 (200 MHz); $2,575 (233 MHz)
Approximate Street Price at Publication: From $1,595 (166 MHz); $1,895 (200 MHz); $2,395 (233 MHz)

DESKTOP MANUFACTURER: COMPAQ

Model: Deskpro 4000 Pentium II
Physical: White desktop or medium tower case; 200W or greater power supply
Motherboard and Processor: Intel Pentium II CPU, 233, 266, or 300 MHz and higher; 16- or 32-MB SDRAM (max 384 MB)
Cache: 512K integrated secondary cache
Floppy/Hard Drives: 1.44-MB floppy drive; 2.1- to 3.2-GB SMART Ultra ATA hard drive
Video: Matrox MGA/1064 SG PCI card with 2-MB SGRAM (upgradable to 4 MB)
Multimedia: 24x CD-ROM drive (IDE); embedded audio in some systems; systems also available without CD or sound
Modem: Optional; Compaq Netelligent 10/100 TX embedded network interface
Bundled Software: Windows NT 4.0; Insight Personal Edition; computer setup utility; Compaq Diagnostics
Warranty: Three-year limited warranty with first year on site; twenty-four-hour toll-free support; online support
Suggested List Price at Publication: From $2,656 (233 MHz); $3,281 (266 MHz); $3,806 (300 MHz)
Approximate Street Price at Publication: From $2,495 (233 MHz); $3,095 (266 MHz); $3,595 (300 MHz)

DESKTOP MANUFACTURER: COMPAQ

Model: Deskpro 4000N
Physical: White desktop slimline case; intended network workstation
Motherboard and Processor: Intel Pentium MMX CPU, 166, 200, or 233 MHz; 16- or 32-MB SDRAM (max 256 MB)
Cache: 256K integrated secondary cache
Floppy/Hard Drives: 1.44-MB floppy drive; 2.1- to 3.2-GB SMART Ultra ATA hard drive
Video: S3 Trio 64 V2/GX2 with 2-MB SGRAM (at maximum)
Multimedia: Optional on some models
Modem: Optional; Compaq Netelligent 10/100 TX embedded network interface
Bundled Software: Windows NT 4.0; Insight Personal Edition; computer setup utility; Compaq Diagnostics
Warranty: Three-year limited warranty with first year on site; twenty-four-hour toll-free support; online support
Suggested List Price at Publication: From $1,600 (166 MHz); $1,975 (200 MHz); $2,039 (233 MHz)
Approximate Street Price at Publication: From $1,495 (166 MHz); $1,695 (200 MHz); $1,929 (233 MHz)

DESKTOP MANUFACTURER: COMPAQ

Model: Deskpro 4000S
Physical: White small desktop slimline case; intended network workstation
Motherboard and Processor: Intel Pentium MMX CPU, 166 or 200 MHz; 16- or 32-MB SDRAM (max 256 MB)
Cache: 256K integrated secondary cache
Floppy/Hard Drives: 1.44-MB floppy drive; 2.1-GB enhanced IDE hard drive
Video: S3 Trio 64 V2/GX embedded with 2-MB SGRAM (at maximum)
Multimedia: Slimline 20x CD-ROM drive (optional)
Modem: Optional; Compaq Netelligent 10/100 TX embedded network interface
Bundled Software: Windows 95; Insight Personal Edition; computer setup utility; Compaq Diagnostics
Warranty: Three-year limited warranty with first year on site; twenty-four-hour toll-free support; online support

Suggested List Price at Publication: From $1,526 (166 MHz); $1,681 (200 MHz); $2,025 (233 MHz)
Approximate Street Price At Publication: From $1,399 (166 MHz); $1,549 (200 MHz); $1,895 (233 MHz)

DESKTOP MANUFACTURER: COMPAQ

Model: Deskpro 6000 Pentium II
Physical: White desktop or medium tower case; 200W or greater power supply
Motherboard and Processor: Intel Pentium II CPU, 233, 266, or 300 MHz; 16- or 32-MB SDRAM (max 384 MB)
Cache: 512K integrated secondary cache
Floppy/Hard Drives: 1.44-MB floppy drive; 2.1- to 3.2-GB Ultra SCSI hard drive
Video: Matrox Millennium AGP 2 with 4-MB WRAM (upgradable to 16 MB)
Multimedia: 24x CD-ROM drive with embedded audio
Modem: None; Compaq Netelligent 10/100 TX embedded network interface
Bundled Software: Windows NT 4.0; Insight Personal Edition; computer setup utility; Compaq Diagnostics
Warranty: Three-year limited warranty with first year on site; twenty-four-hour toll-free support; online support
Suggested List Price at Publication: From $3,941 (233 MHz); $4,283 (266 MHz); $5,743 (300 MHz)
Approximate Street Price at Publication: From $3,595 (233 MHz); $3,995 (266 MHz); $4,495 (300 MHz)

COMPAQ PRESARIO

This lineup of Compaq home personal computer systems is in direct competition with the IBM Aptivas and Hewlett-Packard Pavilions and is indirectly positioned against other bundles from Acer (Aspire), Packard Bell, and NEC. The Presario is one of the oldest "home office" series of personal computers on the market – the first models appeared in an all-in-one design of 486SX class systems back in the early '90s. It has been wise of Compaq to abandon that form factor (which they did around 1996) because it was limiting and made those systems more difficult to upgrade and repair.

Even the current Presarios, like home-PC packages from their competitors, are not particularly customizable. They come with a huge complement of extras, at least some of which the folks in the marketing department assume you're going to want. Maybe they're right, but maybe not. These are systems which have been physically designed with flair, although they're not quite as dramatic as the Aptiva Stealth series. Some newer Presarios – the 4528s, for example – include innovative features which are likely to appear in other PCs before long, including multi-media volume controls built right into the case, and a compact disc player without a tray – it sucks the disk in just like the CD player in your car.

These are attractive home PCs from a major builder with a good pedigree. But the fact that they are often sold in the deep discount column, and contain special systems engineering, means that your vendor may be either unwilling or even downright unable to assist you in case of trouble. And like many other manufacturers, Compaq now offers on-site warranty only for the first ninety days after purchase. After that, it is not at all shy about charging a "per call" credit card fee for any phone support outside the guarantee. If you don't plan to disturb all that special hardware and software by adding your own programs and devices later, these computers are great right out of the box. If you do have special tasks you want to undertake that aren't on Compaq's menu, you might want to look at systems without quite so many extras.

Also, take care when purchasing one of these to ask for one of Compaq's Presario monitors. A favourite trick of vendors is to price these systems bare and then make up profit on the monitor. But special features such as a duplexing microphone that supports the telephone software are built into most Presario monitors. So don't accept a cheaper, third-party product if you want to be sure the whole package is going to work properly.

The way these systems are sold to computer stores also makes them confusing to evaluate: Compaq offers selected models to some vendors – one line of Presarios to department stores and mass marketers and other lines to independent computer outlets. This creates difficulty when you are trying to compare one model in one store against its counterpart model in another. Many major computer and printer manufacturers, including IBM, Hewlett-Packard, NEC, and Packard Bell, are guilty of this "dual channel" distribution. Of course, it enables the builder's salespeople to offer special deals to different kinds of resellers, but it also burdens the end-user with one more unnecessary consideration when trying to make an already difficult purchase.

DESKTOP MANUFACTURER: COMPAQ

Model: Presario 2200
Physical: Black desktop; steady-state 75W power supply
Motherboard and Processor: 180-MHz Cyrix processor; 16-MB DRAM (expandable to 48 MB DRAM required)
Cache: 256K pipeline burst cache (upgradable to 512K)
Floppy/Hard Drives: 1.44-MB floppy drive; 1.6-GB hard drive
Video: 2-MB MPEG video
Multimedia: 8x CD-ROM drive; sound card; speakers sold separately with optional monitor
Modem: 33.6-Kbps/14.4-Kbps internal data/fax modem (upgradable to K56flex)
Bundled Software: Windows 95; Microsoft Works, Money 97, Bookshelf, Encarta 97; Sim City 2000 Network Edition
Warranty: Compaq one-year limited warranty – one-year parts and one-year carry-in labour with first ninety-days on site; twenty-four-hour toll-free tech support
Suggested List Price at Publication: $1,400
Approximate Street Price at Publication: $1,100
Additions: Compaq Windows 95 keyboard; Compaq mouse; slimline Compaq case

DESKTOP MANUFACTURER: COMPAQ

Model: Presario 4528
Physical: White minitower; steady-state 75W power supply
Motherboard and Processor: 233-MHz Pentium processor with MMX technology; 32-MB DRAM (expandable to 64 MB, DRAM DIMM required)
Cache: 256K pipeline burst cache (upgradable to 512K)
Floppy/Hard Drives: 1.44-MB floppy drive; 3.2-GB hard drive
Video: Accelerated 64-bit graphics with Direct3D; 1-MB video memory (upgradable to 2 MB); MPEG-2 video playback
Multimedia: 24x (max) CD-ROM drive; 16-bit stereo sound; Dolby Digital Surround Sound (AC-3) and JBL 3D VirtualTheater; JBL Pro speakers (sold separately with Compaq monitor)
Modem: 33.6-Kbps/14.4-Kbps internal data/fax modem (upgradable to K56flex)
Bundled Software: Windows 95; Microsoft Works, Money 97,

Bookshelf, Encarta 97; Sim City 2000 Network Edition
Warranty: Compaq one-year limited warranty – one-year parts and one-year carry-in labour with first ninety days on site, plus twenty-four-hour toll-free technical support during warranty
Suggested List Price at Publication: $2,595
Approximate Street Price at Publication: $2,095
Additions: Compaq Windows 95 keyboard; Compaq mouse; 1 open ISA slot, 1 open PCI/ISA combo slot, 1 ISA slot with modem; 4 drive bays (1 open bay); 2 USB connectors

DESKTOP MANUFACTURER: COMPAQ

Model: Presario 4540
Physical: White minitower; steady-state 75W power supply
Motherboard and Processor: 200-MHz Pentium processor; 16-MB DRAM (expandable to 48 MB, DRAM DIMM required)
Cache: 256K pipeline burst cache (upgradable to 512K)
Floppy/Hard Drives: 1.44-MB floppy drive; 2.1-GB hard drive
Video: Accelerated 64-bit graphics with Direct3D; 1-MB video memory (upgradable to 2 MB); MPEG-2
Multimedia: 16x (max) CD-ROM drive; sound card; JBL Pro speakers (sold separately with optional monitor)
Modem: 33.6-Kbps/14.4-Kbps internal data/fax modem (upgradable to K56flex)
Bundled Software: Windows 95; Microsoft Works, Money 97, Bookshelf, Encarta 97; Sim City 2000 Network Edition
Warranty: Compaq one-year limited warranty – one-year parts and one-year carry-in labour with first ninety days on site, plus twenty-four-hour toll-free technical support during warranty
Suggested List Price at Publication: $1,649
Approximate Street Price at Publication: $1,595
Additions: Compaq Windows 95 keyboard; Compaq mouse; 1 open ISA slot, 2 USB connectors

DESKTOP MANUFACTURER: COMPAQ

Model: Presario 4550
Physical: White minitower; steady-state 75W power supply
Motherboard and Processor: Pentium processor with MMX technol-

ogy; 32-MB DRAM (expandable to 48 MB, DRAM DIMM required)
Cache: 256K pipeline burst cache (upgradable to 512K)
Floppy/Hard Drives: 1.44-MB floppy drive; 3.2-GB hard drive; Iomega Zip drive
Video: Accelerated 64-bit graphics with Direct3D; 1-MB video memory (upgradable to 2 MB); MPEG-2 video playback
Multimedia: 16x (max) CD-ROM drive; 16-bit stereo sound; Dolby Digital Surround Sound (AC-3) and JBL 3D VirtualTheater; JBL Pro speakers (sold separately with Compaq monitor)
Modem: 33.6-Kbps/14.4-Kbps internal data/fax modem (upgradable to K56flex)
Bundled Software: Windows 95; Microsoft Works, Money 97, Bookshelf, Encarta 97; Sim City 2000 Network Edition
Warranty: Compaq one-year limited warranty – one-year parts and one-year carry-in labour with first ninety days on-site, plus twenty-four-hour toll-free technical support during warranty
Suggested List Price at Publication: $2,089
Approximate Street Price at Publication: $1,995
Additions: Compaq Windows 95 keyboard; Compaq mouse; 1 open ISA slot, 1 open PCI/ISA combo slot, 1 ISA slot with modem; 4 drive bays (1 open bay); 2 USB connectors

DESKTOP MANUFACTURER: COMPAQ

Model: Presario 4660
Physical: Minitower case; steady-state 145W power supply
Motherboard and Processor: Pentium II 300 MHz; 64-MB DRAM (expandable); (DRAM DIMM required)
Cache: Internal 32K, external 512K
Floppy/Hard Drives: 1.44-MB floppy drive; 8.0-GB hard drive
Video: PCI 32-bit accelerated graphics (64-bit with 2-MB video memory); 1-MB EDO video memory (upgradable to 2 MB); MPEG-2
Multimedia: 16x (max) CD-ROM drive; integrated 16-bit stereo sound; Spatializer 3D Surround Sound; simultaneous, 2-way (full-duplex) speakerphone; JBL Pro stereo speakers (sold separately with optional monitor)
Modem: Internal 56-Kbps data/fax modem
Bundled Software: Windows 95; Microsoft Works; CorelDraw 5; Compton's Interactive Encyclopedia 96; Quicken SE Multimedia; PGA Tour 96; Compaq Utilities

Warranty: Compaq one-year limited warranty – one-year parts and one-year carry-in labour with first ninety days on site
Suggested List Price at Publication: $3,080
Approximate Street Price at Publication: $2,895
Additions: Windows 95 keyboard; mouse; 2 PCI slots, 2 ISA slots, 1 PCI/ISA combo slot; 2 open drive bays; 2 USB connectors

DESKTOP MANUFACTURER: COMPAQ

Model: Presario 4824
Physical: White minitower case; steady-state 165W power supply
Motherboard and Processor: 233-MHz Intel Pentium II processor; 32-MB RAM (expandable to 256 MB)
Cache: 512K internal pipeline burst cache
Floppy/Hard Drives: 1.44-MB floppy drive; 6.5-GB hard drive
Video: Accelerated 64-bit graphics with Direct3D; 2-MB SyncGraphics memory (upgradable to 4 MB); MPEG-2
Multimedia: 24x CD-ROM; 16-bit stereo sound; Dolby Digital (AC-3) and JBL 3D VirtualTheater; speakers (sold separately with Presario 1425, 1525, or 1725 monitor)
Modem: K56flex internal modem
Bundled Software: Windows 95; Microsoft Works, Bookshelf, Encarta 97, Money 97; Internet applications; Intel video capture utility
Warranty: One-year limited warranty (one-year parts and one-year carry-in labour, ninety days on site); one-year twenty-four-hour toll-free telephone support
Suggested List Price at Publication: $2,795 (estimated)
Approximate Street Price At Publication: $2,449
Additions: Compaq Windows 95 keyboard; Compaq mouse; PCI slots and ISA slots, composite video and audio left and right

DESKTOP MANUFACTURER: COMPAQ

Model: Presario 4840MT
Physical: Minitower case; steady-state 165W power supply
Motherboard and Processor: 266-MHz Intel Pentium II processor; 32-MB DRAM (expandable to 384 MB)
Cache: 512K internal pipeline burst cache
Floppy/Hard Drives: 1.44-MB floppy drive; 6.5-GB hard drive

Video: ATI Rage Pro video card with AGP (accelerated graphics port) and ATI motion compensation; 4-MB SyncGraphics video memory; MPEG-2
Multimedia: DVD-ROM drive (supports CDs/CD-ROMs); 16-bit stereo sound; Dolby Digital (AC-3) and JBL 3D VirtualTheater; speakers (sold separately with Presario FX500 or 1725S monitor)
Modem: K56flex internal modem
Bundled Software: Windows 95; Microsoft Works, Bookshelf, Encarta 97, Money 97; Internet applications; Intel video capture utility
Warranty: One-year limited warranty (one-year parts and one-year carry-in labour, ninety days on site)
Suggested List Price at Publication: $3,499 (estimated)
Approximate Street Price at Publication: $3,000
Additions: Compaq Windows 95 keyboard; Compaq mouse; PCI slots and ISA slots, composite video and audio left and right

DESKTOP MANUFACTURER: COMPAQ

Model: Presario 4860
Physical: Black minitower case; steady-state 165W power supply
Motherboard and Processor: 333-MHz Intel Pentium II processor; 64-MB DRAM (expandable to 384 MB)
Cache: 512K internal pipeline burst cache
Floppy/Hard Drives: 1.44-MB floppy drive; 8.0-GB hard drive
Video: ATI Rage Pro video card with AGP (accelerated graphics port) and ATI motion compensation; 4-MB SyncGraphics video memory; MPEG-2
Multimedia: DVD-ROM drive (supports CDs/CD-ROMs); 16-bit stereo sound; Dolby Digital (AC-3) and JBL 3D VirtualTheater; speakers (sold separately with Presario FX500 or 1725S monitor)
Modem: K56flex internal modem
Bundled Software: Windows 95; Microsoft Works, Bookshelf, Encarta 97, Money 97; Internet applications; Intel video capture utility
Warranty: One-year limited warranty (one-year parts and one-year carry-in labour, ninety days on site)
Suggested List Price at Publication: $3,718
Approximate Street Price at Publication: $3,495
Additions: Compaq Windows 95 keyboard; Compaq mouse; PCI slots and ISA slots, 1 PCI/ISA combo slot; 6 drive bays; 2 USB connectors; 3 RCA input jacks (one composite video and audio left and right)

COMPAQ PROLIANT/PROSIGNIA SERVERS

Anyone who truly appreciates computer technology has to have a soft spot in his or her heart for the Compaq family of servers. I know I do. Throwbacks to the old mainframe days when everything seemed to work perfectly, these systems are built to support networks and are manufactured with this in mind. Of course, they're priced with this in mind too, but only because they contain extras that systems in other sectors of the market don't have. Look at the available pre-sale documentation, for example. It is complete. It may be a bit technical, but this is a time when you appreciate extra information. Both the Proliants and Prosignias are intended to be used in networking solutions – so it doesn't make sense to spend the extra money on one as a stand-alone station, unless (as some people do) you happen to like extra quality.

These computers have traditionally been available bare, without even such essentials as CD-ROMs, although in 1998 most have at least these preinstalled. No sound cards or modems, though. By the time you have built one into a complete system, it's easy to find yourself staring at a $5,000 invoice. And that's without a monitor.

Higher-priced versions in the series will support exotic tasks and configurations such as RAID (redundant array of independent drives) setups and fast, wide SCSI drives, and allow the creation of what is known as a fault-tolerant environment. Unless you have a situation that demands these capabilities, the Proliants and Prosignias, as well as their competitors from Digital, NEC, AST, IBM, and Dell, are likely to be beyond you. So appreciate these computers for their design, special capabilities, excellent pedigree, and three-year support, but remember your needs if you're thinking of purchasing one. If you can afford one, especially in the recently reduced Prosignia series, and have a suitable application, go for it. Otherwise, look carefully at whether you can justify server quality and expense.

Note: because of the level of manufacturer engineering in server PCs in general, these computers do not respond as quickly to changing technology. Thus they usually lag behind those hot rods the guy down the street is putting together. The upside, however, is increased reliability. A large manufacturer with corporate clients is not able to integrate components into its systems until they are fully tested and documented.

Compaq is now well positioned in this market, with its $9.6 billion acquisition in early 1998 of Digital Equipment making it the second largest computer company in the world.

DESKTOP MANUFACTURER: COMPAQ

Model: Proliant series
Physical: Mid- to floor tower cases; rack mount options
Motherboard and Processor: Pentium MMX, Pentium Pro, and Pentium II 200- to 300-MHz and higher CPU; 16- to 64-MB ECC RAM; dual processor capable; customizable
Cache: 256–512K and higher level 2 cache
Floppy/Hard Drives: 1.44-MB floppy drive; SCSI and fast ultra wide SCSI hard drives from 2 to 9.1 GB and larger; hot pluggable drives available in most models
Video: 2- to 4-MB SDRAM
Multimedia: Internal 16x or 24x CD-ROM
Modem: Optional; Compaq Netelligent 10/100 Base-T network interface
Bundled Software: Windows 95 or Windows NT 4.0; Smart Start; Compaq Insight Manager; Auto Server Recovery; Compaq Utilities
Warranty: Three-year parts and labour, first year on site; Compaq Prefailure warranty
Suggested List Price at Publication: $5,850 (PII 233); $7,764 (PII 266); $9,100 (PII 300)
Approximate Street Price at Publication: $4,895 (PII 233); $6,895 (PII 266); $8395 (PII 300)

DESKTOP MANUFACTURER: COMPAQ

Model: Prosignia series
Physical: Compaq medium tower and floor towers
Motherboard and Processor: Intel Pentium MMX, Pentium Pro, and Pentium II CPU; 16- to 64-MB RAM (max. 208 to 256 MB); 200W power supply; customizable
Cache: 256–512K external cache
Floppy/Hard Drives: EIDE or SCSI and fast ultra wide SCSI hard drives from 2 to 9.1 GB; hot pluggable drives available in most models
Video: 2- to 4-MB SDRAM video card
Multimedia: Internal 8x, 16x, or 24x CD-ROM
Modem: None; Compaq Netelligent 10/100 Base-T network interface
Bundled Software: Windows 95/98 or Windows NT; Compaq network utilities

Warranty: Three-year parts and labour, first year on site
Suggested List Price at Publication: From $3,380 (PII 233)
Approximate Street Price at Publication: From $3,199 (PII 233)

DELL

Based in Round Rock, Texas, Dell advertises itself as the world's leading direct marketer of personal computers. And yes, there is indeed a Mr. Dell, Michael Dell to be exact, the entrepreneur who started this company back in the 1980s when the idea of "remote marketing" – selling systems over the telephone and by mail – was something of a novelty in PC retailing. As his company grew and became able to claim status as a large-scale builder (it is a Fortune 500 corporation today), it also became able to offer the price and support advantages of a large organization. Now it plays both sides of the fence, providing the support, stability, and volume pricing of an international manufacturer as well as the flexibility of a custom builder who will put together a system to your needs, using up-to-date components.

In the '90s, with the explosion of the Internet and increased consumer familiarity with computers, Dell's remote marketing strategy has been right on the money. The company promotes its products aggressively on the World Wide Web and through print and other media advertising, and is doing very well, having posted profitable quarters for several years in a row. Along with IBM and Compaq, it is one of the the best-known computer companies in the world.

Dell's desktop computer products can be divided into three categories: general home/office systems (the Dimension series), network workstations (the OptiPlex G series and the Workstation 400s), and server systems (the Poweredge 2100, 2200, 4100, 4200, and 6100 lines). As of publication, Dell's corporate promo sheet stated that approximately 90 percent of its revenues are derived from sales to other Fortune 500 companies, and that it now sells computers in over 140 countries, with a total employment of almost 15,000 people.

As far as its individual systems are concerned, Dell's flagship Dimension series computers are very competitively priced – most of them offered with Microsoft Office, loaded with very current components, and customizable to your specifications. The prices are slightly higher than those of most local assemblers, but remember there is a pretty large company in the background here, even if it is a long way away. Still, the remote marketing scenario is not without its disadvantages. Don't forget the $75 to $150 shipping charges that must be added when considering this company's advertised prices. A recent call confirmed that there is no place in Canada to actually see one of the Dimension systems in action, though I suspect the company would make special arrangements for quantity orders, or corporate or server purchasers.

DESKTOP MANUFACTURER: DELL

Model: Dimension XPS D266
Physical: Minitower; Dell Soft 200W power supply
Motherboard and Processor: Pentium II 266 MHz; 32-MB SDRAM standard (upgradable to 384 MB)
Cache: 32K level 1 cache, 512K level 2 cache
Floppy/Hard Drives: 1.44-MB floppy drive; 4.3-, 6.4-, or 8.4-GB EIDE (SCSI drives also available)
Video: STB 4-MB AGP video card (other options available)
Multimedia: 32x (max) CD-ROM; Yamaha or Creative Labs AWE64 Value wavetable card; speakers
Modem: 56-Kbps data/fax modem optional
Bundled Software: Windows 95 or Windows NT 4.0; Microsoft Office 97 Small Business Edition, Microsoft Home Essentials
Warranty: Three-year limited warranty standard; various optional support plans available
Suggested List Price at Publication: $2,069 (15" monitor included)
Approximate Street Price at Publication: $2,069 (15" monitor included)
Additions: Shipping charges apply; configuration charges may apply

DESKTOP MANUFACTURER: DELL

Model: Dimension XPS II (D300)
Physical: Minitower; Dell Soft 200W power supply
Motherboard and Processor: Pentium II 300 MHz; 64-MB SDRAM standard (upgradable to 384 MB)
Cache: 512K level 2 cache
Floppy/Hard Drives: 1.44-MB floppy drive; 4.3-, 6.4-, or 8.4-GB EIDE (SCSI drives also available)
Video: STB 4-MB AGP video card (other options available)
Multimedia: 32x (max) CD-ROM; Yamaha or Creative Labs AWE64

Value wavetable card; speakers
Modem: 56-Kbps data/fax modem optional
Bundled Software: Windows 95 or Windows NT 4.0; Microsoft Office 97 Small Business Edition, Microsoft Home Essentials
Warranty: Three-year limited warranty standard; various optional support plans available
Suggested List Price at Publication: $2,879 (17" monitor included)
Approximate Street Price at Publication: $2,879 (17" monitor included)
Additions: Shipping charges apply; configuration charges may apply

DESKTOP MANUFACTURER: DELL

Model: Dimension XPS II (D333)
Physical: Minitower; Dell Soft 200W power supply
Motherboard and Processor: Pentium II 333 MHz; 32-MB SDRAM standard (upgradable to 384 MB)
Cache: 512K level 2 cache
Floppy/Hard Drives: 1.44-MB floppy drive; 4.3-, 6.4-, or 8.4-GB EIDE (SCSI drives also available)
Video: STB 4-MB AGP video card (other options available)
Multimedia: 32x (max) CD-ROM; Yamaha or Creative Labs AWE64 Value wavetable card; speakers
Modem: 56-Kbps data/fax modem optional
Bundled Software: Windows 95 or Windows NT 4.0; Microsoft Office 97 Small Business Edition, Microsoft Home Essentials
Warranty: Three-year limited warranty standard; various optional support plans available
Suggested List Price at Publication: $3,079 (17" monitor included)
Additions: Shipping charges apply; configuration charges may apply

DESKTOP MANUFACTURER: DELL

Model: Dimension XPS MMX (M233)
Physical: Minitower; Dell Soft 200W power supply
Motherboard and Processor: Pentium with MMX 233 MHz; 32-MB SDRAM standard (upgradable to 384 MB)
Cache: 512K level 2 cache
Floppy/Hard Drives: 1.44-MB floppy drive; 4.3-, 6.4-, or 8.4-GB EIDE (4-GB SCSI drives also available)

Video: 4-MB Virge video card (other options available); 15" monitor included
Multimedia: 32x (max) CD-ROM; Sound Blaster card; speakers
Modem: 56-Kbps data/fax modem optional
Bundled Software: Windows 95 or Windows NT 4.0; Microsoft Office 97 Small Business Edition
Warranty: Three-year limited warranty standard; various optional support plans available
Suggested List Price at Publication: $2,049 (monitor included)
Approximate Street Price at Publication: $2,049 (monitor included)
Additions: Shipping charges apply; configuration charges may apply

DESKTOP MANUFACTURER: DELL

Model: OptiPlex Ga 233/266 (L,M,T)
Physical: OptiFrame chassis: low-profile (145W power supply), full desktop case; midtower cases available
Motherboard and Processor: Pentium II 233 or 266 MHz; 32-MB SDRAM
Cache: 512K integrated level 2 cache
Floppy/Hard Drives: 1.44-MB floppy drive; 2.1-GB or higher Ultra DMA hard drive; 4/8-GB Travan4 tape drives optional
Video: Integrated S3 Trio 64 V2 PCI with 2-MB video memory; optional Matrox Millennium II PCI with 4-MB WRAM PCI video memory
Multimedia: 24x (max) EIDE CD-ROM drive optional; Creative Labs AWE32 value card or Vibra 16x sound cards optional
Modem: Optional 56-Kbps data/fax modem; 3Com Ethernet card included
Bundled Software: Windows NT 4.0 or Windows 95
Warranty: Three-year limited warranty standard; various optional support plans available
Suggested List Price at Publication: $1,869 (233 MHz); $2,069 (266 MHz)
Approximate Street Price at Publication: $1,869 (233 MHz); $2,069 (266 MHz)
Additions: Shipping charges apply; configuration charges may apply

DESKTOP MANUFACTURER: DELL

Model: OptiPlex Ga 300 (L,M,T)
Physical: OptiFrame chassis: low-profile (145W power supply), full desktop case; midtower cases available
Motherboard and Processor: Pentium II 300 MHz; 32-MB SDRAM
Cache: 512K integrated level 2 cache
Floppy/Hard Drives: 1.44-MB floppy drive; 4.3-GB or higher Ultra DMA hard drive; 4/8-GB Travan4 tape drives optional
Video: Integrated S3 Trio 64 V2 PCI with 2-MB video memory; optional Matrox Millennium II PCI with 4-MB WRAM PCI video memory
Multimedia: 24x (max) EIDE CD-ROM drive optional; Creative Labs AWE 32 value card or Vibra 16x sound card optional
Modem: Optional 56-Kbps data/fax modem; 3Com Ethernet card included
Bundled Software: Windows NT 4.0 or Windows 95
Warranty: Three-year limited warranty standard; various optional support plans available
Suggested List Price at Publication: $2,219
Approximate Street Price at Publication: $2,219
Additions: Shipping charges apply; configuration charges may apply

DESKTOP MANUFACTURER: DELL

Model: OptiPlex Ga 333 (L,M,T)
Physical: OptiFrame chassis: low-profile (145W power supply), full desktop case; midtower cases available
Motherboard and Processor: Pentium II 333 MHz; 32-MB SDRAM
Cache: 512K integrated level 2 cache
Floppy/Hard Drives: 1.44-MB floppy drive; 4.3-GB or higher Ultra DMA hard drive; 4/8-GB Travan4 tape drives optional
Video: Integrated S3 Trio 64 V2 PCI with 2-MB video memory; optional Matrox Millennium II PCI with 4-MB WRAM PCI video memory
Multimedia: 24x (max) EIDE CD-ROM drive optional; Creative Labs AWE32 value card or Vibra 16x sound cards optional
Modem: Optional 56-Kbps data/fax modem; 3Com Ethernet card included
Bundled Software: Windows NT 4.0 or Windows 95

Warranty: Three-year limited warranty standard; various optional support plans available
Suggested List Price at Publication: $2,329
Approximate Street Price at Publication: $2,329
Additions: Shipping charges apply; configuration charges may apply

DESKTOP MANUFACTURER: DELL

Model: OptiPlex Gn (L,M,T)
Physical: OptiFrame chassis: low-profile (145W power supply), full desktop case; midtower cases available
Motherboard and Processor: Pentium with MMX, 233 or 266 MHz; 32- to 256-MB EDO RAM
Cache: 256K level 2 pipeline burst cache
Floppy/Hard Drives: 1.44-MB floppy drive; 2.1-GB or higher Ultra DMA hard drive; 4/8-GB Travan4 tape drives optional
Video: Integrated S3 Trio 64 V2 PCI with 2-MB video memory; optional Matrox Millennium II PCI with 4-MB WRAM PCI video memory
Multimedia: 24x (max) EIDE CD-ROM drive optional; Creative Labs AWE32 Value card or Vibra 16x sound card optional
Modem: Optional 56-Kbps data/fax modem
Bundled Software: Windows NT 4.0 or Windows 95
Warranty: Three-year limited warranty standard; various optional support plans available
Suggested List Price at Publication: $1,329 (233 MHz); $1,519 (266 MHz)
Approximate Street Price at Publication: $1,329 (233 MHz); $1,519 (266 MHz)
Additions: Ethernet network cards included in some models, optional in others; shipping charges apply; configuration charges may apply

DIGITAL EQUIPMENT WORKSTATIONS

These business class PCs are in competition with workstations from other large builders such as IBM and NEC, and are targeted at "price conscious mainstream business users" (the 3100s), "value conscious customers worldwide" (the 3010s), and "advanced users of productivity business applications" (the 5100s). They accompany Digital's lineup of Venturis and Celebris computers, which were introduced a few years ago. The recent merger of Digital Equipment with Compaq Computer of Houston, Texas, now means that its PCs come from the second largest computer company in the world, which will likely affect Digital's marketing and distribution, and may even jeopardize the existence of some models.

Currently DEC desktops are only available through a tightly controlled network of authorized resellers, as is the case with most of its competitors. This strategy protects a manufacturer's ability to support its products, but can also serve to keep its prices higher, even though the specifications of these systems are not noticeably different from others in the same tier.

If you have the inclination to find and purchase a Digital desktop and pay the extra dollars for it, you may now feel encouraged that you are buying into a strong new alliance. On the other hand, Digital's recent marriage to Compaq calls into question the stability of some of its workstations over the longer term. Only time will tell.

DESKTOP MANUFACTURER: DIGITAL EQUIPMENT

Model: Digital PC 3000 and 5000 series
Physical: Tower and desktop cases; 200-300W power
Motherboard and Processor: Intel Pentium, Pentium Pro, and Pentium II 200- to 300-MHz processors
Cache: 256–512K cache
Floppy/Hard Drives: 1.44-MB floppy drive; 2.5- to 10-GB and larger enhanced IDE and SCSI hard drives
Video: 2- to 4-MB 32-bit video
Multimedia: CD-ROM/sound optional
Modem: Optional; Ethernet and other network interfaces included in some models
Bundled Software: Windows 95 or Windows NT 4.0; Digital Serverworks Network Tools
Warranty: One-year on-site warranty
Suggested List Price at Publication: \$1,899 (3100/P200); \$2,299 (5100/P200)
Approximate Street Price at Publication: \$1,849 (3100/P200); \$2,249 (5100/P200)

DIGITAL EQUIPMENT SERVERS

In competition with other "tier one" servers from its new business partner, Compaq, and IBM, this American manufacturer's Prioris systems enjoy a reputation for reliability and support in the world of networking, where they are usually called upon to control large numbers of workstations in medium-sized and corporate business environments. These are not computers to take home to the kids. As with all entries in this end of the market, the Prioris systems are engineered to support specialty applications in addition to LANs (local area networks), WANs (wide area networks), corporate intranets, and other environments where computers need to share information on a single server – which absolutely must not fail, or, at least, must be set up to ensure that network users connected to it will never be thrown into disarray.

Digital has been a major player in this marketplace ever since the early days of personal computing, when it was known for its manufacture of minicomputers, a business that has been rocked by the power of microcomputers in the '90s. Networking and corporate sales form a logical market niche for a company with this history. If you're con-sidering one of these servers, you should seek more pre-sale information than can be included in a general-audience consumer guide such as this one. You may feel that Digital's experience with complex computer environments, and its new position in the marketplace, makes it more attractive than ever. On the other hand, since many of its products have now become redundant to those offered by its new partner, it is also possible that some of its products will be altered or even discontinued in the foreseeable future.

DESKTOP MANUFACTURER: DIGITAL EQUIPMENT

Model: Prioris ZX/HX 6000 server series; XL 5000/6000; XLe 6180/MX 6200 servers
Physical: Medium and floor tower cases; up to 300W power; rack mounts and other server options available
Motherboard and Processor: Intel Pentium, Pentium Pro, and Pentium II 200- to 300-MHz processors; single, dual, or quad processors accepted in various models; customizable
Cache: 256–512K cache
Floppy/Hard Drives: 1.44-MB floppy drive; 2.5- to 10-GB and larger enhanced IDE and SCSI hard drives

Video: 2- to 4-MB 32-bit video
Multimedia: 12x CD-ROM in most models; no sound
Modem: Optional; Ethernet and other network interfaces included in most models
Bundled Software: Windows 95 or Windows NT 4.0; Digital Serverworks Network Tools
Warranty: One-year on-site warranty
Suggested List Price at Publication: From $5,039 base price (MX 6266); from $5,626 (XL P200); other models from $3,820 base price
Approximate Street Price at Publication: From $4,795 base price (MX 6266); from $5,395 (XL P200)

HEWITT RAND

A multinational company with a presence in the United States, Canada, and other countries around the Pacific rim, Hewitt Rand sells three lines of generic computers in Canada, variously intended for business use, the academic tender market, networking, and home/small-office computing. All of these systems are ordinary in design, allowing the introduction of conventional components. The cases are attractive and large enough in most models to accommodate extra internal devices. It's doubtful whether the 686 systems are a good buy when compared for price and performance against direct competitors, although it's difficult to find another company that exactly occupies Hewitt Rand's place in the market. This company is large enough to call itself a multinational, yet not well enough known to reap the full rewards of that distinction. It bundles some systems with Hewitt Rand 15" and 17" monitors, and advertises assembly in Canada as an advantage. You can have these computers custom configured at the time of purchase, and it's worth noting that most models are Novell certified, which means that, even if you do not intend to use them in a networking environment, a builder has gone to the trouble of having its PCs subjected to standards tests, and that it will guarantee levels of quality and types of parts to keep them compatible. Hewitt Rand also offers a new line of servers with RAID and multiprocessor options.

Although Hewitt Rand would probably like to be thought of as an alternative to manufacturers such as Acer, AST, and even Dell, its systems are in competition with generic PCs made by other national manufacturers such as Patriot, Batra, and Bondwell. The generic design of Hewitt Rand PCs, combined with their certifications and international presence (even if it is a low-profile one), makes them unique in the Canadian marketplace. They are a good choice if you are seeking a computer that is a notch above those of the locally assembled market but not quite of the same stature as one from a major multinational manufacturer.

DESKTOP MANUFACTURER: HEWITT RAND

Model: Maxxima MMX/Maxxima P II series
Physical: ATX medium tower case; 200 or 250W power supplies
Motherboard and Processor: Pentium MMX or Pentium II 166- to 333-MHz; 16- or 32-MB SDRAM or EDO RAM (max 128 MB); BIOS antivirus protection; customizable
Cache: 512K level 2 pipeline burst cache
Floppy/Hard Drives: 1.44-MB floppy drive; 2.1-GB enhanced IDE hard drive and larger
Video: 2-MB S3 Virge 3D DX video card; other cards optional
Multimedia: 16x CD-ROM; 3D wave table sound card; external multimedia speakers with adapter
Modem: 33.6- or 56-Kbps US Robotics modem
Bundled Software: Windows 95/98
Warranty: Two-year parts-and-labour warranty
Approximate Street Price at Publication: From $1,199 (166 MMX); $1,995 (266 Pentium II)

DESKTOP MANUFACTURER: HEWITT RAND

Model: Proform home series
Physical: Desktop or minitower case
Motherboard and Processor: Cyrix M2 MMX 200 or 233 MHz; customizable 16-MB (200) or 32-MB (233)
Cache: 512K pipeline burst cache
Floppy/Hard Drives: 1.44-MB floppy drive; 2.1-GB enhanced IDE hard drive
Video: 1-MB video with MPEG
Multimedia: 16x CD-ROM; sound card; external multimedia speakers with adapter
Modem: 33.6-Kbps data/fax modem
Bundled Software: Windows 95/98

Warranty: One-year parts-and-labour return-to-depot warranty
Suggested List Price at Publication: \$1,399 (200 MHz); \$1,599 (233 MHz)
Approximate Street Price at Publication: \$1,329 (200 MHz, 14" monitor included); \$1,549 (233 MHz, 14" monitor included)
Note: Available in black

DESKTOP MANUFACTURER: HEWITT RAND

Model: Server series
Physical: Medium and floor towers
Motherboard and Processor: Pentium II and Pentium Pro 200 to 333 MHz; 32-MB RAM and higher; max 1-GB DIMMS
Cache: 512K pipeline burst cache
Floppy/Hard Drives: 1.44-MB floppy drive; enhanced IDE hard drives and SCSI hard drives
Video: S3 Trio 64 V2 MPEG video card
Multimedia: 12x CD-ROM; sound card; speakers optional
Modem: Optional
Bundled Software: Windows 95/98; Windows NT; networking utilities
Warranty: Two-year parts-and-labour warranty; warranty options available
Suggested List Price at Publication: Contact manufacturer
Approximate Street Price at Publication: Contact manufacturer

HEWLETT-PACKARD KAYAK

The new Kayak business class workstations from Hewlett-Packard are a notch above the company's phased-out Vectras and the current small business Brioline. Available in three classes – the XAs, XUs, and XWs – with processors ranging from 180-MHz Pentium MMX to 333-MHz and higher Pentium IIs as of publication, these computers are for the most part network ready, and come in various high performance configurations: both desktop and midtower designs, most containing Matrox Millennium video cards, others with fast wide SCSI hard drives for use in shared data environments. All include multimedia CD-ROM (24x) and a one-year on-site warranty with years two and three return-to-depot. Like the Vectras, these business class systems come at higher prices and configurations than many home and small office users will want or be prepared to pay for, but for their intended market, they are an attractive new lineup indeed.

DESKTOP MANUFACTURER: HEWLETT-PACKARD

Model: Kayak XA/XU/XW
Physical: Desktop; mini- or medium tower case/CSA power supply
Motherboard and Processor: Pentium II 233 MHz to 333 MHz
Cache: 512K and higher
Floppy/Hard Drives: 1.44-MB floppy drive; 2.1-GB, 4.5-GB, or 9.1-GB ultra wide SCSI hard drive
Video: Matrox Millennium II card installed in AGP slot; Cirrus Logic (some models); up to 1,600 x 1,200 (some models)
Multimedia: HP 24x (max) IDE CD-ROM; integrated Sound Blaster Pro, full-duplex stereo audio solution; built-in speaker and ergonomic volume control; MPC3 and Direct Sound III compatible
Modem: Optional
Bundled Software: Windows NT Workstation 4.0; HP TopTOOLS; Microsoft Internet Explorer; Netscape Communicator; McAfee Web Scan and Virus Scan; Adobe Acrobat Reader; AutoDesk WHIP! plug-in; other software in various models
Warranty: Three-year limited warranty (one year on site, next business day; two-year carry-in, parts and labour)
Suggested List Price at Publication: From $3,077 (XA 233 PII); $5,121 (XU 266 PII); $10,350 and up (XW series)
Approximate Street Price at Publication: From $2,199 (XA 233 PII); $4,795 (XU 266 PII); $10,350 and up (XW series)

HEWLETT-PACKARD PAVILION

In competition with Compaq's Presarios, IBM's Aptivas, the NEC Ready PC series, and the Acer Aspires, Hewlett-Packard's Pavilions are complete home computer systems from one of the most respected builders in the business. There is a manageable number of these systems available (about five models at the time of publication), ranging from the Pavilion 5120 to the 7370. Undoubtedly, new variations will appear throughout 1998.

These are the only systems from a tier one builder that still come with one full year of on-site warranty, Compaq and IBM having throttled that portion of their home PC guarantees back to ninety days and NEC retreating to six months. In systems from all of these companies, the remaining months of warranty are covered by a return-to-depot condition: you have to take a failed component to an authorized service centre and leave it there for repair.

There is a substantial preinstalled software package included with the Pavilions (over fifty titles!), including an exclusive imaging program complete with hundreds of photos and images you can customize or use in desktop publishing and wordprocessing applications. Note that the 7170 and 7295 systems came with only 28.8- or 33.6-Kbps fax/modems and 8x CD-ROMS, but soon into 1998 these outdated features will probably have been replaced by more up-to-date specifications, or the models perhaps completely replaced by the 8000 series or some variation of that lineup.

As with other home packages, these computers perform best with their own monitors, which have integrated speakers attached to both sides. While the Pavilions used to be near the top of the price group when compared to their direct competitors, they have recently (in early 1998) been reduced. This, and their longer warranty, make them worth considering if you are looking for a packaged PC.

DESKTOP MANUFACTURER: HEWLETT-PACKARD

Model: Pavilion 7000, 7100, 7200, and the current 7400 series
Physical: Medium tower case
Motherboard and Processor: 120- to 200-MHz Intel Pentium processors; 16-MB, 24-MB, or 32-MB RAM
Cache: 16K primary cache, 256K pipeline burst secondary cache (on some models)
Floppy/Hard Drives: 1.44-MB floppy drive; 1.62- to 4.0-GB hard drive
Video: 1-MB to 6-MB EDO video RAM (Premium 3Dfx Interactive dual 64-bit Voodoo graphics card on 7295V model); MPEG for full-screen, full-motion video
Multimedia: 4x, 6x, 8x, or 16x (max) CD-ROM drive; sound card; HP/Altec Lansing stereo speakers
Modem: Internal 33.6-Kbps fax/modem
Bundled Software: Windows 95; Hewlett-Packard application bundle
Warranty: One-year limited on-site warranty
Suggested List Price at Publication: $2,623 (7410); $2,973 (7420)
Approximate Street Price at Publication: $2,095 (7410); $2,995 (7420)
Additions: Windows 95 keyboard; mouse; Storm Technologies Easy-Photo drive (on some models); Iomega Zip drive (on some models)

DESKTOP MANUFACTURER: HEWLETT-PACKARD

Model: Pavilion 8000 series (8140, 8160, 8175, 8180)
Physical: Medium tower design
Motherboard and Processor: 200MMX MHz Pentium or 233MMX, 266MMX MHz Pentium II processors; 32- or 48-MB RAM
Cache: 32K primary cache, 256K pipeline burst cache
Floppy/Hard Drives: 1.44-MB floppy drive; 4.3- or 6.0-GB EIDE hard drive
Video: ATI 3D Rage II+ video card; 2-MB EDO video memory; MPEG for full-screen, full-motion digital video
Multimedia: 24x (max) CD-ROM drive; wave table sound and 16-bit, 3D stereo sound card; Polk Audio stereo speakers with Power Port technology
Modem: K56flex internal modem
Bundled Software: Windows 95; Microsoft Works; Quicken SE; reference package; games package; Intel Video Phone Receive; 8180 model includes thirty-day trial of AirMedia Live (wireless news, financial services tool)
Warranty: One-year, on-site limited hardware warranty; ninety-day limited software warranty; twenty-four-hour phone support
Suggested List Price at Publication: $2,551 (8140); $2,895 (8160); $3,325 (8175)
Approximate Street Price at Publication: $1,995 (8140); $2,295 (8160); $2,595 (8175)
Additions: Windows 95 keyboard; two-button mouse (wireless RF mouse on 8180 model); universal serial bus (USB) for easy plug and play; 6 expansion slots (3 PCI, 2 ISA, and 1 ISA/PCI)

HEWLETT-PACKARD VECTRA AND BRIO

The now disappearing Vectras and their replacements, the Brios, are from premium builder Hewlett-Packard and are offered in ranges extending from the entry-level VE series through to the XU and the 500 Vectras, as well as three classes of Brios: business systems, advanced business systems, and business communication systems. As you might expect from a company which is secure, at least for the moment, in its place in the industry, all of these PCs are conservative in the "hardware for dollar" column, but have scored better than average in independent service surveys. That is undoubtedly what justifies their pricing. The current Brios run from 200-MHz Pentium MMX PCs to Pentium II

333s, and compete with systems from other builders of stature – Compaq's Deskpros, IBM's PCs, Digital's 3000s, Dell's OptiPlexes, and NEC's Enterprises.

Many of the Vectras and Brios include manufacturer-specific advantages, such as soft powerdown – the ability to turn a system on and off by using the spacebar on the keyboard. Some also allow you to power on and off remotely via a network, in keeping with their intended use as business PCs and workstations. Included software is usually Microsoft Office or Word, Microsoft Publisher, and "Connected On-Line Backup" – a program which automatically backs up your hard drive via modem or Internet connection. Variations on this theme are bound to appear in one form or another in other computers soon, but it's worth noting that software that performs this task is now available on the World Wide Web for free. Considering their price, performance, and support, the Brios are tier one business systems that won't break any price barriers unless their manufacturer experiences a major hiccup. They are of good quality, sold at premium prices, and aimed at companies that are already networking or intend to do so in the future.

DESKTOP MANUFACTURER: HEWLETT-PACKARD

Model: Brio Business/Advanced Business Series
Physical: Desktop and medium tower designs
Motherboard and Processor: Intel Pentium MMX and Pentium II processors, 166 to 333 MHz; 16-, 32-, or 64-MB EDO or SDRAM
Cache: 256–512K level 2 cache
Floppy/Hard Drives: 1.44-MB floppy drive; 2.5- to 4.0-MB and larger enhanced IDE hard drives; SCSI hard drives and controllers optional
Video: 2- to 4-MB Super VGA video card
Multimedia: Internal CD-ROM; 16-bit sound card; headphones with some models, Labtech external speakers in some others
Modem: 56K fax/modems in some Brios; optional in others
Bundled Software: Windows 95; Microsoft Word, Publisher, Office in selected models; Connected OnLine Backup
Warranty: Hewlett-Packard three-year return-to-depot parts warranty (first year on site)
Suggested List Price at Publication: $1,643 (MMX 166 MHz); $2,555 (PII 266 MHz); $3,784 (PII 333 MHz)
Approximate Street Price at Publication: $1,549 (MMX 166 MHz); $2,395 (PII 266 MHz); $3,595 (PII 333 MHz)

Additions: Brio 14" ($333 list price), 15" ($392 list price) and 17" ($688 list price) monitors available for the series

IBM APTIVA

Introduced in the early '90s, Aptivas are premium home and small office bundles from the world's pre-eminent computer manufacturer. While the series has undergone several changes since the first 486s were introduced, as of publication they were available in three issues, from the least expensive E series, through the mid-range L series, to the top-of-the-line S models. Jammed with software and goodies such as voice recognition, IBM Home Director, Lotus SmartSuite, and Video Phone software, this group of PCs changes about as rapidly as any lineup from a large manufacturer can – sometimes several times each year.

At the top of the ladder the S series are systems sometimes known as "Stealth PCs" because of their sleek black design. Bose speakers are mounted on the sides of a 15" or 17" monitor, and a subwoofer, K56-flex modem, 24x CD-ROM or DVD, and cordless mouse come with models in the 233- to 300-MHz range. This is designer computing at its zenith. The L series PCs are of a similar design but with a reduced complement of programs and lower specifications – smaller hard drives and slower processors. The E series are most conventional in appearance and internal design (consider this to be in their favour), at 166 to 233 MHz as of publication, with new issues bound to appear throughout '98. All of the Aptiva computers, especially the S and L lines, are expensive and highly proprietary, as a close look at them will confirm. The S series are unlike any other PC I know of, designed with a separate unit which contains the floppy drive and a pop-up CD-ROM which sits under the monitor. The CPU tower is independent and may be positioned on or off the desk. While this unusual setup is eyecatching, it is not without disadvantages. If the CD or floppy on one of these systems acts up, you know that only the manufacturer is going to be able to repair it properly. This definitely affects your support and upgrade options. On the other hand, if you place a high value on design and appearance, these systems will surely catch your attention. Note also that IBM only offers these systems with Aptiva monitors – the CPUs are not sold separately. Still, they are of good quality and well supported – this is state of the art prepackaged computing. If you happen to like everything included in the bundle, great; if not, you're probably paying for extras you neither need nor want.

DESKTOP MANUFACTURER: IBM

Model: Aptiva E26/E46
Physical: Medium tower case; separate speakers
Motherboard and Processor: K6 233 MHz (E26); K6 266 MHz (E46); 32-MB SDRAM
Cache: 512K cache (256K in E26)
Floppy/Hard Drives: 1.44-MB floppy drive; 3.2- or 4.0-GB (E46) hard drive
Video: 2-MB SGRAM (E46 only); MPEG-2
Multimedia: 24x CD-ROM; sound; external speakers; microphone
Modem: Internal 56-Kbps fax/modem
Bundled Software: Windows 95; games; Lotus SmartSuite; Freelance Graphics; RingCentral Telephony package; and more
Warranty: One-year warranty; IBM "Owner Privileges" support plan comes with some models
Suggested List Price at Publication: $2,395 (E26)
Approximate Street Price at Publication: $1,999 (E26)
Additions: Customizable Aptiva EZ Buttons keyboard (4 buttons); IBM ScrollPoint mouse; USB connectors; IBM monitor required

DESKTOP MANUFACTURER: IBM

Model: Aptiva S61
Physical: Black split-system design (minitower/media console)
Motherboard and Processor: 266-MHz Pentium II processor with MMX; 32-MB SDRAM
Cache: 512K external cache
Floppy/Hard Drives: 1.44-MB floppy drive; 6.4-GB hard drive
Video: ATI 3D Rage Pro graphics accelerator (2x AGP); Aptiva Ultimate Arcade 3D graphics; 4-MB video RAM
Multimedia: 20x (max) CD-ROM drive; MPEG-2; 300-MIP Crystal Clear audio processor; integrated Bose audio with Dolby Digital Sound, TrueSpace processing system, and Acoustimass
Modem: Internal K56flex fax/modem
Bundled Software: Windows 95; MechWarrior 2: Mercenaries, HeliCops; IBM voice recognition software; Aptiva Photo Director (IBM/Kodak); RingCentral telephony package
Warranty: One-year return-to-depot warranty (first ninety days on site); IBM online support; toll-free fax-back system

Suggested List Price at Publication: \$3,999 (with 15" monitor); \$4,349 (with 17" monitor)
Additions: Customizable Aptiva EZ Buttons keyboard (4 buttons); IBM ScrollPoint mouse; USB connectors; Home Director starter kit; IBM monitor required

DESKTOP MANUFACTURER: IBM

Model: Aptiva S62
Physical: Black split-system design (minitower/media console); CSA power supply
Motherboard and Processor: 266-MHz Pentium II processor with MMX; 32-MB SDRAM
Cache: 512K cache
Floppy/Hard Drives: 1.44-MB floppy drive; 6.4-GB hard drive
Video: ATI 3D Rage Pro graphics accelerator (2x AGP); Aptiva Ultimate Arcade 3D graphics; 4-MB video RAM
Multimedia: DVD-ROM II with movie playback, also serves as 20x (max) CD-ROM drive; MPEG-2; 300-MIP Clear audio processor; integrated Bose audio with Dolby Digital, TrueSpace processing system, and Acoustimass sound
Modem: Internal K56flex fax/modem
Bundled Software: Windows 95; MechWarrior 2: Mercenaries, Heli-Cops; IBM voice recognition software; Aptiva Photo Director (IBM/ Kodak); RingCentral Telephony package
Warranty: One-year return-to-depot warranty (first ninety days on site); IBM online support; toll-free fax-back system
Suggested List Price at Publication: \$4,699 (17" monitor included)
Approximate Street Price at Publication: \$4,499 (17" monitor included)
Additions: Customizable Aptiva EZ Buttons keyboard (4 buttons); IBM ScrollPoint mouse; USB connectors; IBM monitor required

IBM PC 300

Is it safe to say that, along with their Apple counterparts, these are the descendants of the little machines that helped start it all? IBM still issues a wide range of systems in its PC line, all of them of excellent quality and backed by strong warranty and support. The 300s are IBM's offering for the office, and are often the chosen brand of Fortune 1,000 corporations and large institutions. In Canada, they are in direct competition with Compaq's Deskpros, Dell's Dimensions and OptiPlexes, and Digital Equipment's PC 3000 and 5000 series. In the U.S. and around the world, other competitors lurk in the wings, but the different incarnations of IBM's PC have remained remarkably stable in a business which is known for products that come and go.

There are all sorts of reasons why these systems have retained their place near the top. They are price competitive, if you take the time and trouble to compare everything in them and weigh factors such as failure rate, warranty, and support. A wander through IBM's web page tells a lot about this lineup. From the marketing perspective, there is no doubt that IBM's corporate view of the world puts some people off, but the benefits included with its PCs offset this: IBM's Asset Care (a diagnostic program which tells you about your system and what's going on inside it), SMART hard drives which warn of impending failures, laser etching of key components, Wake On LAN (the system logs onto a network automatically on powerup), and other networking advantages. These systems are not intended for the home market; without full multimedia features or a modem they belong in a networked business environment. But for their intended use, they remain near the top of the price, performance, and support pyramid.

DESKTOP MANUFACTURER: IBM

Model: IBM PC 300/350/365 series; IBM GL/XL/PL series
Physical: Desktop and midtower cases; 200–230W and higher power supply
Motherboard and Processor: Intel Pentium MMX 166- to 233-MHz and Pentium II 233- to 300-MHz processors; 32- to 64-MB SDRAM
Cache: 512K secondary cache
Floppy/Hard Drives: 1.44-MB floppy drive; 2.5- to 4.3-GB and larger EIDE and UDMA hard drives; some models with SCSI hard drives and controllers
Video: 2- to 4-MB SDRAM or WRAM; Matrox Millennium S/VGA card in some models
Multimedia: Internal 6x–32x CD-ROM; some models can be purchased bare
Modem: Optional; internal Ethernet network adapter in some models
Bundled Software: Windows 95/98 or Windows NT 4.0 or higher; IBM Utilities

Warranty: One-year on-site warranty; IBM toll-free support
Suggested List Price at Publication: From $1399 (300 GL); $2,489 (300 XL); $1,729 (300 PL)
Approximate Street Price at Publication: From $1,329 (300 GL); $2,295 (300 XL); $1,679 (300 PL)

IBM SERVERS

It is here that the line between the personal computer and its bigger brothers starts to blur. The distinction between these "PC" servers from IBM and the domain of the minicomputer is getting hard to identify. But these computers offer more than enough to ooh and ahh over by way of specifications and pedigree, even if you don't have the money to afford one, or the application to put it to good use. A browse through IBM Canada's website tells the story. Have a look at the exploded version of any of the 300 or 500 series designs and specs; now that's a computer. That's pre-sale information. Unfortunately, though, that's a high price! With the ante at about $3,000, even an entry-level system from this group is more to gape at than purchase unless you're setting up an intranet for a bank. What *do* they do with those huge profits, anyway?

Certainly for smaller, or even medium-sized, cost-conscious companies, some of the Compaq, NEC, or Dell servers are more competitively priced. Still, all of this doesn't prevent us from admiring the three-year on-site warranty, the IBM tech-support army, the extra networking features, and the cutting-edge position of the manufacturer. If you can afford one, why not? Otherwise, these servers are in a financial as well as a technological class by themselves.

DESKTOP MANUFACTURER: IBM

Model: IBM servers
Physical: IBM medium and full tower cases
Motherboard and Processor: Intel Pentium MMX, Pentium Pro, and Pentium II processors, 200- to 300-MHz; 32- to 64-MB ECC, EDO, or SDRAM; dual processors in some models; customizable
Cache: 512K and higher external level 2 cache
Floppy/Hard Drives: 1.44-MB floppy drive; 2.5- to 4.0-GB and larger enhanced IDE and fast wide SCSI hard drives and adapter; rack mount hardware available
Video: 2- to 4-MB Super VGA video card

Multimedia: Internal CD-ROM; other multimedia features optional
Modem: As required; internal Ethernet network adapter in most models
Bundled Software: Windows 95, Windows NT 4.0, or IBM OS/2 or Novell Netware; IBM network utilities
Warranty: Three-year on-site limited warranty; IBM toll-free tech support
Suggested List Price at Publication: From $2,799 base price (PC 310)
Approximate Street Price at Publication: From $2,699 base price (PC310)

IPC SYSTEMS

A trademark in Canada of distributor 3D microcomputers, IPC systems are aimed at the generic PC market, seemingly the low end of the price and specifications spectrums. As of early 1998, I could find only one other new PC that had a 1-megabyte video card in it; Bondwell's 166M home package. The raw cost between a 1-MB and 2-MB component as of publication was only about $20, but it is exactly because of details like these that the IPC systems occupy their special niche as nationally manufactured and supported PCs for less than $600 (monitor not included).

Potential problems loom here, perhaps more on the marketing side of the equation than because of lack of quality or support. After all, these PCs are much like the Batras, Ultinets, or Pines, the chief differences being in specifications and presentation. A danger arises with the lowest-cost IPC systems, though, for novices entering the market at too low a level without fully realizing the limitations of a small hard drive, slow processor, or basic video card. As long as you are fully aware of what those ultralow prices and specifications mean, these systems provide computing opportunities to people and businesses that might not otherwise be able to afford them. They may not be aimed at the high end of the market, but are they ever affordable. Probably these PCs are a good bet for a youngster, or for use as a low-cost secondary system. The alternative is to have one of these customized for you, which the company will be happy to do.

DESKTOP MANUFACTURER: IPC

Model: IPC-120
Physical: Desktop case
Motherboard and Processor: Intel Pentium 120-MHz processor

Cache: 256K external cache
Floppy/Hard Drives: 1.44-MB floppy drive; 1.0-GB enhanced IDE hard drive
Video: 1-MB Super VGA video card
Multimedia: 6x CD-ROM; 16-bit generic sound card; amplified speakers
Modem: Optional
Bundled Software: Windows 95
Warranty: Two-year parts-and-labour return-to-depot warranty
Suggested List Price at Publication: $599 base system (phasing out)
Approximate Street Price at Publication: $599 base system

DESKTOP MANUFACTURER: IPC

Model: IPC-150
Physical: Desktop case
Motherboard and Processor: Intel Pentium 150-MHz processor; 16-MB EDO RAM; customizable
Cache: 256K external cache
Floppy/Hard Drives: 1.44-MB floppy drive; 1.7-GB enhanced IDE hard drive
Video: 1-MB Super VGA video card
Multimedia: 20x CD-ROM; 16-bit generic sound card; amplified speakers
Modem: Optional
Bundled Software: Windows 95
Warranty: Two-year parts-and-labour return-to-depot warranty
Suggested List Price at Publication: $789 base system (phasing out)
Approximate Street Price at Publication: $789 base system

DESKTOP MANUFACTURER: IPC

Model: IPC-200x
Physical: Minitower case
Motherboard and Processor: Intel Pentium MMX 200-MHz processor; 32-MB EDO RAM; customizable
Cache: 512K external cache
Floppy/Hard Drives: 1.44-MB floppy drive; 1.7-GB enhanced IDE hard drive
Video: 2-MB ATI Super VGA video card

Multimedia: 16x CD-ROM; 16-bit generic sound card; amplified speakers
Modem: Optional
Bundled Software: Windows 95
Warranty: Three-year parts-and-labour warranty (first year on site, second and third return to depot)
Suggested List Price at Publication: From $1,049
Approximate Street Price at Publication: From $1,049

DESKTOP MANUFACTURER: IPC

Model: IPC-233 PII
Physical: Minitower case
Motherboard and Processor: Intel Pentium II processor; 32-MB SDRAM; customizable; faster processors available
Cache: 512K external cache
Floppy/Hard Drives: 1.44-MB floppy drive; 2.0-GB enhanced IDE hard drive
Video: 4-MB RAM Virge Super VGA video card
Multimedia: 32x CD-ROM; sound card/amplified speakers
Modem: Optional
Bundled Software: Windows 95
Warranty: Three-year parts-and-labour warranty (first year on site, second and third return to depot)
Suggested List Price at Publication: From $1,349
Approximate Street Price at Publication: From $1,349

MYNIX

Founded in 1989, Mynix Computer's corporate statement says that it is aiming at the high-end PC market with the support of seven international branches. Reviewed in December '97 by CCP Labs, the generic Mycomp 200 offers advantages over other generic PCs in its class: Novell certification and quality components. It includes a USR modem at 33.6 Kbps, although in 1998 systems this is likely to be replaced by a 56-Kbps model. The Quantum Fireball ST 3.2 Ultra DMA hard drive and Matrox Millennium II video card with 4 MB of WRAM (Matrox's version of VRAM) are also from respected manufacturers.

Priced in the middle of the generic Canadian PC pack, these systems are aimed at cost-conscious businesses and corporations that want network reliability. The company also advertises that it is active in the component and connectivity sides of the business. Competing against companies such as Hits, Compucon, and STD, these systems are also up against larger adversaries such as Hewitt Rand which are already a presence in the national market. These mid-priced generics under the names Prima and Vantage are "bare computer" options if you are setting up a network in a small or medium-sized company or if you want a built-to-order system with a third party behind it.

DESKTOP MANUFACTURER: MYNIX

Model: Mycomp
Physical: Medium tower; 200W power
Motherboard and Processor: Intel Pentium or Pentium II processor; 32-MB EDO SDRAM; Award BIOS; or build to order
Cache: 512K level 2 pipeline burst cache
Floppy/Hard Drives: 1.44-MB floppy drive; Quantum Fireball ST 3.2-GB Ultra DMA hard drive
Video: Matrox Millennium II video card with 4-MB WRAM
Multimedia: Internal BTX 24x CD-ROM; BTX 1853L sound card; speakers
Modem: US Robotics 33.6-Kbps internal fax/modem
Bundled Software: Windows 95/98
Suggested List Price at Publication: $1,865
Approximate Street Price at Publication: From $1,795

NEC POWERMATE ENTERPRISE AND ENTERPRISE II

Perhaps having taken note of the success of direct marketer Dell in recent years, Nippon Electronics Corporation has begun selling its business and value class systems the same way, promoting them through a "NEC NOW" telephone and Internet sales program and supporting them with a network of authorized dealers who will consult with users and businesses when services such as networking or special configurations are required. Although this is a new venture for the Japanese manufacturer, its alliance with selected "after-sale vendors" sets it apart from others in the direct marketing field.

The Enterprises are business class systems, in competition with Dell's OptiPlex series, Compaq's Deskpros, Hewlett-Packard's Vectras, and IBM's 300s. Their pricing places them in reach of the larger SOHO (small office/home office) market, although some models may be out of reach of small companies. As of publication, the Enterprise software complement contained no applications but was heavy on utilities. This, along with the company's formidable size and reputation and a full first-year on-site warranty, with years two and three return-to-depot, are what you're paying extra for.

One of the notable advantages to the new NEC Direction series, and a plus to other direct-marketed systems, is the inclusion of up-to-date components. By building systems to user orders (or at least, predictions of user orders) instead of in huge manufacturing runs, custom built PCs allow you to order the fastest available CD-ROM and newest DVD options, highest performance video cards, and best Zip drive backups. Even though they are priced well above generic systems from national marketers in Canada, you may wish to pay the extra money for either an Enterprise workstation or a built-to-order NEC if you want to deal with a large manufacturer or if networking is in your future.

DESKTOP MANUFACTURER: NEC

Model: NEC Direction series
Physical: Desktop or tower designs; 200W switchable power supplies
Motherboard and Processor: Intel Pentium II 233-, 266-MHz, and higher processors; 32- to 64-MB SDRAM (2 DIMMS, expandable to 384 MB; build to order
Cache: 512K cache
Floppy/Hard Drives: 1.44-MB floppy drive; 2.1-, 3.2-, 6.4-GB hard drives; IDE hard drives; 4-GB or 8-GB Seagate Travan tape drives optional; Iomega Zip drives optional
Video: 64-bit graphics accelerator Super VGA video cards with 4-MB SGRAM (upgradable to 8 MB) optional
Multimedia: Internal CD-ROM; Windows sound system; external speakers
Modem: Internal US Robotics x2 56-Kbps fax/modem; Intel Pro 100 10/100 Ethernet network adapters optional
Bundled Software: Windows 95 or Windows NT 4.0; applications and utilities to order
Warranty: NEC limited warranty; NEC support
Approximate Street Price at Publication: $2,349 (PII 233; 15" monitor included); $3,379 (PII 333; 17" monitor included)

DESKTOP MANUFACTURER: NEC

Model: Powermate Enterprise/Enterprise II series
Physical: Desktop or minitower design; 200W switchable power supply
Motherboard and Processor: Intel Pentium MMX/Pentium II processors; 16- to 64-MB RAM sockets (expandable)
Cache: 512K pipeline burst cache
Floppy/Hard Drives: 1.44-MB floppy drive; 2.1-, 3.2-, 6.4-GB Ultra DMA IDE hard drives; 4- or 8-GB Travan tape drives optional; Iomega 100-MB Zip drives optional
Video: 2-MB SGRAM 64-bit graphics accelerator Super VGA video card; 4-MB EDO Diamond Stealth 2000 Pro add-on card is optional upgrade
Multimedia: Internal 24x CD-ROM; FM Synthesis Business audio card on some models; Creative Labs Sound Blaster 32 wave table sound card optional
Modem: Internal US Robotics x2 56-Kbps fax/modem; Ethernet network adapter optional
Bundled Software: Windows 95/98 or Windows NT 4.0; NEC Select Install CD; Cybermedia First Aid Autofix; Magic Eye System Health Monitoring; Intel Landisk Client Manager
Warranty: NEC three-year limited warranty; (first year on site)
Approximate Street Price at Publication: From $1,295

NEC READY PCs

One of the true innovators in the personal computer business, NEC is almost amazing in its diversity, poised on the edge of associated fields such as supercomputing and robotics. They have added digital video discs to the most recent issues in this series, as well as a design feature in which the CD or DVD and floppy drive are housed in a detachable media unit which also shows the time, date, and record of any waiting fax and voice messages. Intel's video phone software and hardware bundle allows video conferencing via the Internet, and the NEC "Connections" package is described as a premium quality speakerphone, fax, and voice-mail centre. Also included is NEC's WebWay, the company's own Internet solution, which connects you to other NEC users and provides information and support for their products.

Ready PC descriptions also remind readers that monitor, speakers, and microphone are sold separately, so, as always when buying a large manufacturer's packaged PC, be sure you buy the recommended peripherals, otherwise all that neat stuff you're paying for may not work properly. These systems are in the top end of the home PC pack, positioned against Compaq's Presarios, IBM's Aptivas, and Hewlett-Packard's Pavilions. They are covered by a one-year limited warranty, with the first six months on site.

If you have the money and the inclination for a home system that will take you well into the future, these systems are a good choice, but be sure to buy one containing the fastest processor you can afford. You may grow accustomed to the features in these "packages" (I used to own a similar computer a few years ago), and might find it hard to migrate to a different manufacturer. You can later reinvent a generic system that a dealer or consultant has put together for you, but letting a complex home bundle go – trading it in, selling it, or as happened to me, having it stolen – is a major upset. So get the most powerful PC you can, to ensure you'll be supported well into the future. Then, have some fun getting into all the neat extras included in the package.

DESKTOP MANUFACTURER: NEC

Model: Ready 9840 series
Physical: Minitower, white case; 200W power supply (115V/220V switch selectable)
Motherboard and Processor: 233-MHz Pentium II processor; 64-MB SDRAM
Cache: 512K pipeline burst cache
Floppy/Hard Drives: 1.44-MB floppy drive; 6.4-GB E/IDE hard drive
Video: Accelerated 64-bit PCI graphics controller with MPEG
Multimedia: 24x IDE CD-ROM; 16-bit, 3D Wavetable surround sound; speaker system
Modem: Internal 56-Kbps data/fax/voice modem; hands-free full-duplex speakerphone
Bundled Software: Windows 95; Microsoft Works, Encarta 96, Publisher, Arcade; Quicken SE; McAfee Web Scan and Virus Scan; or updated NEC software pack
Warranty: One-year limited warranty (first six months on site); optional extended warranty available: three-year on-site service (next-business-day reponse)
Approximate Street Price at Publication: $2,399 (15" monitor included)
Additions: Windows 95 104-key keyboard; NEC/Microsoft 2-button

mouse; 5 expansion slots (2 PCI slots, 2 ISA slots, 1 shared ISA/PCI slot); 6 drive bays (4 external, 2 internal)

DESKTOP MANUFACTURER: NEC

Model: Ready 9850
Physical: Minitower case; 200W power supply (115V/220V switch selectable)
Motherboard and Processor: 266-MHz Pentium II processor; 64-MB SDRAM
Cache: 512K synchronous pipeline burst cache
Floppy/Hard Drives: 1.44-MB floppy drive; 6.4-GB E/IDE hard drive (32-bit PCI enhanced IDE interface); internal Iomega 100-MB Zip drive available
Video: Accelerated 64-bit graphics with MPEG
Multimedia: 24x (max) IDE CD-ROM drive; 16-bit, 3D Wavetable surround sound; speaker system
Modem: Internal 56/14.4-Kbps x2 data/fax/voice modem (US Robotics); hands-free full-duplex speakerphone
Bundled Software: Windows 95; Microsoft Works, Encarta 97, Publisher, Money, Bookshelf, Arcade; Blockbuster Movie Guide; POD (MMX), Sega Sonic (MMX); Family Doctor (MMX), Ultimate Human Body Experience (MMX), Quicken SE; McAfee Web Scan and Virus Scan; NEC help software; or updated NEC software pack
Warranty: One-year limited warranty (first six months on site); optional extended warranty program
Approximate Street Price at Publication: $2,699 (15" monitor included)
Additions: Windows 95 104-key keyboard; NEC/Microsoft 2-button mouse; 5 expansion slots (2 PCI slots, 2 ISA slots, 1 shared ISA/PCI slot); 2 USB ports; 5 drive bays (3 external, 2 internal)

DESKTOP MANUFACTURER: NEC

Model: Ready 9870
Physical: Beige or charcoal medium tower design; 200W power supply
Motherboard and Processor: 300-MHz Pentium II processor; 64-MB SDRAM (expandable to 256 MB)

Cache: 512K cache
Floppy/Hard Drives: 1.44-MB floppy drive; 6.4-GB IDE hard drive
Video: 3D High Performance with 4-MB video memory
Multimedia: 16-bit, 3D Wavetable surround sound
Modem: Internal 56/14.4-Kbps x2 data/fax/voice modem; hands-free full-duplex speakerphone
Bundled Software: Windows 95; Microsoft Works, Word 97, Encarta 97, Publisher, Money, Bookshelf, Arcade, Entertainment Pack; NewSoft Presto!; Jonny Quest LE; You Don't Know Jack; Mayo Clinic Family Health; ABCs of Windows; McAfee Web Scan and Virus Scan; NEC help software or NEC updated software pack
Warranty: One-year limited warranty (first six months on site); optional extended warranty available
Approximate Street Price at Publication: \$3,299 (15" monitor included)
Additions: NEC ErgoSelect Win95 keyboard (104 keys plus multimedia buttons); Microsoft IntelliMouse; 6 expansion slots (3 PCI, 2 ISA, 1 shared ISA/PCI); 2 USB ports; 4 drive bays (3 external, 1 internal)

PACKARD BELL

According to its promotional literature, Packard Bell was the world sales leader in the home PC market in 1996 (source: International Data Corp.). It is also a manufacturer with a controversial past, having been the target of a lawsuit filed by competitor Compaq accusing it of putting used components in its systems. It has also been hit with at least one class action from customers who felt that it did not fully honour its obligations to them. These jolts have had their effect on the company's image. But in 1996 its white knight appeared in the form of Japanese giant NEC (Nippon Electronics Corporation), which merged with it to form Packard Bell NEC. Exactly what is going to happen to the Packard Bell trademark in the long run is unclear, but for the immediate future it's safe to assume that these computers will remain a big presence in the consumer market.

Packard Bell has traditionally courted the home user, and has sold its systems aggressively across the board: through department stores, high-tech supercentres, catalogue companies, the Internet, and a limited distribution and dealer network in Canada. Perhaps its huge variety of PCs – the company's website lists over sixty different models grouped into four categories: the Legends, Pack-Mates, Multimedias, and Platinum series – has had something to do with its ability to sell and support its systems satisfactorily. Just deciding on one requires research. As with other "split" lines of home computers, confusion can arise when similar, but differently named, models are available from different vendors at different prices. This marketing strategy makes it difficult to compare a PC in one store against a slightly altered version of the same thing in another. One or two standardized lines here would benefit resellers and buyers alike, and probably the manufacturer as well.

All of the Packard Bell systems are aggressively priced for the items they include. Among the home PCs offered by other multinationals (the IBM Aptivas, the NEC Ready PC series, the Compaq Presarios, and Acer Aspires), Packard Bell offers among the most features and software for the money. But their reputation is still in drydock. The current corporate assertion is that the company has repledged its commitment to service and support. It certainly has some digging to do to get out from under all of those Packard Bell hate pages on the World Wide Web. It will be interesting to see how the market responds to the company's initiative in '98.

As far as specific features are concerned, each of these systems is conventionally designed with a separate multimedia monitor, attractive medium tower or less common and less desirable desktop case, 33.6 or 56K modem, and CD-ROM or DVD. Watch for them to be advertised at very sharp prices without a monitor, and be careful to insist on a 15" or 17" Packard Bell display if you decide to buy. As is the case with other prepackaged home PCs, this protects you against one manufacturer pointing the finger at another if such things as your voice and telephone applications act up.

The list of programs these systems ship with is also impressive: among them, Packard Bell's introductory "Navigator" (a graphical menu which presents other programs in the system by category), standbys such as Microsoft Word and Microsoft Works, Janna Contact Management, the Reuters Money Network, the Ultimate Human Body, an interesting presentation/graphics package called the Third Dimension, and all kinds of other games and utilities. If you're the kind of purchaser who is inclined to offer a manufacturer a second chance, these systems do indeed offer a lot of features for the price.

DESKTOP MANUFACTURER: PACKARD BELL

Model: Legend series
Physical: Medium tower or Slimline desktop design

Motherboard and Processor: 166- to 233-MHz Pentium MMX; 16- to 32-MB EDO RAM (expandable to 256 MB)
Cache: 256–512K secondary cache
Floppy/Hard Drives: 1.44-MB floppy drive; 2.1- to 6.4-GB and larger IDE hard drive
Video: 3D graphics and video accelerator with 2- to 4-MB memory; MPEG-2 video; S/VGA video resolution output up to 1,600 x 1,200 (monitor dependent)
Multimedia: 16x–24x CD-ROM drive; optional DVD drive on some models; 16-bit sound card; Intel Video Phone and Proshare on some models (camera sold separately); speakers and microphone sold separately (integrated into 15" or 17" PB NEC monitor)
Modem: Internal 33.6- or 56-Kbps x2 modem (US Robotics)
Bundled Software: Windows 95; Microsoft Word 97, Works, Money, Encarta 97; PB NEC utilities and Internet tools, among others
Warranty: One-year limited warranty for hardware defects; ninety days on-site service for registered users
Suggested List Price at Publication: Contact manufacturer
Approximate Street Price at Publication: Contact manufacturer

DESKTOP MANUFACTURER: PACKARD BELL

Model: Multimedia series
Physical: Tower or desktop design; sleep button; sliding panel protects drives and power button
Motherboard and Processor: 200- to 266-MHz Pentium MMX or 266-MHz Pentium II (Platinum) processor; 32-MB EDO or SDRAM (expandable to 128 MB)
Cache: 256–512K pipeline burst level 2 cache
Floppy/Hard Drives: 1.44-MB floppy drive; 4.3-GB (Multimedia) or 7.0-GB (Platinum) hard drive
Video: Diamond Multimedia AS hardware MPEG-2 video
Multimedia: 24x (max) CD-ROM drive; DVD drive available for some models; Intel Video Phone available for some models
Modem: Internal 56-Kbps modem
Bundled Software: Windows 95; Microsoft Word 97, Works, Money, Encarta 97; utilities and Internet tools; KiddoNet; Planet Oasis; other programs
Warranty: One-year limited warranty for hardware defects; ninety days on-site service for registered users

Approximate Street Price at Publication: $1,899 (5606, P233 MMX); 15" monitor included

DESKTOP MANUFACTURER: PACKARD BELL

Model: Pack-Mate series
Physical: Medium tower or Slimline desktop design
Motherboard and Processor: 166- to 233-MHz Pentium MMX; 16- to 32-MB EDO RAM (expandable to 256 MB)
Cache: 256–512K secondary cache
Floppy/Hard Drives: 1.44-MB floppy drive; 2.1- to 6.4-GB and larger IDE hard drive
Video: 3D graphics and video accelerator with 2- to 4-MB memory; MPEG-2 video; S/VGA video resolution output up to 1,600 x 1,200 (monitor dependent)
Multimedia: 16x–24x CD-ROM drive; optional DVD drive on some models; 16-bit sound card; Intel Video Phone and Proshare on some models (camera sold separately); speakers and microphone sold separately (integrated into 15" or 17" PB monitor)
Modem: Internal 33.6- or 56-Kbps x2 modem (US Robotics)
Bundled Software: Windows 95; Microsoft Word 97, Works, Money, Encarta 97; PB NEC utilities and Internet tools, among others
Warranty: One-year limited warranty for hardware defects; ninety days on-site service for registered users
Approximate Street Price at Publication: $1,799 (model 7836, P233 MMX); 15" monitor included
Additions: MediaSelect keyboard features easy access to CD-ROM, phone, speakers, volume, and more; Microsoft IntelliMouse

DESKTOP MANUFACTURER: PACKARD BELL

Model: Platinum/Platinum Supreme series
Physical: Tower design; 6 expansion slots (3 PCI, 1 PCI/ISA, 2 ISA) and 6 device bays; 2 PCI local bus IDE interfaces support up to 4 devices; sleep button on tower; sliding panel protects the drives and power button
Motherboard and Processor: 266-MHz Pentium II; 32-MB SDRAM (expandable to 256 MB); Pentium MMX 233–266 MHz
Cache: 512K secondary cache

Floppy/Hard Drives: 1.44-MB floppy drive; 5.1- to 7.0-GB hard drive
Video: 3D graphics and video accelerator with 4-MB video memory; MPEG-2 video; S/VGA video resolution output up to 1,600 x 1,200 (monitor dependent)
Multimedia: 24x (max) CD-ROM drive; optional DVD drive on some models; 16-bit sound card; Intel Video Phone and Proshare on some models (camera sold separately); speakers and microphone sold separately (integrated into 15" or 17" PB monitor)
Modem: Internal 56-Kbps x2 modem (US Robotics)
Bundled Software: Windows 95; Microsoft Word 97, Works, Money, Encarta 97; PB NEC utilities and Internet tools, among others
Warranty: One-year limited warranty for hardware defects; ninety days on-site service for registered users
Approximate Street Price at Publication: $2,499 (Platinum 3000A, P233 MMX); 15" monitor included
Additions: MediaSelect keyboard features easy access to CD-ROM, phone, speakers, volume, and more; Microsoft IntelliMouse

PATRIOT

According to its published corporate statement, the mission of "Canada's computer company" is to manufacture quality desktop and server systems, sell them nationally and internationally, and place Canada among the world leaders in technological advancement. An admirable goal! This privately owned Canadian company, headquartered in Markham, Ontario, produces generic computers as well as a line of CAD servers and a "Computers 4 Kids" package. It also produces large "builds" of PCs – an interesting way of assembling and selling large numbers of systems quickly at a very low price. A "build" is a manufacturing run of 500 or 1,000 or more computers with a specific marketing scheme in mind. Patriot systems have variously appeared in print and television advertising campaigns offering a lot of computer at eye-catching cost. This is a unique method of gaining a pre-eminent place in the computer market; when Patriot puts together so manysystems of the same specs at one time, and sells them fast at a low overhead, purchasers can reap impressive price rewards. One issue offered in early '97 was a multimedia Pentium package complete with printer, software, and monitor for $1,095. Systems like these might also appeal to a user who wants as little to do with his or her computer vendor as possible; you can call a direct number (sometimes these orders are not even handled by Patriot but by a telephone marketing company instead), order the package, and have it arrive on your doorstep a week or so later.

Patriot also customizes single systems to user specifications. In these cases it is in direct competition with several other national companies building generics. In its "Computers 4 Kids" campaign, developed in association with the Children's Miracle Network and Corel Corporation, the company donates $50 to the Children's Miracle Network Hospital or foundation in your area. It will also provide you with a "Point" certificate which you can give to the school of your choice, allowing it a free Patriot PC for educational use for every fifteen Point certificates collected. This is a commendable and creative marketing plan, and if you are charitably inclined, might influence you to purchase one of these family packages. Patriot offers these Computers 4 Kids systems via lease, and even though their intention is philanthropic, it is always a good idea to look very carefully at all of the items and specs included in any package, and at the *total* amount it will cost over time. If you take all factors into consideration and still like the idea of this marketing plan, this is a good way to make a donation to the hospital or school of your choice.

DESKTOP MANUFACTURER: PATRIOT

Model: CAD Star; CAD Star Plus; CAD Star Professional Workstations
Physical: Desktop, minitower, medium tower, and floor tower cases; customizable
Motherboard and Processor: Intel Pentium Pro 180-MHz, Dual Pentium Pro 200-MHz, and Pentium II CPUs; 32-MB or 64-MB RAM (max 512-MB RAM)
Cache: 256–512K pipeline burst cache
Floppy/Hard Drives: 1.44-MB floppy drive; 2.5- to 4.0-GB and larger enhanced IDE or SCSI hard drives using Adaptek ultra wide SCSI controller (some models)
Video: Matrox Millennium video cards with 4-MB WRAM
Multimedia: Internal CD-ROM; sound card and speakers available
Modem: 56-Kbps fax/modem in some models; integrated Ethernet network adapter
Bundled Software: Windows 95/98, Windows NT 4.0
Warranty: Two-year next-day on-site warranty; toll-free seven-day/twenty-four-hour phone support
Approximate Street Price at Publication: $3,595 (dual PII 233-MHz package; 17" monitor included)

DESKTOP MANUFACTURER: PATRIOT

Model: Desktop computers; server computers; Computers 4 Kids
Physical: Desktop, slimline, minitower, medium tower, and floor tower cases
Motherboard and Processor: Intel Pentium MMX and Pentium II processors; 32-MB or 64-MB EDO or SDRAM; or build to order
Cache: 256–512K pipeline burst cache
Floppy/Hard Drives: 1.44-MB floppy drive; 2.5- to 4.0-GB and larger enhanced IDE hard drive
Video: 2-MB and larger video card (various)
Multimedia: 16x or 24x internal CD-ROM; sound card; speakers
Modem: 33.6- or 56-Kbps fax/modem
Bundled Software: Windows 95; various software bundles available
Warranty: One-year return-to-depot warranty
Approximate Street Price at Publication: $3,599 (Pentium II Computers 4 Kids package; monitor included)

PINE

Located in the same market tier as Batra, IPC, and Bondwell Computers, Pine markets generic PCs nationally. They are cost competitive and flexible in design; they will accept industry-standard components and are easy to upgrade and repair. They're a reasonable buy for individuals and companies desiring a lower-priced product and a minimum of software and support.

Watch for these systems to change from month to month alongside new technology. They rate highly on the price/performance index but, those sharp numbers mean little profit is available to either vendor or manufacturer, so get a clear idea of exactly where you're going when you buy one. Be prepared for the usual terrain in this end of the market: rudimentary documentation, basic components, and the chance that you'll have to pay for support if software and hardware issues arise on the "edge" of the warranty. Take special note that prices quoted on generic computer systems in general are usually cash discounted and may vary in different parts of the country. These guys have borrowed a thing or two from the local assemblers, and while this is not necessarily bad, it means you have to be sure to read all the fine print.

Last but not least, you've got to love the tree/series marketing tie-in: Evergreen, Sequoia, and Cedar – easily the most outdoorsy model names in all of personal computerdom.

DESKTOP MANUFACTURER: PINE

Model: Cedar series
Physical: White medium tower case; 250W power supply
Motherboard and Processor: Intel Pentium 233 MMX processor; 32-MB SDRAM; customizable
Cache: 512K level 2 cache
Floppy/Hard Drives: 1.44-MB floppy drive; 4.1-GB Ultra DMA hard drive
Video: 4-MB 64-bit MPEG Super VGA video card
Multimedia: 24x CD-ROM; 16-bit 3D sound card with wave table; separate 80W speakers
Modem: 56-Kbps fax/modem with voice
Bundled Software: One-month unlimited Internet access; Windows 95 included in advertised price
Warranty: Two-year return-to-depot warranty; toll-free tech support
Suggested List Price at Publication: From $1,499
Approximate Street Price at Publication: From $1,499

DESKTOP MANUFACTURER: PINE

Model: Evergreen series
Physical: White medium tower case; 250W power supply
Motherboard and Processor: Intel Pentium 166 MMX processor; 16-MB SDRAM; customizable
Cache: 512K level 2 cache
Floppy/Hard Drives: 1.44-MB floppy drive; 1.7-GB enhanced IDE hard drive
Video: 2-MB 64-bit MPEG Super VGA video card
Multimedia: 24x CD-ROM; 16-bit 3D sound card; separate speakers
Modem: 33.6-Kbps fax/modem
Bundled Software: One-month unlimited Internet access; no operating system in advertisement
Warranty: Two-year return-to-depot warranty; toll-free support
Suggested List Price at Publication: From $999
Approximate Street Price at Publication: From $1,095

DESKTOP MANUFACTURER: PINE

Model: Sequoia series
Physical: White ATX medium tower case; 250W power supply; customizable
Motherboard and Processor: Intel Pentium II 233 and higher processor; 32-MB SDRAM; LX chipset
Cache: 512K level 2 cache
Floppy/Hard Drives: 1.44-MB floppy drive; 4.1-GB Ultra DMA hard drive
Video: ATI Graphic Expression plus 4-MB SDRAM MPEG Super VGA video card
Multimedia: 24x CD-ROM; Creative Labs AWE 64 sound card; separate 80W speakers
Modem: 56-Kbps fax/modem with voice
Bundled Software: One-month unlimited Internet access; Windows 95 included in advertised price
Warranty: Two-year return-to-depot warranty; toll-free tech support
Suggested List Price at Publication: From $1,999
Approximate Street Price at Publication: From $1,999

SIDUS

This Markham, Ontario, computer manufacturer and parts distributor is perhaps best known for the systems it "OEMs" or assembles in large quantities for corporate and government clients and for distribution through its own dealer network. Sidus has had notable success marketing its wares internationally, especially in the former Soviet Union and other Eastern Bloc countries. Its PCs are generic but command added value because of some network certifications, much in the same vein as STD Computing of London, Ontario, Patriot, and Hewitt Rand. These computers can be built to order in small quantities as well, incorporating up-to-the-minute technology, and offering some price advantages as a result. But among systems from Canadian assemblers, their prices are in the mid to top end of the pack, and there is some question as to whether the slightly higher tag is worth paying when compared to the killer prices from small, local assemblers and other aggressive national builders such as Batra, Patriot, and IPC, even though some of these competitors may not provide the stability of a publicly traded company as Sidus does.

DESKTOP MANUFACTURER: SIDUS

Model: Sidus systems
Physical: Desktop, minitower, and medium tower cases to order
Motherboard and Processor: Pentium MMX/Pentium II processors from 166 MHz; customizable
Cache: 256–512K cache (to order)
Floppy/Hard Drives: 1.44-MB floppy drive; 2.5- to 4.0-GB and larger enhanced IDE and SCSI hard drive (to order)
Video: 2- to 4-MB and larger VGA video card (built to order)
Multimedia: Internal CD-ROM; sound card; speakers (built to order)
Modem: Internal fax/modem; Ethernet network adapter (built to order)
Bundled Software: Operating system (included to order)
Warranty: One-year limited warranty; tech support available; additional warranty available
Suggested List Price at Publication: From $1,295 (estimated)
Approximate Street Price at Publication: From $1,295

STD/COMPUPARTNER

The company profile on its home page states that STD is a Canadian corporation founded in Markham, Ontario, in 1984. It has since expanded across the country to sites in Vancouver, Edmonton, Hull, London, Quebec City, Halifax, and other cities, producing PCs at seven of its twelve locations. The company sells variously to corporations, governments, and institutions, as well as homes and businesses. Its promotional literature cites a study which shows it to rank fourth in Canada among PC vendors, although it is not clear exactly what that term means; does STD compare itself to all vendors or just to manufacturers selling direct?

CCP Labs gave STD an Editor's Choice in late 1997, which marks it as a manufacturer of Canadian generic computer systems to be watched. Its prices put it in competitive reach of other national assemblers in the same tier as Just Imagine, Hewitt Rand, IPC, and Bondwell, to name a few. STD's three-year warranty is notable, with the first year on site. These unbundled PCs are worth considering if you're looking for pure performance without extra frills, in a system from a Canadian company.

DESKTOP MANUFACTURER: STD/COMPUPARTNER

Model: Performance TX series
Physical: Chenbro midtower case; 145W power supply
Motherboard and Processor: Intel Pentium MMX 166- to 200-MHz processors; 430 VX chipset; 16-MB EDO RAM (max 128 MB)
Cache: 512K level 2 cache
Floppy/Hard Drives: Panasonic 1.44-MB floppy drive; 2.0-GB EIDE hard drive
Video: ATI 3D Expression Mach 64D PCI with 2-MB RAM
Multimedia: Panasonic 24x CD-ROM; Opti 16-bit sound card; 120W speakers; microphone
Modem: Linkskey 33.6-Kbps Rockwell chipset voice/fax modem
Bundled Software: Windows 95; Microsoft Plus, Internet Explorer, Internet Phone
Warranty: Three-year limited warranty; first year on site
Suggested List Price at Publication: From $1,650
Approximate Street Price at Publication: From $1,650

DESKTOP MANUFACTURER: STD/COMPUPARTNER

Model: Ultra LX ATX series
Physical: Desktop case; 145W power supply
Motherboard and Processor: Intel Pentium MMX and Pentium II processors; 32- to 128-MB EDO or SDRAM; or build to order
Cache: 512K level 2 cache
Floppy/Hard Drives: Panasonic 1.44-MB floppy drive; 2.0-GB EIDE hard drive
Video: S3 Virge video card with 2-MB RAM (expandable to 4 MB)
Multimedia: Panasonic 24x CD-ROM; Opti 16-bit sound card; 120W speakers
Modem: Linkskey 33.6-Kbps or K56flex Rockwell chipset voice/fax modem
Bundled Software: Windows 95; Microsoft Plus, Internet Explorer, Internet Phone
Warranty: Three-year limited return-to-depot warranty
Suggested List Price at Publication: From $1,650
Approximate Street Price at Publication: $1,650 to $1,900

DESKTOP MANUFACTURER: STD/COMPUPARTNER

Model: Valueline II series
Physical: Desktop case; 145W power supply
Motherboard and Processor: Intel Pentium MMX 166/200/233-MHz processor; 32-MB EDO RAM (max 512 MB)
Cache: 512K level 2 cache
Floppy/Hard Drives: Panasonic 1.44-MB floppy drive; 3.2-GB UIDE hard drive
Video: ATI 3D Expression Mach 64D video card with 2-MB RAM
Multimedia: Panasonic 24x CD-ROM; Opti 16-bit sound card; 120W speakers
Modem: Linkskey 33.6-Kbps or K56flex Rockwell chipset voice/fax modem
Bundled Software: Windows 95; Microsoft Plus, Internet Explorer, Internet Phone
Warranty: Three-year limited return-to-depot warranty
Suggested List Price at Publication: From $1,350
Approximate Street Price at Publication: From $1,350

ULTINET

Of all of the national assemblers of generic PCs in Canada, this Toronto company is probably the most technically oriented in its advertising and marketing. Its systems are also among the most aggressively priced, and its print ads are filled with specification details complicated enough to throw even expert PC shoppers into a muddle. The combined effect of their presentation can be confusing, even though it is intended to distinguish these systems from the competition by way of performance and price.

These are generic systems pure and simple, but on the cutting edge of the market. Pricing is as sharp as any you'll find from even small, local assemblers, but remember, tiny margins should always make you suspicious about after-sale support. Note that the Ultinet 233 Pentium MMX was awarded an Editor's Choice in CCP Test Labs' December '97 survey. This company has been around for a while and isn't shy about promoting itself. If you want a generic PC from a local builder grown big, look here. But, as always when buying at this overheated end of the market, be very thorough about each and every aspect of the transaction: assembly timing, deposit, method of payment, included software and options, delivery, and after-sale warranty and support.

DESKTOP MANUFACTURER: ULTINET

Model: Ultinet Editor's Choice series
Physical: Medium tower case; CSA power supply
Motherboard and Processor: Intel Pentium II; TX/LX chipset; 64-MB SDRAM; Pentium II 233 MHz, Pentium 333 MHz
Cache: 512K pipeline burst cache
Floppy/Hard Drives: 1.44-MB floppy drive; 6.4-GB UDMA hard drive; other hard drives available
Video: Matrox Millennium II or ATI X-PERT with 2-MB SGRAM and higher
Multimedia: 32x CD-ROM; Sound Blaster; speakers
Modem: 56K fax/modem
Bundled Software: Windows 95/98; CD bundle
Warranty: Two-year parts-and-labour return-to-depot warranty (upgradable to on-site); three-year labour warranty
Approximate Street Price at Publication: $2,564 (PII 233); $2,694 (PII 266); $2,926 (PII 300); $3,229 (PII 333); prices include Viewsonic 773 .26-mm dot pitch 17" monitor

DESKTOP MANUFACTURER: ULTINET

Model: Ultinet level two and three packages
Physical: Desktop; minitower; medium tower cases to order; customizable
Motherboard and Processor: Intel Pentium MMX or Pentium II processors 32- to 128-MB SDRAM
Cache: 512K pipeline burst cache
Floppy/Hard Drives: 1.44-MB floppy drive; Quantum Fireball ST UDMA 4.1-GB and other hard drives
Video: Matrox Millennium II with 4-MB WRAM; customizable
Multimedia: Panasonic 24x CD-ROM; Creative Labs Sound Blaster AWE 64; stand-alone speakers
Modem: US Robotics 56-kbps internal fax/modem
Bundled Software: Windows 95
Warranty: Two-year parts-and-labour return-to-depot warranty (upgradable to on-site); three-year labour warranty
Suggested List Price at Publication: From $1,295
Approximate Street Price at Publication: From $1,095

MONITORS

ACER

In addition to the sleek multimedia monitors it sells with its Aspire series, Acer also offers the AcerView series, a line of displays designed for use with its own business class desktops and with third-party or generic computer systems from other manufacturers. Six representative models available in Canada are the 34T/35c/54e/56c/76c/78ie and, with a 21" diagonal (19.8" viewable area), the 98i. The 14" 34T and 15" 54e are the company's entries at the low end of the market, with 1,024 x 768 maximum resolution and basic controls (the 34T analogue and the 54e digital). Product spec sheets advertise that these are low-radiation monitors, but some models list MPR-II, a recognized reduced-emission standard, as optional. If you are concerned about emissions, enquire about this before buying. Also, the 17" models offer a viewable area diagonal of only 15.6" or 15.7", which is lower than that of some competitors, although whether this reduction in size will mean much to you is something to decide only after viewing a floor model.

These monitors are priced in the middle tier of the market and offer average features for price. Consider one for use with a locally assembled PC, but be sure to evaluate any of the 17" issues for size before you buy. Note that the warranty on the multimedia series is improved if you purchase one with an Aspire PC, the first ninety days being covered by the company's second-day turnaround replacement or repair.

MONITOR MANUFACTURER: ACER

Model: AcerView 34T/35c
Physical/Screen Size: 14"/13.1" viewable
Resolution: 1,024 x 768

Dot Pitch: .28 mm
Refresh Rate: 50–90 Hz
Radiation: MPR-II low-radiation compliant
Warranty: One-year parts-and-labour return-to-depot warranty
Approximate Street Price at Publication: $369 (35c)

MONITOR MANUFACTURER: ACER

Model: AcerView 54e/56c
Physical/Screen Size: 15" diagonal/13.7" viewable
Resolution: 1,024 x 768
Dot Pitch: .28 mm
Refresh Rate: 50–110 Hz
Radiation: MPR-II low-radiation compliant
Special Features: On-screen digital controls
Warranty: One-year parts-and-labour return-to-depot warranty
Approximate Street Price at Publication: $409 (56c)

MONITOR MANUFACTURER: ACER

Model: AcerView 76c
Physical/Screen Size: 17" diagonal/15.7" viewable
Resolution: 1,280 x 1,024 non-interlaced
Dot Pitch: .28 mm
Refresh Rate: 50–120 Hz
Radiation: MPR-II low-radiation feature optional
Special Features: On-screen digital controls; flat square screen design
Warranty: One-year parts-and-labour return-to-depot warranty
Approximate Street Price at Publication: $799

MONITOR MANUFACTURER: ACER

Model: Aspire multimedia series 33s/54s/77is
Physical/Screen Size: 14" diagonal/13.1" viewable (33s); 15" diagonal/14.7" viewable (54s); 17" diagonal/13.6" viewable (77is)
Resolution: 1,024 x 768 interlaced (33s); 1,024 x 768 non-interlaced (54s); 1,280 x 1,024 non-interlaced (77is)
Dot Pitch: .28 mm (33s); .27 mm (54s); .28 mm (77is)

Refresh Rate: 50–90 Hz (33s); 50–110 Hz (54s and 77is)
Special Features: All models: unidirectional microphone, headphone jack; 6-W-per-channel stereo speakers (33s); 10-W-per-channel stereo speakers, twenty user-programmable display modes (54s); 6-W speakers, twenty user-programmable display modes (77is)
Warranty: With Acer system: one-year carry-in warranty (ninety-day second-day replacement); stand-alone: one-year return-to-depot warranty
Approximate Street Price at Publication: From $499

APPLE

With six displays available as of early 1998, Apple continues its tradition of offering high performance products that are also compatible with PCs on the Windows/Intel side of the market. There are two 20" and three 17" monitors, as well as one 15" monitor in this lineup, available in two types: the ColorSyncs and Multiple Scans. The ColorSyncs contain Sony Trinitron aperture grilles and are designed to comply with Apple's ColorSync technology, a colour identification system that enables specially equipped printers and monitors to reproduce colours accurately and uniformly.

Selected displays (the Multiple Scan 15AV, 17" ColorSync AV, and 20" ColorSync AV) come with multimedia features: speakers, microphone and headphone jacks, and, in some cases, multiple connectors to accept different video inputs.

All six Apple displays are performance products – the viewable areas in them are large in relation to their physical diagonals. The 17" ColorSync AV, for example, has a viewable area of 16.1 inches and the 20" ColorSync a viewable area of 19.1 inches, so these monitors present a bigger picture than most of their counterparts in the Wintel computer group. Other properties, such as low radiation emission and on-screen software controls, make this group, from the entry level 15AV (Apple no longer offers any 14" monitors) to the top-of-the-line 20" ColorSync AV, attractive and feature rich, and, as might be expected, higher in price than mainstream 17" and 20" displays. While it is unlikely these monitors will gain much of a foothold in the larger conventional PC market, dedicated Apple users will undoubtedly continue to enjoy them, and pay a premium for them, as long as Apple remains a separate standard in the personal computer world.

MONITOR MANUFACTURER: APPLE

Model: 17" ColorSync
Physical/Screen Size: 17" diagonal/16.1" viewable
Resolution: 1,280 x 1,024 at 75 Hz
Dot Pitch: .25 mm
Refresh Rate: 40–120 Hz
Radiation: MPR-II low-radiation compliant
Special Features: Energy Star compliant
Warranty: One-year parts-and-labour warranty
Approximate Street Price at Publication: $999

MONITOR MANUFACTURER: APPLE

Model: 17" ColorSync AV
Physical/Screen Size: 17" diagonal/16.1" viewable
Resolution: 1,280 x 1,024 at 75 Hz
Dot Pitch: .25 mm
Refresh Rate: 40–120 Hz
Radiation: MPR-II low-radiation compliant
Special Features: Energy Star compliant
Warranty: One-year parts-and-labour warranty
Approximate Street Price at Publication: $1,049

MONITOR MANUFACTURER: APPLE

Model: 20" ColorSync AV
Physical/Screen Size: 20" diagonal/19.1" viewable
Resolution: 1,600 x 1,200
Dot Pitch: .26 mm
Refresh Rate: 48–120 Hz
Radiation: MPR-II low-radiation compliant
Special Features: Energy Star compliant; AV features
Warranty: One-year parts-and-labour warranty
Approximate Street Price at Publication: $2,599

MONITOR MANUFACTURER: APPLE

Model: Multiple Scan 15AV
Physical/Screen Size: 15" diagonal/13.75" viewable
Resolution: 1,024 x 768
Dot Pitch: .28 mm
Refresh Rate: 56–75 Hz
Radiation: MPR-II low-radiation compliant
Special Features: Energy Star compliant; AV features
Warranty: One-year parts-and-labour warranty
Approximate Street Price At Publication: $569

MONITOR MANUFACTURER: APPLE

Model: Multiple Scan 720
Physical/Screen Size: 17" diagonal/16.1" viewable
Resolution: 1,280 x 1,024
Dot Pitch: .28 mm
Refresh Rate: 40–160 Hz
Radiation: MPR-II low-radiation compliant
Special Features: EPA Energy Star compliant
Warranty: One-year parts-and-labour warranty
Approximate Street Price at Publication: $929

COMPAQ

With a recently expanded line of monitors intended for its Deskpros and servers and, secondarily, as third-party products for the generic market, Compaq now offers three distinct lines of displays. The first of these are the Presario Multimedia 1500 and more recent 1600. As with IBM's Aptivas, Hewlett-Packard's Pavilions, and other bundled home and small office computer systems, Presario PCs should be married to Compaq's intended monitors. Compared with competitors in this field, the 1600s seem average, with speakers mounted on the sides and a built-in duplexing microphone. Take a very good look at one when you are considering a Presario, or any other bundled PC for that matter; if it's part of the package, it may influence which computer you choose.

Compaq also offers two lines of stand-alone monitors, the Value series V50 (15"), V70 (17"), and V90 (19"), as well as the Performance line P50 (15"), P70 (17"), P110 (21"), and QVision 210 (21"). Value line displays are garden-variety multisync monitors in 15", 17", and 19" formats, with .28-mm dot pitch and capable of 1,024 x 768 (V50) and 1,280 x 1,024 (V70) resolutions. They are MPR-II emission rated and have digital controls, Energy Star power-saving features, and antiglare/antistatic screens. But while that partial list may sound like a lot of features, those specifications are almost all standard in 1998 for monitors from significant manufacturers – in many cases at lower prices. This is not to say that the Value line is far overpriced, only that it is slightly high. Perhaps this is offset by Compaq's size and reputation, and by its first-year on-site warranty.

The V70s are covered by an additional two-year return-to-depot warranty, while the V50's is one-year on-site only. The new addition to this lineup, the V90, is notable for its unusual 19" (18" viewable) size, which is 23 percent larger, the literature says, than most conventional 17" monitors, although the spec sheet on their website might have been more precise in that comparison by citing whether they were comparing 15.6" or 15.8" viewable diagonals. Advertising aside, the V90 is one of the best new products to hit Compaq's display lineup for some time, and compares favourably in price and performance if you are looking for a premium, large-screen product. With a .26-mm dot pitch, 1,600 x 1,200 resolution at 60/75 Hz, Mac interface, and space-saving design, this is a good buy. It is also covered by a first-year on-site and years two and three return-to-depot warranty, as is its smaller cousin, the V70. There is even a multimedia option kit. If you can afford one, this is one of the most interesting of Compaq's Value line products.

In addition to its entry-level V series, Compaq also offers a performance group of monitors in 15", 17", and 21" sizes. These are multisync products with Trinitron tubes and intended for corporate and performance computing environments. With a three-year (first year on-site) warranty, Macintosh compatibility, .26- and .28-mm dot pitches, and fast refresh rates, these are intended for CAD/CAM, financial, publishing, and other professional applications. They are priced accordingly.

MONITOR MANUFACTURER: COMPAQ

Model: P50/P70
Physical/Screen Size: 15" diagonal/13.6" viewable (P50); 17" diagonal/15.6" viewable (P70)
Resolution: Up to 1,280 x 1,024 (P50); up to 1,600 x 1,200 (P70)
Dot Pitch: .28 mm (P50); .26 mm (P70)

Refresh Rate: 48–160 Hz; 85 Hz in preset modes
Radiation: MPR-II low-radiation compliant
Special Features: Mac compatible; flat square screen; on-screen controls; Energy Star compliant
Warranty: Three-year limited warranty (first year on site)
Suggested List Price at Publication: $532 (P50); $1,199 (P70)
Approximate Street Price at Publication: $489 (P50); $1,079 (P70)

MONITOR MANUFACTURER: COMPAQ

Model: P110
Physical/Screen Size: 21″ diagonal/19.1″ viewable
Resolution: Up to 1,600 x 1,200
Dot Pitch: .26 mm
Refresh Rate: 48–160 Hz; 85 Hz in preset modes
Radiation: MPR-II low-radiation compliant
Special Features: Mac compatible; flat square screen; on-screen controls; universal serial bus (USB) port; Energy Star compliant
Warranty: Three-year parts-and-labour warranty (first year on site)
Suggested List Price at Publication: $2,665
Approximate Street Price at Publication: $2,395

MONITOR MANUFACTURER: COMPAQ

Model: Presario Multimedia 1425 multimedia series
Physical/Screen Size: 14″ diagonal/13.2″ viewable
Resolution: 1,024 x 768 non-interlaced
Dot Pitch: .28 mm
Refresh Rate: 75 Hz
Special Features: Side-mounted JBL speakers, multidirectional duplexing microphone for 4000 and 8000 series Presarios; Energy Star compliant
Warranty: One-year return-to-depot warranty (first ninety days on site)
Suggested List Price at Publication: $468
Approximate Street Price at Publication: $429

MONITOR MANUFACTURER: COMPAQ

Model: Presario Multimedia 1525 multimedia series
Physical/Screen Size: 15" diagonal/13.5" viewable
Resolution: 1,024 x 768 non-interlaced
Dot Pitch: .28 mm
Refresh Rate: Up to 75 Hz
Special Features: Side-mounted JBL speakers, multidirectional duplexing microphone for 4000 and 8000 series Presarios; Energy Star compliant
Warranty: One-year return-to-depot warranty (first ninety days on site)
Suggested List Price at Publication: $585
Approximate Street Price at Publication: $529

MONITOR MANUFACTURER: COMPAQ

Model: Presario Multimedia 1725/1725s multimedia series
Physical/Screen Size: 17" diagonal/15.6" viewable
Resolution: 1,280 x 1,024 non-interlaced
Dot Pitch: .28 mm
Refresh Rate: Up to 75 Hz
Special Features: Side-mounted JBL speakers, multidirectional duplexing microphone for 4000 and 8000 series Presarios; 1725s for Presario 4840; Energy Star compliant
Warranty: One-year return-to-depot warranty (first ninety days on site)
Suggested List Price at Publication: $1,072
Approximate Street Price at Publication: $949

MONITOR MANUFACTURER: COMPAQ

Model: Presario Multimedia FX500 multimedia series
Physical/Screen Size: 15" diagonal/13.8" viewable
Resolution: 1,024 x 768 non-interlaced
Dot Pitch: .28 mm
Refresh Rate: 85 Hz
Special Features: Side-mounted JBL speakers, multidirectional duplexing microphone for 4000 and 8000 series Presarios; one-touch controls; universal serial bus (USB) ports to connect peripherals; Energy Star compliant

Warranty: One-year return-to-depot warranty (first ninety days on site)
Suggested List Price at Publication: $756
Approximate Street Price at Publication: $679

MONITOR MANUFACTURER: COMPAQ

Model: Presario Multimedia FX700 multimedia series
Physical/Screen Size: 17" diagonal/16.0" viewable
Resolution: 1,280 x 1,024 non-interlaced
Dot Pitch: .28 mm
Refresh Rate: Up to 75 Hz
Special Features: Side-mounted JBL speakers, multidirectional duplexing microphone for 4800 series Presarios; one-touch controls; universal serial bus (USB) ports to connect peripherals; Energy Star compliant
Warranty: One-year return-to-depot warranty (first ninety days on site)
Suggested List Price at Publication: $1,132
Approximate Street Price at Publication: $995

MONITOR MANUFACTURER: COMPAQ

Model: Presario V400/410/410e series
Physical/Screen Size: 14" diagonal/13.2" viewable
Resolution: 1,024 x 768 non-interlaced
Dot Pitch: .28 mm
Refresh Rate: 75 Hz
Special Features: Side-mounted JBL speakers, duplexing microphone; Energy Star compliant
Warranty: One-year return-to-depot warranty (first ninety days on site)
Suggested List Price at Publication: $351 (V410)
Approximate Street Price at Publication: $319 (V410)

MONITOR MANUFACTURER: COMPAQ

Model: QVision 210
Physical/Screen Size: 21" diagonal/19.5" viewable
Resolution: Up to 1,600 x 1,200
Dot Pitch: .26 mm
Refresh Rate: 48–160 Hz; 85 Hz in preset modes

Radiation: MPR-II low-radiation compliant
Special Features: Flat square screen; on-screen controls; Energy Star compliant
Warranty: Three-year limited warranty (first year on site)
Suggested List Price at Publication: $3,259
Approximate Street Price at Publication: $2,895

MONITOR MANUFACTURER: COMPAQ

Model: V50/V70
Physical/Screen Size: 15" diagonal/13.7" viewable (V50); 17" diagonal/15.6" viewable (V70)
Resolution: 1,024 x 768 (V50); 1,280 x 1,024 (V70) non-interlaced
Dot Pitch: .28 mm
Refresh Rate: 47–115 Hz
Radiation: MPR-II low-radiation compliant
Special Features: Mac compatible; on-screen controls (V70); flat square screen; user-programmable graphics modes; Energy Star compliant
Warranty: One-year on-site parts-and-labour warranty (V50); three-year parts, one-year on-site labour warranty (V70)
Suggested List Price at Publication: $492 (V50)
Approximate Street Price at Publication: $459 (V50)

MONITOR MANUFACTURER: COMPAQ

Model: V90
Physical/Screen Size: 19" diagonal/18" viewable
Resolution: Up to 1,600 x 1,200
Dot Pitch: .26 mm
Refresh Rate: 48–160 Hz; 85 Hz in preset modes
Radiation: MPR-II low-radiation compliant
Special Features: Mac compatible; flat square screen; on-screen controls; language selection; universal serial bus (USB) port; Energy Star compliant
Warranty: Three-year parts, one-year on-site labour warranty
Suggested List Price at Publication: $1,332
Approximate Street Price at Publication: $1,195

DAEWOO/DAYTEK

A look at this Korean giant's company profile offers background to its size and diversity. Founded with US$10,000 in 1967 to manufacture and export nylon shirts to Southeast Asia, Daewoo exported over $13 billion in goods in 1996 and manufactured a line of products which included automobiles, construction equipment, ships, and electronic components. Boasting a leading share of 13.1 percent of Canada's monitor market, Daewoo subsidiary Daytek offers fifteen products, including the DT 1400/1500/1700/2000 series as well as its Vista V15, V17, and V19 models. This is a wide range of displays, even though the company is best known for its entries at the low end of the market. They are often sold with generic computer systems, or OEM-manufactured for other companies to put their names on and sell.

Several of the Dayteks are Apple compatible, and their lowest-end products can be compared to the Orchestra, TTX, and Magitronics monitors. Some issues include Samsung picture tubes, but this is a wide product range, so treat each one separately. You might want to enquire about picture- tube type when you buy. Otherwise, with such a large presence in the Canadian market, Daytek monitors are perhaps a better bet than some of their lesser-known and more thinly distributed (although slightly cheaper) rivals. As far as the higher-end Vista series is concerned, they do not yet enjoy the performance reputation of established players such as Mitsubishi and NEC.

MONITOR MANUFACTURER: DAEWOO

Model: DT-1436A/D/DM2/M2
Physical/Screen Size: 14" diagonal/13.5" viewable (estimated)
Resolution: 1,024 x 768
Dot Pitch: .28 mm
Refresh Rate: 40–90 Hz
Radiation: Some models MPR-II low-radiation compliant
Special Features: Energy Star compliant
Warranty: Three-year return-to-depot warranty
Suggested List Price at Publication: $299 (1436A); $349 (1436DM2)
Approximate Street Price at Publication: $239 (1436A); $279 (1436DM2)

MONITOR MANUFACTURER: DAEWOO

Model: DT-1531/1536/D/A/D
Physical/Screen Size: 15" diagonal/13.8" viewable
Resolution: 1,024 x 768
Dot Pitch: .28 mm
Refresh Rate: 40–120 Hz (may vary according to model)
Radiation: MPR-II low-radiation compliant
Special Features: Flat square screen; on-screen display; some models available in black; Energy Star compliant
Warranty: Three-year parts-and-labour return-to-depot warranty
Suggested List Price at Publication: $359 (1531) (estimated)
Approximate Street Price at Publication: $299

MONITOR MANUFACTURER: DAEWOO

Model: DT-1726D
Physical/Screen Size: 17" diagonal/16" viewable
Resolution: 1,600 x 1,200
Dot Pitch: .26 mm
Refresh Rate: 50–150 Hz
Radiation: MPR-II low-radiation compliant
Special Features: Mac compatible; microprocessor controls; Energy Star compliant
Warranty: Three-year return-to-depot warranty
Suggested List Price at Publication: $749 (estimated)
Approximate Street Price at Publication: $629

MONITOR MANUFACTURER: DAEWOO

Model: DT-2000M/2102M
Physical/Screen Size: 20" diagonal/19" viewable (estimated)
Resolution: 1,600 x 1,280 non-interlaced
Dot Pitch: .28 mm
Refresh Rate: 40–90 Hz
Special Features: Flat square screen; digital controls; degaussing; pincushioning; Energy Star compliant
Warranty: Three-year return-to-depot warranty

Suggested List Price at Publication: $2,099 (2102) (estimated)
Approximate Street Price at Publication: $1,899 (2102)

MONITOR MANUFACTURER: DAEWOO

Model: Vista V15/V17/V19
Physical/Screen Size: 15"/17"/19" diagonal
Resolution: 1,280 x 1,024 non-interlaced (V15/V19); 1,600 x 1,200 (V17)
Dot Pitch: .26mm (V15); .25 mm (V17); .28 mm (V19)
Refresh Rate: 50–120 Hz (may vary with model)
Radiation: MPR-II low-radiation compliant
Special Features: On-screen display; Diamondtron tube in V17; Energy Star compliant
Warranty: Three-year parts-and-labour return-to-depot
Suggested List Price at Publication: $499 (V15); $899 (V17); $1,399 (V19) (estimated)
Approximate Street Price at Publication: $350 (V15); $829 (V17); $1,229 (V19)

IBM

With one 14" model in its lineup of monitors, IBM offers G and P series displays as well as 15" and 17" multimedia products sold with Aptiva computers. Aptiva monitors are bundled with those PCs and are specifically intended for use with them, so don't attempt to mix and match even if a vendor allows it. If you want to buy an Aptiva, and you have an old monitor (or even a nice new one) sitting at home, don't be tempted. Sell it, trade it in, or give it to your favourite charity so you can get the proper piece with your new bundled PC; that way, you'll know that all of the multimedia and telephone applications will work. More important, you'll know who to call if they don't. As has been advised elsewhere in this guide, this is true for all home/small office computer bundles, including the Compaq Presarios, NEC Ready series, AST Advantages, Hewlett-Packard Pavilions, and Acer Aspires. It doesn't make sense to mix components when you are already paying extra for the integration provided by a manufacturer.

As far as its stand-alone monitors are concerned, IBM's G and P series are intended for use with its servers and 300 series PCs, and are available in the G42/G52/G72 models as well as the professional

P50/P70/P200/P201 ones. The Gs are the entry levels, the Ps contain Sony Trinitron tubes and come with a three-year warranty.

While IBM monitors enjoy a good reputation among service people in general and have the backing of IBM (a fact perhaps more important to corporate users than to individuals), they are not especially price competitive. All are multisync products, with dot pitches of .26 mm or .28 mm, with the large-screen, niche-market P200/201s containing a .31-mm Sony tube. Most are MPR-II low-emission compliant. Note also that four or five models are available in attractive black cases, if you're design conscious or already happen to own a black PC. Unless you specifically want IBM's name, however, or have been instructed by a corporate superior to purchase one, these displays are best married to Big Blue's own PCs in large business environments. While the occasional generic-computer user may want to insist on one, several other third-party monitor manufacturers offer more specifications for the dollar.

MONITOR MANUFACTURER: IBM

Model: G42
Physical/Screen Size: 14" diagonal/13.2" viewable
Resolution: 1,024 x 768; 800 x 600 non-interlaced
Dot Pitch: .28 mm
Refresh Rate: 50–100 Hz; 60–75 Hz in preset modes
Radiation: MPR-II low-radiation compliant
Special Features: Multifrequency monitor; Energy Star and Nutek compliant
Warranty: One-year return-to-depot warranty
Suggested List Price at Publication: $399
Approximate Street Price at Publication: $359

MONITOR MANUFACTURER: IBM

Model: G51
Physical/Screen Size: 15" diagonal/ 13.6" viewable
Resolution: 1,024 x 768; 800 x 600 non-interlaced
Dot Pitch: .28 mm
Refresh Rate: 50–100 Hz; 60–75 Hz in preset modes; 85 Hz at 800 x 600
Radiation: MPR-II low-radiation compliant

Special Features: Multifrequency monitor; Energy Star compliant
Warranty: One-year return-to-depot warranty
Suggested List Price at Publication: $499
Approximate Street Price at Publication: $459

MONITOR MANUFACTURER: IBM

Model: G52
Physical/Screen Size: 15" diagonal/13.6" viewable
Resolution: 1,280 x 1,024 maximum; 1,024 x 768 non-interlaced
Dot Pitch: .28 mm
Refresh Rate: 50–120 Hz; 60–75 Hz in preset modes; 85 Hz at 800 x 600
Radiation: MPR-II low-radiation compliant
Special Features: Multifrequency monitor; Energy Star compliant; available in black
Warranty: Three-year return-to-depot warranty
Suggested List Price at Publication: $559; $599 (black)
Approximate Street Price at Publication: $495; $529 (black)

MONITOR MANUFACTURER: IBM

Model: G72
Physical/Screen Size: 17" diagonal/15.7" viewable
Resolution: 1,600 x 1,200 maximum; 1,024 x 768 non-interlaced
Dot Pitch: .28 mm
Refresh Rate: 50–120 Hz; 70–85 Hz in preset modes; 85 Hz at 800 x 600
Radiation: MPR-II low-radiation compliant
Special Features: Multifrequency monitor; Energy Star compliant; available in black
Warranty: Three-year return-to-depot warranty
Suggested List Price at Publication: $949
Approximate Street Price at Publication: $895

MONITOR MANUFACTURER: IBM

Model: P70
Physical/Screen Size: 17" diagonal/15.9" viewable
Resolution: 1,600 x 1,200 non-interlaced

Dot Pitch: .26 mm
Refresh Rate: 50–120 Hz; 70–85 Hz in preset modes; 85 Hz at 800 x 600
Radiation: MPR-II low-radiation compliant
Special Features: Multifrequency monitor; Trinitron tube; Energy Star compliant
Warranty: Three-year express maintenance warranty
Suggested List Price at Publication: $1,243
Approximate Street Price at Publication: $1,179

MONITOR MANUFACTURER: IBM

Model: P200/201
Physical/Screen Size: 20" diagonal/19.1" viewable
Resolution: Up to 1,600 x 1,200 non-interlaced
Dot Pitch: .31 mm (P200); .26 mm (P201)
Refresh Rate: 50–160 Hz; 85 Hz in preset modes
Radiation: MPR-II low-radiation compliant
Special Features: Flat square screen; Trinitron tube; Energy Star compliant
Warranty: Three-year express maintenance warranty
Suggested List Price at Publication: $2,695 (P200); $2,995 (P201) (estimated)
Approximate Street Price at Publication: $2,395 (P200); $2,395 (P201)

MAG INNOVISION

With its North American head office in Santa Ana, California, MAG Innovision has made inroads in the small office and corporate computer markets with products which are beginning to compete with those of larger companies such as Panasonic, Sony, and NEC. While it recently (in 1994) acquired Princeton Graphics, a company that continues to produce monitors under its original name, MAG's Innovisions remain common among generic-computer sellers, who often offer them as upgrades over "lowest-cost" products from Daytek, TTX, and Orchestra.

With a lineup of about fifteen products, the MAGs can be divided loosely into three groups: the Technitron series, the DJ series, and the V2 series, with each lineup sharing common features and aimed at a specific market. The V2s are the company's least expensive models, ranging from the 410 to the 720. The DJ series (about eight models in all) are "new and improved," notably offering MAG's JAG Control, a "one-touch" fine-tuning system. The Technitron series, at the top, feature Sony Trinitron picture tubes and use microprocessor-based digital controls to manage display attributes. Many of these models are Apple compatible. But even with this kind of variety in its overall lineup, MAG is still best known as a tier two manufacturer. In that class it is a leader, with a good reputation for service and support, and an eye on the higher ground of the business and corporate markets. For use with generic computer systems, or even brand-name PCs being used in small offices, these monitors are recommended for their reputation, reasonable cost, and support.

MONITOR MANUFACTURER: MAG INNOVISION

Model: DJ 530/700/702/702E/707/717/800/920 series
Physical/Screen Size: 15" diagonal (530/700/707/800/920); 17" diagonal (702/702E/717)
Resolution: 1,024 x 728; up to 1,600 x 1,200 (some models)
Dot Pitch: .28 mm (530/700/702E/707/800/920); .26 mm (702/717)
Refresh Rate: 50–120 Hz (530/700/702E/707/800/920); 50–166 Hz (717)
Radiation: MPR-II low-radiation compliant
Special Features: Plug and play; Energy Star compliant; on-screen display
Warranty: Three-year parts, CR (cathode raytube), and labour warranty
Suggested List Price at Publication: $415 (530); $805 (700); $1,015 (717)
Approximate Street Price at Publication: $415 (530); $769 (700); $969 (717)

MONITOR MANUFACTURER: MAG INNOVISION

Model: Technitron DX500T/DX700T/DX715T series
Physical/Screen Size: 15" diagonal (DX500T/DX700T); 17" diagonal (DX715T)
Resolution: 1,280 x 1,024 non-interlaced
Dot Pitch: .25 mm
Refresh Rate: 50–100 Hz (DX500T/DX700T); 50–160 Hz (DX715T)
Radiation: MPR-II low-radiation compliant
Special Features: Plug and play; Energy Star compliant; on-screen display

Warranty: Three-year parts, two-year CRT, one-year labour warranty
Suggested List Price at Publication: $485 (DX500T); $1,119 (DX715T)
Approximate Street Price at Publication: $485 (DX500T); $969 (DX715T)

MONITOR MANUFACTURER: MAG INNOVISION

Model: V2 410/510/710/720 series
Physical/Screen Size: 14" (410/510); 17" (710/720)
Resolution: 1,024 x 768; up to 1,280 x 1024 (some models)
Dot Pitch: .28 mm
Refresh Rate: 50–100 Hz (410/510); 50–120 Hz (710/720)
Radiation: MPR-II low-radiation compliant
Special Features: Plug and play; Energy Star compliant; on-screen display
Warranty: Three-year parts, one-year CRT, one-year labour warranty
Suggested List Price at Publication: $355 (410); $495 (510); $695 (710); $739 (720)
Approximate Street Price at Publication: $269 (410); $459 (510); $679 (710); $710 (720)

MAGITRONIC

Established in 1985, Magitronic describes itself as a supplier of OEM computer components with manufacturing facilities in Norcross, Georgia; Los Angeles, California; and Toronto. Its monitors are sold throughout the Western hemisphere and in Asia. Self-described as a "second tier" builder, Magitronic produces a modest lineup, including the 1400/1450 series 14" models, a 15" model 1500, a 17" model 1700, and a 19" diagonal model 2000. These monitors all carry a three-year return-to-depot limited warranty. A new 19" model is being introduced in mid '98.

Magitronic's products are definitely positioned according to price, and as such they are a favourite of local PC assemblers who want to be able to advertise features for dollar. It's worth noting that these monitors have nothing to do with products from another builder of a similar name, MAG, which is known for its mostly higher-performance and higher-priced displays. Magitronic is more in competition with companies such as Daytek, TTX, and Orchestra. They offer satisfactory monitors at the low end of the generic market, with features in accordance with that price range.

MONITOR MANUFACTURER: MAGITRONIC

Model: 1400
Physical/Screen Size: 14" diagonal/13.3" viewable
Resolution: 1,024 x 768 maximum
Dot Pitch: .28 mm
Refresh Rate: 55 Hz
Radiation: MPR-II low-radiation compliant
Special Features: Energy Star compliant
Warranty: Two-year parts-and-labour, one-year CRT warranty
Suggested List Price at Publication: $259
Approximate Street Price at Publication: $219
Note: Product being phased out

MONITOR MANUFACTURER: MAGITRONIC

Model: 1450
Physical/Screen Size: 14" diagonal/13.3" viewable
Resolution: 1,024 x 768 maximum
Dot Pitch: .28 mm
Refresh Rate: 55–100 Hz
Radiation: MPR-II low-radiation compliant
Special Features: Energy Star compliant
Warranty: Three-year parts-and-labour warranty
Suggested List Price at Publication: $259
Approximate Street Price at Publication: $219

MONITOR MANUFACTURER: MAGITRONIC

Model: 1500
Physical/Screen Size: 15" diagonal/13.9" viewable
Resolution: 1,280 x 1,024 maximum
Dot Pitch: .28 mm
Refresh Rate: 30–65 Hz
Radiation: MPR-II low-radiation compliant
Special Features: Energy Star compliant
Warranty: Three-year all parts-and-labour warranty
Suggested List Price at Publication: $349
Approximate Street Price at Publication: $289

MONITOR MANUFACTURER: MAGITRONIC

Model: 1701
Physical/Screen Size: 17" diagonal/15.8" viewable
Resolution: 1,280 x 1,024
Dot Pitch: .28 mm
Refresh Rate: 30–69 Hz
Radiation: MPR-II low-radiation compliant
Special Features: Energy Star compliant; on-screen display
Warranty: Three-year parts-and-labour, one-year CRT warranty
Suggested List Price at Publication: $619 (estimated)
Approximate Street Price at Publication: $549

MONITOR MANUFACTURER: MAGITRONIC

Model: 2000
Physical/Screen Size: 19" diagonal
Resolution: 1,600 x 1,280
Dot Pitch: .28 mm
Refresh Rate: Up to 80 Hz
Radiation: MPR-II low-radiation compliant
Special Features: Energy Star compliant
Warranty: Three-year labour, two-year parts, one-year CRT warranty
Suggested List Price at Publication: Contact manufacturer
Approximate Street Price at Publication: Contact manufacturer

MITSUBISHI

Founded in the 1920s and strengthened early by contracts from companies such as Westinghouse to produce electrical appliances in Japan, this world leader in visual electronics has variously manufactured escalators, elevators, railway and subway equipment, even nuclear power generators. Today it has a strong presence in the semiconductor industry, as well as in large-screen video manufacturing, having supplied some of those really big screens to baseball and sports stadiums. Yet with all that history and those varied products in its past, Mitsubishi remains, almost curiously, a leader in computer monitor technology, its lineup being ranked with NEC and Panasonic as one of the best high-performance display groups available. The company's best-known Diamond Scans and Diamond Pros have been around at least since the early '90s, and this range is supplemented by the niche-market Megaview series – presentation monitors with great big (up to 40" diagonals and more) screens and great big prices. The Diamond Scans and Pros aren't cheap either, but have a loyal following among graphics-oriented computer users who want performance. Most popular are the 17" Diamond Pros, 67TXV/87TXM/Diamond Pro 700. All having .25-mm dot pitches and resolution maximums at 1,600 x 1,280, these monitors look good and are protected by a three-year warranty. Expect to pay extra for these and other features such as the included Mac interface, edge-to-edge picture technology, low emission ratings, and a new design which Mitsubishi says uses 30 percent fewer components. Often married to high-performance generic systems, or brand-name professional workstations for graphics and financial applications, the Diamond Scans and Diamond Pros remain one of the best groups of performance monitors available. They are priced accordingly.

MONITOR MANUFACTURER: MITSUBISHI

Model: Diamond Scan 15VX
Physical/Screen Size: 15" diagonal/13.8" viewable
Resolution: Up to 1,024 x 768 at 75 Hz
Dot Pitch: .28 mm
Refresh Rate: 50–100 Hz
Radiation: MPR-II low-radiation compliant
Warranty: Three-year parts, labour, and CRT warranty
Suggested List Price at Publication: $499
Approximate Street Price at Publication: $499

MONITOR MANUFACTURER: MITSUBISHI

Model: Diamond Scan 20LP
Physical/Screen Size: 20" diagonal/19" viewable
Resolution: 1,024 x 768
Dot Pitch: .31 mm
Refresh Rate: 45–90 Hz
Radiation: MPR-II low-radiation compliant
Special Features: Digital controls
Warranty: Three-year parts, labour, and CRT warranty

Suggested List Price at Publication: $2,499
Approximate Street Price at Publication: $2,499

MONITOR MANUFACTURER: MITSUBISHI

Model: Diamond Scan 20M
Physical/Screen Size: 20" diagonal/18.5" viewable
Resolution: 800 x 600
Dot Pitch: .31 mm
Refresh Rate: 45–90 Hz
Radiation: MPR-II low-radiation compliant
Warranty: Three-year parts, labour, and CRT warranty
Suggested List Price at Publication: $2,249
Approximate Street Price at Publication: $2,249

MONITOR MANUFACTURER: MITSUBISHI

Model: Megaview 29
Physical/Screen Size: 29" diagonal/27" viewable
Resolution: 640 x 480
Dot Pitch: .76 mm
Refresh Rate: 45–100 Hz
Radiation: MPR-II low-radiation compliant
Warranty: One-year parts, labour, and CRT warranty
Suggested List Price at Publication: Contact manufacturer
Approximate Street Price at Publication: Contact manufacturer

MONITOR MANUFACTURER: MITSUBISHI

Model: Megaview 33
Physical/Screen Size: 33" diagonal/31.2" viewable
Resolution: 800 x 600
Dot Pitch: .83 mm
Refresh Rate: 40–120 Hz
Radiation: MPR-II low-radiation compliant
Warranty: One-year warranty
Suggested List Price at Publication: $6,750
Approximate Street Price at Publication: $5,495

MONITOR MANUFACTURER: MITSUBISHI

Model: Megaview 37 Plus
Physical/Screen Size: 37" diagonal/35" viewable
Resolution: 1,024 x 768
Dot Pitch: .85 mm
Refresh Rate: 40–120 Hz
Radiation: MPR-II low-radiation compliant
Warranty: One-year parts, labour, and CRT warranty
Suggested List Price at Publication: $9,800
Approximate Street Price at Publication: $9,200

MONITOR MANUFACTURER: MITSUBISHI

Model: Megaview PRO 37
Physical/Screen Size: 37" diagonal/35" viewable
Resolution: 1,280 x 1,024
Dot Pitch: .85 mm
Refresh Rate: 40–120 Hz
Radiation: MPR-II low-radiation compliant
Warranty: One-year parts, labour, and CRT warranty
Suggested List Price at Publication: $14,200
Approximate Street Price at Publication: $12,950

NEC

Perhaps the best known maker of high quality monitors in the world, Nippon Electronics Corporation of Japan produces several lines, including its Multisync A series, XV+ series, E (Enterprise) series, M (Multimedia) series, and P (Professional) series. You are most likely to run across the XVs, Ms, and the new Es when shopping for a display for home or office; the Ps are aimed at the specialty markets in business and graphics, with features to burn at much higher prices. Indeed, all of NEC's products reside at the high end of the price spectrum, in competition with builders such as Panasonic, Mitsubishi, and Sony, as well as certain products from challengers MAG and Samsung.

NEC includes Chromaclear (increased depth and colour saturation) and Opticlear (glare reduction) technologies in most of its monitors, MPR-II low-radiation compliance, as well as an easy to use On-Screen Manager to adjust and control images.

With a long history at the top of the market, NECs are still the monitor of choice for those who can afford them – and in some cases even for shoppers who can't. That is to say, it's not uncommon for computer purchasers to want an NEC monitor badly enough to sacrifice other specs in a configuration just to be able to afford one. I must say, I can't entirely blame them. If you place emphasis on the way your system displays its text and graphic images, an NEC might be for you. Look especially at the XV series. On the other hand, an alternative to NEC's multimedia line might be a premium product from another manufacturer and a separate set of speakers.

MONITOR MANUFACTURER: NEC

Model: Multisync A500
Physical/Screen Size: 15" diagonal/13.8" viewable
Resolution: 1,600 x 1,200 at 60 Hz
Dot Pitch: .28 mm
Refresh Rate: 56–100 Hz
Radiation: MPR-II low-radiation compliant
Special Features: On-Screen Manager; Mac compatible
Warranty: Three-year warranty
Suggested List Price at Publication: $495 (estimated)
Approximate Street Price at Publication: $429

MONITOR MANUFACTURER: NEC

Model: Multisync A700
Physical/Screen Size: 17" diagonal/15.6" viewable
Resolution: 1,280 x 1,024 at 65 Hz
Dot Pitch: .28 mm
Refresh Rate: 56–100 Hz
Radiation: MPR-II low-radiation compliant
Special Features: On-Screen Manager; Mac compatible
Warranty: Three-year warranty
Suggested List Price at Publication: $995 (estimated)
Approximate Street Price at Publication: $849

MONITOR MANUFACTURER: NEC

Model: Multisync E500
Physical/Screen Size: 15" diagonal/13.8" viewable
Resolution: 1,280 x 1,024 at 65 Hz
Dot Pitch: .25 mm
Refresh Rate: 55–120 Hz
Radiation: MPR-II low-radiation compliant
Special Features: On-Screen Manager; Mac compatible
Warranty: Three-year warranty
Suggested List Price at Publication: $595 (estimated)
Approximate Street Price at Publication: $495

MONITOR MANUFACTURER: NEC

Model: Multisync E700
Physical/Screen Size: 17" diagonal/15.6" viewable
Resolution: 1,600 x 1,200 at 65 Hz
Dot Pitch: .25 mm
Refresh Rate: 55–120 Hz
Radiation: MPR-II low-radiation compliant
Special Features: On-Screen Manager; Mac compatible
Warranty: Three-year warranty
Suggested List Price at Publication: $1,095 (estimated)
Approximate Street Price at Publication: $979

MONITOR MANUFACTURER: NEC

Model: Multisync M500
Physical/Screen Size: 15" diagonal/13.8" viewable
Resolution: 1,280 x 1,024 at 65 Hz
Dot Pitch: .28 mm
Refresh Rate: 55–120 Hz
Radiation: MPR-II low-radiation compliant
Special Features: On-Screen Manager; Mac compatible
Warranty: Three-year warranty
Suggested List Price at Publication: $649 (estimated)
Approximate Street Price at Publication: $539

MONITOR MANUFACTURER: NEC

Model: Multisync M700
Physical/Screen Size: 17" diagonal/15.6" viewable
Resolution: 1,280 x 1,024 at 65 Hz
Dot Pitch: .25 mm
Refresh Rate: 55–120 Hz
Radiation: MPR-II low-radiation compliant
Special Features: On-Screen Manager; Mac compatible
Warranty: Three-year warranty
Suggested List Price at Publication: $1,095 (estimated)
Approximate Street Price at Publication: $995

MONITOR MANUFACTURER: NEC

Model: Multisync P750
Physical/Screen Size: 17" diagonal/15.6" viewable
Resolution: 1,600 x 1,200 at 75 Hz
Dot Pitch: .25 mm
Refresh Rate: 55–160 Hz
Radiation: MPR-II low-radiation compliant
Special Features: On-Screen Manager; Mac compatible
Warranty: Three-year warranty
Suggested List Price at Publication: $1,295
Approximate Street Price at Publication: $1,195

MONITOR MANUFACTURER: NEC

Model: Multisync P1150
Physical/Screen Size: 21" diagonal/19.6" viewable
Resolution: 1,600 x 1,200 at 75 Hz
Dot Pitch: .28 mm
Refresh Rate: 55–160 Hz
Radiation: MPR-II low-radiation compliant
Suggested List Price at Publication: $2,295
Approximate Street Price at Publication: $2,095

MONITOR MANUFACTURER: NEC

Model: Multisync XM29 Multimedia
Physical/Screen Size: 29" diagonal/27" viewable
Resolution: Up to 1,024 x 768 at 60 Hz
Dot Pitch: .75 mm
Refresh Rate: 40–120 Hz
Radiation: MPR-II low-radiation compliant
Special Features: MS plug-and-play compatible; Energy Star compliant
Warranty: One-year warranty
Suggested List Price at Publication: $3,995
Approximate Street Price at Publication: $3,700

MONITOR MANUFACTURER: NEC

Model: Multisync XV15+
Physical/Screen Size: 15" diagonal/13.8" viewable
Resolution: 1,280 x 1,024 at 60 Hz
Dot Pitch: .25 mm
Refresh Rate: 55–100 Hz
Radiation: MPR-II low-radiation compliant
Special Features: On-Screen Manager; Intelligent Power Manager; Mac compatible
Warranty: Three-year warranty
Suggested List Price at Publication: $695 (estimated)
Approximate Street Price at Publication: $595

MONITOR MANUFACTURER: NEC

Model: Multisync XV17+
Physical/Screen Size: 17" diagonal/15.6" viewable
Resolution: 1,280 x 1,024 at 76 Hz
Dot Pitch: .25 mm
Refresh Rate: 55–100 Hz
Radiation: MPR-II low-radiation compliant
Special Features: On-Screen Manager; Intelligent Power Manager (IPM); Mac compatible

Warranty: Three-year warranty
Suggested List Price at Publication: $1,095 (estimated)
Approximate Street Price at Publication: $995

ORCHESTRA

This twelve-year-old company, with U.S. headquarters in Garden Grove, California, advertises its mission as bringing value to the peripheral market by offering competitive pricing. This is in line with the market position of its products, which are favourites among small and medium-sized local assemblers of generic PCs who want to be able to advertise a best price. A competitor to Magitronic and especially Daytek, neither of whom have anywhere near the whimsy in their product names, the Orchestra lineup comprises about ten 14", 15", and 17" monitors ranging from the entry-level Bugle at .39-mm dot pitch to two Tuba II 17s at .26 and .28 mm. Notable is the Tympani 17", with a dot pitch of .42 mm. This must be one of the lowest-cost, lowest-specification 17" products on the market, although this is not to say it is recommended. Anything over a .31-mm dot pitch presents a grainy picture, which can be murder on the eyes before long. But the price is low, so if you notice that one of those generic PC advertisements includes a 17" monitor at a price you can hardly believe, chances are not bad it will include one of these.

The company's mid-range products – the Cornet, French Horn, and Trombone series – are average monitors suitable for use with basic home and small office PCs.

MONITOR MANUFACTURER: ORCHESTRA

Model: Bass Drum
Physical/Screen Size: 17" diagonal/15.9" viewable
Resolution: 1,600 x 1,280 non-interlaced
Dot Pitch: .28 mm
Refresh Rate: 50–90 Hz
Radiation: MPR-II low-radiation compliant
Special Features: Mac compatible; Energy Star compliant
Warranty: Two-year return-to-depot limited warranty
Suggested List Price at Publication: Contact manufacturer
Approximate Street Price at Publication: Contact manufacturer

MONITOR MANUFACTURER: ORCHESTRA

Model: Bugle/Cornet series
Physical/Screen Size: 14" diagonal/13.2" viewable (Bugle); 14" diagonal/13.4" viewable (Cornet)
Resolution: 1,024 x 768 interlaced
Dot Pitch: .39 mm (Bugle); .28 mm (Cornet)
Refresh Rate: 50–90 Hz
Special Features: Energy Star compliant
Warranty: One-year parts-and-labour return-to-depot warranty
Suggested List Price at Publication: $399 (Cornet)
Approximate Street Price at Publication: $249 (Cornet)

MONITOR MANUFACTURER: ORCHESTRA

Model: Horn
Physical/Screen Size: 15" diagonal/13.9" viewable
Resolution: 1,280 x 1,024 non-interlaced
Dot Pitch: .28 mm
Refresh Rate: 50–90 Hz
Radiation: MPR-II low-radiation compliant
Special Features: Microprocessor digital on-screen controls; edge-to-edge display; Energy Star compliant
Warranty: One-year return-to-depot warranty
Suggested List Price at Publication: $499
Approximate Street Price at Publication: $379

MONITOR MANUFACTURER: ORCHESTRA

Model: Trombone/Trumpet series
Physical/Screen Size: 14" diagonal/13.4" viewable
Resolution: 1,280 x 1,024 non-interlaced (Trombone); 1,024 x 768 (Trumpet)
Dot Pitch: .28 mm
Refresh Rate: 50–90 Hz
Special Features: Mac compatible; Energy Star compliant
Warranty: One-year parts-and-labour return-to-depot warranty
Suggested List Price at Publication: $399 (Trumpet)
Approximate Street Price at Publication: $249 (Trumpet)

MONITOR MANUFACTURER: ORCHESTRA

Model: Tuba II
Physical/Screen Size: 17" diagonal/15.9" viewable
Resolution: 1,600 x 1,200 non-interlaced
Dot Pitch: .26 mm or .28 mm
Refresh Rate: 50–120 Hz
Radiation: MPR-II low-radiation compliant
Special Features: Mac compatible; flat square screen; digital controls; Energy Star compliant
Warranty: Two-year parts-and-labour warranty
Suggested List Price at Publication: $1,095
Approximate Street Price at Publication: $749

MONITOR MANUFACTURER: ORCHESTRA

Model: Tympani
Physical/Screen Size: 17" diagonal/15.9" viewable
Resolution: 1,024 x 768 non-interlaced
Dot Pitch: .42 mm
Refresh Rate: 50–90 Hz
Special Features: Analogue controls; Energy Star compliant
Warranty: One-year parts-and-labour warranty
Suggested List Price at Publication: $999
Approximate Street Price at Publication: $649

PANASONIC

A company which has not always been known to be price competitive on the computer side of its business (think of its notebook PCs), Panasonic has nevertheless manufactured some very successful products (think of its dot matrix printers and computer components) over the years, at the very top of the performance-for-price pyramid. Its current crop of monitors comes close to this territory. As of publication, the company offered several displays in Canada, including the P15, P17, and S21 as well as the PF17, PM15, and PM17.

All of these are multisync monitors, meaning they can handle various frequencies, or types, of monitor signals, and most include a Mac interface. Only four of them can rightly be called high-performance monitors on the PC side, if your definition of that term is the ability to display resolutions of 1,600 x 1,200 – hardly a requirement in most office and home computer applications. The PM15s and 17s are equipped with dome speakers and microphone for multimedia, while the .24-mm-pitch PF70 is described as "perfectly flat," a feature very much worth considering if a big, clear image is important to you. Flat-screen monitors in general are preferred for the way they present information to your peripheral vision. All of these displays are MPR-II low-radiation compliant and come from a company that manufactures its own picture tubes, or at least has a parent company make them for it. Panasonics also have an excellent reputation among service people. With these features in mind, and their recent, more competitive price structure, these monitors, particularly the S15 and S70 models, are recommended.

MONITOR MANUFACTURER: PANASONIC

Model: PanaFlat PF70
Physical/Screen Size: 17" diagonal
Resolution: 1,600 x 1,280
Dot Pitch: .24 mm
Refresh Rate: Up to 160 Hz
Radiation: MPR-II low-radiation compliant
Special Features: Very flat screen; on-screen control functions; Mac compatible
Warranty: One-year parts-and-labour warranty
Suggested List Price at Publication: $1,399
Approximate Street Price at Publication: $1,249

MONITOR MANUFACTURER: PANASONIC

Model: PanaMedia PM15 Multimedia
Physical/Screen Size: 15" diagonal/14" viewable
Resolution: 1,280 x 1,024 at 65 Hz
Dot Pitch: .27 mm
Refresh Rate: 50–120 Hz
Radiation: MPR-II low-radiation compliant
Special Features: Windows 95 Plug and Play; dome speakers
Warranty: Three-year return-to-depot warranty (estimated)
Suggested List Price at Publication: $579
Approximate Street Price at Publication: $529

MONITOR MANUFACTURER: PANASONIC

Model: PanaMedia PM17
Physical/Screen Size: 17" diagonal/16" viewable
Resolution: 1,280 x 1,024 non-interlaced
Dot Pitch: .27 mm
Refresh Rate: 60–120 Hz
Radiation: MPR-II low-radiation compliant
Special Features: Windows 95 Plug and Play; dome speakers
Warranty: Three-year warranty
Suggested List Price at Publication: $999
Approximate Street Price at Publication: $929

MONITOR MANUFACTURER: PANASONIC

Model: PanaSync Pro P21/PanaSync S21
Physical/Screen Size: 21" diagonal/20" viewable
Resolution: 1,600 x 1,200 at 75 Hz (P21); 1,280 x 1,024 (S21)
Dot Pitch: .25 mm (P21); .27 mm (S21)
Refresh Rate: 50–160 Hz (P21); 50–150 Hz (S21)
Radiation: MPR-II low-radiation compliant
Special Features: Windows 95 Plug and Play
Warranty: Three-year warranty
Suggested List Price at Publication: $2,215 (P21); $1,569 (S21)
Approximate Street Price at Publication: $2,150 (P21); $1,469 (S21)

MONITOR MANUFACTURER: PANASONIC

Model: PanaSync S70
Physical/Screen Size: 17" diagonal/16" viewable
Resolution: 1,280 x 1,024
Dot Pitch: .27 mm
Refresh Rate: 50–120 Hz
Radiation: MPR-II low-radiation compliant
Special Features: Windows 95 Plug and Play
Warranty: Three-year warranty
Suggested List Price at Publication: $699
Approximate Street Price at Publication: $629

PRINCETON GRAPHICS

Princeton Graphics has been in the computer display business for twenty years. The company started building monitors in the early '80s, offering some of the first-ever third-party monochrome TTL products intended for use with early IBM and Compaq PCs. It also participated in the introduction of early EGA (enhanced graphics adapter) and multisync, or multiple frequency capable, monitors in the mid-'80s. In 1994, the company was acquired by MAG Innovision, although its products continue to be offered under the Princeton name in its EO and Ultra series as well as an interesting hybrid PC/TV called the Arcadia Home Monitor.

The EO series are generic PC-class monitors with fast refresh rates at 75 Hz in resolutions up to 1,600 x 1,200. They include plug-and-play technology and compatibility with a new VESA (Video Electronics Standards Association) standard known as Display Data Channels (DDC1 and DDC2). The slightly lower priced Ultra series can also be driven into the 1,600 x 1,200 range, although at a lower frequency of 66 Hz. Both lines include PreVu Onscreen picture adjustments and MPR-II radiation emissions compliance.

Perhaps the most innovative of this company's issues are its Arcadia Home Monitors, four models of televisions which mix the clarity of a computer monitor with the size (27"–31") and signal compatibilities of a television. These double as ordinary TVs for use with a cable connection, VCR, or DVD player, as well as being big-screen PC monitors. While this "convergence" end of the monitor marketplace is still new, it's bound to grow quickly. If you're considering one of these combination products, be sure to consider its practicality. If you are looking for large-screen output from a PC, these may be a good bet. Two alternative approaches are to (a) adapt a conventional TV to your PC, but the output will be poor, or (b) buy a big-screen PC monitor, but even 19" and 20" diagonals in the computer world are quite expensive. With these options in mind, it would seem that the "two-in-one" displays Princeton is offering, even at their substantial price, could be a good choice for computer users of the future.

MONITOR MANUFACTURER: PRINCETON GRAPHICS

Model: Arcadia AR 2.7/AR3.1
Physical/Screen Size: 27" diagonal (AR2.7)/31" diagonal (AR3.1)
Resolution: 800 x 600

Dot Pitch: .83 mm
Refresh Rate: 38 Hz
Special Features: Energy Star compliant; on-screen display monitor/ TV inputs
Warranty: One-year parts, CRT, and labour warranty
Suggested List Price at Publication: $1,112 (AR2.7); $1,999 (AR3.1)
Approximate Street Price at Publication: $1,112 (AR2.7); $1,799 (AR2.7)

MONITOR MANUFACTURER: PRINCETON GRAPHICS

Model: EO40/50/70
Physical/Screen Size: 14" diagonal/13.4" viewable (EO40); 15" diagonal/13.8" viewable (EO50); 17" diagonal/15.8" viewable (EO70)
Resolution: 1,280 x 1,024 non-interlaced; 1,024 x 768 (EO40)
Dot Pitch: .28 mm
Refresh Rate: 50–120 Hz; 40–120 Hz (EO40)
Radiation: MPR-II low-radiation compliant
Special Features: Flat square screen (EO50 and EO70 only); Mac and SPARC station compliant with optional adapter
Warranty: Three-year limited parts, CRT, and labour warranty
Suggested List Price at Publication: $429 (EO50); $665 (EO70)
Approximate Street Price at Publication: $379 (EO50); $649 (EO70)

MONITOR MANUFACTURER: PRINCETON GRAPHICS

Model: Ultra 72
Physical/Screen Size: 17" diagonal/15.8" viewable
Resolution: 1,280 x 1,024
Dot Pitch: .28 mm
Refresh Rate: 55–90 Hz
Radiation: MPR-II low-radiation compliant
Warranty: One-year parts, CRT, and labour warranty
Suggested List Price at Publication: $739
Approximate Street Price at Publication: $649

MONITOR MANUFACTURER: PRINCETON GRAPHICS

Model: Ultra 80
Physical/Screen Size: 20" diagonal
Resolution: 1,600 x 1,200
Dot Pitch: .28 mm
Refresh Rate: 50–200 Hz
Radiation: MPR-II low-radiation compliant
Warranty: Three-year parts, two-year CRT, one-year labour warranty
Suggested List Price at Publication: $1,529
Approximate Street Price at Publication: $1,495

SAMSUNG

This Korean giant is a household name throughout the world and offers a wide range of equipment, much like Mitsubishi and Tatung. With revenues in excess of $80 billion and interests ranging from heavy industry to semiconductors, Samsung started as a noodle and dried fish trading company in 1938. Its current crop of monitors includes the SyncMaster S/B/MB/MP/NE series, to name a few. Models you are likely to encounter in Canada are the 400b/500s/700s/500b/700b and 700p. These are standard 14", 15", and 17" Super VGA products, all advertising Mac compatibility but requiring an adapter which the company's literature says is available for free. Confirm this with your dealer. All of these monitors offer 1,280 x 1,024 resolutions in the 65- to 80-Hz range and the usual plug-and-play features and MPR-II compliance. The SyncMaster 700bs and 700ps are graphics-oriented with a wide variety of digital on-screen controls: the usual contrast, brightness, HV size and position, as well as pin balance, rotation, colour selection, vertical linearity, and some other terms you'll probably want to look up in the manual.

Attractively priced, particularly the 500s and 700s, these monitors are commonly found in the generic computer market and, less often, sitting on top of brand-name systems in offices where the administration has a mandate to purchase from a bigger company. With a three-year "Advanced Replacement" warranty covering the CRT (cathode ray tube) as well as general parts and labour, the SyncMasters are better supported than many others in the third-party market. While they are average in the price-for-features column, the company name and guarantee position them well against other mid-range displays.

MONITOR MANUFACTURER: SAMSUNG

Model: SyncMaster 400b/400s
Physical/Screen Size: 14" diagonal/13.12" viewable
Resolution: 1,024 x 768
Dot Pitch: .28 mm
Refresh Rate: 50–120 Hz
Radiation: MPR-II low-radiation compliant
Special Features: Energy Star compliant
Warranty: Three-year warranty
Suggested List Price at Publication: $239 (400s)
Approximate Street Price at Publication: $239 (400s)

MONITOR MANUFACTURER: SAMSUNG

Model: SyncMaster 500b/500s
Physical/Screen Size: 15" diagonal/13.8" viewable
Resolution: Up to 1,280 x 1,024 non-interlaced
Dot Pitch: .28 mm
Refresh Rate: 50–160 Hz (varies with model)
Radiation: MPR-II low-radiation compliant
Special Features: Multimedia models available; Mac compatible; Energy Star compliant
Warranty: Three-year warranty
Suggested List Price at Publication: $429 (500b); $379 (500s)
Approximate Street Price at Publication: $400 (500b); $359 (500s)

MONITOR MANUFACTURER: SAMSUNG

Model: SyncMaster 700b/700p/700s series
Physical/Screen Size: 17" diagonal/15.8" viewable (most models)
Resolution: Up to 1,600 x 1,280; 1,024 x 768 (most models)
Dot Pitch: .26 mm; .28 mm (some models)
Refresh Rate: 50–120+ Hz
Radiation: MPR-II low-radiation compliant
Special Features: Multimedia models available; Mac compatible; on-screen display controls (some models); Energy Star compliant
Warranty: Three-year warranty
Suggested List Price at Publication: $779 (700b); $949 (700p); $699 (700s)

Approximate Street Price at Publication: $749 (700b); $895 (700p); $659 (700s)

SONY

One of the highest profile manufacturers of monitors in the world, Sony has long been famous for its Trinitron picture-tube technology, which it uses in its own displays and also sells to several other companies. Its lineup is divided into six groups, three of which might be described as specialty, or niche-market, products and three – the ES, GS, and PS series – intended for more common home and business computer applications.

In competition with other manufacturers of similar stature in the field – Panasonic, Mitsubishi, and NEC – as well as some brand-name computer builders such as IBM and Compaq (some of which use Sony's parts), this Japanese giant has recently become one of the more competitive, offering its 17" ES series at dealer prices that in turn support a retail price of under $995 in Canada. In the last two years, however, there have been reports of the renowned tubes in some of Sony's 15" monitors displaying a thin, wavering line about two-thirds of the way down from the top of the screen. Whether this was the result of a defect in a single manufacturing run or a longstanding problem is not clear. Certainly the company's 17" products enjoy as good a reputation as ever, as well as a reduced price.

All of Sony's monitors, in particular the ES and GS lines, remain popular and competitive at the high end of the generic computer market, as well as being companions to brand-name PCs when a corporation views Sony's displays as a better buy than those from a PC manufacturer. The 17" 200 ES and 200 GS, the second of which has an unusual multimedia "monitoring" speaker as well as a built-in headphone jack, are worth considering if you are buying a high-end generic or brand-name business class PC.

MONITOR MANUFACTURER: SONY

Model: CPD-100 ES/CPD-200 ES
Physical/Screen Size: 15" diagonal/14" viewable (100 ES); 17" diagonal/16" viewable (200 ES)
Resolution: 1,280 x 1,024 non-interlaced (100 ES); 1,024 x 768 (200 ES)
Dot Pitch: .25 mm

Refresh Rate: 50–120 Hz
Radiation: MPR-II low-radiation compliant
Special Features: On-screen display; Mac compatible; Trinitron tube; Energy Star compliant
Warranty: One-year parts, labour, and CRT warranty (certain restrictions apply)
Suggested List Price at Publication: $499 (100 ES); $899 (200 ES)
Approximate Street Price at Publication: $499 (100 ES); $899 (200 ES)

MONITOR MANUFACTURER: SONY

Model: CPD-100 GS/CPD-200 GS
Physical/Screen Size: 15" diagonal/14" viewable (100 GS); 17" diagonal/16" viewable (200 GS)
Resolution: 1,280 x 1,028 non-interlaced
Dot Pitch: .25 mm
Refresh Rate: 50–120 Hz
Radiation: MPR-II low-radiation compliant
Special Features: On-screen display; digital controls; Mac compatible; space-saver design; mono speaker and built-in microphone; range of digital controls on the 200 GS, including zoom and volume control; Energy Star compliant
Warranty: Three-year parts, labour, and CRT warranty (certain restrictions apply)
Suggested List Price at Publication: $1,049 (200 GS)
Approximate Street Price at Publication: $1,049 (200 GS)

MONITOR MANUFACTURER: SONY

Model: (PS series) GDM 200/GDM 400/GDM 500
Physical/Screen Size: 17" diagonal/16" viewable (GDM 200); 19" diagonal/18" viewable (GDM 400); 21" diagonal/19.8" viewable (GDM 500)
Resolution: Up to 1,600 x 1,280
Dot Pitch: .25 mm
Refresh Rate: 48–160 Hz
Radiation: MPR-II low-radiation compliant
Special Features: A wide range of on-screen controls, including sizing, zoom, and multilanguage options; Mac compatible; Energy Star compliant

Warranty: One-year parts-and-labour warranty (GDM 200/GDM 400); three-year warranty (GDM 500)
Suggested List Price at Publication: $1,229 (GDM 200); $1,829 (GDM 400); $2,799 (GDM 500)
Approximate Street Price at Publication: $1,229 (GDM 200); $1,829 (GDM 400); $2,799 (GDM 500)

TTX

Started in 1985, with offices around North America and full-service facilities in Canada in Vancouver, Calgary, Winnipeg, Toronto, and Montreal, this Canadian company is a common producer of monitors under its own name, and also manufactures displays for other companies to sell. As of early 1998, it produced about twelve mainstream products in the 14", 15", and 17" classes, with a few extra models in the 20" and 21" niche market and point-of-sale markets.

These monitors are most likely to appear with generic, or locally assembled, PCs. The majority of them are MPR-II low-radiation compliant, although according to the company's website its two 14" models are not. The biggest group in the lineup comprises TTX's 17" monitors, with six models available as of publication. The company must be heeding reports which state that in 1998, 17" diagonal products will finally surpass 14s in market share, ranking behind only 15" models. These displays are well priced for the features they offer, and evenly matched when compared to competitive monitors from multinational corporations such as Daewoo.

MONITOR MANUFACTURER: TTX

Model: 7565E
Physical/Screen Size: 17" diagonal/15.7" viewable
Resolution: 1,280 x 1,024 at 60 Hz
Dot Pitch: .28 mm
Refresh Rate: 50–90 Hz
Radiation: MPR-II low-radiation compliant
Special Features: On-screen display
Suggested List Price at Publication: $799
Approximate Street Price at Publication: $549

MONITOR MANUFACTURER: TTX

Model: 8195XE
Physical/Screen Size: 21" diagonal/20" viewable
Resolution: 1,600 x 1,280
Dot Pitch: .26 mm
Refresh Rate: 50–160 Hz
Special Features: On-screen display; Energy Star compliant
Suggested List Price at Publication: $2,295
Approximate Street Price at Publication: $1,799

MONITOR MANUFACTURER: TTX

Model: 8565
Physical/Screen Size: 15" diagonal/13.7" viewable
Resolution: 1,280 x 1,024 at 60 Hz
Dot Pitch: .28 mm
Refresh Rate: 50–90 Hz
Radiation: MPR-II low-radiation compliant
Special Features: On-screen display
Suggested List Price at Publication: $429
Approximate Street Price at Publication: $319

MONITOR MANUFACTURER: TTX

Model: 8765
Physical/Screen Size: 17" diagonal/16" viewable
Resolution: 1,280 x 1,024 non-interlaced
Dot Pitch: .28 mm
Refresh Rate: 50–120 Hz
Radiation: MPR-II low-radiation compliant
Special Features: On-screen display; high contrast CRT
Suggested List Price at Publication: $799
Approximate Street Price at Publication: $589

MONITOR MANUFACTURER: TTX

Model: 8995
Physical/Screen Size: 19" diagonal/18" viewable
Resolution: 1,600 x 1,200 at 75 Hz
Dot Pitch: .26 mm
Refresh Rate: 50–125 Hz
Radiation: MPR-II low-radiation compliant
Special Features: Microprocessor-based digital controls; flat square screen
Suggested List Price at Publication: $1,299
Approximate Street Price at Publication: $1,059

VIEWSONIC

Founded in 1987 by entrepreneur James Chu, Viewsonic Corporation entered the monitor market around 1991 and has since gained recognition as a tier two builder in competition with MAG Innovision and even some Panasonic and Sony products. With several awards from both publications and individual reviewers, Viewsonic displays are available in four groups in Canada through regular distribution: the E2 series, Professional series, Graphics series, and niche-market Viewpanel series, which are active-matrix colour-panel desktop displays. It is the E2 series you are most likely to encounter in the general home and small office computer markets. They are available in the usual 14", 15", and 17" issues at prices which place them a step above the Dayteks and Tatungs, and are often offered as an upgrade when being sold with a locally assembled PC, or as a slightly lower-cost mate to a brand-name system such as a Compaq Deskpro.

The Graphics series are aimed at the discriminating user who will pay extra for features and perhaps take a chance on a lesser-known name, while the Professional models are likely to be purchased by users who take the trouble to research the market carefully. In all, the Viewsonic monitors, especially the E2 series, fare well in the review literature and are average in price for the features they offer.

MONITOR MANUFACTURER: VIEWSONIC

Model: 15GA/GS, 17GA/G773
Physical/Screen Size: 15" diagonal/14" viewable (15GA/GS); 17" diagonal/16" viewable (17GA/G773)

Resolution: 1,280 x 1,024 non-interlaced
Dot Pitch: .27 mm; .26 mm (G773)
Refresh Rate: 65–110 Hz in preset modes; up to 160 Hz (G773)
Radiation: MPR-II low-radiation compliant
Special Features: Digital controls; PC and Mac compatible; flat square screen; plug and play; GA series monitors have built-in multimedia features: speakers, headphone jack, microphone
Warranty: Three-year limited warranty
Suggested List Price at Publication: \$499 (15GA); \$459 (15GS); \$839 (17GA)
Approximate Street Price at Publication: \$499 (15GA); \$459 (15GS); \$799 (17GA)

MONITOR MANUFACTURER: VIEWSONIC

Model: E641/E655
Physical/Screen Size: 14" diagonal/13.2" viewable (E641); 15" diagonal/13.9" viewable (E655)
Resolution: 1,024 x 768 non-interlaced (E641); 1,280 x 1,024 non-interlaced (E655)
Dot Pitch: .28 mm
Refresh Rate: 67–85 Hz; 87–100 Hz (E655) in preset modes
Radiation: MPR-II low-radiation compliant
Special Features: Digital controls; PC and Mac compatible; flat square screen (E655); plug and play
Warranty: Three-year limited warranty
Suggested List Price at Publication: \$269 (E641); \$399 (E655)
Approximate Street Price at Publication: \$269 (E641); \$399 (E655)

MONITOR MANUFACTURER: VIEWSONIC

Model: E771/E771+/E771B
Physical/Screen Size: 17" diagonal/16" viewable
Resolution: 1,280 x 1,024 non-interlaced
Dot Pitch: .27 mm
Refresh Rate: 66–110 Hz in preset modes
Radiation: MPR-II low-radiation compliant
Special Features: Digital controls; PC and Mac compatible; flat square screen; plug and play; E771+ and E771B have built-in multimedia

features: speakers, headphone jack, microphone; available in black
Warranty: Three-year limited warranty
Suggested List Price at Publication: $669 (E771); $769 (E771B)
Approximate Street Price at Publication: $669 (E771); $769 (E771B)

PRINTERS

ALPS INK JET

Alps Electric USA is a wholly owned subsidiary of Alps Electric Limited of Tokyo, Japan. In addition to making printers, the company produces a line of other computer peripherals, including conventional and specialty keyboards, scanner keyboards, keypads, mice, and Playstation gaming products. As of publication, two of the company's models are the 2010, a stand-alone ink jet, and the MD 4000, a printer and scanner combination. Both come in PC or Mac interface versions, and require 8 megabytes of memory to manage accompanying software. Available through dealers who may purchase them in Canada from Serviceworks or other distributors, Alps printers are advertised as an improvement over conventional ink jet technologies. According to the company's literature, this is because of the exclusive "Micro Dry" ink in them, which fuses colour onto the paper or media surface instead of spraying or bubbling it. The intended result is a sharper picture which won't smudge. These printers also print in a range of metallic colours, unusual at this end of the market, as well as at a very sharp 1,600 x 600 greyscale resolution.

There are quite a lot of features here, but for some reason, the recognition of this manufacturer in Canada is low. While the company has been around long enough, and is large enough to inspire confidence in its service and support and the availability of its consumables – it's a $4-billion Fortune International 500 concern – its presence in the market could use improvement. Nevertheless, these printers offer many features if you are willing to pay the higher price for them.

PRINTER MANUFACTURER: ALPS

Model: MD 1000
Physical/Type: Colour dry ink
Paper Handling: 100 sheets
Bundled Software: Hanes T-Shirt maker; Sierra On-Line Print Artist; Adobe PhotoDeluxe (Macintosh only); Mac/Windows drivers
Print Characteristics: 1,200 x 600 dpi black, 600 x 600 dpi colour
Warranty: One-year limited warranty
Suggested List Price at Publication: $780
Approximate Street Price at Publication: $459
Notes: Prints on standard paper, greeting cards, transparencies, T-shirt transfers; 8-MB RAM and Windows 3.1, Windows 95, or Mac OS 7.01 required

PRINTER MANUFACTURER: ALPS

Model: MD 2010
Physical/Type: Colour dry ink
Print Speed: 2 ppm black, 3 to 5 minutes per page colour
Paper Handling: Sheet feeder included
Bundled Software: Windows 95 and Windows 3.x drivers
Print Characteristics: 1,200 x 600 dpi black, 600 x 600 dpi colour
Warranty: One-year parts-and-labour warranty
Suggested List Price at Publication: $559
Approximate Street Price at Publication: $395
Note: Dry ink technology

PRINTER MANUFACTURER: ALPS

Model: MD 2300
Physical/Type: Photo-quality dry ink printing
Print Speed: 15 to 20 ppm black, 1 to 2 ppm colour
Memory: 32-KB buffer
Paper Handling: 100 sheets paper/20 envelopes
Bundled Software: Drivers and utilities
Print Characteristics: 1,200 x 600 dpi black, 600 x 600 dpi colour
Warranty: One-year parts-and-labour warranty
Suggested List Price at Publication: $1,568

Approximate Street Price at Publication: $1,195
Notes: 16-MB RAM required, 32 MB recommended; Windows 3.1 or Windows 95, Mac OS 7.01

PRINTER MANUFACTURER: ALPS

Model: MD 4000
Physical/Type: Colour printer/scanner combination
Print Speed: 1 minute per page black, 3 to 5 minutes per page colour
Memory: 32-KB buffer
Paper Handling: 100-sheet feeder
Accessories: Media sample kit included
Bundled Software: Mac or Windows 3.x/Windows 95 drivers
Print Characteristics: 1,200 x 600 dpi black, 600 x 600 dpi colour
Warranty: One-year parts-and-labour warranty
Suggested List Price at Publication: $1,002
Approximate Street Price at Publication: $795
Notes: 8-MB RAM required; sheet-feed scanner scans at 600 dpi

BROTHER LASER

Appearing in a range of about ten models, Brother's HL series have been available since the company entered the laser printer business in the early '90s. At the bottom of the group, the 720s and 730s are aimed at homes and small offices, with a superior set of specifications for their approximately $500 and $600 respective price tags. Perhaps this is to compensate for Brother's position as a relative newcomer in this market, major players like NEC and Hewlett-Packard having been in the game since the '70s. Advertising a straight paper path, a feature which used to be an unusual advantage but which has now become more common in lasers under $1,000, the low-cost HLs have shown early wear and tear on their feed roll assemblies, requiring replacement parts sooner than might be expected (as reported to me by one mechanic). Otherwise, this is a competitive group of products, with toner and drum costs putting the per-page cost of their outputs in the $.02–$.03 range at 5-percent coverage, which is about normal.

Whether the higher-level HLs such as the 1060s are making inroads among corporate and institutional customers is debatable. At prices over $1,000, the market veers sharply toward Hewlett-Packard and

Lexmark. An extra which Brother has included with several of its current models is a piece of software designed to make email printing easier. According to the literature, this package allows you to print messages directly from Microsoft Explorer or Netscape Navigator more quickly and easily than by using browser/email software on its own. It remains to be seen whether this addition and other features in the office-grade HLs will be enough to alter the public's perception of Brother as a manufacturer which belongs at the low end of the market.

PRINTER MANUFACTURER: BROTHER

Model: 720/730/730 Plus, 730DX/730DX Plus
Physical/Type: Desktop monochrome laser
Print Speed: 6 ppm
Memory: .5- or 1-MB RAM resident, max 2 MB
Paper Handling: 100-sheet straight paper path
Accessories: Brother Internet Software Suite
Bundled Software: Windows 95 and Windows 3.x drivers, Mac drivers come in Mac/serial interface
Print Characteristics: 600 x 600 dpi
Warranty: Two-year limited warranty
Suggested List Price at Publication: $569 (730DX); $599 (730DX Plus)
Approximate Street Price at Publication: $499 (730DX); $529 (730DX Plus)

PRINTER MANUFACTURER: BROTHER

Model: 760/760 Plus, 760DX/760DX Plus
Physical/Type: Desktop monochrome laser
Print Speed: 6 ppm
Memory: 1-MB RAM, max 33 MB
Paper Handling: 200-sheet straight paper path
Accessories: Optional Mac interface
Bundled Software: Surf 'n' Print software, font manager, Windows 95 and Windows 3.x drivers
Print Characteristics: 1,200 x 600 dpi; 61 fonts
Warranty: Two-year limited warranty
Suggested List Price at Publication: $669 (760DX); $699 (760DX Plus)

Approximate Street Price at Publication: $629 (760DX); $649 (760DX Plus)
Note: Brother Internet Software Suite with some models

PRINTER MANUFACTURER: BROTHER

Model: 1060/1660
Physical/Type: Desktop monochrome laser
Print Speed: 10 ppm (1060); 17 ppm (1660)
Memory: 2-MB RAM, max 32 MB (1060); 4-MB RAM, max 66 MB (1660)
Paper Handling: Dual sheet feeding at 200 sheets each; 150- and 500-sheet trays (1660 model)
Accessories: Optional Mac interface; optional Ethernet in 1660
Bundled Software: Windows 95 and Windows 3.x drivers
Print Characteristics: 1,200 x 600 dpi
Suggested List Price at Publication: $799 (1060); $1,899 (1660)
Approximate Street Price at Publication: $769 (1060); $1,595 (1660)
Notes: Advanced photoscale technology; multiple printer languages; in 1660: PCMCIA card slot, font card slot, 87 fonts, high resolution control

CANON BUBBLE JET

With ink jet printer sales mushrooming from four million units sold in 1992 to twenty-one million in 1995, all of the major players in this market have been riding a wave of popularity which has been self-propelling, financing further research and development into better print quality. In 1998 we are all reaping the rewards of this cycle: ink jets are hot, and pioneer Canon has been well positioned in this group of products from the beginning with its Bubble Jets, a name which has endured and is even sometimes mistakenly used to describe ink jets in general. In a similar fashion as the products of its competitors, Canon Bubble Jets use a technology which positions tiny drops of ink in a matrix of holes, then heats them so they bubble out onto the page in the pattern of a desired character, rather than squirting them out in streams.

As of early 1998, the wide range of models in the BJC series started with the entry-level 240 at about $225 street price and included the BJC 250, 260, 620, 4000, 4200, 4200 Photo, 4300, and 4304 Photo, and the BJC 7000s. The company can also be counted on to introduce new models and variations on its existing ones throughout 1998. Also notice the "Photo" designation following some models. Canon offers an optional "Photo Kit" for many of its products. This package contains a special ink cartridge for better-quality pictures. Photo-designated models already include this, but offering it as an option for others is also a good idea. It allows you to move into photo printing, with its increased costs, when you want to. This flexibility is especially attractive to cost-conscious purchasers searching at the low end of the market, who are provided room to adapt as their printing applications demand. Canon also offers its bubble jet printing technology in a line of MultiPASS products, the C2500, C3000s, and C5000s, which are multi-function units that fax, copy, and scan.

As far as durability is concerned, there have been reports of early printhead replacements in some of these printers. As the most important and expensive single component in the whole machine, a printhead should be built to last; if it fails, it's a toss-up whether or not the printer will be worth fixing. Otherwise, these are well-supported printers from a globally recognized manufacturer and carry a three-year program of warranty and support. They produce a quality output for the dollar. Priced in the lowest tier when compared feature for feature with competitors from Lexmark and Hewlett-Packard, Bubble Jets are primarily a home lineup, a position Canon would undoubtedly like to expand into the small and medium-sized business markets in the future.

PRINTER MANUFACTURER: CANON

Model: BJC-80
Physical/Type: Portable bubble jet, ink on demand
Print Speed: 4.5 ppm black, 2 ppm colour
Memory: 34-KB buffer
Paper Handling: Built-in sheet feeder/30 sheets
Accessories: Manufacturer's accessories available
Bundled Software: Windows 95 and Windows 3.x drivers included; TrueType font-pack disk
Print Characteristics: 720 x 360 dpi black, 720 x 360 dpi colour
Warranty: One-year limited warranty with InstantExchange warranty program
Suggested List Price at Publication: $499
Approximate Street Price at Publication: $429

PRINTER MANUFACTURER: CANON

Model: BJC-240
Physical/Type: Bubble jet, ink on demand
Print Speed: 4 ppm black, 1 ppm colour
Memory: 40-KB buffer
Paper Handling: Built-in sheet feeder/100 sheets
Accessories: Manufacturer's accessories available
Bundled Software: Canon drivers and utilities
Print Characteristics: 720 x 360 dpi black, 360 x 360 dpi colour
Warranty: One-year InstantExchange warranty program
Suggested List Price at Publication: $249
Approximate Street Price at Publication: $199

PRINTER MANUFACTURER: CANON

Model: BJC-250
Physical/Type: Bubble jet, ink on demand
Print Speed: 1/2 ppm colour at 10 cpi, 4 ppm black
Memory: 40-KB buffer
Paper Handling: Built-in sheet feeder/100 sheets
Accessories: Manufacturer's accessories available
Bundled Software: Canon drivers and utilities
Print Characteristics: 720 x 720 dpi black, 720 x 720 dpi colour
Warranty: One-year limited warranty
Suggested List Price at Publication: $295
Approximate Street Price at Publication: $229

PRINTER MANUFACTURER: CANON

Model: BJC-620
Physical/Type: Bubble jet, ink on demand
Print Speed: 3 ppm black, 1.7 ppm colour at 10 cpi
Memory: 60-KB buffer
Paper Handling: Built-in sheet feeder/100 sheets at paper weight 17 lb; envelopes 15 sheets; transparencies 50 sheets
Accessories: Manufacturer's accessories available

Bundled Software: Canon Creative on two CD-ROM set; Microsoft Windows Printing System
Print Characteristics: 720 x 720 dpi black, 720 x 720 dpi colour
Warranty: One-year InstantExchange warranty program
Suggested List Price at Publication: Contact manufacturer
Approximate Street Price at Publication: Contact manufacturer

PRINTER MANUFACTURER: CANON

Model: BJC-4200
Physical/Type: Bubble jet, ink on demand
Print Speed: 1 ppm colour at 10 cpi
Memory: 26-KB buffer
Paper Handling: Built-in sheet feeder/100 sheets at paper weight 20 lb; letter 100 sheets; legal 100 sheets; envelopes 15 sheets
Accessories: Manufacturer's accessories available
Bundled Software: Canon Creative on two CD-ROM set; Color Advisor 2.0; Visual Guide Super Solver
Print Characteristics: 720 x 360 dpi
Warranty: One-year InstantExchange warranty program
Suggested List Price at Publication: $395
Approximate Street Price at Publication: $299

PRINTER MANUFACTURER: CANON

Model: BJC-4200 Photo
Physical/Type: Bubble jet, ink on demand
Print Speed: 5 ppm black, 1 ppm colour (optional BC-20 cartridge)
Memory: 26-KB buffer
Paper Handling: Built-in sheet feeder/100 sheets
Accessories: Manufacturer's accessories available
Bundled Software: Canon drivers and utilities; Canon Creative with Web-Record
Print Characteristics: 720 x 360 dpi photo quality
Warranty: One-year limited warranty
Suggested List Price at Publication: $375
Approximate Street Price at Publication: $299

PRINTER MANUFACTURER: CANON

Model: BJC-4300
Physical/Type: Bubble jet, ink on demand
Print Speed: 5 ppm black, 2 ppm colour
Memory: 26-KB buffer
Paper Handling: Built-in sheet feeder/100 sheets at paper weight 20 lb; letter 100 sheets; legal 100 sheets
Bundled Software: Canon drivers and utilities; Windows 95 and Windows 3.x drivers included
Print Characteristics: 720 x 360 dpi black, 720 x 360 dpi colour
Warranty: One-year limited warranty with InstantExchange warranty program
Suggested List Price at Publication: $375
Approximate Street Price at Publication: $295

PRINTER MANUFACTURER: CANON

Model: BJC-4304/4304 Photo
Physical/Type: Bubble jet, ink on demand
Print Speed: 5 ppm black, 2 ppm colour
Memory: 26-KB buffer
Paper Handling: Built-in sheet feeder/100 sheets
Bundled Software: Canon drivers and utilities; Canon Creative on two CD-ROM set
Print Characteristics: 720 x 360 dpi black, 720 x 360 dpi colour
Warranty: One-year limited warranty with InstantExchange warranty program
Suggested List Price at Publication: $379 (4304) (estimated)
Approximate Street Price at Publication: $329 (4304) (estimated)

PRINTER MANUFACTURER: CANON

Model: BJC-4550
Physical/Type: Bubble jet, ink on demand, 11" x 17"
Print Speed: 510 cps (characters per second) high-speed black (BC-20 cartridge), 346 cps high-quality black (BC-21 cartridge), 1 ppm high-quality colour at 10 cpi
Memory: 64-KB buffer

Paper Handling: Built-in sheet feeder/100 sheets; letter 100 sheets; legal 100 sheets; envelopes 50 sheets
Accessories: Manufacturer's accessories available
Bundled Software: Canon drivers and utilities; Canon Creative on two CD-ROM set
Print Characteristics: 720 x 360 dpi black
Warranty: One-year InstantExchange warranty program
Suggested List Price at Publication: $469
Approximate Street Price at Publication: $469

PRINTER MANUFACTURER: CANON

Model: BJC-7000
Physical/Type: Colour desktop bubble jet
Print Speed: 5 ppm black, 3.5 ppm colour
Memory: 64-KB buffer
Paper Handling: Plain paper; edge-to-edge printing
Accessories: Manufacturer's accessories available
Bundled Software: Canon Creative 3; Canon drivers and utilities
Print Characteristics: 1,200 x 600 dpi black, 1,200 x 600 dpi colour
Warranty: One-year limited warranty with InstantExchange warranty program
Suggested List Price at Publication: $749
Approximate Street Price at Publication: $699

PRINTER MANUFACTURER: CANON

Model: MultiPASS C2500
Physical/Type: Colour bubble jet; plain paper fax and copier
Print Speed: Up to 5 ppm black, 3 to 8 ppm colour
Paper Handling: 150 sheets
Accessories: Manufacturer's accessories available
Bundled Software: Canon Creative on two CD-ROM set; Desktop Manager v1.3
Print Characteristics: 720 x 360 dpi
Warranty: Two-year InstantExchange warranty program
Suggested List Price at Publication: Contact manufacturer
Approximate Street Price at Publication: Contact manufacturer

PRINTER MANUFACTURER: CANON

Model: MultiPASS C3000
Physical/Type: Bubble jet printer; plain paper fax and copier
Print Speed: Up to 5 ppm black (using BC-20), 2 ppm colour
Paper Handling: Built-in cut-sheet feeder/100 sheets
Accessories: Manufacturer's accessories available
Bundled Software: Canon drivers and utilities; Canon Creative with WebRecord
Print Characteristics: 720 x 360 dpi
Warranty: One-year limited warranty with InstantExchange warranty program
Suggested List Price at Publication: $689
Approximate Street Price at Publication: $639

PRINTER MANUFACTURER: CANON

Model: MultiPASS C5000
Physical/Type: Bubble jet printer; plain paper fax/copier/scanner
Print Speed: Up to 5 ppm black, up to 2 ppm colour
Paper Handling: 100 sheets letter/legal/A4; 50 sheets transparencies; 10 sheets back print film; 10 sheets envelopes
Accessories: Manufacturer's accessories available
Bundled Software: Canon drivers and utilities; MultiPASS desktop manager; Canon Creative
Print Characteristics: 720 x 360 dpi (BC-20 black)
Warranty: One-year limited warranty
Suggested List Price at Publication: $879

EPSON DOT MATRIX

One of the oldest product lines in the whole personal computer marketplace, Epson's dot matrix printers have been around since the early '80s, when their original FX and LX models were connected to IBM's and Compaq's first PCs. The group has undergone various changes through the years, and now comprises about five models in Canada, from the low-end 9-pin FX to the higher-priced and more fully featured LQ series. These do not compete so closely for the heavy industrial users of the higher-end Okidatas and Fujitsus, and it's questionable how many of them are selling into regular home and business applications when superior ink jet technology is available at the same price. In whatever market is left for them, the Epson impact printers are most directly competitive with the Panasonics. Both manufacturers are similar when compared feature for feature.

Epson is recognized as a company which helped pioneer this field many years ago, and its printers are known to be both reliable and common, the latter being important when it comes to buying ribbons. Many other products use Epson-compatible supplies, so the chances are better than average you'll be able to find what you need easily, perhaps even manufactured by a third party at a lower price. In all, these impact printers are an average product line with a good pedigree, but have fallen out of favour in the general home and small office markets because of competition from the ink jets.

PRINTER MANUFACTURER: EPSON

Model: LQ-570+/2170 (130 column)
Physical/Type: 80-, 130-column 24-pin dot matrix
Print Speed: 330 cps draft; 112 cps letter quality
Memory: 8-KB buffer
Paper Handling: Push/pull tractor feed
Accessories: Fabric, film ribbon; cut-sheet feeder; Mac serial interface; envelope feeder
Bundled Software: Manufacturer's drivers and utilities
Suggested List Price at Publication: $489 (LQ-570+); $1,049 (2170)
Approximate Street Price at Publication: $429 (LQ-570+); $1,049 (2170)

PRINTER MANUFACTURER: EPSON

Model: LQ-670
Physical/Type: Impact dot matrix
Print Speed: 300 cps (10 cpi) high-speed draft; 250 cps (10 cpi), 300 cps (12 cpi) draft
Memory: 64-KB user selectable buffer
Paper Handling: Push/pull tractor feed; straight paper path
Accessories: Optional Ethernet server; manufacturer's accessories
Bundled Software: Manufacturer's drivers and utilities
Print Characteristics: 10, 12, 15 cpi scalable fonts
Warranty: Two-year limited parts-and-labour warranty

Suggested List Price at Publication: $639
Approximate Street Price at Publication: $549
Note: Up to five-part forms

PRINTER MANUFACTURER: EPSON

Model: LQ-870/LQ-2170
Physical/Type: 80-, 130-column 24-pin dot matrix
Print Speed: 300 cps (10 cpi) high-speed draft; 138 cps (15 cpi) letter quality; 413 cps (15 cpi) condensed
Memory: 8-KB buffer
Paper Handling: Continuous-form tractor feed, smart park
Accessories: Sheet feeder; serial interface; other accessories available
Bundled Software: Windows 95 and Windows 3.x drivers and manufacturer's utilities
Print Characteristics: Scalable fonts; bitmapped fonts; 10, 12, 15 cpi and proportional spacing
Warranty: Two-year warranty
Suggested List Price at Publication: $889 (LQ-870); $1,049 (LQ-2170)
Approximate Street Price at Publication: $695 (LQ-870); $829 (LQ-2170)
Note: Up to 5 copies

PRINTER MANUFACTURER: EPSON

Model: LX-300
Physical/Type: 9-pin impact dot matrix
Print Speed: 264 cps (12 cpi) draft: 53 cps (12 cpi); 44 cps (10 cpi) near letter quality
Memory: 4-KB buffer
Paper Handling: Single sheets: 7.2" to 10.1"; continuous: 4.0" to 10.0"; no. 6 envelopes: 6.5" to 3.6"; no. 10 envelopes: 9.5" to 4.1"; labels: continuous sheet
Accessories: Optional colour kit; sheet feeders; other accessories
Bundled Software: Windows 95 and Windows 3.x drivers and manufacturer's utilities
Print Characteristics: Character matrix: 9 x 9 draft mode; bitmapped font: 18 x 20 near letter quality mode
Warranty: Two-year limited warranty in Canada and the U.S.
Suggested List Price at Publication: $339

Approximate Street Price at Publication: $289
Note: Up to three-part forms

EPSON INK JET

From Epson America, the North American arm of Japanese giant Seiko Epson, comes the well-known Stylus line of ink jet printers, the early ancestors of which appeared when ink jet technology was new, around 1991. Well reviewed and competitively priced, the Stylus series uses the company's own version of the ink jet printing process – Piezo Electric technology – which, Epson advertises, will render up to a startling 1,400 dpi by printing smaller and rounder dots of colour. This product line starts with the Stylus Color 400 series at the bottom and progresses through the 600 and 800 models to the Stylus Photo. It also includes two niche-market products, the Stylus Color 3000, a full-bleed colour comping device, and the 1520, a large-format printer intended for architectural drawings, plans, and other images on wide paper.

Awarded a technology excellence seal from *PC Magazine* in 1996 for the Piezo Electric innovation, and reviewed second in 1997 by the *Toronto Star*'s "Fast Forward" section in a detailed comparison to the Hewlett-Packard PhotoSmart, the Canon 4300, and the Lexmark 7000, the Stylus Photo scores well. As of publication, its price was on the high side, at just over $700 street, and its special paper was more expensive than its three closest competitors', at a whopping $3.00+ per sheet. These prices are offset somewhat by the lower, $40 cost of its replacement cartridges. All in all, the Stylus series is recommended. The company is well enough known that support and software drivers for its products will be easy to find and deal with, and its prices, if slightly high, are competitive with those of Hewlett-Packard and Lexmark.

PRINTER MANUFACTURER: EPSON

Model: Stylus Color 400
Physical/Type: Four-colour (CMYK) ink jet
Print Speed: Up to 4 ppm black, up to 3 ppm colour
Memory: 10-KB buffer
Paper Handling: Input paper tray 100 sheets/10 envelopes; output paper tray: 30 sheets
Accessories: Serial interface; transfers and other media available from the manufacturer

Bundled Software: Windows 95 and Windows 3.x drivers; Look Your Best; Adobe PhotoDeluxe; Jump Start Guide
Print Characteristics: 720 x 720 dpi
Warranty: One-year limited warranty in Canada and the U.S.
Suggested List Price at Publication: $299
Approximate Street Price at Publication: $279

PRINTER MANUFACTURER: EPSON

Model: Stylus Color 600
Physical/Type: Four-colour ink jet
Print Speed: 6 ppm black, 4 ppm colour
Memory: 32-KB buffer
Paper Handling: 100 sheets input tray, 30 sheets output tray
Accessories: Media types, network interfaces; other manufacturer's accessories available
Bundled Software: Windows 95 and Windows 3.x, Mac OS drivers and manufacturer's utilities; Look Your Best
Print Characteristics: 1,440 x 720, 360 x 360, 180 x 180 dpi
Warranty: Two-year warranty
Suggested List Price at Publication: $479
Approximate Street Price at Publication: $399
Note: Serial and parallel interfaces included

PRINTER MANUFACTURER: EPSON

Model: Stylus Color 800
Physical/Type: Four-colour ink jet
Print Speed: Up to 8 ppm black, up to 7 ppm colour
Memory: 32-KB buffer
Paper Handling: 100 sheets, 10 envelopes
Accessories: Ethernet, LocalTalk network interfaces; cards and other media available from the manufacturer
Bundled Software: Windows 3.x and Windows 95, Mac OS drivers
Print Characteristics: 1,440 x 720 dpi, 360 x 360 dpi, 180 x 180 dpi
Warranty: Two-year limited warranty in Canada and the U.S
Suggested List Price at Publication: $579
Approximate Street Price at Publication: $495
Notes: Mac interface included; QuickDry ink; AcuPhoto half-toning

PRINTER MANUFACTURER: EPSON

Model: Stylus Color 1520
Physical/Type: Four-colour ink jet
Print Speed: Up to 6 ppm black, up to 5 ppm colour
Memory: 64-KB buffer
Paper Handling: Input paper tray: 100 sheets/10 envelopes; output paper tray: 30 sheets
Accessories: Ethernet and LocalTalk network interfaces; serial interface; other manufacturer's accessories
Bundled Software: Windows 95 and Windows 3.x drivers and manufacturer's utilities
Print Characteristics: 1,440 x 720 dpi, 720 x 720 dpi, 360 x 360 dpi, 180 x 180 dpi
Warranty: Two-year limited warranty
Suggested List Price at Publication: $1,259
Approximate Street Price at Publication: $1,129

PRINTER MANUFACTURER: EPSON

Model: Stylus Color 3000
Physical/Type: Four-colour ink jet
Print Speed: Up to 7 ppm black, 7 ppm colour
Memory: 64-KB buffer
Paper Handling: Input paper tray: 100 sheets/10 envelopes; output paper tray: 30 sheets
Accessories: Ethernet and LocalTalk network interfaces; serial interface; other manufacturer's accessories
Bundled Software: Windows 95 and Windows 3.x drivers and manufacturer's utilities; Mac interface included on specified model
Print Characteristics: 1,440 x 720 dpi, 720 x 720 dpi, 360 x 360 dpi, 180 x 180 dpi
Warranty: Two-year limited warranty
Suggested List Price at Publication: $3,249 (Mac and PC models)
Approximate Street Price at Publication: $2,699 (Mac and PC models)
Additions: Separate Mac and PC models available

PRINTER MANUFACTURER: EPSON

Model: Stylus Photo
Physical/Type: Drop-on-demand Micro Piezo ink jet
Print Speed: Photos at 720 x 720 dpi: 3" x 5" 90 seconds; 8" x 10" under 6 minutes
Memory: 64-KB buffer
Paper Handling: Input paper tray: 100 sheets/10 envelopes; output paper tray: 30 sheets
Accessories: Transparencies, glossies, cards, iron-on transfers, Adobe PostScript Level 2; other manufacturer's accessories
Bundled Software: Windows 95 and Windows 3.x, Mac OS drivers; Digital Darkroom with Live Picture and LivePix, FlashPix
Print Characteristics: 720 x 720 dpi, 360 x 360 dpi, 180 x 180 dpi, 6-colour mix
Warranty: Two-year limited warranty in Canada and the U.S.
Suggested List Price at Publication: $699
Approximate Street Price at Publication: $599

EPSON LASER

It would seem that Epson has anticipated the encroachment of the ink jet on the laser printer market, for as of publication the company offers only two electrophotography lasers, both intended for business applications and office workgroups, and offering features beyond the needs of most home computer users and many small businesses.

The EPL 1200 has a whopping 6 megabytes of RAM and a 1,250-sheet paper tray, provides simultaneous performance for up to four computers, and has a substantial toner cycle of 6,000 pages. The EPL 2000 is a large workgroup/network printer able to produce 20 pages per minute and print on media up to 13" x 19". Accessories for both products include a range of paper intake trays for large and small pages and envelopes, optional Mac interfaces, and Ethernet network capabilities (10 Base-T is included with the EPL 2000). Competing against Hewlett-Packard, NEC, and Lexmark at this higher end of the market, Epson is challenged to make its presence known in a market of better recognized competitors. To users, the more widely known manufacturers offer advantages in terms of consumable availability and price, as well as accessibility to service. Companies with smaller market shares often present better pricing, however, and both of these products from Epson are quite competitive when compared fairly to their better known counterparts. This may help the company gain ground in the business-class printing market in the future. Otherwise it will continue to remain best known for its wide range of ink jets.

PRINTER MANUFACTURER: EPSON

Model: EPL-N1200
Physical/Type: Laser electrophotography
Print Speed: 12 ppm
Memory: Standard: 6-MB RAM; maximum: 64 MB (using standard 72-pin SIMMs)
Paper Handling: Standard tray: 250 sheets; optional lower paper cassette: 500 sheets (up to two lower paper cassettes); maximum paper capacity: 1,250 sheets using two lower trays; standard output tray: 250 sheets
Print Characteristics: True 600 x 600 dpi
Warranty: One-year limited warranty
Suggested List Price at Publication: $1,879
Approximate Street Price at Publication: $1,649

PRINTER MANUFACTURER: EPSON

Model: EPL-N2000
Physical/Type: Laser electrophotography
Print Speed: 20 ppm letter or A4, long-edge feed
Memory: Standard: 4-MB RAM; maximum: 68 MB
Paper Handling: Standard universal tray: 150 sheets; standard lower paper cassette: 500 sheets; optional lower paper cassette: 250 or 500 sheets; maximum paper capacity: 1,150 sheets using optional lower paper trays
Print Characteristics: 600 x 600 dpi
Warranty: One-year limited warranty
Suggested List Price at Publication: Contact manufacturer
Approximate Street Price at Publication: Contact manufacturer

FUJITSU DOT MATRIX

With one of the best names at the workhorse end of the impact printer market, Fujitsu is still selling some of its dot matrix products in the

$1,000+ range. If that surprises you, it's perhaps because you're not aware of the thousands of data-crunching computer setups still pumping away in the back rooms of all kinds of large companies and institutions.

These printers were never a leader in Canada in the home or small office markets; even low-priced ones back in the good old matrix printer days (the late '80s) sold in the $400+ range. Fujitsu's pricing for its current models places them more in competition with Okidata than it does with Panasonic and Epson, neither of which is known for offering the same range of high-performance impact printers.

Fujitsu's DL series printers are indeed capable of some startling speed – up to 600 characters per second – which also carries a hefty price tag. So these printers are aimed at a niche market. If you have the application, they are among the best in their class for high-volume accounting and database reporting.

PRINTER MANUFACTURER: FUJITSU

Model: DL3700/3800
Physical/Type: 24-pin impact dot matrix; 80 column (3700), 130 column (3800)
Print Speed: 400 cps/333 cps high-speed draft; 360 cps/300 cps draft; 120 cps/100 cps letter; 240 cps/200 cps correspondence/report
Memory: 128-KB buffer
Paper Handling: Standard friction-based platen, two-position (push/pull) continuous-form tractor on rear or top and paper parking
Accessories: Optional four-colour kit, sheet feeder; other manufacturer's accessories available
Bundled Software: Windows 95 and Windows 3.x drivers and utilities
Print Characteristics: Up to five-part forms; draft, near letter quality, high speed; eight bitmapped and three outline fonts
Warranty: Two-year depot warranty
Suggested List Price at Publication: $755 (3700); $925 (3800)
Approximate Street Price at Publication: $649 (3700); $795 (3800)

PRINTER MANUFACTURER: FUJITSU

Model: DL6400/6600
Physical/Type: 24-pin impact dot matrix, 130 column
Print Speed: 504 cps draft; 336 cps near letter quality; 168 cps letter

Memory: 128-KB buffer
Paper Handling: Straight paper path, friction, bi-directional tractor, bottom feeding
Accessories: Cut-sheet feeder, rear tractor, stacker, colour upgrade
Bundled Software: Windows 95 and Windows 3.x drivers and utilities
Print Characteristics: Up to five-part forms; draft near letter quality, high speed; eight bitmapped and three outline fonts; bar code printing
Warranty: Two-year depot warranty
Suggested List Price at Publication: $2,395 (6400); $2,595 (6600)
Approximate Street Price at Publication: $2,095 (6400); $2,395 (6600)
Notes: Serial and parallel interfaces included; up to 8 copies

FUJITSU LASER

This huge Japanese electronics company – Fujitsu is the third-largest computer manufacturer in the world, with global revenues of over $49 billion – has a strong presence in the mainframe and supercomputer industries as well as other sectors of the personal computer market, including the production of hard drives, chips, and all kinds of other components. In the general printer market in Canada, Fujitsu offers its DL series dot matrix printers and a range of four PrintPartner lasers – the PP10V, PP14AV, PP14PRO, and PP14NET – intended mostly for business and corporate applications. All of these are true lasers, with generous 250- or 550-sheet intake bins and lots of memory; 3 megabytes come standard in the lowest-cost 10V model, with 11 megabytes in the network-intended 14 ADV, PRO, and NET series. The 10V includes both parallel and serial ports, a combination which used to be more common in lasers than it is today. The higher-level 14s either include or will accept duplexing options to allow them to print on both sides of a sheet. They offer a large, 30,000-sheet duty cycle (at 5-percent coverage) and Fujitsu's FEIT image-enhancing technology. All are covered by a "no excuses" exchange warranty, which, according to its literature, means the company promises to ship you a replacement via Federal Express within forty-eight hours of a verifiable failure. If you're researching the purchase of one of these lasers, be sure to get the facts straight about the terms of this warranty: try the info sheet on its website (www.fujitsu.com; enter a search for "printer warranty"). In its description on the Internet, Fujitsu states it wants a credit card number before they'll get the ball rolling, but exactly what this precaution is for is not made clear.

In the corporate market, these printers compete with the Hewlett-Packards, NECs, and Lexmarks. Also, Fujitsu's relatively low profile among mainstream dealers has implications for the availability and price of consumables and service. It is possible that a company of this stature has a strong idea about where it wants to be in this market and is not particularly concerned about every last home-office printer sale. As a result, although these lasers are durable and come from a well-respected giant, they reside in a niche market and, with the exception of the 10V model, deserve a very close comparison to their lower-cost competitors before winning your vote.

PRINTER MANUFACTURER: FUJITSU

Model: PrintPartner 10V
Physical/Type: Laser electrophotography
Print Speed: 10 ppm
Memory: Standard: 3-MB RAM; maximum: 67 MB using industry-standard 72-pin SIMMs via two expansion slots
Paper Handling: Standard: letter-sized cassette tray with 250-sheet capacity; manual feed optional
Accessories: Legal-sized cassette tray with 250-sheet capacity; second hopper with adjustable letter/legal cassette tray, 500-sheet capacity; multi-function feeder: 100 sheets or 30 envelopes; other manufacturer's accessories
Bundled Software: Windows 95 and Windows 3.x drivers and utilities
Print Characteristics: User selectable: 300 dpi, 600 dpi, 1,200 dpi class (600 x 2,400 dpi)
Warranty: Eighteen-month parts-and-labour warranty (first year free warranty plus on-site exchange)
Suggested List Price at Publication: $1,095
Approximate Street Price at Publication: $895

PRINTER MANUFACTURER: FUJITSU

Model: PrintPartner 14ADV/ADV Duplex
Physical/Type: Laser electrophotography
Print Speed: 14 ppm
Memory: Standard: 11-MB RAM; maximum: 67 MB using industry-standard 72-pin SIMMs via two expansion slots
Paper Handling: Standard: letter-sized cassette tray with 550-sheet capacity; multi-function feeder: 100 sheets or 30 envelopes; manual feed

Accessories: Legal-sized cassette tray with 550-sheet capacity; second hopper with adjustable letter/legal cassette tray, 500-sheet capacity; duplex unit; LocalTalk and Ethernet interface board; other manufacturer's accessories
Bundled Software: Windows 95 and Windows 3.x drivers and utilities
Print Characteristics: User selectable: 300 dpi, 600 dpi, 1,200 dpi class (600 x 2,400 dpi)
Warranty: Eighteen-month parts-and-labour warranty (first year on-site exchange)
Suggested List Price at Publication: $1,695 (14ADV)
Approximate Street Price at Publication: $1,395 (14ADV)

PRINTER MANUFACTURER: FUJITSU

Model: PrintPartner 14V
Physical/Type: Laser electrophotography
Print Speed: 14 ppm
Memory: Standard: 3-MB RAM; maximum: 67 MB using industry-standard 72-pin SIMMs via two expansion slots
Paper Handling: Standard: letter-sized cassette tray with 250-sheet capacity
Accessories: Legal-sized cassette tray with 250-sheet capacity; second hopper with adjustable letter/legal cassette tray, 500-sheet capacity; multi-function feeder: 100 sheets or 30 envelopes
Bundled Software: Windows 95 and Windows 3.x drivers and utilities
Print Characteristics: User selectable: 300 dpi, 600 dpi, 1,200 dpi class (600 x 2,400 dpi)
Warranty: Eighteen-month parts-and-labour warranty (first year on-site exchange)
Suggested List Price at Publication: $1,295
Approximate Street Price at Publication: $1,095

GENICOM/TEXAS INSTRUMENTS

In September 1996, Texas Instruments sold its printer section to Genicom, an American manufacturer with a substantial presence in the field and a well-known supplier of high-tech printing solutions and data integration products to large companies. With several issues of ultra fast line printers, serial dot matrix printers, page printers, and colour lasers, the company and its product lines are included in a general PC product guide such as this one chiefly because one or two of its models are indeed intended for the business market. The Genicom serial dot matrix printers carry substantial price tags, run at speeds of up to 700 characters per second, and are intended for corporate database and number crunching. The network and colour lasers in the lineup are in a class by themselves, competitive with some of the QMS products, but well out of the specification and price range for companies other than the institutions and large corporations that have the specific requirements and big budgets for them.

PRINTER MANUFACTURER: GENICOM

Model: 3812/3840/3840EM
Physical/Type: High-speed impact dot matrix
Print Speed: Up to 600 cps
Memory: 64-KB buffer
Paper Handling: Front or bottom feed form handling; switchable dual paper paths
Accessories: Optional sheet feeders and receiving bins for various media; international character sets; assorted emulations and interfaces available
Bundled Software: Windows 95 and Windows 3.x drivers; other drivers and network utilities available
Warranty: One-year parts-and-labour warranty; warranty options available
Suggested List Price at Publication: $4,009 (3812)
Approximate Street Price at Publication: $3,495 (3812)

PRINTER MANUFACTURER: GENICOM

Model: Laser
Physical/Type: Microlaser 30/40 laser
Print Speed: Up to 30 and 40 ppm
Memory: 8- to 16-MB RAM (expandable)
Paper Handling: Large capacity paper trays
Accessories: Optional letter, legal, and universal trays; various media handling and networking options
Bundled Software: Windows NT and networking drivers and utilities
Print Characteristics: Up to 1,200 x 1,200 dpi

Warranty: One-year parts-and-labour warranty; warranty options available
Suggested List Price at Publication: Contact manufacturer
Approximate Street Price at Publication: Contact manufacturer

HEWLETT-PACKARD INK JET

As of early 1998, Hewlett-Packard (HP) maintains its strong presence in the home and small office printer markets by offering more than fifteen different models of ink jets, ranging from the 600 series (which may be phased out by the time of publication) up to the 1000s and the professional grade 1600s. Flagship models in early '98 are the 700s and PhotoSmarts, designed with the graphically oriented user in mind. Like other colour ink jet printer manufacturers, Hewlett-Packard has undoubtedly been happy to see the continued growth of the World Wide Web. If you want to be able to browse the Internet and print exactly what you see, these are the answer.

The 722C and some other models come with the company's Creative Solutions software, which is a printer assistant/presentation package designed to help you manipulate and print graphics of different types.

In an in-depth comparison (in *The Toronto Star's* "Fast Forward" section) with Epson's Stylus Photo, Canon's 4300, and Lexmark's 7000, the Hewlett-Packard PhotoSmart fared well in the categories of speed, special photo paper cost, cartridge cost, resolution, and print quality. It was the most expensive of the four competitors, but was the overall winner. This is not to say that all of HP's ink jets are as competitive. This is a fiercely contested market right now, so before making any decisions, take comparable models of at least the big four – Epson, Lexmark, HP, and Canon – into consideration. But be sure to include the HPs; with such a large offering, as well as a good support reputation, they are often a best buy, depending on what else is available during the same month in this fast-changing market.

Also, be aware that since Hewlett-Packard printers are so well known, resellers sometimes offer certain models as loss leaders. And remember, any vendor can be asked to match a competitor's price, although whether he or she will is another story. If you do buy one of these at a killer discount, don't expect much help from the store or supercentre that paid $479 for it and has to resell it at $495; you'll likely be referred to HP. This is not the end of the world, but can be inconvenient. These ink jets are supported by the manufacturer or one of its authorized repair centres, but consider this when deciding where to buy. As is the case with all deeply discounted printers, and indeed with personal computer equipment in general, find out ahead of time exactly what you'll have to do and where you'll have to go if it fails.

PRINTER MANUFACTURER: HEWLETT-PACKARD

Model: DeskJet 340
Physical/Type: Portable colour ink jet
Print Speed: Up to 3 ppm
Memory: 48-KB input buffer
Paper Handling: 30-sheet paper tray
Accessories: Optional serial interface; multi-voltage power adapter included; other manufacturer's accessories available
Bundled Software: Windows 95 and Windows 3.x drivers and utilities
Print Characteristics: 600 x 600 dpi black, 300 x 300 dpi colour
Warranty: One-year parts-and-labour return-to-authorized-service-centre warranty
Suggested List Price at Publication: $460
Approximate Street Price at Publication: $395

PRINTER MANUFACTURER: HEWLETT-PACKARD

Model: DeskJet 670C
Physical/Type: Beige desktop colour ink jet
Print Speed: Up to 4 ppm black, up to 1.5 ppm colour
Memory: 512-KB
Paper Handling: 100-sheet paper tray
Accessories: Optional serial interface; multi-voltage power adapter included; other manufacturer's accessories available
Bundled Software: Windows 95 and Windows 3.x drivers and utilities
Print Characteristics: 600 x 600 dpi black, 600 x 300 dpi colour
Warranty: One-year parts-and-labour return-to-authorized-service-centre warranty; express exchange available in Canada and the U.S.
Suggested List Price at Publication: $348
Approximate Street Price at Publication: $295

PRINTER MANUFACTURER: HEWLETT-PACKARD

Model: DeskJet 692C
Physical/Type: Beige desktop colour ink jet
Print Speed: Up to 5 ppm black, up to 1.7 ppm colour, up to 4 mpp photo
Memory: 512-KB buffer (estimated)
Paper Handling: Two paper trays
Accessories: Optional HP colour photo kit printer cartridge; other manufacturer's accessories available
Bundled Software: Windows 95 and Windows 3.x drivers and utilities included
Print Characteristics: 600 x 600 dpi black, 300 x 300 dpi colour
Warranty: One-year parts-and-labour return-to-authorized-service-centre warranty; express exchange available in Canada and the U.S.
Suggested List Price at Publication: $409
Approximate Street Price at Publication: $349

PRINTER MANUFACTURER: HEWLETT-PACKARD

Model: DeskJet 694C
Physical/Type: Beige desktop colour ink jet
Print Speed: Up to 5 ppm black, up to 1.7 ppm colour
Memory: 512-KB buffer
Paper Handling: 100-sheet paper tray
Accessories: Optional serial interface; multi-voltage power adapter included; other manufacturer's accessories available
Bundled Software: Windows 95 and Windows 3.x drivers and utilities included
Print Characteristics: 600 x 600 dpi black, 600 x 300 dpi colour
Warranty: One-year parts-and-labour return-to-authorized-service-centre warranty; express exchange available in Canada and the U.S.
Suggested List Price at Publication: $395 (estimated)
Approximate Street Price at Publication: $349

PRINTER MANUFACTURER: HEWLETT-PACKARD

Model: DeskJet 890 Cxi/Cse
Physical/Type: Beige desktop colour ink jet

Print Speed: Up to 5 ppm black, up to 1.7 ppm colour, up to 4 mpp photo
Memory: 512-KB buffer
Paper Handling: 150-sheet paper tray
Accessories: Optional HP photo colour print cartridge; serial interface; multi-voltage power adapter included; other manufacturer's accessories available
Bundled Software: Windows 95 and Windows 3.x and Mac drivers and utilities included
Print Characteristics: 600 x 600 dpi black, 300 x 300 dpi colour
Warranty: One-year parts-and-labour return-to-authorized-service-centre warranty; express exchange available in Canada and the U.S.
Suggested List Price at Publication: $668
Approximate Street Price at Publication: $595

PRINTER MANUFACTURER: HEWLETT-PACKARD

Model: DeskJet 1000 Cxi/1000 Cse
Physical/Type: Beige desktop colour ink jet, 11" x 17"
Print Speed: Up to 4.5 ppm black, up to 3.5 ppm colour
Memory: 512-KB buffer
Paper Handling: 150 sheets, 15 envelopes, 60 cards
Accessories: Optional trays; network and serial interfaces; other manufacturer's accessories available
Bundled Software: Windows 95 and Windows 3.x drivers included; Corel PrintHouse (Calendar Creator) with 1000 Cxi model
Print Characteristics: 600 x 600 dpi black, 300 x 300 dpi colour (600 x 600 with colour resolution enhancement, CRE); billboard up to 4', booklet printing, mirrored printing, duplexing
Warranty: One-year parts-and-labour return-to-authorized-service-centre warranty; express exchange available in Canada and the U.S.
Suggested List Price at Publication: $825 (1000 Cxi)
Approximate Street Price at Publication: $729 (1000 Cxi)
Note: HP RealLife Photo Imaging (requires Pentium 100 and 50-MB hard disk space, 16-MB RAM)

PRINTER MANUFACTURER: HEWLETT-PACKARD

Model: DeskJet 1100C
Physical/Type: Desktop colour ink jet, 11" x 17"
Print Speed: 6.5 ppm black, 5 ppm black and colour, 2 ppm colour
Memory: 2-MB RAM
Paper Handling: 150 sheets, 15 envelopes, 60 cards
Accessories: Optional trays; network and serial interfaces; other manufacturer's accessories available
Bundled Software: Windows 95 and Windows 3.x drivers included; Corel PrintHouse (Calendar Creator) with 1000 Cxi model
Print Characteristics: 600 x 600 dpi black, 600 x 600 dpi colour
Warranty: One-year parts-and-labour return-to-authorized-service-centre warranty; express exchange available in Canada and the U.S.
Suggested List Price at Publication: Contact manufacturer
Approximate Street Price at Publication: Contact manufacturer
Note: HP RealLife Photo Imaging (requires Pentium 100 and 50-MB hard disk space, 16-MB RAM)

PRINTER MANUFACTURER: HEWLETT-PACKARD

Model: DeskJet 1600c/cn/cm
Physical/Type: Desktop colour ink jet stand-alone and network printers
Print Speed: Up to 9 ppm black, up to 4 ppm colour
Memory: 4-MB RAM; expandable to 100 MB
Paper Handling: 180-sheet paper tray; 500-sheet tray optional
Accessories: Transparencies, network interfaces, Adobe PostScript Level 2, and other manufacturer's accessories
Bundled Software: Windows 95 and Windows 3.x drivers included; Mac-compatible (cm series only)
Print Characteristics: 600 x 600 dpi black, 600 x 300 dpi colour; Intellifont, Adobe, bitmap, TrueType fonts
Warranty: One-year parts-and-labour return-to-authorized-service-centre warranty; express exchange available in Canada and the U.S.
Suggested List Price at Publication: $2,353 (1600c)
Approximate Street Price at Publication: $1,995 (1600c)
Notes: cn and cm have network interfaces included; "out of ink" sensor; cm is Mac compatible

HEWLETT-PACKARD LASER

Arguably the best-known family of printers in the world, the more than ten models in Hewlett-Packard's LaserJet series start with the entry-level 6Ls and extend all the way up to its network-ready 5Si corporate monsters and colour lasers for over $5,000.

Since their introduction over ten years ago, Hewlett-Packard LaserJets have undergone constant revisions. Although there has been a certain symmetry to the introduction of new models and features, the product line can be confusing. In the beginning came the LaserJet, a truly innovative product aimed at business applications, with a price tag of over $2,000 and promoted largely by its connection to the superior Apple computers of the day. It was followed by the LaserJet Series 2s and the small office 2Ps, and then by the Series 3s and the small office 3Ps. In the '90s the line was further diversified, and now starts with the L series at the bottom. These are inexpensive home printers in the $500 to $550 range, printing at six pages per minute and providing 1 megabyte of RAM. Next up the ladder are the P models, which are faster and have improved paper handling, more memory, more maximum memory, and some extra features such as an infrared connection. The LaserJet Ms are the mid-range office products, while the 5, 5 Plus, and Si series are intended for larger businesses and workgroup environments respectively.

All of these printers carry the advantage of coming from the best-known manufacturer in the business. As with HP's ink jets, this creates dividends in the consumable, service, and compatibility departments. Although some competitors, such as Lexmark's Optras or Okidata's L series, are more feature rich for the dollar, Hewlett-Packard's popularity means it's easier to find third-party support and toners and drums. HP's better-than-average service reputation is another important advantage. Also, particularly at the low end of the market, the 6Ls and 6Ps are often treated as a commodity by resellers large and small, so the pricing on them can be very sharp. You can take advantage of this, but be sure (as described in the notes on HP's ink jets) that you are buying an authorized HP product and you know what you'll have to do to get it fixed. There is a temptation for vendors to bring "grey market" equipment into Canada from the United States or from offshore without Hewlett-Packard's knowledge. Buying one of these, while saving you as much as $100 or more, can leave you holding the bag – or at least having to ship the thing back to its distribution source for warranty.

PRINTER MANUFACTURER: HEWLETT-PACKARD

Model: LaserJet 4V/4MV
Physical/Type: Beige desktop monochrome laser
Print Speed: 16 ppm
Memory: 4-MB RAM; expandable to 66 MB
Paper Handling: Two paper trays: 350-sheet capacity
Accessories: Optional 500-sheet letter, legal, A4 tray; 250-sheet legal tray; other manufacturer's accessories available
Bundled Software: Windows 95 and Windows 3.x drivers included
Print Characteristics: 600 x 600 dpi black
Warranty: One-year parts-and-labour return-to-authorized-service-centre warranty; on-site options available
Suggested List Price at Publication: $3,228 (4V); $4,678 (4MV)
Approximate Street Price at Publication: $2,795 (4V); $4,095 (4MV)

PRINTER MANUFACTURER: HEWLETT-PACKARD

Model: LaserJet 5/5N/5M
Physical/Type: Beige desktop monochrome laser
Print Speed: 12 ppm
Memory: 4-MB RAM; expandable to 66 MB
Paper Handling: Two paper trays: 350-sheet capacity
Accessories: Optional 500-sheet paper feeder; power envelope feeder; infrared adapter duplex printing assembly; HP PrinterPal fax assembly; other manufacturer's accessories available
Bundled Software: Windows 95 and Windows 3.x drivers and utilities included; Mac drivers and utilities (5M only)
Print Characteristics: 600 x 600 dpi black
Warranty: One-year parts-and-labour return-to-authorized-service-centre warranty: on-site upgrades available
Suggested List Price at Publication: $1,809 (5); $2,322 (5N); $8,800 (5M)
Approximate Street Price at Publication: $1,495 (5); $1,949 (5N); $7,995 (5M)

PRINTER MANUFACTURER: HEWLETT-PACKARD

Model: LaserJet 6L
Physical/Type: Beige desktop monochrome laser

Print Speed: 6 ppm
Memory: 1-MB RAM; expandable to 9 MB
Paper Handling: 100-sheet vertical paper bin
Accessories: Manufacturer's accessories available
Bundled Software: Windows 95 and Windows 3.x drivers included
Print Characteristics: 600 x 600 dpi black
Warranty: One-year parts-and-labour return-to-authorized-service-centre warranty; express exchange available in Canada and the U.S.
Suggested List Price at Publication: $619 (estimated)
Approximate Street Price at Publication: $539

PRINTER MANUFACTURER: HEWLETT-PACKARD

Model: LaserJet 6P/MP
Physical/Type: Beige desktop monochrome laser
Print Speed: 8 ppm
Memory: 2-MB RAM; expandable to 50 MB
Paper Handling: Two paper trays: 350-sheet capacity
Accessories: Optional network interfaces; memory; other manufacturer's accessories available
Bundled Software: Windows 95 and Windows 3.x drivers and utilities included; Mac utilities and drivers (MP only)
Print Characteristics: 600 x 600 dpi black
Warranty: One-year parts-and-labour return-to-authorized-service-centre warranty; express exchange available in Canada and the U.S.
Suggested List Price at Publication: $686
Approximate Street Price at Publication: $539

LEXMARK INK JET

Originally the Information Products division of IBM, this company was taken over in 1991 by a New York investment firm with the goal of establishing itself as an independent presence in the office equipment business. It's reasonable to say that they have achieved that goal; they've become a major force in the home and office printer markets, particularly in the ink jet printer market in 1998.

Lexmark's Jetprinters range through the 1000, 1020, 2030, 2050, 2055, 2070, 3000, 4079, 7000, 7200 and 7200Vs, with a few variation models in the lineup as well. Most are housed in dramatic, black, space-saving designs with vertical intake trays that accommodate about fifty sheets. A pull-out pan in front accommodates your finished work.

Lexmark's corporate statement says they have one of the fastest manufacturing cycles in the printer business – meaning they can bring new technology to market quickly – and this is certainly supported by the appearance of so many new products from them each year. As of publication, their flagship colour ink jets were the 7000/7200 models, printing up to 1,200 x 1,200 dpi, with the 7200 selling for about $550 on the street. An in-depth review of this product in *The Toronto Star* in late 1997 rated it slightly behind Hewlett-Packard's PhotoSmart and Epson's Stylus Photo, but ahead of Canon's 4300 printer overall. At 1,200 x 1,200 dpi, it ranked above its four major competitors in resolution, but simple arithmetic does not necessarily win. When evaluated for a combination of colour, sharpness of detail, and graininess – the overall look of a printed photo – the Lexmark scored below both the Epson Stylus Photo and the HP. From a price perspective, the 7200 ranked in the mid- to low-range, at a street value of $550. It is also worth noting that not one but two test 7200s shipped to one reviewer left smudge marks on the paper. These could have been isolated problems.

All of these factors considered, the Lexmark colour ink jet family is worth a look, but as with any printer, try to view some output examples before buying. Judging the work coming from a printer is a subjective exercise. You are the one who is going to have to be satisfied. If the output suits you, the Jetprinters are price sensitive, and popular enough to ensure that support and supplies will be accessible. Compare them to the Canons and Epsons for economy-minded applications in small offices and at home.

PRINTER MANUFACTURER: LEXMARK

Model: Jetprinter 1000
Physical/Type: Desktop single-cartridge colour ink jet
Print Speed: Up to 3.5 ppm black, up to 1.5 ppm colour
Paper Handling: 30-sheet vertical paper bin
Accessories: Accepts Lexmark colour and black-ink cartridges; other manufacturer's accessories available
Bundled Software: Windows 95 and Windows 3.x drivers included
Print Characteristics: 600 x 600 dpi black, 600 x 600 dpi colour
Suggested List Price at Publication: $249
Approximate Street Price at Publication: $195

PRINTER MANUFACTURER: LEXMARK

Model: Jetprinter 2030/2050
Physical/Type: Desktop dual-cartridge colour ink jet
Print Speed: Up to 3 ppm black, up to 2 ppm colour, up to 2 mpp high-quality colour
Paper Handling: 30-sheet vertical paper bin
Accessories: Accepts Lexmark colour and black-ink cartridges; other manufacturer's accessories available
Bundled Software: Windows 95 and Windows 3.x drivers and utilities included
Print Characteristics: 600 x 300 dpi
Warranty: One-year parts-and-labour return-to-authorized-service-centre warranty; express exchange available in Canada and the U.S.
Suggested List Price at Publication: $319 (2030)
Approximate Street Price at Publication: $259 (2030)

PRINTER MANUFACTURER: LEXMARK

Model: Jetprinter 3000
Physical/Type: Desktop single-cartridge colour ink jet
Print Speed: 4 ppm black, up to 1.5 ppm colour
Paper Handling: 30-sheet vertical paper bin
Accessories: Accepts Lexmark colour or black-ink cartridges; other manufacturer's accessories available
Bundled Software: Windows 95 and Windows 3.x drivers and utilities included
Print Characteristics: 600 x 300 dpi
Warranty: One-year parts-and-labour return-to-authorized-service-centre warranty; express exchange available
Suggested List Price at Publication: $329
Approximate Street Price at Publication: $295

PRINTER MANUFACTURER: LEXMARK

Model: Jetprinter 7000
Physical/Type: Black desktop dual-cartridge colour ink jet
Print Speed: Up to 8 ppm black, up to 3 ppm colour
Paper Handling: 30-sheet vertical paper bin

Accessories: Accepts Lexmark colour or black-ink cartridges; other manufacturer's accessories available
Bundled Software: Windows 95 and Windows 3.x drivers and utilities included
Print Characteristics: Up to 1,200 x 1,200 dpi
Warranty: One-year parts-and-labour return-to-authorized-service-centre warranty; express exchange available in Canada and the U.S.
Suggested List Price at Publication: $489
Approximate Street Price at Publication: $449

LEXMARK OPTRA LASER

The Lexmark Optra family of laser printers underwent some changes toward the end of 1997, including the introduction of four new models and price reductions on some existing products. This does not distinguish the lineup from its competitors – change is a fact of life in the printer business – but the revamps make the current group of Optras more competitive and comprehensive than before. In Lexmark's mission statement, the company says it wants to offer lasers with specific features designed for specific parts of the market. This strategy has resulted in the Optra E series (low-end, home and small office printers), the S series (mid-range business class printers), and the N and SC series (high-end network-ready products for corporate and institutional use). On the bottom, the E series are about even when matched feature for feature with competitors Hewlett-Packard, NEC, and Okidata. The mid-range Lexmarks, the Optra S and ST 1600 series (S 1620/1620N, S 1650/1650N, ST 1650/1650, and the S 2420/2420N and S 2450/2450N) are worth a look if you are setting up a business – they are feature rich and backed by a large enough company and support team to be a threat to market king HP. Most of the S series come with a 4-MB RAM standard, and run in the 8 to 12 page-per-minute range. They are quiet, with large enough duty cycles (the recommended number of pages printed in a month) to keep you from having to run to the toner store too often, though this does not necessarily indicate a low cost per page.

There is a choice of on-site or LexExpress warranties, the former available as an option at extra cost with the S 1600s and S 2420s. These printers are also advertised as being environmentally friendly, though this term is sometimes used in the computer business more as a marketing grab than as an indication of any real benefit to the future of the planet. But the Optras boast ozone-free printing, power-saving features, and an "operation resource" program for processing returnable print cartridges, so the environmental schtick here sounds legitimate.

With all of these features, and sharp prices aimed at buying a bigger piece of the small and medium-sized business markets, the Lexmark Optras are a recommended alternative to the HP LaserJets.

PRINTER MANUFACTURER: LEXMARK

Model: Optra C
Physical/Type: Beige desktop colour laser
Print Speed: Up to 12 ppm black; 3 ppm colour
Memory: 8-MB RAM (expandable)
Paper Handling: 350-sheet horizontal paper tray
Accessories: Network options; special paper handling and envelope options
Bundled Software: Windows 95 and Windows 3.x drivers included
Print Characteristics: 600 x 600 dpi
Warranty: One-year parts-and-labour return-to-authorized-service-centre warranty
Suggested List Price at Publication: $7,988
Approximate Street Price at Publication: $7,099

PRINTER MANUFACTURER: LEXMARK

Model: Optra E+/EX
Physical/Type: Beige desktop monochrome laser
Print Speed: Up to 6 ppm black
Memory: 2-MB RAM (expandable)
Paper Handling: 150-sheet paper tray
Accessories: Serial interface; special paper handling and envelope options; postscript option
Bundled Software: Windows 95 and Windows 3.x drivers included; printer utilities
Print Characteristics: 600 x 600 dpi
Warranty: One-year parts-and-labour return-to-authorized-service-centre warranty
Suggested List Price at Publication: $699 (Optra E+)
Approximate Street Price at Publication: $579 (Optra E+)

PRINTER MANUFACTURER: LEXMARK

Model: Optra N 240/245
Physical/Type: Beige desktop monochrome laser
Print Speed: Up to 24 ppm black
Memory: 4-MB RAM (240 model, expandable); 16-MB RAM (245 model, expandable)
Paper Handling: 1,000-sheet horizontal paper tray
Accessories: Network options; special paper handling and envelope options; duplexing options
Bundled Software: Windows 95 and Windows 3.x drivers included
Print Characteristics: 600 x 600 dpi black
Warranty: One-year parts-and-labour return-to-authorized-service-centre warranty; on-site options available
Suggested List Price at Publication: $4,899 (240); $5,929 (245)
Approximate Street Price at Publication: $4,099 (240); $5,299 (245)

PRINTER MANUFACTURER: LEXMARK

Model: Optra S 1250/1250N
Physical/Type: Beige desktop monochrome laser
Print Speed: Up to 12 ppm black
Memory: 4-MB RAM (expandable)
Paper Handling: 350-sheet horizontal paper tray
Accessories: Network options; special paper handling and envelope options; duplexing options, Ethernet adapter included with the 1250N; other manufacturer's accessories available
Bundled Software: Windows 95 and Windows 3.x drivers included; networking software; printer utilities
Print Characteristics: 1,200 x 1,200 dpi black
Warranty: One-year parts-and-labour return-to-authorized-service-centre warranty; on-site options available
Suggested List Price at Publication: $1,807 (1250); $2,321 (1250N)
Approximate Street Price at Publication: $1,499 (1250); $1,929 (1250N)

PRINTER MANUFACTURER: LEXMARK

Model: Optra S 1650/1650N
Physical/Type: Beige desktop monochrome laser

Print Speed: Up to 16 ppm black
Memory: 4-MB RAM (expandable)
Paper Handling: 350-sheet horizontal paper tray
Accessories: Network options; special paper handling and envelope options; duplexing options, Ethernet adapter included with the 1650N; other manufacturer's accessories available
Bundled Software: Windows 95 and Windows 3.x drivers included; networking software; printer utilities
Print Characteristics: 1,200 x 1,200 dpi black
Warranty: One-year parts-and-labour return-to-authorized-service-centre warranty; on-site options available
Suggested List Price at Publication: $1,999 (1650) (estimated); $2,584 (1650N)
Approximate Street Price at Publication: $1,695 (1650); $2,249 (1650N)

PRINTER MANUFACTURER: LEXMARK

Model: Optra S 2450/2450N
Physical/Type: Beige desktop monochrome laser
Print Speed: Up to 24 ppm black
Memory: 4-MB RAM (expandable)
Paper Handling: 1,250-sheet horizontal paper tray
Accessories: Network options; special paper handling and envelope options; duplexing options, Ethernet adapter included with the 2450N; other manufacturer's accessories available
Bundled Software: Windows 95 and Windows 3.x drivers included; networking software; printer utilities
Print Characteristics: 1,200 x 1,200 dpi black
Warranty: One-year parts-and-labour return-to-authorized-service-centre warranty; on-site options available
Suggested List Price at Publication: $3,999 (2450); $4,659 (2450N)
Approximate Street Price at Publication: $3,495 (2450); $4,195 (2450N)

PRINTER MANUFACTURER: LEXMARK

Model: Optra S for Mac
Physical/Type: Beige desktop monochrome laser
Print Speed: Up to 5 ppm black
Paper Handling: 350-sheet horizontal paper tray

Accessories: Network options; special paper handling and envelope options; duplexing options
Bundled Software: OS 7 drivers; AppleTalk network and printer utilities; other manufacturer's accessories available
Print Characteristics: 1,200 dpi black
Warranty: One-year parts-and-labour return-to-authorized-service-centre warranty; on-site options available
Suggested List Price at Publication: $2,598
Approximate Street Price at Publication: $2,295

PRINTER MANUFACTURER: LEXMARK

Model: Optra SC 1275/1275N
Physical/Type: Colour laser
Print Speed: Up to 12 ppm black, up to 3 ppm colour
Memory: 16-MB RAM (expandable)
Paper Handling: 350-sheet horizontal paper tray
Accessories: Network options; special paper handling and envelope options; duplexing options, Ethernet adapter included with the 1275N; other manufacturer's accessories available
Bundled Software: Windows 95 and Windows 3.x drivers included; networking software; printer utilities
Print Characteristics: 600 dpi black, 600 dpi colour
Warranty: One-year parts-and-labour return-to-authorized-service-centre warranty; on-site options available
Suggested List Price at Publication: $6,999 (1275); $7,799 (1275N)
Approximate Street Price at Publication: $6,199 (1275); $7,299 (1275N)

NEC INK JET

With three products in its lineup as of publication, NEC has become a player in the heated home and small office colour ink jet markets. Head to head with tough competitors Lexmark, Canon, Epson, and Hewlett-Packard, the company has its work cut out for it as it tries to increase its market share with the SuperScript 100C, 150C, and 750C. The two lower-priced models, the 100C and 150C, offer average features in their classes, printing at resolutions of 600 x 300 dpi, with the entry-level 100C producing 300 x 300 dpi in colour at up to three minutes per page. The 750C offers graphic black and midnight black outputs. The advertised advantage here is more shades of grey and sharper text, though this feature seems similar to other dual-cartridge printing systems which produce colours from one reservoir and black from another when printing a composite document such as a page from the Internet. The 100C is very competitively priced and seems poised to gain NEC a reputation in the student market, even though it offers very basic specifications. As with competitor Canon's 200 series, be sure you are satisfied with the speed and colour quality of an entry-level printer before buying. All of the SuperScripts are covered by NEC's one-year, limited overnight replacement warranty, with an optional Service Xpress extended support plan available for the 150C and 750C. Enquire about the conditions of this enhanced support plan from an authorized vendor.

PRINTER MANUFACTURER: NEC

Model: SuperScript 100C
Physical/Type: Desktop colour ink jet
Print Speed: Up to 3 ppm black, up to 3 mpp colour
Memory: 128-KB RAM
Paper Handling: 40-sheet paper tray
Accessories: Special media (ink jet and glossy papers; transparencies and T-shirt transfers) available
Bundled Software: Windows 95 and Windows 3.x drivers and utilities included
Print Characteristics: 300 x 300 dpi black, 600 x 300 dpi colour
Warranty: One-year parts-and-labour return-to-authorized-service-centre warranty; overnight express exchange available in Canada and the U.S.; Service Xpress plan available
Suggested List Price at Publication: $195 (estimated)
Approximate Street Price at Publication: $179

PRINTER MANUFACTURER: NEC

Model: SuperScript 150C
Physical/Type: Desktop colour ink jet
Print Speed: Up to 3 ppm black, up to 3 mpp colour
Memory: 128-KB RAM
Paper Handling: 40-sheet paper tray
Accessories: Special media (ink jet and glossy papers; transparencies and T-shirt transfers) available

Bundled Software: Windows 95 and Windows 3.x drivers and utilities included; The Print Shop Software; Color Project Pak; Sesame Street Art Workshop
Print Characteristics: 600 x 300 dpi black, 600 x 300 dpi colour
Warranty: One-year parts-and-labour return-to-authorized-service-centre warranty; overnight express exchange available in Canada and the U.S.; Service Xpress plan available
Suggested List Price at Publication: $229
Approximate Street Price at Publication: $195

PRINTER MANUFACTURER: NEC

Model: SuperScript 750C
Physical/Type: Desktop colour ink jet
Print Speed: Up to 6 ppm black, up to 2 ppm colour
Memory: 1-MB RAM
Paper Handling: 40-sheet paper tray
Accessories: Special media (ink jet, glossy, and photo papers; transparencies and T-shirt transfers) available; NEC photo kit and photo cartridge
Bundled Software: Windows 95 and Windows 3.x drivers and utilities included; The Print Shop Software; Color Project Pak; Sesame Street Art Workshop
Print Characteristics: 600 x 600 dpi black, 600 x 600 dpi colour
Warranty: One-year parts-and-labour return-to-authorized-service-centre warranty; overnight express exchange available in Canada and the U.S.; Service Xpress plan available
Suggested List Price at Publication: $295
Approximate Street Price at Publication: $269

NEC LASER

First issued in the mid-1980s, the NEC Silentwriter series is one of the oldest lines of this kind of products still available. As of early 1998, the 1760 and 1765 Silentwriters were current and aimed at business and corporate markets where speed and networking are important parts of the printing equation. As such, these products are out of reach of the budgets of many small business and home purchasers, although they have a good reputation, and come from a major manufacturer.

Accompanying the Silentwriters are the SuperScripts, starting with the 1260 and 1260N models and including the 660 Plus, 850, 750C and

100Cs. At just over $1,000, the 1260 is one of the fastest personal lasers in its class, offering twelve pages per minute, 600 x 600 dpi resolution, a 250-sheet paper intake tray, and optional 500-sheet tray and network interface. This is a fast, capable business printer in sheep's clothing. Its features and available options place it in a very competitive position versus Hewlett-Packard's 6P and Lexmark's mid-range Optra. It is intended for use in home setups as well as small and even medium-sized offices. Most SuperScripts ship with Adobe's Print Gear software, which is designed to speed up network printing, an advantage to users who hope to connect two or more PCs to their printer in the future. As a series of printers from a well-known builder which offers good market coverage for consumables and support, the SuperScripts, especially the 1260, are worth a look.

PRINTER MANUFACTURER: NEC

Model: SuperScript 660 Plus
Physical/Type: Desktop laser
Print Speed: 6 ppm
Memory: 256-KB RAM; max 4-MB
Paper Handling: 150-sheet universal tray; 5 envelopes
Accessories: Additional paper feed trays; other manufacturer's accessories available
Bundled Software: Windows 95 and Windows 3.x drivers included; NEC "Business Essentials" CD-ROM; line user guide
Print Characteristics: 600 x 600 dpi; 53 TrueType fonts
Warranty: Two-year overnight replacement warranty (some restrictions apply)
Suggested List Price at Publication: $459 (estimated)
Approximate Street Price at Publication: $395

PRINTER MANUFACTURER: NEC

Model: SuperScript 860
Physical/Type: Desktop laser
Print Speed: 8 ppm
Memory: 1-MB RAM; max 5-MB
Paper Handling: 200-sheet universal tray; 5 envelopes
Accessories: Additional paper feed trays; RAM; other manufacturer's

accessories available
Bundled Software: Windows 95 and Windows 3.x drivers included; NEC "Solutions on CD" CD-ROM
Print Characteristics: 600 x 600 dpi; 78 Type 1 fonts
Warranty: Two-year overnight replacement warranty (some restrictions apply)
Suggested List Price at Publication: $649 (estimated)
Approximate Street Price at Publication: $549

PRINTER MANUFACTURER: NEC

Model: SuperScript 1260/1260N
Physical/Type: Desktop laser
Print Speed: 12 ppm
Memory: 2-MB RAM; max 16-MB
Paper Handling: 250-sheet universal tray
Accessories: Additional paper feed trays; RAM; network interface upgrade kit option and other manufacturer's accessories available
Bundled Software: Windows 95, Windows NT, and Windows 3.x drivers included; ATM Adobe Type Manager; Mac drivers through Ethertalk with network interface upgrade kit option
Print Characteristics: 600 x 600 dpi; 124 levels of greyscale
Warranty: One-year parts-and-labour warranty
Suggested List Price at Publication: $1,045 (1260); $1,659 (1260N)
Approximate Street Price at Publication: $979 (1260); $1,449 (1260N)

OKIDATA DOT MATRIX

Okidata first made its name in the computer printer business by selling specialty card-reading and impact products to banks and large institutions. Its history has propelled it through the shakedown in the matrix printer market, where it remains a presence with competitors Fujitsu and Epson for invoicing and accounting. As business printers, the Microlines have not been as affected as the lower-end Panasonics and Epsons by the appearance of the ink jets.

Ranging from the ML 184 Turbo, a small, beige slimline printer common in countertop business applications, through the ML 320/321 series, to the 520/521 and the high-speed Pacemark series, the 9-pin Microlines have been issued in two emulations over the years. An "emulation" is a printer type which you select when installing a piece of software. Because Okidatas were often used in large computer environments in the past, they were built in two types: those with Okidata emulation and those with Epson/IBM. This is worth noting if you're considering one of these; most programs will work easily with the Epson/IBM version of these printers, so check what software you plan to use before buying. In the past, the Microlines earned a reputation as being well supported, reliable office-grade printers, but reports of changes in the quality of the 320 series have surfaced in the past year.

The 24-pin Microlines – the 390/391 and 590/591 – are intended more for a fast, readable original than for greater hitting power. Nine-pin printers are actually preferred when it comes to hammering through several copies. The fewer, larger pins in them have a greater impact and produce a clearer carbon. The greater number of pins in a 24-pin product define characters on the top sheet better. Still, the 390s and 590 24-pin matrixes are fast, running at draft speeds of up to 600 characters per second. They too are aimed at corporations and institutions that require high speed and reliability and will pay a premium price for these features.

PRINTER MANUFACTURER: OKIDATA

Model: Microline 180/182/184/192 Plus and Turbo series
Physical/Type: Beige desktop 80-column 9-pin dot matrix
Print Speed: 200 cps draft; 50 cps NLQ (near letter quality); 240 cps high-speed draft; 300 cps super-speed draft
Paper Handling: Continuous-form tractor feed
Accessories: Serial interface; sheet feeder (some models); roll paper stand (some models) and other manufacturer's accessories available
Bundled Software: Windows 95 and Windows 3.x drivers included
Warranty: One-year parts-and-labour return-to-authorized-service-centre warranty; express exchange warranty available
Suggested List Price at Publication: $429
Approximate Street Price at Publication: $379
Notes: Okidata or IBM/Epson emulation; 110V or 220V power supply

PRINTER MANUFACTURER: OKIDATA

Model: Microline 320/321 T and D series
Physical/Type: Beige desktop 80- and 136-column 9-pin dot matrix

Print Speed: 75 cps NLQ; 300 cps utility; 390 cps high-speed draft; 435 cps super-speed draft
Memory: 28-KB buffer
Paper Handling: Continuous-form tractor feed
Accessories: Serial interface; sheet feeder; paper stand; pull tractor; other manufacturer's accessories available
Bundled Software: Windows 95 and Windows 3.x drivers included
Print Characteristics: Gothic, courier, scalable fonts
Warranty: Three-year parts-and-labour return-to-authorized-service-centre warranty; on-site options available
Suggested List Price at Publication: $599 (320); $879 (321)
Approximate Street Price at Publication: $495 (320); $729 (321)
Notes: Okidata or IBM/Epson emulation; 110V or 220V power supply

PRINTER MANUFACTURER: OKIDATA

Model: Microline 390/391 series
Physical/Type: Beige desktop 80- and 136-column 24-pin dot matrix
Print Speed: 315 cps draft; 180 cps NLQ (estimated); 400 cps high-speed draft (estimated)
Memory: 28-KB buffer
Paper Handling: Continuous-form tractor feed
Accessories: Serial interface; sheet feeder; paper-feeding attachments; other manufacturer's accessories available
Bundled Software: Windows 95 and Windows 3.x drivers included
Print Characteristics: Gothic, courier, scalable fonts
Warranty: Three-year parts-and-labour return-to-authorized-service-centre warranty; on-site options available
Suggested List Price at Publication: $699 (390); $929 (391)
Approximate Street Price at Publication: $569 (390); $729 (391)
Notes: Okidata or IBM/Epson emulation; 110V or 220V power supply

PRINTER MANUFACTURER: OKIDATA

Model: Microline 395/395C series
Physical/Type: Beige desktop 80- and 136-column 24-pin dot matrix
Print Speed: 486 cps draft; 242 cps NLQ; 607 cps high-speed draft
Memory: 28-KB buffer (estimated)
Paper Handling: Continuous-form tractor feed

Accessories: Serial interface; sheet feeder; pull tractor; bottom push tractor; other manufacturer's accessories available
Bundled Software: Windows 95 and Windows 3.x drivers included
Print Characteristics: Gothic, courier, scalable fonts
Warranty: Three-year parts-and-labour return-to-authorized-service-centre warranty; on-site options available
Suggested List Price at Publication: $929 (395); $1,799 (395C)
Approximate Street Price at Publication: $729 (395); $1,599 (395C)
Notes: Okidata or IBM/Epson emulation; 110V or 220V power supply

PRINTER MANUFACTURER: OKIDATA

Model: Microline 520/521 series
Physical/Type: Beige desktop 80- and 136-column 9-pin dot matrix
Print Speed: 325 cps draft; 80 cps NLQ; 435 cps high-speed draft
Memory: 28-KB buffer (estimated)
Paper Handling: Continuous-form tractor feed
Accessories: Serial interface; sheet feeder; pull tractor; bottom push tractor; other manufacturer's accessories available
Bundled Software: Windows 95 and Windows 3.x drivers included
Print Characteristics: Gothic, courier, scalable fonts
Warranty: Three-year parts-and-labour return-to-authorized-service-centre warranty; on-site options available
Suggested List Price at Publication: $699 (520); $959 (521)
Approximate Street Price at Publication: $599 (520); $829 (521)
Notes: Okidata or IBM/Epson emulation; 110V or 220V power supply

PRINTER MANUFACTURER: OKIDATA

Model: Microline 590/591 series
Physical/Type: Beige desktop 80- and 136-column 24-pin dot matrix
Print Speed: 360 cps draft; 120 cps NLQ; 450 cps high-speed draft
Memory: 28-KB buffer
Paper Handling: Continuous-form tractor feed
Accessories: Serial interface; sheet feeder; paper stand; colour kit; other manufacturer's accessories available
Bundled Software: Windows 95 and Windows 3.x drivers included
Print Characteristics: Gothic, courier, scalable fonts
Warranty: Three-year parts-and-labour return-to-authorized-service-

centre warranty; on-site options available
Suggested List Price at Publication: $849 (590)
Approximate Street Price at Publication: $729 (590)
Notes: Okidata or IBM/Epson emulation; 110V or 220V power supply

PRINTER MANUFACTURER: OKIDATA

Model: Pacemark 3410
Physical/Type: Beige 136-column 9-pin dot matrix
Print Speed: 420 cps draft; 105 cps NLQ; 550 cps high-speed draft
Memory: 64-KB RAM
Paper Handling: Continuous-form tractor feed
Accessories: Serial interface; sheet feeder; paper stand
Bundled Software: Windows 95 and Windows 3.x drivers included
Print Characteristics: Gothic, courier, scalable fonts
Warranty: Three-year parts-and-labour return-to-authorized-service-centre warranty
Suggested List Price at Publication: $2,399
Approximate Street Price at Publication: $2,199
Notes: Okidata or IBM/Epson emulation; 110V or 220V power supply

OKIDATA LED

LED (light-emitting diode) printing is a "laser-like" technology, included in Okidata's page printer series. It has been available for several years, starting with the appearance of the OL 400s about 1991. Producing a similar, though slightly lighter, output than most true laser printers, this process uses an LED panel instead of a laser and mirrors to etch an image, based on instructions from a computer, onto an electrostatic drum. The drum then attracts fine black toner powder, which is baked, or fused, onto the page. This printing system is similar to conventional lasers – so much so that these printers are sometimes advertised as lasers, though really they are different. Not all of Okidata's page printers have used this technology in the past; some of their current models do. The company's promotional literature states that the LED system is cheaper to maintain than a regular laser printer, but reviewers and repair people report that when all factors are considered, the savings are minimal. Most LED printers – those from Okidata and Panasonic – present a different consumable schedule, requiring low-cost toner every 2,500–3,500 copies (at 5-percent coverage) and then quite an expensive drum (in the $300 range) every 12,000–15,000 copies. This actually makes the per-page cost of operating these products even slightly higher than for some competitors, while the opportunity to purchase third-party or remanufactured consumables is not as great as it is when feeding a more common printer.

The baby of this family – the Okipage 4W – is a unique entry in the page printer field, having been variously described as the smallest and the least expensive 600 dpi–class page printer available. It is a Windows-only product, and, as with other LEDs, its output is distinguishable from true 600-dpi lasers.

Watch for Okidata page printers, especially the little 4W, on the shelves of mass marketers. At the retail level, these printers were once a favourite loss leader of aggressive resellers in Canada, sometimes being sold even below wholesale. This made them popular (if you could get in the door early enough to grab one of the promotional models) but less attractive for vendors to handle. I have not seen them advertised so aggressively recently, so perhaps the company has somehow moved to slow this practice.

Okidata's lower-end page printers are competitive in recognition with the Brother HL series, and prominent in the under-$500 non–ink jet field, a notch below the Hewlett-Packard 6Ls and Lexmark Optras in price. Take a good look at the output before buying; if you're looking for a low-priced letter-quality printer with sharper output than an ink jet, consider the 4W.

PRINTER MANUFACTURER: OKIDATA

Model: Okipage 4W
Physical/Type: Beige desktop LED
Print Speed: 4 ppm
Memory: 128-KB RAM
Paper Handling: 100-sheet paper tray
Bundled Software: Windows 95 and Windows 3.x drivers included
Print Characteristics: 600 dpi "class"
Warranty: One-year limited warranty with overnight exchange; five-year limited warranty on LED assembly
Suggested List Price at Publication: $369
Approximate Street Price at Publication: $309

PRINTER MANUFACTURER: OKIDATA

Model: Okipage 6E/6EX
Physical/Type: Desktop LED
Print Speed: 6 ppm black
Memory: 1-MB RAM; expandable to 18 MB
Paper Handling: 100-sheet paper tray
Accessories: Optional RAM; legal and letter universal trays; multipurpose feeder; other manufacturer's accessories available
Bundled Software: Windows 95 and Windows 3.x drivers and utilities included
Print Characteristics: 600 dpi "class" (OP 6 model), true 600 dpi (OP 6EX model)
Warranty: One-year limited warranty with overnight exchange; five-year warranty on LED assembly
Suggested List Price at Publication: $799
Approximate Street Price at Publication: $629
Notes: Serial and parallel interface; 110V or 220V power supply

PRINTER MANUFACTURER: OKIDATA

Model: Okipage 16N
Physical/Type: Desktop monochrome laser
Print Speed: 16 ppm
Memory: 2-MB RAM; expandable to 66 MB
Paper Handling: 500-sheet universe paper tray
Accessories: Optional RAM; legal and letter universal trays; multi-purpose feeder; other manufacturer's accessories available
Bundled Software: Windows 95 and Windows 3.x drivers and utilities included
Print Characteristics: 600 x 600 dpi black
Warranty: One-year return-to-depot limited warranty; on-site warranty options available
Suggested List Price at Publication: $1,599
Approximate Street Price at Publication: $1,429
Notes: Serial and parallel interface; 110V or 220V power supply; HP 4/IBM/Epson emulation

PRINTER MANUFACTURER: OKIDATA

Model: OL 810E
Physical/Type: Desktop monochrome laser
Print Speed: 8 ppm
Memory: 2-MB RAM; expandable to 34 MB
Paper Handling: 250-sheet universal paper tray
Accessories: Optional RAM; legal and letter universal trays; multipurpose feeder; other manufacturer's accessories available
Bundled Software: Windows 95 and Windows 3.x drivers and utilities included
Print Characteristics: 600 x 1,200 dpi black
Warranty: One-year limited warranty with overnight exchange; five-year warranty on LED assembly
Suggested List Price at Publication: $1,129
Approximate Street Price at Publication: $969
Notes: Serial and parallel interface; 110V or 220V power supply; HP 4/IBM/Epson emulation

PANASONIC DOT MATRIX

These printers have a long history in a section of the market which has shrunk rapidly in the face of competition from ink jet printers to become a specialty group in the late 1990s. In the late '80s, Panasonic was a clear leader in home-printing applications with its 1011/1012 and 2410/2420, 9- and 24-pin models. These sold routinely for between $175 and $400 in several narrow- (80-column) and more expensive wide-carriage (130-column) issues. Now, as might be expected, the company offers a smaller lineup aimed at the accounting and invoicing applications to which matrix printers have been relegated. Panasonic's wide-carriage 9-pin models are lower in price than the faster Okidatas and Fujitsus, and sell in the $400–$550 range. Narrow-carriage products run at about $250–$400. Some of these are colour upgradable: you must purchase a four-colour ribbon, which the printhead assembly raises and lowers during operation, yielding a combination of up to sixteen colours. However, the output of these printers is no match for even an inexpensive ink jet. Add to this the fact that their paper handling is limited to connected tractor-fed paper, and it's easy to see why these printers have lost ground.

If you are considering buying an impact printer, note that

Panasonics, which are also available in Canada under the Raven label, are best known for their location at the mid to low end of the price scale, below the Okidatas and Fujitsus. Those two lines of higher-performance and higher-priced products have a more secure position among corporate and institutional purchasers, which now dominate the matrix printer market.

PRINTER MANUFACTURER: PANASONIC

Model: 3626
Physical/Type: Impact dot matrix
Printer Speed: 300 cps draft; 100 cps letter quality; 80 cps super letter quality
Memory: 40-KB buffer
Paper Handling: Push/pull tractor
Accessories: Cut-sheet feeder; serial interface; colour kit; other manufacturer's accessories available
Bundled Software: Manufacturer's utilities to control all printer functions; Windows 95 and Windows 3.1 drivers included
Print Characteristics: Bit image (dot matrix) to 360 x 360 dpi
Warranty: Two-year limited parts-and-labour warranty
Suggested List Price at Publication: $729
Approximate Street Price at Publication: $595

PANASONIC LED

Panasonic, a division of multifaceted Japanese giant Matsushita (pronounced "Matooshta"), has offered several different page and laser printer designs over the years. Its early "true lasers", quite a few of which are still in use today, had a bigger presence a few years ago than its lineup today. Owners of those old issues will be well aware that, while of good quality, they had high per-page costs due to the large number of consumables (count 'em, five!) they needed to keep functioning.

In 1994, the company introduced personal page printers: the 500 and 600 LED series. These and Okidata's OL series are the best-known "non-laser" letter-quality printers now available, the Panasonics being notable for their space-saving "bookshelf" design. This form factor is appealing in some ways, but is not without disadvantages. The vertical paper tray, which accommodates about 100 sheets, can also funnel bits of debris into the printer and compromise the life of its drum. How serious this is depends on the environment in which it's being used. Other features in these printers are their 300 x 600 dpi (1,200 dpi in the LS-6) resolution and very quiet, ozone-free operation. But with only 256K of RAM in the 6100 and 512K in the 6500, other printers in this price range are more competitive. One megabyte has become a standard; you can expect to run out of memory when printing websites off the Internet if you are running with anything less.

All in all, these are unique, space-saving products, but recommended only if that is an important consideration. Otherwise, they are light on features. Note too that they are available in Canada, as are many other Panasonic printer products, under the Raven label. There is no material difference between equivalent products with these brand names, and in fact Serviceworks, the Canadian distributor of the Raven series based in Vancouver, B.C., has offices across the country, providing distributor-level service and support.

PRINTER MANUFACTURER: PANASONIC

Model: 6100/6500
Physical/Type: Desktop LED; upright desktop design
Print Speed: 6 ppm
Memory: 256-KB (6100); 512-KB RAM (6500); expandable to 4.5 MB
Paper Handling: 100 sheets imput; 50 sheets out
Bundled Software: Windows 95 drivers and manufacturer's utilities; 6100 model, Windows only
Print Characteristics: 300 x 300 dpi (6100); 600 x 600 dpi, 1,200 dpi in enhanced mode (6500)
Warranty: One-year parts-and-labour warranty
Suggested List Price at Publication: $525 (6100); $650 (6500)
Approximate Street Price at Publication: $429 (6100); $539 (6500)

QMS LASER

This U.S. manufacturer of high-end or "business class" printers offers a wide range of well-supported monochrome and colour lasers, as well as other connectivity products including mixed-platform networked printing systems, sophisticated document-handling technologies, and remote network management. If this sounds like QMS is a leading-edge company with most of its products above the requirements and budgets of small businesses, that is indeed its market position.

The corporate statement on QMS's home page describes some of the industry milestones it has pioneered since being founded in 1977: developing the first desktop colour laser, the first laser to use artificial intelligence, and the first Postscript colour printer. Its laser printers for the colour business market are the QMS Magicolor CX series, and the 2 CX, 2 EX, and WX. It also offers a range of high-performance monochrome lasers which start at 1,200 dots per inch, twenty-page-per-minute printing and go up from there. At publication, the QMS entry-level monochrome was $3,999 (U.S. dollars), which is competitive in this marketplace. Still, these printers are not for the home, or even the small, cost-conscious business. A possible exception is the Magicolor 2CX, which, at U.S. $3,499, brings the price of colour laser printing into a more affordable range. If you have trouble finding a vendor who handles them, don't be shy about calling the manufacturer. As is often the case with specialized computer products, a builder's representative will often know more about his lineup than a retailer.

It's also worth noting that the recent, remarkable abilities of inexpensive ink jets to print photo-quality pictures are taking their toll on the colour laser market. Still, among graphics professionals and in certain corporate environments, a colour or fast networkable multiplatform laser is a must. The current line of products from this American manufacturer is well supported and highly recommended for these specialty applications.

PRINTER MANUFACTURER: QMS

Model: 2060 BX
Physical/Type: Monochrome laser
Print Speed: Up to 20 ppm black
Memory: 20-MB RAM; expandable to 128 MB
Paper Handling: 250-sheet horizontal multipurpose paper tray
Accessories: Duplexing options; networking and envelope-feeding options; a wide range of other options available
Bundled Software: QMS CrownNet; DECnet TCPIP; LocalTalk; Windows drivers; other QMS utilities
Print Characteristics: 1,200 x 1,200 dpi black
Warranty: One-year parts-and-labour on-site warranty
Suggested List Price at Publication: $3,599
Approximate Street Price at Publication: $3,299

PRINTER MANUFACTURER: QMS

Model: 2060 EX
Physical/Type: Monochrome laser
Print Speed: Up to 20 ppm black
Memory: 48-MB RAM; expandable to 128 MB
Paper Handling: 250-sheet horizontal multipurpose paper tray
Accessories: Networking and envelope-feeding options; a wide range of other options available
Bundled Software: QMS CrownNet; DECnet TCPIP; LocalTalk; Windows drivers; other QMS utilities
Print Characteristics: 600 x 600 dpi colour (2 CX); 2,400 x 600 dpi colour (2 EX)
Warranty: One-year parts-and-labour on-site warranty
Suggested List Price at Publication: $4,899 (2 CX); $6,999 (2 EX)
Approximate Street Price at Publication: $4,599 (2 CX); $6,395 (2 EX)

PRINTER MANUFACTURER: QMS

Model: 2060 GX
Physical/Type: Monochrome laser
Print Speed: Up to 20 ppm black
Memory: 16-MB RAM; expandable to 128 MB
Paper Handling: 250-sheet horizontal multipurpose paper tray
Accessories: Duplexing options; networking and envelope-feeding options; a wide range of other options available
Bundled Software: QMS CrownNet; DECnet TCPIP; LocalTalk; Windows drivers; other QMS utilities
Print Characteristics: 1,200 x 1,200 dpi black
Warranty: One-year parts-and-labour on-site warranty
Suggested List Price at Publication: $4,199
Approximate Street Price at Publication: $3,899

PRINTER MANUFACTURER: QMS

Model: 2425 Turbo/Turbo EX series
Physical/Type: Monochrome large workgroup tabloid-sized laser
Print Speed: Up to 24 ppm black
Memory: 40-MB RAM; expandable to 128 MB

Paper Handling: 250-sheet horizontal multipurpose paper tray
Accessories: Duplexing options; networking and envelope-feeding options; a wide range of other options available
Bundled Software: QMS CrownNet; DECnet TCPIP; LocalTalk; Windows drivers; other QMS utilities
Print Characteristics: 1,200 x 1,200 dpi black
Warranty: One-year parts-and-labour warranty
Suggested List Price at Publication: $7,699 (Turbo EX)
Approximate Street Price at Publication: $7,099 (Turbo EX)
Notes: Many advanced features to accommodate network printing requirements

PRINTER MANUFACTURER: QMS

Model: Magicolor 2 CX/2 EX
Physical/Type: Colour laser
Print Speed: Up to 16 ppm black, 4 to 8 ppm colour
Memory: 24-MB RAM (2 CX); 80-MB RAM (2 EX); expandable
Paper Handling: 250-sheet horizontal multipurpose paper tray
Accessories: Networking and envelope-feeding options; a wide range of other options available
Bundled Software: QMS CrownNet; DECnet TCPIP; LocalTalk; Windows drivers; other QMS utilities
Print Characteristics: 600 x 600 dpi colour (2 CX); 2,400 x 600 dpi colour (2 EX)
Warranty: One-year parts-and-labour on-site warranty
Suggested List Price at Publication: $4,899 (2 CX); $6,999 (2 EX)
Approximate Street Price at Publication: $4,599 (2 CX); $6,395 (2 EX)
Note: Many advanced features to accommodate colour graphics printing

GLOSSARY

Access Time – The time (measured in milliseconds) a hard drive takes to locate information on a specified track on its disk. Normally stated as an average.

Aftermarket – A term used to describe goods or services that are offered as additions to a product after it has been purchased.

AGP (Accelerated Graphics Port) – A video card interface design developed by Intel that allows data from a video card to access a system's main memory directly. This design provides for the increased speed required by newer computer applications involving multimedia and video.

Analogue Signal – A type of communication characterized by the continuous transmission of information; as opposed to a digital signal, which is characterized by the transmission of separated and distinct pieces of information.

ANSI (American National Standards Institute) – An organization that oversees the establishment of data transmission and signalling codes.

Application – A specific computer task or computer program. Application software differs from operating system software, which plays a greater role in the internal control of a computer and its connected components. Examples of applications are wordprocessing, spreadsheet, and database programs; combinations of these are sometimes known as integrated applications.

ASCII (American Standard Code for Information Interchange) – A set of numeric values used to represent characters in the alphabet and other common symbols, which has become an established basic transmission standard.

Asynchronous Data Transmission – A communication standard in which the timing used to control the passage of each character is independent of the transmission timing of other characters.

ATA (Advanced Technology Attachment) – A design commonly used to describe devices (such as IDE hard drives) with integrated or built-in controllers. This has appeared in various refinements, sometimes referred to as ATAPI (AT attachment packet interface), ATA-2, and Ultra ATA. These describe both the data transfer and physical connection characteristics of an AT device.

Autoexec File – A part of a computer program containing instructions which a system automatically reads and runs, usually at the time the computer is turned on.

Backup – A copy of a data file, computer program, or other information, made in case the original is lost, damaged, or otherwise misplaced.

Bandwidth – The amount of information that can be handled by a computer, computer component, or communications network in a fixed amount of time. Often used in reference to telephone and other systems which make up the Internet. For digital devices, bandwidth is usually expressed in bits or bytes per second; for analogue devices, the unit is cycles per second, or hertz (Hz).

Baud – The transfer rate of any group of like symbols in one second. This does not precisely refer to bits per second, and so is no longer commonly used to describe the data transfer speeds of today's faster modems. See also Bits per Second.

Beta Version – A trial or test version of a new piece of computer hardware or software.

Binary Code – The numeric system of 0s and 1s used by computers and other electronic devices to encode and transmit information. See also Digital Data.

BIOS (Basic Input/Output System) – Information, normally stored in the read-only memory (ROM) of a computer, that enables it to manage its peripherals (hard drive, video subsystem, memory configuration, and keyboard), as well as keep track of rudimentary data such as the time and date.

Bit – A contraction of "binary digit." A unit of information represented by a 0 or 1. See also Byte.

Bits per Second (bps) – The number of electronic data bits passing between two devices in one second. Often used (in the Kbps or kilobytes per second variant) to describe data transfer rates between modems. See also Baud.

Boot – The act of turning on a computer and starting its operating system, enabling it to perform other computing tasks.

Boot Disk – A disk that contains the operating system files or information necessary for a computer to start, recognize its components, and prepare for other computing tasks.

Bubble Jet Printer – Developed by Canon, a printer whose technology is a variation on conventional ink jet printing. In a bubble jet printer, heated ink bubbles through small apertures in the printhead and onto a piece of paper or other medium.

Buffer – A section of memory, in a computer system, computer component, or printer, that has been reserved for a specific task.

Bundling – The practice of including extra items in the sale of a product. Software and peripherals such as scanners and printers are commonly bundled with PCs.

Bus Mouse – A mouse that connects to a port or opening (usually a 0.25"-diameter DIN plug) that is connected by a card or cable directly to a computer's expansion bus.

Byte – A group of bits, which together carry specific information. A byte is often composed of eight bits.

Cache Memory – A small amount of memory set aside for repetitive tasks and designed to enhance the speed of a computer. Cache may be found in various parts of a system, including its processor chip (CPU), hard drive, and motherboard.

CAD/CAM (Computer-Aided Design/Computer-Aided Manufacturing) – An application or program that allows the design, drawing, and viewing of an object, and secondarily, its fabrication or manufacture in a computer-controlled environment.

CD-ROM (Compact Disc–Read-Only Memory) – A data storage disc, usually 5.25" in diameter (other sizes have been introduced but are not common), which can hold up to 1 gigabyte of digital information in the form of sound files, text, or pictures. Most CDs accommodate about 630 megabytes of data (about 435 1.44-MB floppy disks' worth). Data on a CD-ROM is recorded once, and may be read at any time by a computer with a CD-ROM drive. Usually, these drives in personal computers are also able to play music CDs.

Characters per Second (cps) – The number of characters that a printer is capable of printing in one second. Most often used to measure the speed of dot matrix printers.

Chipset – A collection of circuits on one or more microchips which share a group of functions or tasks. Chipsets commonly control the activities of components such as video cards or modems, and in current microcomputers are also found on motherboards to assist the CPU in important tasks related to data management and flow.

Circuit Board – A small card or board, found in a computer or other electronic device, on which electronic circuits or paths are printed or etched. Circuit boards often contain secondary components such as chips or electrical parts which help regulate the passage of data.

Controller Card – A circuit card, normally plugged into a slot on a computer's motherboard, that controls a device such as a hard drive or CD-ROM drive. Controller cards are available in a wide range of design types and sizes.

CPU (Central Processing Unit) – A microchip that controls the speed and basic functions of a computer. It is responsible for the arithmetic manipulation (adding and subtracting) of bits during all operations, as well as the management of other kinds of data flowing to and from the computer's subsystems.

DAT (Digital Audio Tape) Drive – A storage device that writes information in digital form on a specially designed tape. DAT drives are often used to back up data.

Data File – An organized assembly of information that can be stored and retrieved by a computer or other electronic device.

Database Software – A computer program designed to manipulate and store data in a system of records or files, and then print that data in lists, tables, or other formats.

Debugging – The act of checking a program, piece of computer hardware, or complete computer system to determine whether any operational problems exist, and if so, where they are located.

Digital Data – Information that has been broken into discrete values for purposes of recording or transmission; as opposed to analogue data, which is continuous.

DIN (Deutsch Industrie Norm) Plug – A round plug common on keyboards and mice, 0.5" in diameter for older keyboards and 0.25" (Mini DIN) for some mice, newer keyboards, and other peripherals.

Directory – A section of a hard drive or other storage device that is set apart and designated to hold specific data. The principal directory of a hard drive is commonly known as its main or "root" directory, while other sections are called subdirectories.

Dot Matrix Printer – A printer that operates by causing a series of pins (usually 9 or 24) in its printhead to hammer through an inked ribbon and leave an impression on a sheet of paper. Sometimes called an impact printer.

Dot Pitch – The distance between the dots that make up a picture. Most often used in descriptions of computer monitors, and measured in 100ths of a millimetre between dots of the same colour: e.g., .26-mm dot pitch. The smaller a monitor's dot pitch, the sharper its image.

Driver – A piece of software that enables a computer to recognize and work with a specific component or subsystem.

Duplexing/Print Duplexing – The ability of a printer to print on both sides of a single sheet of paper. A duplexing option or attachment is a common accessory to business class and network-ready laser printers.

DVD (Digital Video Disc) Drive – A drive, similar to a CD-ROM, that stores and reads large amounts of data. Current DVDs hold up to 30 gigabytes of digital information, enabling the drive to store and replay half an hour or more of full-motion video.

Emulation – The presentation of information by a computer peripheral (such as a printer) to other parts of a system, in a recognized format established by another brand of peripheral.

Encryption – The encoding of data to prevent its unauthorized viewing or use. Encryption is commonly employed in Internet applications that involve financial transactions and in the transfer of confidential information.

ESDI (Enhanced Small Device Interface) – A disk drive connection standard introduced by a consortium of manufacturers in the 1980s. ESDI drives are now obsolete, having been replaced by SCSI, IDE, and enhanced IDE (or EIDE) drives.

Expansion Bus – A communication pathway in a computer into which boards or devices can be plugged, and which provides for the transfer of data between its subsystems and processor, or CPU. Expansion bus access is typically provided through slots on a PC's motherboard. While different expansion bus designs have appeared over the years, those in current systems are usually of the PCI (peripheral component interconnect) type.

Floppy Disk – A magnetically encodable disk which data can be written to and read from. Also called a floppy. Older, 5.25" floppy disks came in two formats: 360 kilobytes and 1.2 megabytes. Newer, 3.5" disks hold approximately 1.44 MB of data.

Floppy Drive – A data storage device that can write to and read from floppy disks. Current floppy drives take 1.44-MB 3.5" disks; new drive designs able to read special 120-MB disks are also becoming popular.

Game Port – An oblong, 15-pin female connector on the back of a personal computer into which a joystick or other device can be plugged for use with games and entertainment software. Often included on sound cards.

Generic – In connection with microcomputers, this term is often used to describe a component which can easily be replaced by another part of the same specifications from another manufacturer. The term is also used to describe complete computer systems which are assembled from generic parts.

Gigabyte (GB) – An information block of 1,024 megabytes (1,073,741,824 bytes). This term is commonly used to describe the data capacities of storage devices such as hard drives in personal computers.

Grey Scale – A measurement of the number of different shades of grey used to make up a "black-and-white" picture.

GUI (Graphical User Interface) – A software design characteristic that presents choices and information in a graphical, as opposed to a text-based, form.

Hard Drive – A storage device, normally containing internal, non-removable platters, on which data is magnetically encoded. Hard drive capacities in current computer systems range from 2.5 to 10 gigabytes.

Host/Remote Software – A program designed to be run on two computers, allowing one system (the remote) to call the other (the host) through a network connection or a telephone line. The remote can then read information on the host's hard drive and access its resources.

Hotpluggable Device – A component that can be plugged into, and unplugged from, a computer without the system being shut down or configured or its hardware or software modified to accept the device.

Hypertext – Text or information embedded in a document or program, which, when selected or activated, automatically displays additional information of related interest.

IDE/EIDE (Integrated Drive Electronics/Enhanced Integrated Drive Electronics) – A class of hard drives, common in current personal computers, which have controlling electronics built into them. The introduction of the IDE/EIDE drives has lowered manufacturing costs and saves physical space in the PCs into which they are installed.

Ink Jet Printer – A printer that ejects ink in streams or "jets" from small apertures in its printhead onto paper or other media.

Interface – A connection point between two electronic components, two pieces of software, or a computer program and the person using it.

Interlacing – A technique whereby a computer monitor displays a picture by first drawing every second line and then filling in the remaining lines to complete the frame. See also Non-Interlacing.

Internet – The series of local, regional, national, and international computer networks, including the World Wide Web, linked together in a global system of shared information.

ISP (Internet Service Provider) – A company or individual with computer and communications equipment that is specially set up to provide personal computer users access to the Internet.

Kilobyte (KB; K) – A data block of 1,024 bytes. Commonly used to describe memory and file sizes in personal computers. Not to be confused with a kilobit (Kb), which is used to describe modem and network data transfer speeds. Many subsystems that used to be measured in "K" or "KB" are now described using larger units – megabytes (MB), gigabytes (GB), or even terabytes (TB).

LAN (Local Area Network) – A collection of two or more computers that are connected by a cable or other communication system so they can share data.

Laptop Computer – A type of portable computer common in the 1980s but replaced in the 1990s by the notebook. Despite the specific meaning of this term to describe larger, heavier – over 10 lb (4.5 kg) – products, it remains in use as a generic label for all small portable computers.

Laser Printer – A printer that uses one or more lasers to produce images sent to it by a computer or other electronic device. It does this by accepting precise instructions that describe the image or text being reproduced, electrostatically attracting toner onto a sheet of paper according to those instructions, and then fusing or baking the toner onto the page to create a finished print.

LED Printer – Similar in principle to laser printers, LED printers use a "light-emitting diode" to draw an image on a page to which toner can then be attracted and fused for a finished print.

Local Bus – The information pathways on a motherboard that connect its processor (CPU), BIOS, and RAM. Faster than a system's expansion bus, the local bus was exploited in many 486 motherboards, which were designed to allow other computer components such as the video and hard drive controller cards to access it as well. Some of these connections met a manufacturing standard known as "VESA local bus." See also VESA.

Megabyte (MB) – A data block of 1,024 kilobytes (1,048,576 bytes). Commonly used to describe RAM and hard drive storage sizes in personal computers. Not to be confused with a megabit (Mb), which is used to describe the data transfer speed of a network, or sometimes the capacity of a single RAM chip.

Microchip – A piece of silicon or other semiconducting material on which electronic circuitry is printed or etched, and which provides for the management of very small amounts of electricity. Usually smaller than 2" x 2", and produced in varieties of shapes and designs for different computing functions, microchips are sometimes plugged directly into a system's motherboard, or into circuit boards which in turn are plugged into expansion bus slots.

Microprocessor – A small chip made of semiconducting material and containing circuits which control a computer or other electronic device. This term is sometimes used to describe a system's CPU, but some microprocessors contain data management properties in addition to CPU circuitry.

MIDI (Musical Instrument Digital Interface) – A data transmission and connection standard used by electronic devices such as keyboards and sound cards, and characterized by a specific connector type and by the inclusion of specific musical data during transmission. MIDI music transmissions include values defining a note's pitch, length, and volume, and often include other data defining attributes such as attack and delay.

Minicomputer – A mid-range system that is faster and more capable than a microcomputer. Minicomputers are typically used to manage networks and store data that can be accessed by large numbers of connected PCs. As the latter have gained in power and speed, the difference between these two types of systems has become less distinct.

Modem – A contraction of "modulation/demodulation." An internal or external computer component that enables a system to send and receive data over telephone lines or other information networks. Current PC modems run at 33.6 or 56 Kbps (kilobits per second).

Monitor – Any device on which data being processed by a computer are displayed. The terms monitor and display are sometimes used interchangeably, but they actually refer to different items: the display is the screen on which information appears, while the monitor is the entire unit in which the screen is housed.

Motherboard – The main board in a computer on which electronic circuits are printed or etched, and which commonly contains a system's microprocessor, logic chipset, cache, ROM, and BIOS. Motherboards also provide apertures into which memory chips (RAM) can be plugged; expansion bus slots into which other circuit cards can be plugged; IDE connectors for hard drives and CD-ROMs; and serial, parallel, and keyboard ports to allow communication with peripherals.

Mouse – A small, palm-sized computer input device designed to manage the movement of the cursor on a system's monitor, and to provide for the execution of user instructions and choices.

MPEG (Motion Picture Experts Group)/MPEG-2 – Video compression standards named after the group of industry experts who collaborated to define them, MPEG and MPEG-2 transmissions use compressed data. Only the changes between frames of moving pictures (as opposed to all data making up each frame) are stored and sent. This reduction in necessary information allows MPEG and MPEG-2 devices to transmit and display near-video-quality motion pictures.

MTBF (Mean Time Between Failure) – The length of time expected to pass before a computer component will fail.

Multimedia – A combination of components in a computer enabling it to process and display sound and moving pictures (video). These usually include a CD-ROM or DVD drive, sound card, speakers, and video card with graphics capabilities.

Non-Interlacing – A monitor technique of displaying a picture by drawing every line in a single pass, without resorting to interlacing. A non-interlaced monitor is more stable (flickers less), faster, and more desirable than an interlaced monitor.

Notebook Computer – A type of portable computer technically smaller than a laptop, approximately the size of a piece of paper and weighing under 10 lb (4.5 kg). Largely a marketing label from portable computer manufacturers, "notebook" has not become the standard as expected, and is still interchangeable with the term "laptop."

OEM (Original Equipment Manufacturer) – A company that assembles computer equipment using its own or another manufacturer's components, in order to sell the equipment under another name, either to a user or to another company for resale.

Operating System – A program (or set of programs) that controls a computer's components and systems, manages its general operation, and enables it to run other, task-oriented software known as applications.

Parallel Port – An oblong, 25-pin female connector on the back of a personal computer, into which a parallel cable (a connecting cable that carries data in organized packets) can be plugged. Usually used to connect a printer, a parallel port can also accommodate other devices such as an external tape backup or Zip drive.

PCI (Peripheral Component Interconnect) – An expansion bus design, common in Pentium-level computer motherboards, that connects slots into which peripheral controller cards can be plugged to send data to the CPU chip, memory (RAM), logic chipset, and other fundamental systems.

PCL (Printer Control Language) – A computer language, originally developed for use in Hewlett-Packard's LaserJets, which resides in a printer and helps it process and print information.

PCMCIA (Personal Computer Memory Card International Association) – A design standard common in but not exclusive to notebook computers. This term describes the physical and electronic form of devices that can be plugged into systems containing a PCMCIA port.

Peripheral – An external component or device (such as a printer, keyboard, mouse, or backup drive) which is connected to a computer.

Pipeline (Burst) Cache – A small amount of memory in a computer or computer component, designed to handle the repetitive submission of information. "Pipeline" refers to the way in which the cache sends data in "bursts," as opposed to other types of cache memory, which send data in sequential form.

Plotter – A printing device designed to produce CAD drawings, architectural plans, and blueprints. Plotter images are usually rendered by a series of coloured pens or stylae, which are directed to exact locations on an X-axis (horizontal)/Y-axis (vertical) grid across a bed on which paper is positioned.

PnP (Plug-and-Play) Device – A component that is automatically recognized and accepted by the system into which it is introduced.

Power Supply – A computer assembly that accepts power directly from an external supply (e.g., an alternating-current plug on the wall).

Print Spooler – A program that allocates some of a computer's resources (notably its memory) to help manage jobs being sent to a printer.

Proprietary Part/Proprietary Program – A computer component, part, or program that is designed for a specific model or series of equipment.

PS/2 Mouse – A mouse with a small (0.25" diameter), round DIN plug, often used with a notebook computer, but which may be connected to any computer with a compatible PS/2 port.

Push Programming – Programming enhancements or features, such as special information, sound, animation, and even video, that are automatically sent to or from a computer connected to the Internet.

RAID (Redundant Array of Independent Drives) – An assembly of storage drives and other special equipment designed to provide constant access and backup in networked computer environments, as well as to support the network automatically if one of its subsystems fails.

RAM (Random-Access Memory) – The main memory in a computer, which is cleared each time the system is turned off, and which accepts data submitted to the system during a computing session. Measured in megabytes, 16, 32, 48, and 64 MB being common in current personal computers. RAM chips are available in different types, shapes, and sizes.

RISC (Reduced Instruction Set Chip) Processor – A processor designed to recognize a specific, limited set of instructions which affect how efficiently it processes data.

ROM (Read-Only Memory) – Computer memory that contains permanently stored information that is not normally changed.

Scanner – A device with the ability to recognize, encode, and communicate information automatically. Typically, scanners read text on a page or magnetic bars, dots, or other codes on objects or labels.

SCSI (Small Computer Standard Interface) – (Pronounced "scuzzy.") A design standard defining the form and operation of certain components of a computer. A SCSI interface or connection is characterized by 8-bit parallel data transfer, typically through a SCSI card that is able to support several devices (such as a hard drive or compact disc drive) at once. SCSI connections are generally faster and thus more desirable than other interface types such as IDE/EIDE.

Serial Mouse – A mouse that plugs into a serial port on the back of a computer.

Serial Port – An external connector (usually a DB 9-pin or DB 25-pin male) on the back of a personal computer. Serial ports deliver data one bit at a time, and are commonly used to connect an external modem, barcode reader, or other input device, as well as some networking cables. They are often referred to as COM ports.

Server – A computer or other device which manages the activities and resources of other computers or peripherals connected to it. Servers can store all of the data in a network and manage access to it from connected stations, or they may act as traffic managers between computers which process data independently.

SIMM (Single In-line Memory Module) Chip – Any of several types of memory chip, including DRAM (dynamic random-access memory), FPM (fast page memory), and EDO (extended data out), and coming in various sizes, such as 8, 16, and 32 megabytes and larger.

Software – A collection of numbered instructions causing a computer to perform a specific task.

Sound Card – A card or circuit in a personal computer, which enables it to recognize and process audio data from a microphone, CD, or other input device and transfer that data to external speakers or headphones. More sophisticated sound cards recognize speech, allow the creation of music, and provide output to computer-compatible musical MIDI (musical instrument digital interface) devices.

Touch Pad – A pointing device similar in function to a mouse, which allows a computer user to move a cursor or pointer around a screen by sliding his or her finger around on a small, sensitive pad.

Trackball – A pointing device similar in function to a mouse, which presents a ball that can be rotated in order to move a cursor or pointer around a screen.

Transfer Rate – The speed at which data is transferred from one device to another. Often measured in KBps (kilobytes per second), Kbps (kilobits per second), MBps (megabytes per second), or Mbps (megabits per second).

USB (Universal Serial Bus) Port – A new serial connection design that enables data transmission rates of up to 12 megabits per second and connection of up to 127 devices, as well as connection to hotpluggable and plug-and-play devices. Expected to become standard on most new PCs issued in 1998.

VESA (Video Electronic Standards Association) – A standard set by a consortium of manufacturers of video cards and monitors. VESA is used to describe a bus design on some motherboards, as well as controller cards and other components which these motherboards will accept.

WAN (Wide Area Network) – A group of connected computers, in different geographical locations, which can share data and programs. The Internet may be thought of as a very large WAN. By contrast, computers in a LAN, or local area network, are situated within the same building or site.

World Wide Web – An important part of the Internet, the World Wide Web is a global network of "server" computers allowing access to shared information in the form of documents, sound, video, and other files that meet a set of common transmission standards. Documents, or "sites," on the Web are typically presented in HTML (Hypertext Markup Language) format, which provides referrals, or "links," to other websites of related interest.

INDEX